TRUST AND DISTRUST IN ORGANIZATIONS

TRUST AND DISTRUST
IN ORGANIZATIONS

Dilemmas and Approaches

RODERICK M. KRAMER AND KAREN S. COOK

EDITORS

VOLUME VII IN THE RUSSELL SAGE FOUNDATION SERIES ON TRUST

Russell Sage Foundation · New York

9382982

The Russell Sage Foundation

The Russell Sage Foundation, one of the oldest of America's general purpose foundations, was established in 1907 by Mrs. Margaret Olivia Sage for "the improvement of social and living conditions in the United States." The Foundation seeks to fulfill this mandate by fostering the development and dissemination of knowledge about the country's political, social, and economic problems. While the Foundation endeavors to assure the accuracy and objectivity of each book it publishes, the conclusions and interpretations in Russell Sage Foundation publications are those of the authors and not of the Foundation, its Trustees, or its staff. Publication by Russell Sage, therefore, does not imply Foundation endorsement.

Library of Congress Cataloging-in-Publication Data

Trust and distrust in organizations : dilemmas and approaches / Roderick M.
    Kramer and Karen S. Cook, editors.
        p. cm. — (The Russell Sage Foundation series on trust ; v. 7)
    Includes bibliographical references and index.
    ISBN 0-87154-485-7
    1. Organizational behavior. 2. Corporate culture. 3. Leadership. 4.
Business ethics. 5. Trust 6. Psychology, Industrial. 7. Industrial management.
I. Kramer, Roderick Moreland. II. Cook, Karen S. III. Series.

HD58.7.T7437 2004
302.3'5—dc22

                                                                2003066814

Text design by Suzanne Nichols

RUSSELL SAGE FOUNDATION
112 East 64th Street, New York, New York 10021
10 9 8 7 6 5 4 3 2 1

To Kevin and Brian, from Karen,

and

To Matthew and Catherine, from Rod

The Russell Sage Foundation Series on Trust

The Russell Sage Foundation Series on Trust examines the conceptual structure and the empirical basis of claims concerning the role of trust and trustworthiness in establishing and maintaining cooperative behavior in a wide variety of social, economic, and political contexts. The focus is on concepts, methods, and findings that will enrich social science and inform public policy.

The books in the series raise questions about how trust can be distinguished from other means of promoting cooperation and explore those analytic and empirical issues that advance our comprehension of the roles and limits of trust in social, political, and economic life. Because trust is at the core of understandings of social order from varied disciplinary perspectives, the series offers the best work of scholars from diverse backgrounds and, through the edited volumes, encourages engagement across disciplines and orientations. The goal of the series is to improve the current state of trust research by providing a clear theoretical account of the causal role of trust within given institutional, organizational, and interpersonal situations, developing sound measures of trust to test theoretical claims within relevant settings, and establishing some common ground among concerned scholars and policymakers.

Karen S. Cook
Russell Hardin
Margaret Levi

SERIES EDITORS

Previous Volumes in the Series

Contents

Contributors

Roderick M. Kramer is William R. Kimball Professor of Organizational Behavior at the Graduate School of Business, Stanford University.

Karen S. Cook is Ray Lyman Wilbur Professor of Sociology and cognizant dean of social sciences at Stanford University.

John Brehm is professor of political science at the University of Chicago.

Robin M. Cooper is a doctorate candidate in the Department of Sociology at Stanford University and is research associate at the Laboratory for Social Research.

John M. Darley is Warren Professor of Psychology and professor of public affairs at Princeton University.

Kurt T. Dirks is associate professor of organizational behavior at the John M. Olin School of Business at Washington University in St. Louis.

Amy C. Edmondson is associate professor of business administration at Harvard University.

Kimberly D. Elsbach is associate professor of management and chancellor's fellow at the Graduate School of Management, University of California, Davis.

Scott Gates is professor of political science at the Norwegian University of Science and Technology and director of the Center for the Study of Civil War at the International Peace Research Institute, Oslo (PRIO).

Dana A. Gavrieli is a graduate student in the School of Business at Stanford University.

Pamela J. Hinds is assistant professor with the Center for Work, Technology, and Organization in the Department of Management Science and Engineering, Stanford University.

Deepak Malhotra is assistant professor in the Negotiations, Organizations, and Markets Unit at Harvard Business School.

Bill McEvily is associate professor of organizational behavior and theory at Carnegie Mellon University.

Gary J. Miller is professor of political science at Washington University in St. Louis.

Stefanie Bailey Mollborn is a doctorate candidate in the Department of Sociology at Stanford University.

J. Keith Murnighan is the Harold H. Hines Jr. Distinguished Professor of Risk Management at the J. L. Kellogg Graduate School of Management at Northwestern University.

Helen Nissenbaum is associate professor of culture and communications and senior fellow of the Information Law Institute at New York University.

Hakan Ozcelik is a doctorate candidate in organizational behavior in the Sauder School of Business at the University of British Columbia.

Sandra L. Robinson is associate professor of organizational behavior and distinguished university scholar chair in the Sauder School of Business at the University of British Columbia.

Daniel P. Skarlicki is associate professor in the Sauder School of Business at the University of British Columbia.

Irena Stepanikova is a doctorate candidate in the Department of Sociology at Stanford University and is a research associate on the Physician-Patient Trust project.

David H. Thom is associate professor of family and community medicine at the University of California, San Francisco.

J. Mark Weber is assistant professor of organizational behavior at the Joseph L. Rotman School of Management at the University of Toronto.

Akbar Zaheer is professor of strategic management at the University of Minnesota.

Roxanne Zolin is assistant professor at the Graduate School of Business and Public Policy at the Naval Postgraduate School, Monterey, California.

Chapter 1

Trust and Distrust in Organizations: Dilemmas and Approaches

RODERICK M. KRAMER AND KAREN S. COOK

FOR MORE than a decade now, the topic of trust has been at the center of scholarly research on organizations. The ascension of trust as a major focus of research in the organizational sciences reflects in no small measure a large body of evidence documenting the substantial and varied benefits that accrue when trust is in place within organizational boundaries. Coupled with this strong evidence of the benefits of trust is an acute appreciation of the problematic nature of organizational trust. Although trust may be a desirable resource, it is often a fragile and elusive one.

Interest in trust as an important dimension of organizational functioning was initially stimulated by a number of influential works on social trust, including most notably Robert Putnam's (1993) provocative findings implicating trust as a critical factor in explaining the origins of civic engagement and the development of democratic regimes in Italian communities. Putnam's argument attracted wide attention and was followed up by Francis Fukuyama's (1995) comparative survey of evidence that trust plays a critical role in societal functioning. In the years following these initial landmark volumes, a number of additional works (for example, Cook 2001; Hardin 2002; Putnam 2000; Sztompka 1999) have added to the stock of studies of trust in the social sciences. Viewed in the aggregate, these contributions converge on the conclusion that trust often constitutes an important resource within social systems.

1

Although much of the initial evidence regarding the benefits of trust as a social resource pertained, strictly speaking, to social systems writ large, the organizational implications of these arguments and empirical findings did not go unnoticed (for example, Kramer and Tyler 1996; Lane and Bachman 1998; Sitkin et al. 1998). Within organizational settings, the virtues of trust as a social resource have been discussed primarily on three levels. The first major theme has been its constructive effect with respect to reducing transaction costs within organizations. Second, the role trust plays in spontaneous sociability among organizational members has been explored. Third, there has been appreciation of how trust facilitates appropriate (that is, adaptive) forms of deference to organizational authorities. Much of the appreciation of the merits of trust as a social resource, it should be noted, followed from a corresponding disenchantment with traditional organizational theories of managerial "command and control." Organizational theories emphasizing authority and hierarchy seemed less readily applicable to the flatter and less centralized organizational forms that began to proliferate in recent decades. Moreover, they were seen as less relevant for organizations embedded in high-velocity environments in which rapid change necessitated swift assessment and action. Finally, the socially differentiated character of contemporary organizations presented special challenges to conventional notions of organizing and managing social relations with harmony.

In concert, these trends helped push theory and research on trust into the mainstream of the academic literature on organizations. In addition, the topic took on new relevance for American citizens after the events of September 11, 2001. Almost immediately, questions were raised about the extent to which they should or could trust the systems on which they rely for well-being and security. Almost immediately, the American public was confronted with a series of sudden assaults on its trust in organizations. The stunning collapse of Enron, Worldcom, and Arthur Andersen, and the Catholic church scandals forced a nationwide search for answers to fundamental questions about trust and trustworthiness. These events, coming so close together and from so many distinct arenas of social life, assaulted our confidence in the trustworthiness of the organizational systems on which we rely. In some cases, these events have generated deep ambivalence and even pervasive distrust, which challenges the fundamental legitimacy of professional and managerial authority.

A primary aim of the present volume is to help us take stock of where we stand on these questions. Construed broadly, the chapters in this book all examine problems and prospects for trust within and across organizational boundaries. In putting this diverse collection together, we had a number of goals. The first was to contribute to the development of a better understanding of the antecedents and consequences of trust in contemporary organizational contexts. Organizational forms and prac-tices are undergoing rapid change and reinvention, raising important new questions about how trust operates across these innovative forms. Thus, one goal of this book is to assess the current state of theory and research on problems of trust and distrust in organizational settings.

We also wanted to bring together scholars who study trust from a vari-ety of different perspectives with a penchant for different kinds of data. In particular, we wanted to bring together in one volume researchers from a wide range of disciplines, including social psychologists, sociologists, political scientists, and economists. Given the complexity of trust-related phenomena in organizations, we felt it was essential to encourage con-versations that cross disciplinary boundaries.

We also included in our volume researchers who, although they may share common theoretical interests, nonetheless approach their ques-tions using different methodologies. Thus, we made an effort to achieve a mix of both quantitative and qualitative methods of research. Finally, and perhaps most important, we were committed to exploring problems and prospects for trust within the context of new, interesting, and impor-tant organizational settings and forms. Thus, we included scholars who study problems of trust and distrust in a variety of diverse and interest-ing contexts, such as doctor-patient relationships, social work relation-ships, geographically dispersed teams, virtual teams, and the Internet. Our emphasis on context was motivated by our strong presumption that the contours of trust and distrust are likely to vary in subtle but important and interesting ways across organizational settings. In their theorizing, academics understandably value and seek parsimonious explanations and generalized accounts of phenomena. As a countermeasure to this push for parsimony and generalization, however, we felt it was impor-tant at this stage of theorizing to seek out the distinctive features of trust-related phenomena as they appear in different organizational arenas. We took seriously Hardin's (2002) argument that trust is a three-part relation defined not only by the characteristics of the truster and trustee, but also the specific transactional domain or context in which their rela-tion is embedded. According to Hardin's (2002) "encapsulated interest" account, an actor A trusts actor B with respect to some specific behavior. Context helps to determine the extent to which A considers B to be trust-worthy in terms of the matter at hand.

Organizing such a diverse set of chapters presented something of a challenge, especially given the deliberately diverse mix of theorists and their distinctive interests and concerns. Obviously there are a number of different cross-cutting dimensions that we might have used to cluster some chapters together and to separate others. We ultimately settled on an organizational scheme that focuses on the context in which the trust relationship is embedded and the challenges surrounding the construction of trust in various settings. In part I are the chapters that deal with trust in relationships that can be classified as primarily hierarchical such as employer-employee, supervisor-worker, professional-client, and doctor-patient relationships. Issues of motivation, monitoring, commitment, and trust loom large in these chapters. At the heart of these investigations are the following questions: Do trust and power really mix—and if so how? What are the determinants of trustworthiness in hierarchical relations? How is trust maintained in the face of power differences?

In part II we move to the more collective level to focus on the role of trust between individuals or organizational agents in teams and networks. How does trust develop in distributed work settings, especially when team members are geographically dispersed? How do we determine the trustworthiness of those we do not see or interact with frequently on a face-to-face basis? Does trust create a safety net for team failure? These are some of the questions addressed in this section of the volume.

In part III we turn to the general challenges of trust building in various environments. What problems do people face in their efforts to create or foster trustworthiness and thus seed trust in social relations? What of betrayal? How do we understand and cope with the many paradoxes of trust? We begin with the chapters that discuss the role of power and hierarchy in trust relations.

Part I: Trust and Hierarchy

Despite the proliferation of new organizational forms, the hierarchical relation remains one of the most important and prevalent forms of organizing found in contemporary organizations. Such relationships are interesting arenas in which to examine trust-related judgments and behaviors because by definition the parties in the relationship are unequal in power or status. Accordingly, the first set of papers examines aspects of trust within hierarchical relationships, an important class of relations in many social and political contexts.

Kurt Dirks and Daniel Skarlicki investigate the importance of trust in leader-follower relationships. In particular, they examine how trust in leaders contributes to effective functioning within groups and organizations. The authors note that although the importance of trust has long been recognized by leadership theorists, there is a dearth of systematic theory and research showing precisely how trust in leaders actually contributes to effective group functioning. In reviewing the extant literature pertaining to this topic, Dirks and Skarlicki note that much of the theory and research to date on trust in leaders is typically *relationship-based* or *character-based*.

Relationship-based trust perspectives emphasize the importance of how followers construe their relationship to a leader. The relationship or the social bond between leaders and followers includes such things as salience of a shared identity, recognition of a common background, and a history of cooperative interaction. Character-based perspectives focus on leaders' characteristics, specifically, the impact of leaders' perceived characteristics on the level of trust followers have in them. According to this perspective, followers' trust in leaders is influenced by their perceptions of the leaders' fairness, trustworthiness, or competence.

Dirks and Skarlicki comment that these perspectives have different implications for thinking about the consequences of trust in leaders. From a relationship-based perspective, leaders and followers exist in an exchange relation, in which positive sentiments and the behaviors those sentiments foster can be reciprocated, resulting in the building of mutual trust over time. In the character-based perspective, followers act in accord with the leader's preferences to the extent that the characteristics they attribute to leaders justify such action. Thus, followers will be willing to engage in behaviors that put them at risk when they attribute competence and benevolence to their leaders.

Despite the fact that some research has tried to untangle these issues, many questions remain. In particular, we know relatively little about what types of trust an organization should focus its efforts on building. For example, are there more advantages to be gained from fostering trust in the top management team, thus creating an organizational culture of trust? Or should more effort be focused on proximal relations (supervisor-subordinate dyads) and let trust build from the ground up? Finally, the authors take on the thorny question of why it is that trust in leaders is so hard to build and sustain? Drawing on existing theory and evidence, they propose that it is important to consider the interdependent effects of leader variables that might influence followers' willingness to engage in some form of desired behavior (such as organizational citizenship behavior, or OCB). For example, it may be essential that a leader be perceived as high in integrity and benevolence in order for followers to engage in OCB.

To evaluate this possibility empirically, Dirks and Skarlicki sampled employees from the financial services department of a large bank. Consistent with their theoretical expectation, the authors found that the relationship between leader integrity and citizenship behavior was strong and positive only when leader and organizational benevolence was high. At moderate or low levels of benevolence, the relationship between leader integrity and such behavior was insignificant, indicating a close link between benevolence and perceived integrity.

John Brehm and Scott Gates examine the complex and problematic trust relations that exist among social work supervisors, the workers they supervise, and the latter's clients. They begin by noting that there is at root a fundamental problem of trust between social work supervisors and the social workers under them. Although supervisors are legally responsible for the actions of those under their supervision, civil service regulations and other legal constraints limit the ability of these supervisors to exercise vigilant and thorough supervision. In a word, they are accountable, yet their hands are in some respects tied. This relationship is further complicated by the fact that the relationship between social workers and those they supervise is protected by confidentiality agreements. Thus, supervisors must work partly in the dark when it comes to knowing how well those they supervise are actually carrying out their duties in a credible and responsible way.

To analyze trust dynamics in this complex relationship, the authors take as an analytic point of departure David Kreps's (1990) well-known trust-honor game. Brehm and Gates introduce a variation of this game, which they call the *trust-honor and reform* game. The game assumes that supervisors confront the choice as to whether to monitor or not monitor their social workers. Social workers in turn can decide to pull or not pull a given case. Pulling a case refers to the discretionary power (based on threat) social workers have to make their clients ineligible for state support when a client does something that merits such action. Clients can respond by either reforming or not reforming their behavior. Issues of trust and distrust reverberate throughout this triadic relationship, as all parties strives to pursue their interests and protect themselves from the prospect of misplaced trust.

Using this basic model as a conceptual platform, Brehm and Gates then show how trust in this complex triadic relationship can be understood in terms of the updating of beliefs among the interdependent actors. In particular, using survey data from social workers and their supervisors, Brehm and Gates attempt to evaluate this model empirically (because of privacy policies, client data unfortunately were not available).

The results of their study suggest that trust between supervisors and their subordinates is contingent in no small measure upon the availability of opportunities for supervisors to interact with and train their subordinates. Second, trust entails support and support entails protection. In particular, they found that subordinates' sense of protection from outside interference was a strong predictor of trust in the supervisor. Thus, the ability of the supervisor to insulate subordinates from debilitating organizational politics and disruptive case interference were found to be very important to the trust-building process. Finally, and perhaps most important, the authors found that trust is consequential in the sense that social workers who trusted their supervisors behaved differently from those who did not. In particular, trust was shown to enhance perceived discretion on the part of the social workers, resulting in a greater expenditure of effort.

Another important form of hierarchical relationship in which trust has long been assumed to be important is the relationship between physicians and their patients. This relationship has been undergoing rapid change in recent years, as medical care has been increasingly delivered in managed-care settings rather than fee-for-service practices. Yet little is currently known about how about such settings actually influence trust and distrust between doctors and those they treat. Accordingly, Karen Cook, Roderick Kramer, David Thom, Irena Stepanikova, Stefanie Bailey Mollborn, and Robin Cooper investigate some of the determinants of perceived trustworthiness in physician-patient relationships in managed-care settings. They conceptualize the relationship between physicians and patients as one of mutual or reciprocal trust, noting that although there has been a fair amount of research on the determinants of patient trust in physicians, much less work has examined the conditions under which physicians trust or distrust their patients, and the consequences of such trust or distrust.

Using qualitative data from interviews and focus groups involving patients and physicians, Cook et al. (2003) find that patients trust physicians who demonstrate care, empathy, and respect for them as individuals, not just as "cases." Important indicators of these sentiments are sustained eye contact, open body language, active listening, as well as the opportunity for the patient to participate in decision making relevant to their treatment. The findings also indicate that certain demographic characteristics such as gender, age, and culture or country of origin matter in the trust relationship because they affect the nature of the interpersonal communication of information. Finally, these authors explore how the features of the managed care settings in which patients receive their health care affect the levels of trust in their physicians. Such factors include a perceived increase in time constraints by both parties, lack of continuity of care, increased diffusion of responsibility and the perceived conflict of interest that emerges when physicians are widely viewed as constrained to offer lower-cost health care options such as fewer diagnostic tests or limitations on access to specific drugs or therapies.

Chapters by Gary Miller and John Darley, respectively, examine the role trust plays in another hierarchical relationship: employer-employee relations. In particular they investigate the effect of trust on the voluntary effort of the workers. There has been a strong presumption in the trust literature that high-trust relationships are more productive than low-trust relationships. The authors explore this general thesis, although they approach the problem of voluntary effort from distinctly different perspectives, Miller draws on insights from rational-choice theory. Darley eschews rational choice to focus on social identity and more emotional determinants of trust.

In his chapter, Gary Miller addresses the important and enduring question of how best to align worker incentives and effort. Specifically, a primary aim of his paper is to examine the nature of the "tit-for-tat" exchange between managers and workers. His focus is on relationships capable of yielding Pareto improvements (all parties are happier) in organizations in which work contracts are based on the monitoring of individual actions rather than outcomes.

In building his argument, Miller first demonstrates the Pareto-suboptimality of effort-based monitoring. Drawing on the work of Akerlof, he suggests that Pareto improvements can be achieved if both supervisors and those they supervise enter into an informal "gift exchange" relation, whereby the supervisors tacitly agree to exchange leniency (relaxed surveillance) for increased voluntary effort by the workers. Supervisors benefit in such an exchange, of course, because of the reduced costs of monitoring. In turn, workers benefit by avoiding having someone breathing down their necks. Employing the Folk Theorem, Miller argues that this tacit arrangement works because each actor can make a credible threat that effectively guarantees or enforces the other's cooperation or compliance. The supervisor has the threat potential to increase monitoring should the worker's effort fall below some desired threshold. The worker in turn has the credible threat of merely "working to rule" (providing only a minimal or suboptimal level of effort). Using this logic, Miller thus argues that what looks on the surface like a process of simple and straightforward gift exchange could actually be the rational response of supervisors and workers to the other's implicit threats. Miller goes on to argue that exchange is one of the sustainable cooperative equilibria in a cooperative game in a repeated game situation.

Miller then examines the "control paradox," whereby more control leads to less effort. He illustrates the implication of his argument in several important domains, including public agencies, congressional oversight, public versus private schools, and regulatory environments. In some ways this is the key issue faced by Brehm and Gates in their study of social workers and their supervisors. Miller concludes by explicating the role trust plays in getting to sustainable cooperation. He notes that there are multiple equilibria in such games, some of which are Pareto-superior. What might help to move to Pareto-improving equilibria? Here trust enters the equation in "switching" equilibria.

An impressive feature of Miller's analysis is how far it carries us without our having to invoke notions of intrinsic motivation. Instead, we can assume simply that the interdependent parties to this exchange relation possess common knowledge about the equilibria being played. Because players are rational, they adjust their behavior to achieve what they desire and to avert the outcome they least desire. In this case, the worker supplies high levels of effort so as to not set off the supervisor's "trigger" for increased monitoring. Voluntary compliance by the worker in turn averts an increase in close monitoring. Both are happier and better off (the meaning of a Pareto improvement).

The contribution by John Darley examines the important question of the role trust plays in organizational performance and success. In order to get the work of the organization done, Darley notes, employees must be willing to comply with organizational rules and directives. They must perform their role. However, success depends on more than this. It also depends on voluntary efforts by workers, including willingness to undertake actions that fall outside their job description or formal organizational role. Motivating employees to perform these "extra-role behaviors" is, of course, at the heart of much organizational theory and research. One class of such behaviors are the organizational citizenship behaviors (OCB) investigated by Dirks and Skarlicki.

Darley reviews existing theory and research relevant to these broad issues and then moves on to address the specific issue of trust. What kind of trust makes a difference in such situations? He notes that some conceptions of trust highlight primarily its calculative dimensions. For example, I trust you simply because I recognize it is in your rational self-interest to fulfill that trust. I can trust you, moreover, because I keep my powder dry (and available) should retaliation for any detected breach of trust be required. In contrast, noncalculative modes of trust, he argues, have their roots in the social relations and ties that obtain between parties. These "noncalculative" conceptions have their theoretical roots primarily in social identity theory. As Darley points out, noncalculative trust helps us understand the conditions under which people feel that a breach or betrayal of trust has occurred. It brings to the surface the identity-based elements of trust and distrust.

Part II: Trust and Distrust in Teams and Networks

In contrast to hierarchical dyadic relationships, in which the parties interact face-to-face and frequently in organizational settings, the chapters in part II examine trust and distrust between individuals in group or collective contexts. Here the parties may be more dispersed geographically or may interact much less frequently face-to-face. In some cases, the actors are anonymous, at least initially.

Chapter 7, by Helen Nissenbaum, focuses on interesting issues of trust on the Internet. Research on the psychological and social complexity of life on the Internet is still in its infancy (see Wallace 1999 and DiMaggio et al. 2001 for a review of the literature). In an important contribution to this growing literature, Nissenbaum articulates the potentially substantial benefits that might accrue should trust online be achieved. At the same time, she notes some of the formidable difficulties associated with securing such trust.

Nissenbaum begins by suggesting that trust online could improve the quality of social life in many spheres, ranging from personal experiences and communal relationships to civic participation. She observes further that if trust can be secured, more people and institutions will accept and use online resources, leading to more investment in online capabilities, resulting in more use, and so on, in a virtuous cycle. Broadly construed, therefore, the Internet might be a significant source of social-capital building.

Although acknowledging these potential benefits of trust online, Nissenbaum then presents an intriguing analysis of some of the inherent features of online life that make such trust problematic. Among the potential obstacles to online trust she notes is the simple fact that for many users and in many parts of the world the Internet remains a relatively new and unfamiliar form of social interaction. Not surprisingly, therefore, there may be an inherent wariness in online transactions.

A second and in some respects more serious problem concerns what Nissenbaum terms *missing identities.* Much of the interaction on the Internet is inherently anonymous. This anonymity is a double-edged sword. On the one hand, it enables people to protect their identities, thereby achieving confidentiality. On the other hand, anonymity reduces greatly the opportunity for the interacting parties to access and verify identity-related information that specifically contributes to the trust-building process.

Another problematic feature of life online is what the author terms *missing personal characteristics.* Many of the differentiating cues that influence our judgments about trustworthiness, she notes, are simply missing from online transactions. For example, in the online environment we typically lack cues that would tell us something about the similarity or familiarity to us or the values we share with those with whom we are interacting online. The prospect of easy misrepresentation of these diagnostic cues—the ability to and ease with which one can lie about one's age, gender, or professional standing or training—is a serious problem, as users of some online advice services have learned.

Finally, the author concludes, the settings or contexts of information exchange on the Internet are themselves somewhat inscrutable. Online users don't know for certain the source of the messages they receive—it is relatively easy to disguise the origins of a message or inflate the credibility of an institution. As with other attributes of life online, however, inscrutability is a double-edged sword. On the one hand, it is equalizing and can liberate people from status-driven patterns of social interaction (dominance, deferral, etc.). In this respect, there is a refreshing sense of egalitarianism about chat rooms. On the other hand, inscrutability means less ready access to crucial information about social and professional roles. An example is provided by help sites where it is hard to evaluate the expertise of the experts volunteering to offer advice or support.

Given the absence of the usual grounds for trust, Nissenbaum next considers, what foundations or bases are available for securing trust online? What steps can we take to sustain trust? The answer lies in enhancing the security of transactions on the Internet. One contributing solution is greater sophistication about access control. If we are assured that the collective is populated by responsible parties, interaction is easier and more spontaneous. A second approach is to increase the transparency of identities. If we can make users' identities transparent enough to interacting parties, they can protect themselves against betrayal and harm. Surveillance is a third weapon.

Nissenbaum concludes by posing the question, Can trust really be secured online? Is security a foundation for online trust? Nissenbaum points out that security experts are engaged in an almost Sisyphean battle in trying to close off every avenue of attack. Much like any fixed defense, the conventional sorts of firewalls and structures currently used to increase security online are inherently vulnerable to circumvention or penetration. They are breachable. As she reminds us, much of our attention has focused on the danger without, whereas far less systematic attention has been paid to the threat posed by insiders. She reminds us that the centurions at the gate may themselves be corrupt or corruptible, prone to wicked mischievousness. Pervasive distrust may be hard to avoid in such contexts.

In "Architects of Trust" Bill McEvily and Akbar Zaheer investigate network facilitators of trust and cooperation among organizational competitors in geographical clusters. Here we move to organizations or their agents as the key actors. A provocative feature of geographical clusters, they note, is that local firms often engage in acts of collaboration with each other, while at the same time competing against each other in downstream product markets. Organizational theorists have generally attributed this phenomenon to the existence of dense and overlapping networks of social, professional, and exchange ties among firms within such clusters. Repeated interactions among cluster members have produced benefits in terms of trust building, including the development of shared understandings, collective identities, and mutual confidence.

Although such an argument may seem compelling on prima facie grounds, McEvily and Zaheer point out that from an empirical perspective, many questions remain unanswered as to how such shared understandings, collective identities, and mutual confidence actually develop. Accordingly, using a qualitative approach, they investigate the development of inter-firm trust in the office furniture manufacturing industry in western Michigan. Among other things, they found that regional institutions played a particularly important role as facilitators of trust among network members. Although unexpected, the authors were able to unpack this relationship, discovering that regional institutions were able to facilitate interaction by organizing conferences, meetings, and setting up subcommittees that brought manufacturers and suppliers together. This study thus provides important evidence for the argument that third parties can act as important conduits of trust among parties.

Roxanne Zolin and Pamela Hinds in chapter 9 explore some of the difficulties in creating and sustaining interpersonal trust in geographically distributed cross-functional work teams. Trust theorists have long argued the benefits of face-to-face interaction and direct experience with others in the trust-building process. As more and more work in organizations is done by individuals who are dispersed geographically, however, it is clear that opportunities for such critical trust-building opportunities will be reduced, and so it becomes important to understand the extent to which trust can and does develop in the absence of such experience. Zolin and Hinds investigate these issues by comparing trust development in geographically collocated versus distributed dyads of student construction-design teams. Using a longitudinal methodology, they sampled trust levels at several points in time, which enabled them to assess changes in trust levels. The authors found that trust levels in distributed dyads changed significantly less than trust levels in collocated teams. Although trust increased more in collocated teams, it also decreased more, consistent with prior research suggesting that trust levels are updated on the basis of direct experience.

Zolin and Hinds also examine how risk perceptions affect trust in geographically dispersed teams. They initially hypothesized that risk would be a significant factor in predicting trust levels for dispersed dyads, so that more risk meant less trust. Their results supported this hypothesis. Viewed in the aggregate, their findings clearly suggest that the dynamics of trust development and maintenance are different in dispersed and collocated teams. However, clearly more research is needed to document how to overcome some of the liabilities of distance for the trust-building process. Zolin and Hinds's results suggest the possibility that if distributed teams could meet initially for a brief period that led to positively structured interaction, then the team members might enjoy a relatively stable sort of trust predicated on the positive group stereotype.

In chapter 10, "Psychological Safety, Trust, and Learning in Organizations," Amy Edmondson defines psychological safety in terms of individuals' perceptions of the degree of interpersonal threat in their group or organizational environments. Thus, psychological safety encompasses people's sense of security when they take risks, such as when they make personal self-disclosures, propose new ideas, or report mistakes. With the presence of psychological safety, there is a kind of tacit mental calculation or assessment as to whether others in a group or organization will give one the benefit of the doubt. Psychological safety thus constitutes a sort of trust in others' willingness to act benevolently toward the self as the self engages in risky behavior of some sort.

Using this definition as a starting point, Edmondson then develops the notion of *team psychological safety*, which can be conceptualized as a form of collective-level psychological safety. The author reviews recent empirical evidence on the impact of psychological safety on group functioning, using data from a variety of real groups ranging from cardiac surgery teams to teams operating in a manufacturing company. On the basis of her findings she identifies a number of antecedents of psychological safety, including important leader behaviors that facilitate the emergence and maintenance of psychological safety within teams. In particular, she suggests there are three leader behaviors that specifically promote psychological safety: accessibility, explicitly inviting input and feedback from others, and modeling openness and fallibility. Many of these same kinds of behaviors, it should be noted, have been implicated in the literature on trust in leaders, suggesting a link between trust and psychological safety. Edmondson also identifies a number of informal, emergent group dynamics that support psychological safety.

Having identified some of the antecedents of team psychological safety, Edmondson then considers some of its consequences, especially with regard to how group members are likely to interact with each other. These include the willingness to seek help, seek feedback, be vocal about errors or concerns, and engage in innovative behavior. To the extent such behaviors facilitate group learning, a strong case can be made for the role psychological safety plays in learning organizations. Future research should explore the nature of the relationship between trust and perceived psychological safety in such organizational contexts. If trust provides psychological safety, trust building may be an essential goal of team training, for example of surgical teams or firefighting teams.

Part III: Challenges to Securing and Sustaining Trust

Given recent examples of breakdowns in trust and trustworthiness (for example, Enron, Tyco, and Arthur Andersen), it seemed appropriate that we conclude the volume with three chapters that address some of the problems of securing and sustaining trust in organizations. In "Managing Images of Trustworthiness in Organizations," Kimberly Elsbach examines this important but largely neglected topic. In particular, she explores the impression-management strategies and self-presentational tactics managers can use to enhance impressions of their trustworthiness. In some respects, she notes, it is hardly surprising that managers accord so much importance to being perceived as trustworthy. In her review of the empirical literature, she documents a number of positive effects of perceived trustworthiness, including enhanced support for and cooperation with trusted managers. Similarly, individuals are more likely to defer to authorities and accept their views as valid when they feel a high level of trust in those authorities (Tyler 1990).

Having established the importance of perceived trustworthiness, Elsbach then elaborates on some of the tactics that can be used by managers to enhance images of their trustworthiness. These include revealing or displaying similarities between oneself and those with whom one works; and revealing dissimilarities between oneself and known untrustworthy others. Impression managers trying to persuade others of their trustworthiness can also display cues or present evidence that they are members of a group that has a reputation for competence, benevolence, or integrity. This allows one to benefit from association with the group. Elsbach notes that impression managers use a variety of physical cues, nonverbal behavior, and language to manipulate impressions of their trustworthiness when interacting with their various constituencies.

Elsbach begins by noting that to possess an image of interpersonal trustworthiness, managers must be perceived by those around them as having a number of attributes, including competence, benevolence, and integrity. But how do managers achieve such attributions? Several antecedent conditions support perceptions of trustworthiness. These include behavioral factors such as behavioral consistency, accurate and open communication, and demonstrating concern. There are also several cognitive factors associated with attributions of trustworthiness, including social categorization and perceived similarity.

Elsbach's analysis reminds us that skillful impression managers may be highly effective at cultivating the illusion of trustworthiness, even when they have little concern with actually being trustworthy. Skillful deceptors may manipulate impressions of trustworthiness in order to commit and conceal wrongdoing and may actually abuse that trust to take advantage of overly trusting or naïve others. The Enron scandal is a good example of how this abuse works in the real world, leading the *Wall Street Journal* to publish a news story with the headline "En-Ruse?" According to the article, Enron executives asked more than seventy low-level employees to go to an empty trading floor and pose as busy sales representatives to impress a group of Wall Street analysts who were visiting the company's headquarters. According to one employee who participated in the lie, "We actually brought in computers and phones, and they told us to act like we were typing or talking on the phone when the analysts were walking through. They told us it was very important for us to make a good impression, and, if the analysts saw that the operation was disorganized, they wouldn't give the company a good rating." To enhance this illusion, the employees even brought in personal pictures to adorn the tops of their desks. The ruse worked. Although the whole charade lasted only ten minutes, it was enough time to create the impression of a dynamic, flourishing trading floor.

Elsbach notes more positively, however, that it is also vitally important for trustworthy and well-intentioned managers to be able to effectively communicate and demonstrate their trustworthiness.

J. Keith Murnighan, Deepak Malhotra, and Mark Weber in "Paradoxes of Trust" examine trust issues in the context of exchange relationships and contracts. In particular, they note that, from an attributional perspective, contracts act as double-edged swords. On the one hand, contracts provide an assurance mechanism, allowing cooperative behavior to be initiated easily. Legal scholars and organizational theorists alike have long noted the power of the "shadow of the law" as a basis for risk taking and presumptive trust in exchange relationships. In a sense the contract allows confidence-building behaviors to occur, giving trust a toehold. At the same time, contracts in certain respects make trust harder to develop because they create ambiguity in the attribution of motive. Because the existence of the contract is common knowledge to the contractees, the others' cooperative or trustworthy behavior can be attributed to the existence of the contract, a situational factor, and not to innate trustworthiness. Therefore, the behavior is less clearly diagnostic of the actor's underlying motivation, intentions, or character. Contracts thus generate situational attributions for others' cooperative behavior, which potentially impede or slow the development of interpersonal trust. Further, trust operates differently in the contract context from what the perspective of rational models of judgment and choice would lead us to expect.

Murnighan, Malhotra, and Weber offer experimental data to support their attributional impetus model. Central to this model, they posit, is the assumption that people sometimes are willing to assume large risks in an effort to develop trust (rather than the sort of gradual incremental risks assumed in many GRIT-type models of trust development) because they recognize that the targets of their trust-building efforts often are likely to judge partial or tentative trusters harshly. One of the important points they make is that people often take risks in their social exchanges in order to build trust (Cook et al. 2003).

In chapter 13, "Untangling the Knot of Trust and Betrayal," Sandra Robinson, Kurt Dirks, and Hakan Ozcelik examine how individuals' initial trust levels influence individuals' responses to their experience with a breach of trust or betrayal. Extant research makes it unclear whether prior trust intensifies the experience of betrayal—a "the higher they are, the harder they fall" sort of argument—or acts to buffer against feelings of betrayal or mitigate the effects. The literature on betrayal suggests to the authors that individual reactions to betrayal are at the very least complex and varied.

They propose that trust might play a role in mitigating responses to such betrayal. Trust, they suggest, might function as an appraisal heuristic. They animate their analysis in terms of two dominant but conflicting logical possibilities. The first is a "love is blind" hypothesis, according to which prior trust would be expected to soften or attenuate the impact of betrayal. This hypothesis follows a kind of "idiosyncrasy credit" logic, whereby we give people some benefit of the doubt on the basis of an accumulated history of otherwise benign and positive experiences. There are several reasons why this might be the case, including cognitive consistency and the possibility that prior trust might influence the construal of actions or inactions linked to betrayal.

Robinson and his colleagues reconcile these opposing predictions and the psychological arguments in favor of them by proposing that prior trust moderates the relationship between the breach experience and the appraisal or interpretation of the breach, resulting in varied emotional and behavioral reactions.

The final chapter, by Roderick Kramer and Dana Gavrieli, looks at the presidency of Lyndon Baines Johnson and suspicion inside the Oval Office to return to the theme of part I and examine the complex relationship between power and trust. Kramer and Gavrieli argue that power affects social-information processing and social interaction in a number of ways that exert deleterious effects on the trust-building and maintenance process. They contend that it becomes harder for those in power to assess others' true loyalty and trustworthiness. Power creates a fog or shroud of attributional ambiguity in interpersonal relationships between the powerful and those over whom they exert power.

To develop this general argument, the authors use published accounts and recently declassified data from secretly recorded White House conversations involving President Lyndon Baines Johnson and his advisers. These conversations, along with supportive archival evidence, provide a rich window into a leader's struggles with problems of trust and distrust in his administration. Using this evidence, Kramer and Gavrieli identify a number of social-information processing biases that can lead to the breakdown of trust within power relationships. One of these is the *sinister attribution bias*, the tendency of social perceivers to overattribute malevolent motives to others, especially those in powerful positions. Another social-information processing bias is the exaggerated perception of conspiracy, the tendency to read coherent connections into individual social actions. The authors elaborate on some of the difficulties that individuals in various positions of power encounter when trying to assess the veridicality of their own perceptions—in other words, power relations complicate the trust-building process. The pervasiveness of power relations in organizational settings makes this obstacle to trust building important to investigate.

Conclusion

Taken together, the chapters in this volume highlight some of the complexities and subtleties of trust-related phenomena in contemporary organizational contexts. They amply demonstrate that trust takes different forms across many different settings, and that trust-building and trust-maintenance processes vary across them as well. These studies highlight the necessity and value of context-specific, "middle range" theories of trust that can be empirically tested.

A major aim of our volume was to highlight the complexities and problematics of trust and distrust in organizational contexts. Our survey does not leave one entirely sanguine about the prospects for trust.

This book had its origins in a rather pleasant academic conference. The setting for that conference was relaxing and convivial. Our conversations about trust had all of the pleasing ambience and casualness of a scientific conference in which abstract ideas were being tossed around with enthusiasm and a certain carefreeness. Recent world events have given the topic of trust more significance and even urgency. There is, we hope, a useful timeliness to our collective musings about trust and distrust.

References

Cook, Karen S., ed. 2001. *Trust in Society*. New York: Russell Sage Foundation.

Cook, Karen S., Toshio Yamagishi, Coye Cheshire, Robin Cooper, Masafumi Matsuda, and Rie Mashima. 2003. "Trust Building via Risk Taking: A Cross-Societal Experiment." Working paper.

DiMaggio, Paul, Eszter Hargittai, W. Russell Neuman, John P. Robinson. 2001. "Social Implications of the Internet." *Annual Review of Sociology* 27(3): 307–36.

Fukuyama, Francis. 1995. *Trust: The Social Virtues and the Creation of Prosperity*. New York: Simon & Schuster/Free Press Paperbacks.

Hardin, Russell, ed. 2002. *Trust and Trustworthiness*. New York: Russell Sage Foundation.

Kramer, Roderick M., and Tom R. Tyler. 1996. *Trust in Organizations: Frontiers of Theory and Research*. Thousand Oaks, Calif.: Sage.

Kreps, David M. 1990. "Corporate Culture and Economic Theory." In *Perspectives on Positive Political Economy*, edited by James E. Alt and Kenneth A. Schepsle. Cambridge: Cambridge University Press.

Lane, Christel, and Reinhard Bachman. 1998. *Trust Within and Between Organizations: Conceptual Issues and Empirical Applications*. New York: Oxford University Press.

Putnam, Robert D. 1993. *Making Democracy Work*. Princeton, N.J.: Princeton University Press.

――――. 2000. *Bowling Alone: The Collapse and Revival of American Community*. New York: Touchstone.

Sitkin, Sim B., Denise M. Rousseau, Ronald Stuart Burt, and Colin Camerer. 1998. "Special Topic Forum on Trust in and Between Organizations." *Academy of Management Review* 23 (special issue).

Sztompka, Piotr. 1999. *Trust: A Sociological Theory*. New York: Cambridge University Press.

Tyler, Tom R. 1990. *Why People Obey the Law*. New Haven, Conn.: Yale University Press.

Wallace, Patricia. 1999. *The Psychology of the Internet*. New York: Cambridge University Press.

PART I

TRUST AND HIERARCHY

Chapter 2

Trust in Leaders: Existing Research and Emerging Issues

KURT T. DIRKS AND DANIEL P. SKARLICKI

RUST IS a crucial element of effective leadership that can impact followers in ways ranging from the mundane to the heroic. For example, trust has been found to explain why some employees effectively complete their jobs and in addition go above and beyond the call of duty in their work without clear recompense. Among the more heroic aspects, trust can help explain why individuals have been willing to follow the visions of leaders, in some cases placing their fate (and sometimes lives) in the hands of leaders in contexts ranging from modern organizations to ancient armies and expeditions.[1]

The recognition of trust as an important issue for leaders clearly is not new. In fact, research over the past four decades and from multiple disciplines has explored the significance of trust in leaders. Until recently, however, surprisingly little research has focused on illuminating *how* trust in leaders contributes to the effective functioning of groups and organizations and how it can be leveraged to meet this objective. In this chapter we first attempt to elucidate some of the research that has been amassed on the topic of trust in leadership. Second, we present new research on several issues: theoretical perspectives on trust in leadership, positive consequences associated with trust in leaders, key issues related to attaining these consequences, and challenges related to the development of trust. Third, for each of these issues we identify some important questions for future research. We conceptualize trust as a psychological state held by the follower involving confident positive expectations about the behavior and intentions of the leader, as they relate to the follower. Hence, in our analysis trust refers to a perception and is measured as such.[2]

21

Theoretical Perspectives

Over the past four decades, trust in one's leader(s) has been an important concept in a number of disciplines, including organizational psychology, management, public administration, organizational communication, and education. In research on the organizational behavior literature, for instance, trust has been identified as an important (although arguably underrecognized) aspect of numerous leadership theories. Transformational and charismatic leaders build trust in their followers (Kirkpatrick and Locke 1996; Podsakoff et al. 1990). Trust is a crucial element of the consideration dimension of effective leader behavior (Fleishman and Harris 1962) and leader-member exchange theory (Schriesheim, Castro, and Cogliser 1999). Other studies show that promoting trust can be important for leader effectiveness (Bass 1990; Hogan, Curphy, and Hogan 1994). In addition to its role in leadership theories, trust has been linked to positive job attitudes, organizational justice, psychological contracts, and effectiveness in terms of communication, organizational relationships, and conflict management.

Although the vastness of this research base can be a potential strength for understanding trust, it can also present a challenge to accessing and making sense of this body of research. In an attempt to integrate some of the research literature regarding the processes by which trust forms, and the nature of the construct itself, we propose that research to date can be viewed in terms of two qualitatively different theoretical perspectives: a *relationship-based* perspective and a *character-based* perspective (Dirks and Ferrin 2002).

The relationship-based perspective focuses on the nature of the leader-follower relationship—more precisely, how the follower understands the nature of the relationship. Some researchers (Konovsky and Pugh 1994; Whitener et al. 1998) describe trust in leadership as operating according to a social-exchange process. For followers their relationship with their leader means that the parties operate on the basis of trust, goodwill, and the perception of mutual obligations and not just on the basis of the standard economic contract (Blau 1964). The social exchange implies a high-quality relationship, and issues of care and consideration in the relationship are central. Researchers have used this perspective in describing how the trust component of leader-follower relationships elicits citizenship behavior (Konovsky and Pugh 1994), underlies transformational leadership (Pillai, Schriesheim, and Williams 1999), and is critical for leader-member exchange relationships (see, for example, Schriesheim, Castro, and Cogliser 1999).

The character-based perspective focuses instead on the follower's perception of the leader's character and how it impacts a follower's vulnerability in a hierarchical relationship (Mayer, Davis, and Schoorman

1995). According to this perspective, trust-related concerns about a leader's character are important because the leader may have authority to make decisions that have a significant impact on a follower and the follower's ability to achieve his or her goals, for example in areas such as promotions, pay, work assignments, and layoffs. This perspective implies that followers make inferences about the leader's characteristics—the presence or absence of such qualities as integrity, dependability, fairness, and ability—and that these inferences have consequences for work behavior and attitudes. Examples of research using this perspective include models of trust based on characteristics of the trustee (Mayer, Davis, and Schoorman 1995), research on perceptions of supervisor characteristics (Cunningham and MacGregor 2000; Oldham 1975), and research on some forms of leader behavior (Jones, James, and Bruni 1975).

To date there has been little empirical recognition of the distinctions between these two perspectives, yet distinguishing between them is important because, as we shall see, they have implications for the way trust develops in the workplace, the consequences of trust, the distinctions between different types of trust, and the possibility of understanding different referents of trust.

Does Trust in Leadership Matter?
Theory and Evidence

Although some individuals may consider it intuitively appealing to consider that trust in leaders is important for individuals, groups, and organizations, social scientists have provided mixed views and evidence on this issue. At one end of the spectrum are those who view trust as having little or no impact (Williamson 1993) and at the other are those who see trust as a concept of substantial importance to organizational effectiveness (Golembiewski and McConkie 1975). In this section we examine some of the theory and evidence for the impact of trust through the lenses of two theoretical perspectives and discuss some unresolved questions.

Consequences of Trust for Individuals

The relationship- and character-based theoretical perspectives describe two different mechanisms by which trust might affect behavior and performance. The relationship-based perspective is grounded in principles of social exchange and deals with employees' willingness to reciprocate care and consideration that a leader expresses in a relationship. In other words, individuals who feel that their leader has demonstrated care and consideration or will do so tend to reciprocate this sentiment in the form of desirable behaviors. Mary Konovsky and Doug Pugh (1994) draw on this logic, suggesting that a social-exchange relationship encourages individuals to spend more time on required tasks and be willing to engage in organizational citizenship behavior (OCB)—to go above and beyond the call of duty.

The character-based perspective focuses on how perceptions of the leader's character impacts a follower's vulnerability in a hierarchical relationship. Specifically, because leaders have the authority to make decisions that have a significant impact on the follower, perceptions about the trustworthiness of the leader can become important to the follower. Drawing on this idea, Roger C. Mayer, James H. Davis, and F. David Schoorman (1995) provide a model proposing that when followers believe their leaders have integrity, capability, or benevolence, they should be more comfortable engaging in behaviors that put them at risk (such as sharing sensitive information). For example, Mayer and Mark Gavin (1999) suggest that when employees believe their leader cannot be trusted (for example, because the leader is perceived as lacking integrity) they will divert energy toward "covering their backs," which can detract from employees' work performance. Both theoretical perspectives suggest that trust may result in higher performance and citizenship behavior, but this end is reached by distinct, and potentially complementary, routes.

Kurt T. Dirks and Don L. Ferrin (2002) conducted a meta-analysis that summarizes the research over the past four decades. They report that trust in leadership had a significant relationship with individual outcomes, including job performance ($r = .16$), organizational citizenship behavior (altruism, $r = .19$), turnover intentions ($r = -.40$), job satisfaction ($r = .51$), organizational commitment ($r = .49$), and a commitment to the leader's decisions ($r = .24$). Data from the samples were drawn from a variety of contexts ranging from financial institutions to manufacturing firms to military units to public institutions. The effect sizes for behavioral and performance outcomes tend to be as high as or higher than the effect sizes observed between similar criteria and other key attitudinal variables such as job satisfaction, organizational commitment, job involvement, and procedural justice (for examples of similar meta-analytic reviews, see Brown 1996; Colquitt et al. 2001; Mathieu and Zajac 1990). Thus, one conclusion of this research is that trust is as important to effective organizational functioning as are the above noted variables, or even more so.

Although there has been considerable research on the relationship of trust and individual outcomes, the literature is limited on several important issues. First, almost all research to date has been based on cross-sectional designs on which the direction of causality cannot be inferred. For instance, rather than trust impacting job performance, it is possible that for some employees, higher job performance inspires increased trust in one's leader. What is needed is experimental and longitudinal research designs that empirically test causality.

Second, few or no studies have explored explicitly *why* trust is related to work outcomes. Empirical research is needed that explores the mediating processes by which trust predicts various individual attitudes and behavior. A corollary of this research question is how relationship- and character-based perspectives differ with respect to how trust relates to various attitudes and behaviors. For example, is trust arising from relationships more powerful and more enduring than trust arising from character assessments? What is the implication of establishing a high level of trust from the character perspective, but a low level from the relational perspective? Are they interchangeable? Under what conditions might one perspective be more important to leader effectiveness than the other?

Third, little research has been directed at understanding the moderating conditions under which trust may have a smaller or greater effect on behaviors. For example, trust is likely to be a stronger predictor of individual performance under conditions where employees work interdependently than when they work independently.

Fourth, almost all of the research has examined the direct (main) effects of trust in leadership on outcomes. As Dirks and Ferrin (2001) noted, trust can have an equally important impact on outcomes by providing a facilitating condition by which other variables (such as incentives) lead to positive outcomes. Research along this line might explore how having trust in leadership provides a condition under which human-resource practices such as incentive systems, feedback, and organizational change may be better received by employees and may ultimately be more effective.

In summary, a better understanding of these issues is likely to help researchers account for greater variance in the relationship between trust and individual outcomes. Last, research is also needed to illuminate the differences between the relationship- and character-based perspectives. An initial step in this direction is Dirks and Ferrin (2002), which indicates that for some variables such as job performance and altruism behavior, the relationship-based perspective may be more predictive, whereas for other variables such as job satisfaction and organizational commitment, the character-based perspective may be more predictive.

Consequences for Groups and Organizations

This research suggests that trust is associated with individual-level effects, although their magnitude might be small to moderate. If trust in leaders indeed has a small to moderate relationship with proximal outcomes such as individual performance, one might ask whether trust in leaders is associated with "bottom-line" benefits for groups and organizations. Three recent studies suggest that it is.

James Davis and colleagues (2000) examined the relationship between trust in a business unit's general manager and organizational performance. They found that trust was significantly related to sales, profits, and employee turnover in a small sample of restaurants. Tony Simons and Judi McLean Parks (2002) investigated whether a senior manager's "behavioral integrity" created collective trust in the senior manager, which in turn translated into higher performance. Using a sample of hotels, they reported that perceptions of behavioral integrity and trust in the senior manager were related to customer satisfaction and profitability. The model explained almost 13 percent of variance in profitability; trust appeared to play a major role in these effects.

Trust in leadership can also be related to bottom-line outcomes for teams and work groups, as demonstrated in Dirks's (2000) study of NCAA basketball teams. Using survey data from players collected early in the season, and statistically adjusting for other potential determinants of team performance (player talent and tenure, coach experience and record, preseason performance, performance in prior years, and trust between team members), trust in the head coach (team leader) accounted for almost 7 percent of the variance in winning percentage. Illustrating the substance of the relationship, the team with the highest trust rating played for the national championship, while the team with the lowest trust score won approximately 10 percent of their remaining games (and the coach was fired at the end of the season). The variance accounted for by different trust levels was nearly equivalent to that accounted for by team-member ability. Moreover, in a context where one would expect trust in one's teammates to be highly crucial for success, trust in leadership proved to be a more important predictor of team performance than was trust in teammates.

In summary, all three studies support the conclusion that trust is related to "bottom-line" effects in terms of group and organizational performance. What is interesting is the magnitude of the effect suggested by the studies—the effect is even stronger than what might be expected on the basis of the data from studies of trust at the individual level and its relationship with seemingly more proximal factors such as individual performance and organizational citizenship behavior. Understanding why this occurs, as well as when trust in leadership is related to group and organizational performance, requires additional theory and research.

Like research at the individual level of analysis, studies of trust at the group and organizational levels need to examine the direction of causality. The results from Dirks (2000) indicate that performance and trust are reciprocally related: past performance impacts trust, which in turn impacts future performance. Second, research might also explore exactly how trust impacts group and organizational performance. We suggest that trust in leadership might impact group or organizational performance in two complementary ways. One way is via increasing individual-level outcomes such as individual performance and citizenship behavior. A second way is suggested by post hoc interviews from Dirks's study of basketball teams. In explaining why trust in the leader is important to team success, one coach offered the following analogy with a team of horses: "In order to pull the wagon, all the horses have to be pulling in the same direction and cadence. Trust helps with that." A player gave the following illustration to make a similar point: "Once we developed trust in Coach————, the progress we made increased tremendously because we were no longer asking questions or were apprehensive. Instead, we were buying in and believing that if we worked our hardest, we were going to get there." These observations illustrate a crucial idea. Trust in leadership allows the individuals in the team or organization to suspend their individual doubts and personal motives and direct their efforts toward a common team goal. In summary, trust in the leader has two complementary effects: it helps maximize individual efforts and performance and it then harnesses those efforts toward achieving a common goal or strategy. These ideas provide only an introduction to a complex issue that deserves further research. For example, it is possible that relationship- and character-based perspectives operate together in this process: the relational elements of trust may inspire individuals to be willing to go above and beyond the character-based factors such as perceived competence and integrity and make individuals willing to take the risk of focusing on attaining a common goal.

Last, research might explore the conditions under which trust in leadership is more or less important. Building on Martin Luther King Jr.'s observation that "the measure of a man is not where he stands in moments of comfort, but where he stands at times of challenge and controversy," from a follower's perspective, trust in leaders may be particularly important in times of challenge and adversity. Our post hoc analysis of the data from the basketball study described above shows that although trust in the leader may indeed be higher for teams that are winning than teams that are losing, the relationship between trust and performance is significantly greater when the team is doing poorly. Specifically, for teams that had been performing well or moderately well, there was little or no relationship between trust and performance. However, for teams that had been performing poorly, the relationship was positive and strong. One interpretation of these results is that trust in the leader may not be salient or may not be seen by employees as critical when the environment is positive (the team is doing well). However, trust is highly relevant to employee performance when the environment is negative (weak economy, organization in decline). Researchers need to investigate under what conditions trust is more or less related to performance.

Emerging Issues: Building Trust in Leadership and Leveraging Its Effects

The previous section reviewed some theories and evidence from existing research. In this section we provide new theory and data, and we raise questions important for developing a more precise understanding of trust in leaders. Specifically, we explore three questions: What type(s) of trust should an organization focus its efforts on building? On what leadership "referent"—or target—should the organization focus its efforts to build trust to achieve beneficial impact? And last, why is trust in leaders so difficult to build and maintain? These factors are important not only for advancing a scientific understanding but also for providing practical guidance for trust development in organizations.

Exploring Different Dimensions of Trust

Recent research suggests that trust is not a uni-dimensional concept but comprises different dimensions. Daniel J. McAllister (1995) suggested that interpersonal trust can be categorized as cognitive-based or affect-based. Cognitive forms of trust are based on perception of the integrity or capability of another party. Affective trust is based on a special relationship with the party that may cause the referent, or trusted person, to demonstrate concern about one's welfare and a feeling of benevolence.[3] Despite the growing evidence of the validity of different trust dimensions, there has been only a limited amount of empirical research exploring the implications of the different dimensions. Theoretically, exploring the different dimensions should provide a more complete and precise understanding of the impact of trust. From a practical perspective, understanding the different dimensions may help leaders better leverage the effects of trust. For example, if a leader wishes to encourage organizational citizenship behavior, which type of trust should he or she focus on building?

To begin exploring this question, it is useful to recognize that the reasons underlying the relationship between trust in leader and employee OCB may vary by dimension. Social-exchange theory suggests that benevolence may predict OCB because the employee perceives that the leader has care and concern for the employee's well-being. One way to reciprocate the leader's benevolence is by engaging in OCB. On the other hand, trust in a leader's integrity may inspire an employee to believe that by engaging in OCB, he or she may derive future benefits because of the leader's adherence to certain values, such as fair treatment.

Although the effects of the different dimensions on OCB may operate independently (see, for example, McAllister 1995), we propose that it may also be important to consider their interdependent effects. Specifically, we propose that one dimension of trust's relationship with OCB may be contingent upon on the level of other dimensions. As noted above, the relationship-based and character-based perspectives suggest that affective forms of trust in leader, such as benevolence, and cognitive forms, such as integrity, may operate via different processes on outcomes such as OCB. In order to elicit OCB, it may be necessary to engage both processes via cognitive and affective forms of trust. For instance, although the leader may be seen as being highly dependable (high integrity), there may be a reluctance to engage in OCB if the leader is deemed to have low care and concern for the employee (low benevolence). Thus we propose that integrity predicts OCB to the degree that benevolence is high, and may be strongest when both are high. This idea implies that a two-way interaction between benevolence and integrity predicts employee OCB.

As part of a larger study, we explored these ideas in a sample of employees of a bank's financial services department. Employees were asked to assess their trust in their manager in terms of integrity and benevolence using Mayer and Davis's (1999) trustworthiness scales. Managers were asked to rate employees' helping OCB using a three-item scale adapted from Van Dyne and LePine (1998). To examine the data we used hierarchical regression following the procedures described in Aiken and West (1991). In step 1, we included two control variables: employees' dependence on their supervisor and tenure. Both variables showed significant bivariate relationships with OCB. In step 2, we entered the main effects for benevolence and integrity. In step 3, we entered the interaction term for benevolence and integrity. The main effects for benevolence and integrity on OCB were not significant. The interaction between benevolence and integrity was significant (beta = .22, p < .05; change in R^2 = .03). A plot of the data indicated that the relationship between integrity and OCB is positive when benevolence is high. At moderate and low levels of benevolence, the relationship between integrity and OCB is not significant.

These ideas and findings present a number of implications, as well as questions for future research. First, the data suggest that in this sample it was not enough for a leader to be trusted in terms of integrity or the extent to which he or she cares about the follower—both dimensions of trust were required in order to predict OCB. This idea presents a challenge to leaders because it suggests that they must develop dual competencies. From a leadership development perspective, it means that leaders must be able to effectively cultivate an image of personal integrity and also be able to establish personal relationships with subordinates. These are likely to require different sets of behaviors.

Clearly, the data we presented above only focused on two specific dimensions and one outcome in one organization. It would be interesting to explore the extent to which different types of trust (including that based on a perception of capability) predict outcomes. Greg Bigley and McAllister (2002) examine how affective trust in a leader may create a "transformation in relational logic" and influence when individuals engage in helping behavior. More specifically, they examine the interactions between affect-based trust and integrity- and competence-based (cognitive) trust. They propose that employees will engage in helping behaviors when both affect- and integrity-based trust in supervisors are high. Employees are also more likely to engage in helping behavior when they feel high levels of affective trust, but believe that the leader has *less* competence—and hence needs their assistance. It may also be interesting to explore whether different types of trust in leaders is required for different organizations or contexts. For example, it may be that some organizations that espouse values of care and concern, such as social service agencies, may require higher levels of affect-based trust in leaders than organizations such as the military, which might need more integrity- and competence-based trust in leaders due to the values they espouse.

Exploring Different Referents of Trust

Perhaps just as important as identifying the type of trust is identifying the exact referent of trust. Much of the literature uses the term "trust in leader" without considering the variation in leadership roles. In order to effectively leverage the benefits of workplace trust, there needs to be a better understanding of which referents, which types of leaders, may be most relevant and important for eliciting high performance and OCB. Under what conditions should an organization focus its efforts on establishing subordinates' trust in supervisors as opposed to building trust in senior management? And what about focusing on trust among coworkers? Although building trust in each of these relationships is likely to be important, limited resources may cause organizations to focus more efforts on some relationships than others.

Arguments from the relationship- and character-based perspectives suggest that trust in different referents might have different consequences. According to social-exchange principles, the relationship-based perspective implies that followers will reciprocate benefits received and that individuals will target their efforts to reciprocate toward the source of the benefit received. For example, trust in a supervisor should be associated with reciprocation primarily aimed at that leader, as opposed to top management. Likewise, efforts to reciprocate trust in senior leadership would be targeted toward senior management or the organization.

Research reviewed by Bass (1990) indicates that supervisors tend to perform activities such as managing performance and day-to-day activities on the job. Senior executives perform more strategic functions such as setting strategic direction, allocating resources to various projects and departments, communicating to employees the goals of the organization, and so on. Given the distinction in the roles of the different leadership referents, reciprocating trust in one's immediate supervisor may be related to job-related outcomes such as increasing job performance or engaging in OCB. For instance, individuals might give extra time to fulfill supervisor requests, or may engage in helping behavior such as staying late to help a supervisor or coworker due to a social exchange process involving a supervisor. In contrast, trust in senior leadership may involve reciprocating to that referent with high commitment to the organization and its mission. The character-based perspective, focusing on concerns about the integrity, reliability, and honesty of specific leaders, would also suggest that understanding which referent is trusted will predict the response or concern toward a specific individual.

A similar argument has been made in the research on organizational justice. Perceptions of fairness of a supervisor have been found to predict agent-referenced outcomes (supervisor-directed citizenship behaviors), whereas perceptions of fairness of policies and procedures predict system-referenced outcomes (organizationally directed citizenship behaviors) (Masterson, Lewis, and Taylor 2000). Thus, insofar as individuals make distinctions between their immediate supervisor and the senior executive team, there may be differences in the consequences of the different referents of trust in leadership.

Dirks and Ferrin (2002) found evidence for these effects. Their analysis showed that trust in supervisor was more strongly related to job-level variables, whereas trust in senior leadership was more strongly related to organizational level variables. For example, they found that job performance related at a significantly higher level with trust in supervisor ($r = .17$) than with trust in senior management ($r = .00$). In contrast, organizational commitment was related at a significantly higher level with trust in senior leadership ($r = .57$) than with trust in supervisor ($r = .44$). The limitation of this research, however, is that it was not able to look at these differences within a single sample to separate the unique variance attributable to trust in each referent. Research is needed to further explore this idea in primary studies.

Future research might also explore whether organizational effectiveness requires trust in multiple referents. Earlier we suggested that trust impacts group or organizational effectiveness by maximizing individual efforts and performance and by harnessing those efforts toward achieving a common goal. Building on our earlier theorizing, we propose that trust in supervisor impacts individual performance and trust in senior management harnesses those efforts toward achieving organizational goals.

Focusing solely on trust in supervisor, however, may overlook other important referents. In many contemporary workplaces employees rely less on a supervisor and exchanges with coworkers have become more important to employees' performance. Exploring trust from the viewpoint of peers is highly relevant in light of the growing presence of lateral relationships in organizations. Thus, research might explore the implications of trust in leaders versus trust in coworkers. The former might result in contributions directed toward the supervisor and the organization, while the latter might result in contributions directed toward coworkers. Examples of consequences might be exchanges of knowledge with coworkers and helping coworkers in need (see McAllister 1995). We suggest that the extent to which trust in and the consequent willingness to engage in exchanges with leaders versus coworkers contributes to individual and group performance is likely to be contingent upon factors such as the extent to which individuals depend upon others to complete their work. In groups where the leader controls resources, sets the strategies, and so forth, trust in leaders will be particularly important, whereas in work contexts where coworkers play an important role in making pivotal decisions, trust in coworkers may be more important. In other words, the party that holds power in the group may be critical to determining which referent of trust is most important. Clearly, in most cases we would expect that some combination of trust in leaders (supervisors, senior management) and trust in coworkers would be helpful, but the conditions under which each one may be most important deserves further research. The answer to this issue would provide guidance on when organizations may, on the margin, focus efforts on establishing trust in each type of referent.

The Challenge of Building and Maintaining Trust in Leadership

The evidence reviewed in an earlier section suggests that trust has numerous individual and organizational benefits. Such findings clearly indicate that building and maintaining trust in leaders is important to effective organizational functioning. Most of the existing research places the responsibility for building and maintaining trust in the hands of the leader. Ellen Whitener and her colleagues (1998) assert that "managers' actions and behaviors provide the foundation for trust and that it is actually management's responsibility to take the first step" (514). Using a relationship-based perspective, these writers proposed five types of behavior that affect trust development: behavioral consistency, behavioral integrity, participative decision making, communication, and demonstrating concern. The evidence reviewed by Dirks and Ferrin (2002) seems to confirm the significance of followers' perceptions of leadership actions and styles. Dirks and Ferrin report substantial relationships between perceptions of leadership actions, including transformational leadership ($r = .72$), interactional justice ($r = .65$), participative decision making ($r = .46$), and failure to meet expectations of subordinates ($r = .40$), as well as others. In short, trust in leadership appears to be associated with a well-established set of leadership actions and behaviors.

What might be more interesting and more puzzling than the leadership behaviors that increase or decrease trust is the challenge of building or maintaining trust in the workplace. A recent survey suggested that almost two thirds of employees report having little or no trust in their employers (AFL-CIO 2001). Another survey found that over 52 percent of employees don't trust the management of their organization and don't believe the information they receive (Katcher 2002). Similarly, in Sandra L. Robinson and Denise M. Rousseau (1994), 55 percent of employees reported that their employer had violated the psychological (informal) contract, resulting in significantly reduced trust.

From the leaders' perspective, we also suspect that many leaders, even though they have developed high levels of trust, may be achieving less trust than they think they deserve. Anecdotal evidence of this comes from the study of college basketball teams (Dirks 2000). After the research was completed, one of the coaches in the study telephoned the first author to inquire about the level of trust in him that his players had reported having in the survey. Even though the data showed that his trust rating was high compared to other coaches in the study, he expressed surprise and disappointment; he had expected it to be higher, given his efforts, and commented, "I don't understand. Why don't they trust me *completely*?" This coach had almost two decades of coaching experience, was the recipient of almost every major coaching award, and felt that he had the best intentions of his players at heart and worked hard at establishing relationships with them. This anecdote reveals that even this highly successful leader, largely trusted by his players, was challenged to achieve the level of trust he desired and expected.

What factors account for the difficulty that leaders face in building and maintaining trust? There are clearly numerous potential answers to this question. The answer may lie within the leader. Some researchers have suggested that leaders are often selected on the basis of technical rather than interpersonal competencies (Hogan, Curphy, and Hogan 1994). If true, this suggests that many leaders do not always possess the competencies or motivation to build trust. The principles for building trust do not appear to be mysterious (following through on commitments, consistency between actions and words, treating people fairly), so possibly many leaders prefer to focus their efforts on other goals.

The answer may also lie partly in the leadership role itself. We feel that this represents one of the more interesting and plausible factors. We label these factors "trust dilemmas" because they point to the many trade-offs involved in maintaining trust in multiple relationships.

As part of research and training sessions with the financial services firm described earlier, we conducted focus groups to investigate the behaviors that build or break trust. As expected, many individuals mentioned trust-building behaviors such as fairness, behavioral integrity, and so on. An unanticipated, interesting theme regarding the implementation of these behaviors arose: roles in organizations, particularly leadership roles, put individuals in dilemmas that make it difficult to consistently engage in trust-building behaviors and often encourage individuals to engage in trust-breaking behaviors. More specifically, the dilemma leaders encounter is that they may have to simultaneously *meet* the expectations of one party and *violate* the expectations of another. For example, a leader might face demands to meet goals set by one's superiors (for example, cut costs), and simultaneously fulfill compensation promises to one's subordinates that conflict with those demands. Or, leaders may feel the need to give special treatment to "stars," high-potential employees while simultaneously having to meet expectations from other employees about treating all subordinates as equals. Or, in trying to manage the perceptions of diverse constituencies, such as various groups of employees, superiors or directors, customers, and stockholders, leaders may represent themselves in inconsistent ways (Simons 2002). When leaders face such "trust dilemmas" they are forced to take an action that sustains the trust of one party but breaks the trust of another.

Several psychological factors associated with attribution processes grounded in the *perceivers* are also likely to accentuate the problem. First, leaders face a high level of scrutiny from followers because followers' outcomes are often dependent on decisions made by leaders (Berscheid et al. 1976). As a consequence of this scrutiny, employees may be particularly likely to notice when managers do not fulfill expectations (Simons 2002). When Roderick Kramer (1996) examined pairs of graduate students and their advisers, he found that the students spent a substantial amount of their time observing the advisers and ruminating on their behavior and motives (three to nine times more time than advisers reported thinking about the students!). In addition, students often drew very negative conclusions about faculty behaviors toward them, even when those behaviors had no intention behind them. In their search for signs of a leader's trustworthiness, perceivers may find trust dilemmas particularly rich in information, since these situations may be seen as revealing a leader's "true" motives as they are put to the test under conflicting pressures.

A second factor involved in the perceptual process builds on a well-established finding from attribution research, that individuals typically discount the extent to which situational factors are the cause of individual behavior as compared to dispositional factors (Gilbert and Malone 1995). In other words, individuals may overattribute the behavior to the leader's disposition—his or her trustworthiness—and not to the dilemma the leader faces. When individuals have an unfulfilled expectation they may be more likely to attribute responsibility to the disposition of the person causing that negative outcome than to situational factors.

Third, trust may be more easily broken than built (Lewicki and Wiethoff 2000). Even a single incident in which a leader violates the expectations of followers can create a significant drop in the level of trust and make followers more sensitive to future actions, which they may interpret as a violation. This phenomenon derives from the bias toward seeing negative information as more diagnostic for making character judgments than positive information (see, for example, Skowronski and Carlston 1989). In other words, humans tend to see negative acts such as breaking a promise, failing to follow through on a commitment, being dishonest, or behaving without integrity as being highly informative about another's character. As noted above, trust dilemmas create the conditions under which a violation of trust is likely.

Another line of inquiry concerns the personal dispositions of subordinates. Some writers (for example, Salam 2000) have argued that such characteristics as integrity and competence will not be sufficient to increase trust in subordinates of certain personalities. The generalized expectation of trustworthiness of others (Mayer, Davis, and Schoorman 1995) would be such a personality trait. In addition to focusing on personality as a main effect on trust, a relevant question is whether the subordinate's personality moderates the trust-in-leader and subordinate-reaction relationship. For example, employees who are high (versus low) on neuroticism and low (versus high) on agreeableness measures tend to have stronger reactions to unfair treatment by their managers (Skarlicki, Folger, and Tesluk 1999). Thus, personality variables associated with one's attribution styles (Kramer 1994) and generalized outlook (such as neuroticism) are likely to be important moderators in terms of understanding the relationship between trust in leader and various outcome variables.

Future research might explore the factors that create difficulty in building trust. We feel that exploring how trust in leaders is built and broken in situations involving "trust dilemmas" may be an interesting direction to take. Research on these would involve identifying the characteristics that make managers more or less likely to get into these dilemmas or who are more or less able to navigate them once they are in them.

The literature on cognitive biases may highlight why some managers are more likely to get into such dilemmas. For example, managers may vary on an overconfidence bias that creates a propensity for them to overcommit to promises that will be difficult to fulfill.

One example of the ability to navigate such situations involves anecdotal and empirical evidence showing that, some managers, even though they understand what behaviors contribute to trust, don't always do the right thing and may even exacerbate a bad situation. For example, a manager has bad news to communicate. Trust experts recommend that, particularly during hard times (layoffs, salary cuts), trust can be enhanced by such actions as providing high-quality face-to-face communication, including giving an adequate explanation for decisions, and treating employees with dignity and respect. Folger and Skarlicki (1998) found, however, that some managers tended to avoid interpersonal contact with employees when delivering bad news, especially when the managers believed they were somehow responsible for it. Because of a reluctance to transmit bad news, leaders may experience anxiety in communicating the truth (Tesser and Rosen 1975). Or managers may wish to avoid confrontation with potentially irate employees who may "shoot the messenger." Some leaders may be tempted to rely on e-mail for communicating messages that would be more effectively communicated in person. From a relational perspective on trust, leaders may be particularly uncomfortable in delivering bad news to individuals with whom they have a strong relationship. The pivotal issue in this case is that some leaders avoid taking precisely the actions that are likely to contribute to trust.

The impression-management literature (see Elsbach, chapter 11 of this volume) might also provide insight into why some leaders are better than others at managing impressions of their character when they are faced with difficult situations. Some managers may be effective at making their trust-creating behaviors visible to subordinates or be better at creating perceptions (warranted or not) that his or her gestures are sincere. This set of ideas may help diagnose a phenomenon that is both puzzling and frustrating for some leaders: despite the fact that they engage in trustworthy behaviors, subordinates do not perceive them as doing so and hence do not trust them more. This suggests that creating trust requires more than just engaging in the behaviors—it also requires managing the followers' perceptions.

One final issue that we have not discussed is of crucial importance: rebuilding trust. Once employees come to distrust a leader, how can trust be restored? Some scholars have suggested that rebuilding trust after a violation involves a different set of processes than building trust initially (Lewicki and Wiethoff 2000). Rebuilding trust may be particularly difficult given the documented bias toward seeing negative information as more diagnostic for making character judgments than positive information (Skowronski and Carlston 1989). This bias means that rebuilding trust in integrity can be extremely difficult and leaders should do what they can to avoid having to do so (see, for example, Kim et al., forthcoming). Although there are some interesting treatments that provide practical guidance for leaders (Galford and Drapeau 2002), currently little scientific work is being done.

Conclusion

Our goal has been to bring into focus some existing and emerging themes in research on trust in leaders. Many of the ideas discussed in this chapter await empirical testing, and the list of topics discussed here is by no means exhaustive. We hope it has become evident to readers that many questions regarding trust in leaders have not been tested, and we hope with this contribution to stimulate further thinking and research on the subject.

Notes

1. The trust and confidence aroused by leaders is a seemingly common theme in historical treatments of events that required followers to undertake extraordinary risks. For examples, see histories of Alexander the Great and his campaign into Asia (Green 1991) and Sir Ernest Shackleton's journey to the Antarctic—and back (Lansing 1959).

2. This perception may frequently be grounded in actual attributes of the other party such as integrity, dependability, or competence, but there is not necessarily a perfect correspondence between perception and "reality."

3. In the framework described earlier, cognitive trust corresponds with the character-based perspective, and affective trust corresponds with the relationship-based perspective.

References

AFL-CIO. 2001. "Workers' Rights in America: What Employers Think About Their Jobs and Employers." Washington, D.C.: Peter D. Hart Associates.

Aiken, Leona S., and Stephen G. West. 1991. *Multiple Regression: Testing and Interpreting Interactions.* 3rd ed. Newbury Park, Calif.: Sage.

Bass, Bernard M. 1990. *Bass and Stogdill's Handbook of Leadership: Theory, Research, and Managerial Applications.* 3rd ed. New York: Free Press.

Berscheid, Ellen, William Graziano, Thomas Monson, and Marshall Dermer. 1976. "Outcome Dependency: Attention, Attribution, and Attraction." *Journal of Personality and Social Psychology* 34: 978–89.

Bigley, Greg, and Daniel J. McAllister. 2002. "Transformations in Relational Logic: How Types of Supervisory Trust Interact to Predict Subordinate OCB." Unpublished manuscript. University of Washington.

Blau, Peter. 1964. *Exchange and Power in Social Life.* New York: Wiley.

Brown, Stephen P. 1996. "A Meta-analysis and Review of Organizational Research on Job Involvement." *Psychological Bulletin* 120(2): 235–55.

Colquitt, Jason, Don Conlon, Michael Wesson, Chris Porter, and K. Yee Ng. 2001. "Justice at the Millennium: A Meta-analytic Review of 25 Years of Organizational Justice Research." *Journal of Applied Psychology* 86(3): 425–45.

Cunningham, J. Barton, and James MacGregor. 2000. "Trust and the Design of Work: Complementary Constructs in Satisfaction and Performance." *Human Relations* 53(12): 1575–91.

Davis, James, F. David Schoorman, Roger C. Mayer, and Hwee Tan. 2000. "The Trusted General Manager and Business Unit Performance: Empirical Evidence of a Competitive Advantage." *Strategic Management Journal* 21(5): 563–76.

Dirks, Kurt T. 2000. "Trust in Leadership and Team Performance: Evidence from NCAA Basketball." *Journal of Applied Psychology* 85(6): 1004–12.

Dirks, Kurt T., and Donald L. Ferrin. 2001. "The Role of Trust in Organizational Settings." *Organization Science* 12(4): 450–67.

———. 2002. "Trust in Leadership: Meta-analytic Findings and Implications for Organizational Research." *Journal of Applied Psychology* 87(4): 611–28.

Fleishman, Edwin, and Edwin F. Harris. 1962. "Patterns of Leadership Behavior Related to Employee Grievances and Turnover." *Personnel Psychology* 15: 43–56.

Folger, Robert, and Daniel P. Skarlicki. 1998. "When Tough Times Make Tough Bosses: Managerial Distancing as a Function of Layoff Blame." *Academy of Management Journal* 41(1): 79–87.

Galford, Robert, and Anne S. Drapeau. 2002. *The Trusted Leader: Bringing the Best in Your People and Your Company.* New York: Free Press.

Gilbert, Daniel T., and Patrick S. Malone. 1995. "The Correspondence Bias." *Psychological Bulletin* 117(1): 21–38.

Golembiewski, Robert, and Mark McConkie. 1975. "The Centrality of Interpersonal Trust in Group Process." In *Theories of Group Processes,* edited by Cary L. Cooper. New York: Wiley.

Green, Peter. 1991. *Alexander of Macedon 356–323 B.C.: A Historical Biography.* Berkeley, Calif.: University of California Press.

Hogan, Robert, Gordon J. Curphy, and Joyce Hogan. 1994. "What We Know About Leadership: Effectiveness and Personality." *American Psychologist* 49(6): 493–504.

Jones, Allan, Lawrence James, and John Bruni. 1975. "Perceived Leadership Behavior and Employee Confidence in the Leader as Moderated by Job Involvement." *Journal of Applied Psychology* 60: 146–49.

Katcher, Bruce. 2002. "How to Improve Employee Trust in Management." Available at: www.HR.com.

Kim, Peter H., Donald Ferrin, Cary Cooper, and Kurt T. Dirks. Forthcoming. "Removing the Shadow of Suspicion: The Effects of Apology Versus Denial for Repairing Competency-Based Versus Integrity-Based Trust Violations." *Journal of Applied Science.*

Kirkpatrick, Shelley A., and Edwin A. Locke. 1996. "Direct and Indirect Effects of Three Core Charismatic Leadership Components on Performance and Attitudes." *Journal of Applied Psychology* 81(1): 36–51.

Konovsky, Mary, and Doug Pugh. 1994. "Citizenship Behavior and Social Exchange." *Academy of Management Journal* 37(3): 656–69.

Kramer, Roderick M. 1994. "The Sinister Attribution Error: Paranoid Cognition and Collective Distrust in Organizations." *Motivation and Emotion* 18(2): 199–231.

———. 1996. "Divergent Realities and Convergent Disappointments in the Hierarchic Relation: Trust and the Intuitive Auditor at Work." In *Trust in Organizations: Frontiers of Theory and Research,* edited by Roderick M. Kramer and Tom R. Tyler. Thousand Oaks, Calif.: Sage.

Lansing, Alfred. 1959. *Endurance: Shackleton's Incredible Voyage.* New York: McGraw-Hill.

Lewicki, Roy J. and Carolyn Wiethoff. 2000. "Trust, Trust Development, and Trust Repair." In *The Handbook of Conflict Resolution: Theory and Practice,* edited by Morton Deutsch and Peter Coleman. San Francisco: Jossey-Bass.

Masterson, Suzanne S., Kyle Lewis, and M. Susan Taylor. 2000. "Integrating Justice and Social Exchange: The Differing Effects of Fair Procedures and Treatment on Work Relationships." *Academy of Management Journal* 43(4): 738–48.

Mathieu, John, and Dennis Zajac. 1990. "A Review and Meta-analysis of the Antecedents, Correlates, and Consequences of Organizational Commitment." *Psychological Bulletin* 108(2): 171–94.

Mayer, Roger C., and James H. Davis. 1999. "The Effect of the Performance Appraisal System on Trust for Management: A Field Quasi-Experiment." *Journal of Applied Psychology* 84(1): 123–36.

Mayer, Roger C., James H. Davis, and F. David Schoorman. 1995. "An Integrative Model of Organizational Trust." *Academy of Management Review* 20(3): 709–34.

Mayer, Roger C., and Mark Gavin. 1999. "Trust for Management and Performance: Who Minds the Shop While the Employees Watch the Boss?" Paper presented at the annual meeting of the Academy of Management, Chicago, Ill., (August).

McAllister, Daniel J. 1995. "Affect- and Cognition-Based Trust as Foundations for Interpersonal Cooperation in Organizations." *Academy of Management Journal* 38(1): 24–59.

Oldham, Greg R. 1975. "The Impact of Supervisory Characteristics on Goal Acceptance." *Academy of Management Journal* 18: 461–75.

Pillai, Rajnandini, Chester A. Schriesheim, and Eric S. Williams. 1999. "Fairness Perceptions and Trust as Mediators for Transformational and Transactional Leadership: A Two-Sample Study." *Journal of Management* 25(6): 897–933.

Podsakoff, Philip, Scott MacKenzie, Robert Moorman, and Richard Fetter. 1990. "Transformational Leader Behaviors and Their Effects on Followers' Trust in Leader, Satisfaction, and Organizational Citizenship Behaviors." *Leadership Quarterly* 1: 107–42.

Robinson, Sandra L., and Denise M. Rousseau. 1994. "Violating the Psychological Contract: Not the Exception but the Norm." *Journal of Organizational Behavior* 15(3): 245–59.

Salam, Sabrina. 2000. "Foster Trust Through Competence, Honesty, and Integrity." In *Handbook of Principles of Organizational Behavior,* edited by Edwin A. Locke. Malden, Mass.: Blackwell.

Schriesheim, Chester A., Stephanie L. Castro, and Claudia C. Cogliser. 1999. "Leader-Member Exchange (LMX) Research: A Comprehensive Review of

Theory, Measurement, and Data-Analytic Practices." *Leadership Quarterly* 10(1, Spring): 63–113.

Simons, Tony. 2002. "Behavioral Integrity: The Perceived Alignment Between Managers' Words and Deeds as a Research Focus." *Organization Science* 13(1): 18–35.

Simons, Tony, and Judi McLean Parks. 2001. "Empty Words: The Impact of Perceived Managerial Integrity on Employees, Customers and Profits." Working paper.

Skarlicki, Daniel P., Robert Folger, and Paul Tesluk. 1999. "Personality as a Moderator in the Relationship Between Fairness and Retaliation." *Academy of Management Journal* 42(1): 100–10.

Skowronski, John J., and Donal E. Carlston. 1989. "Negativity and Extremity Biases in Impression Formation: A Review of Explanations." *Psychological Bulletin* 105(1): 131–42.

Tesser, Abraham, and Sidney Rosen. 1975. "The Reluctance to Transmit Bad News." *Advances in Experimental Social Psychology* 8: 193–232.

Van Dyne, Linn, and Jeffery A. LePine. 1998. "Helping and Voice Extra-role Behaviors: Evidence of Construct and Predictive Validity." *Academy of Management Journal* 41: 108–19.

Whitener, Ellen, Susan E. Brodt, M. Audrey Korsgaard, and Jon M. Werner. 1998. "Managers as Initiators of Trust: An Exchange Relationship for Understanding Managerial Trustworthy Behavior." *Academy of Management Review* 23(3): 513–30.

Williamson, Oliver E. 1993. "Calculativeness, Trust and Economic Organization." *Journal of Law and Economics* 36(1p2): 453–86.

Chapter 3

Supervisors as Trust Brokers in Social-Work Bureaucracies

JOHN BREHM AND SCOTT GATES

T RUST CONSTITUTES a central aspect of human relations, and within the context of organizations it plays a particularly strong role. The success of hierarchical relationships between supervisors and subordinates may hinge on mutual trust, and trust also permeates professional-client relationships. Public bureaucracies, especially those characterized by "street-level bureaucrats" (Lipsky 1980), exhibit aspects of both types of relationships. Consider a social-work bureaucracy: the social worker and client maintain a professional-client relationship, while the social worker and supervisor maintain a hierarchical organizational relationship. Mutual trust in either relationship is shaped by the nature of the other relationship; to consider one relationship, we must consider both.

To better understand trust in a public bureaucracy, and more particularly within the context of a social-work bureaucracy, we proceed with two steps. The first step is to explicate a formal model of trust in a social-work bureaucracy. This model, although quite simple, illustrates the heightened problem of trust in social-work supervision. We then identify a series of testable propositions that are consistent with both the extant organizational psychology literature and the specifics of our game-theoretic treatment. For our second step of research, we analyze a mail-back survey of social workers and case workers in the North Carolina Department of Social Services with the purpose of exploring organizational trust between both the front-line social workers and their supervisors and between the social workers and their clients.

As we demonstrate in our book, *Working, Shirking, and Sabotage* (1997), social workers fall under an important and interesting legal doctrine that

41

makes organizational trust a requirement of paramount importance. This doctrine, *respondeat superiore* ("Let the master answer"), states that the supervisor is legally responsible for the actions of the subordinate. At the same time, the client of the social worker is entitled to protection of his or her privacy, and thus the interactions between social worker and client are covered by unusual confidentiality requirements. Trust inherently permeates the relationship between the supervisor and subordinate as well as that between the social worker and the client.

Both of these relationships manifest themselves in the form of the "principal-agency" problem. One relationship is situated within the organization, involving a supervisor (the principal) who contracts for work from a social worker (an agent). The other principal-agent relationship characterizes the relationship between the social worker and the client. The essence of the principal-agent problem is one of asymmetric information, such that the abilities and preferences of the agent are unknown (adverse selection), and the actions of the agent not entirely observable (moral hazard). The dominant approach in application of these ideas to organizational oversight is to feature the problem of observability of actions, leading to an emphasis upon optimal contracts, or, short of that, a coercive conception of the supervisor. Indeed, most work drawing on a principal-agent perspective tends to apply theories of the firm (for example, Holmstrom 1982) to all hierarchical organizations, private or public. We argue (Brehm and Gates 1997) that although principal-agent theory offers many insights for understanding such relationships, one must be careful in applying models developed for private-sector firms and applying them to public bureaucracies. We share the concerns raised by Gary Miller (chapter 5 of this volume) that overregulation and overemphasis on monitoring and on rules and contracts specifying pecuniary compensation might lead subordinates to work "too" closely to the rule, not accomplishing all that bureaucracies need them to. Likewise, along with Kurt Dirks and Daniel Skarlicki (chapter 2 of this volume), we urge scholars to attend to noninstrumental aspects of the subordinate-supervisor relationship such as the supervisor's reputation for "integrity, dependability, fairness, and ability" (23).

Like firms, public bureaucracies are hierarchies, but these two institutions share only a few important characteristics. Important differences between the private and public sectors necessitate the development of models of hierarchy designed with the special characteristics of public bureaucracy in mind. Unlike firms, public bureaucracies rarely have residuals to distribute; supervisory abilities in the civil service are generally sharply limited; and the public sector tends to rely on socially positive incentives for participation and recruitment (Moe 1984). These differences demonstrate that in order to model the role of trust in a public bureaucracy, specific characteristics of the public sector need to be taken into account. One cannot simply extend the theory of the firm to the public bureaucracy.

This line of research extends our interest in identifying alternative functions of the executive in public bureaucracies. We have argued (Brehm and Gates 1997) that the conception of the supervisor in terms of the coercive principal—meting out rewards, devising contracts, developing monitoring schemes—only weakly fits the conception of the public supervisor. Instead, we suggest that alternative roles are better conceptualizations, including that of task coordinator (Brehm and Gates 1999), teacher (Brehm and Gates 1993), and mission advocate (Carpenter 2001). In particular, our argument here is that supervisors gain effort from their subordinates by cultivating trust, and they cultivate trust through both training and providing political "cover" to protect subordinates from outside political interference. In some senses, this proposition is a perverse reversal of the principal-agency problem: the subordinate provides greater effort when certain principals stay away. But in other senses, this is a reaffirmation of the importance of the "scalar chain" of supervision, this time, thought of not in terms of moving over the head of one's supervisor to the chief but in terms of the chief's defending his or her supervisors. This is a contrast in emphasis to Dirks and Skarlicki (chapter 2 of this volume), who emphasize the equally important role of the dyadic relationship between supervisor and subordinate (a point very much in sympathy with our earlier arguments in Brehm and Gates 1997), the emphasis here being on the relationship of the supervisor and subordinate to other actors outside of the dyad.

At root there is a fundamental problem of trust between supervisors and their subordinate social workers. Not only is the supervisor seriously hampered by civil service regulations, but the preferences of the agents constrain their abilities to supervise their clients, in the very condition where the supervisor is legally responsible for the agent's actions. There is also a critical trust relationship between the social worker and the social worker's clients. Social workers in many states are responsible for administration of the state's welfare, child services, and adult services and also drug and alcohol counseling. Their responsibilities can lead the social worker to remove children from the home, restrain spouses from contact with their family, remove or prolong welfare subsistence checks, or certify for access to state mental health programs. This level of discretion means that the clients are often wary of the actions of the social worker, which creates conditions where a trusting relationship is what prevents the more coercive aspects of the social worker's responsibilities from coming into force. Again, we note the observations in Gary Miller's contribution to this collection (chapter 5) on the positive effects of reducing direct supervision and monitoring.

We examine the role of trust in this network of relationships between the supervisor, social worker, and client. The central questions that we wish to feature with this research are as follows: Under what conditions will the social-work supervisor expand scrutiny of the actions of his or her subordinates? When do supervisors expand the scope of non-monitored activities engaged in by social workers? How do supervisors identify the trustworthiness of their subordinates? How do social workers identify the trustworthiness of their customers? What do social workers do to develop the trust of their clients? Under what conditions do clients trust the recommendations of social workers? The answers to these questions will help us draw conclusions about the role of trust in public bureaucracies.

Conceptualizing Trust

Before examining the role of trust in social-worker bureaucracies, we first provide a brief review of how trust has been conceptualized. Work on trust as applied to organizations can be categorized into two major groups, psychologically based theories and rational-choice theories.[1]

Bridging the two research traditions of organizational psychology and sociology with economic-based principal-agent models is a paper by David Kreps (1990) in which he presents the trust-honor game.[2] The trust-honor game (see figure 3.1) involves two players, a principal and an agent. In our context, consider them to be a boss and worker. The game begins with the worker having to decide whether or not to trust a boss. In turn, the boss decides whether or not to honor the worker's trust, that is, by choosing the cooperative outcome of honor. By honoring the worker's trust, the worker and boss earn payoffs of $10. But the boss can be tempted to abuse the worker's trust and receive a payoff of $15, which gives the worker a loss of –$5. If the worker never trusts the boss they both receive nothing ($0) and the boss has no choice.

This is a version of a one-sided prisoner's dilemma game. We can solve this game by backward induction. In a one-shot game, a boss will opt for the $15 over the $10 and choose to abuse the worker's trust. By looking forward in the game tree and reasoning using backwards induction, the worker will thus not trust the boss. This results in both players' ending up worse off than if they had trusted and honored one another.

Most interactions of this sort are not one-shot games and are played over and over again. Under conditions of repeated play, the losses resulting from distrust and dishonor start to accumulate. Fortunately, the folk-theorem result demonstrates that trust and honor may very well emerge as an equilibrium outcome if both players value the future and see no foreseeable end to the game. The problem with the folk theorem is that it also demonstrates that there are lots of potential equilibria in

Figure 3.1   Kreps's Trust-Honor Game

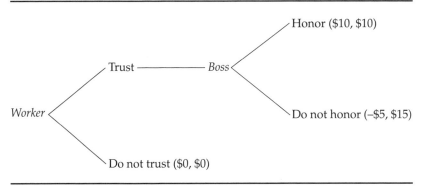

Source: Kreps 1990, 100. Reprinted with the permission of Cambridge University Press.

addition to the cooperative one of trust-honor. The implication is that there is no guide for choosing between different outcomes from the repeated trust-honor game.

Kreps turns to the concept of organizational culture to help guide his analysis around this plethora of equilibria. In games with many equilibria, conventions, organizational norms, and common experiences provide the rules that allow players to distinguish one equilibrium from another. Thomas C. Schelling (1978) refers to these rules as focal points.[3] Game theorists have refined Schelling's theory of focal points in two ways. The first approach features a series of preliminary moves in which players' actions facilitate coordination. Hans Haller and Vincent Crawford (1990) focus, for example, on players' moves made early in the game so as to create a focal point on which to coordinate, despite common knowledge problems. A second approach features extra-game concepts such as psychological (Mehta, Starmer, and Sugden 1994; Bacharach and Bernasconi 1997), organizational, and/or cultural forms (Kreps 1990; Miller 1992; O'Neill 1999) that allow coordination. It is this second approach that we adopt here.

Organizational culture provides the mechanism that identifies these focal points. "It is this psychological network of mutually reinforcing expectations that makes one perfectly feasible outcome (cooperation) occur instead of another perfectly feasible outcome (noncooperation)" (Miller 1992, 207). Trust and honor are by-products of an organizational culture.

Trust, Honor, and Reform: Trust-Honor Redux

The trust-honor game has been used in a variety of contexts to explore the relationship between a supervisor and subordinate. The game provides

Figure 3.2   Trust-Honor-Reform Game

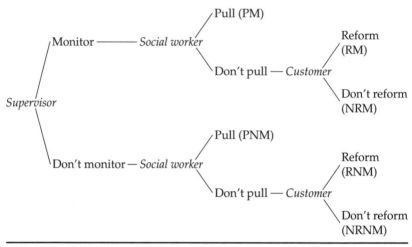

Source: Authors' compilation.

useful insights into organizational culture (Kreps 1990; Miller 1992) and into broader matters (Gibbons 2001). For our purposes of understanding the role of trust in public bureaucracy, we expand the trust-honor game to include three actors—a supervisor, a subordinate social worker, and a client—in the specific context of social work. This game, the trust-honor-reform game, is presented in figure 3.2.

The game begins with a supervisor who has two choices, *to monitor* or *not to monitor* the actions of the subordinate social worker. For our purposes, these actions parallel the *trust, not trust* choices of Kreps's trust-honor game. The social worker moves next with a choice of pulling or not pulling the case from a client. By pulling a case, we mean that the social worker has made the client ineligible for state support.[4] Given that the social worker has not pulled the case, the client can opt either to reform or not reform. By reform, we mean that the client chooses to comply with the social worker's strictures regarding child services, adult services, or drug and alcohol counseling.

This game produces a number of outcomes. First are the two outcomes reflecting decisions by the social worker to pull the case, either with monitoring (PM, for "pull, monitoring") or without monitoring (PNM, for "pull, no monitoring") by the supervisor. Then there are the cases where the client reforms, with (RM, for "reform, with monitoring") or without monitoring (RNM, for "reform, no monitoring"), where, of course, the case has not been pulled. Finally, there are the cases were the client does not reform, abusing the social worker's trust, with monitoring (NRM, for "no reform, monitoring") or without monitoring (NRNM, for "no reform, no monitoring").

To analyze this game, we will play with the relative value of these outcomes for each of the players. We start with a world where all clients are recalcitrant and non-reform is a dominant strategy. The clients also do not want to lose the state benefits, and don't like monitoring: (NRNM > NRM > RNM > RM > PNM > PM).

The social worker wants the client to reform but hates monitoring and would rather pull a case than let it fail: (RNM > PNM > NRNM > RM > PM > NRM). (This is exactly a point noted by Miller [chapter 5 of this volume]: that monitoring is costly not only to the supervisor but also to the subordinate).

The supervisors find monitoring costly, but want reform and would rather pull a case than fail: (RNM > RM > PNM > PM > NRM > NM). The logic is that supervisors prefer that the client reform without monitoring, followed by reform with monitoring, followed by pull with monitoring (such that "if the case is going to be pulled, I would like to know about it"), followed by pull the case without monitoring, followed by not reforming with monitoring ("Hey, at least I tried"), followed by no reform and no monitoring.

If this game is played once as a one-shot game and a client chooses to abuse the trust of the social worker, given complete information the social worker will choose to pull the case, not trusting the client. Moving backward up the game tree, the supervisor will choose to monitor. Take note, in this game the client's decision shapes the nature of the relationship between the supervisor and subordinate social worker. In other words, the professional-client relationship between the street-level bureaucrat (the social worker) and client establishes the nature of the hierarchical relationship within the public bureaucracy. The two relationships are inherently linked in this game, which could be characterized as a two-level game. So with these payoffs in a single-play game, we end up with an equilibrium of [*monitor, pull, no reform*].

Note that the preferences of the supervisor and the social worker are largely the same, the key difference being the distaste that the social worker has for monitoring (which is itself costly to the supervisor). Despite strong, shared preferences by two of the three actors, the outcome of the game hinges on the preferences of the client, with the result that the single-play equilibrium is undesirable to all involved.

Now imagine another scenario where the client sincerely wants to reform and all the other preferences are the same. Analyzing this variation on the game, we again start with the final decision in the one-shot game setting. In this case, since the client has chosen to reform, the social worker chooses to not pull the case, and the supervisor chooses to not monitor. The equilibrium is [*not monitor, not pull, reform*].

Obviously, in the real world we will find some clients of the first type, recalcitrants who will refuse to amend their ways, but we will also find the latter type, who are amenable to reforming their ways. The problem for the social worker is that she never really knows whether or not the client is the type willing to reform or the type who is recalcitrant. In such a situation, the social worker has incomplete information and must rely on her beliefs about the client or the population of clients regarding the propensity for reform. Similarly, since the supervisor's decision to monitor or not depends on the client's decision to reform, a supervisor's beliefs about the propensity to reform will also shape her decision on whether to monitor or not. But also of relevance are the supervisor's beliefs about the social worker's beliefs about the client's propensity to reform. Equilibria in such a game of incomplete information will depend critically on these beliefs. We must take such beliefs, which are critical to any understanding of trust in a public bureaucracy, into account. Indeed, trust is based on beliefs regarding an actor's actions and character (or in game-theoretic terms, an actor's *type*).

Recall how repeating the trust-honor game altered the characterization of the relationship between the supervisor and subordinate from one of no trust (and no honor) to a situation where trust and honor were outcomes sustainable in equilibrium. Repeat our trust-honor-reform game indefinitely and again the folk theorem comes into effect and our game is characterized by an infinite set of equilibria. But with the uncertainty caused by incomplete information regarding the client's type, we can get the [trust, honor, reform] outcome even with a finite number of repetitions.[5] The other implication of repeating this game is that each time the game is played, players are able to update their beliefs, not only beliefs about the other players but also about the organizational-cultural factors that determine focal point equilibria. With repetition, we find the same kinds of focal points operating as with the trust-honor game. The implication is that to understand public bureaucracies, we need to understand the organizational cultures that shape the working relationships therein.

In the context of a public bureaucracy, the updating of beliefs can follow a number of different patterns. Experience with a single client provides information on that client's propensity to reform. Experience with a set of clients allows the social worker (and supervisor) to update beliefs about the general propensity for clients to reform. Players also update their beliefs by watching others play. Supervisors supervise a number of social workers, who in turn are in charge of a number of clients. By watching others like themselves, supervisors and social workers can update their beliefs.

What our game demonstrates is that to understand trust in public bureaucracies we need to understand the nature of beliefs, the updating of beliefs, and the conveyance of information across social workers. These beliefs—social workers' beliefs about clients and supervisors' beliefs about the clients and their beliefs about the beliefs of social workers—serve to provide the entire foundation upon which trust is based. In turn, these belief systems will be supported and enhanced and shaped by the organizational culture of the bureaucracy. The implication is clear, beliefs permeate organizations and constitute the organizational culture and general pattern of decision making in an organization.

"Trust" regularly enters the discussion of potential solutions to repeated games. In some of these games, "trust" merely denotes an expectation of positive reciprocation. Alternatively, "The trust associated with delegation in political institutions is, like the division of labor itself, not an explicit contract but a rule of appropriate behavior. It is sustained by socialization in the structure of rules, and rarely considered as a deliberate willful action" (March and Olsen 1989, 27).

To that end, we expect that the process of socialization into the rules of the organization should be pivotal in cultivating a sense of trust between supervisor and subordinate. The clearer the rules, the more formal processes for socialization there are and the lower the barriers should be toward acquiring the sense of trust of the supervisor in the subordinate. The converse would also hold. Note, however, that clarity about preferences, beliefs, and rules is not sufficient to ensure subordinate compliance; after all, the trust-honor-reform game outlined above is a full-information game, yet the single-shot equilibrium is *untrusting*.

There is another relationship between trust and division of labor. In any complicated hierarchy such as a social-work bureaucracy where policy makers need to delegate decisions to subordinate experts, policy makers are more likely to extend trust to experts who are respected by outsiders, find congruence with the values and personal styles of the policy makers, and "who leave the politics to them, who yearn neither for influence nor for martyrdom" (March and Olsen 1989, 32). As such, we argue that subordinate social workers are more likely to trust those supervisors who can provide for political cover, and protect the subordinates from external influence.

Propositions

From the foregoing overview of our trust-honor-reform game, several themes emerge. Beliefs play a critical role in our study of public bureaucracy. We offer the following propositions:

- The supervisor can broker a climate of trust between the supervisor and the subordinate by providing political "cover." The proposition does not arise directly out of the trust-honor-reform game, but is consistent in that one means to establish a specific culture is to reduce exposure to conflictual external cultures. It is also a variant on the idea of the "scalar chain," introduced in the scientific-management era of organization theory. Henri Fayol (1949) and Luther Gulick (1937) considered it vital that if A is the boss of B and C, and that B is the boss of D, that both A nor C should not deliver orders directly to D, instead going through B.

- The supervisor can broker a climate of trust by better explaining his or her intentions and policies. The clarity of both supervisor and subordinate beliefs should improve the likelihood of achieving trust.

- The greater the shared sense of trust, the greater discretion the subordinate will have.

- Conditional on the subordinate's trust of the supervisor, the more discretion the subordinate has, the more effort he or she will expend on the job. Absent the subordinate's trust of the supervisor, however, the greater the discretion the subordinate has, the less effort he or she will expend.

Key Variables

We identify six main classes of variables: trust, beliefs about clients, supervision, discretion, work, and controls. Of these, two, trust and beliefs about clients, are new to the research agenda, whereas the remaining four were implemented in a prior study of Durham County (North Carolina) Social Services (Brehm and Gates 1997, 109–29).

We define trust of the subordinate by the supervisor as willingness to delegate risky tasks to subordinates without monitoring. By "risky tasks" we mean activities that the subordinate must undertake which entail subordinate choice to provide or withhold services for clients. In other words, we want our study to focus upon social workers' activities that most closely parallel exercise of the authority of the state, and hence the game-theoretic formulation outlined above. These activities would include, among others, decisions about eligibility for programs, reference of clients' cases to other authorities, and recommendations for commitment to medical and other outreach programs.

We define trust of the supervisor by the subordinate as the belief that the supervisor will support the decisions of the subordinate in interactions with third parties, such as the press, supervisors at a parallel level or higher in the hierarchy, and political actors.

Implicitly, these propositions lead to the model depicted in figure 3.3. We treat "trust in the supervisor," "discretion," and "effort" as endogenous variables. We treat "political cover," "attributes of supervision,"

Figure 3.3   Model of Supervisory Trust and Subordinate Effort

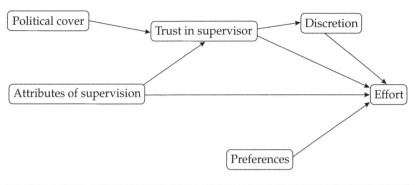

Source: Authors' compilation.

and "subordinate preferences" as exogenous. We will measure the positive, teaching-oriented modes of supervision as well as the coercive ones. We will measure both functional preferences (found in individuals who derive utility, such as a sense of achievement, from the job) and solidary preferences (found in individuals who derive utility, such as self-esteem, from interactions with others on the job).

Data Collection

Our data collection involved a mail-back survey of North Carolina social workers (front-line bureaucrats and their supervisors). (Because of North Carolina privacy guidelines, we could not survey the clients.)

A curious feature of social work in North Carolina is that the state delegates the provision of social services entirely to the county, including the design of the institution itself. In 1946, Herbert Simon criticized the scientific-management school of administration for attributing far too much certainty to the specific form of a hierarchy in organizations (in his example, public health). His criticism was that sometimes organizations would be organized by clientele, sometimes by task, and sometimes by geography (Simon 1946). North Carolina's one hundred county departments of social services include hierarchies organized along all three forms.

We initially contacted the directors of each of the one hundred county departments of social services, thirty of whose directors agreed to participate. The reasons for refusal were varied: some were conducting their own surveys, some had just recently completed surveys, some counties were going through a period of reorganization. The distribution of the counties was quite representative of the state, including urban, farm, mountain, industrial, and ocean counties. The directors supplied us with the list of the names of the employee social workers and their mailing addresses.

We then drew 1,000 names from the list to create a random sample and sent a mail-back questionnaire to 1,000 social workers and case workers. Of these, 511 responded (this response rate is better than most mail-backs, but lower than our response rate for the earlier Durham study).[6]

We measure social-worker and supervisor beliefs about the clients in reference to general parties, not to specific cases (in order to preserve the privacy of social-work clients). We will develop these measures with reference to the clients' willingness to "reform" (along the lines of the game described above): to actively seek employment; to participate in drug, alcohol, or other counseling; to seek shelter from abusive spouses; and such forth.

The remaining four categories of variables are derived from measures previously employed in our study of Durham County Social Services (see chapter 6 of our book *Working, Shirking, and Sabotage* [1997]). We will examine the following specific areas:

- *Supervision:* Studied by means of the social workers' perceptions of the closeness of supervision; whether the supervisor administers rewards and punishments for behavior; whether promotions vary by degree of effort.

- *Work:* The social workers' allocation of time across tasks; assessments of own performance and performance of others.

- *Discretion:* Social workers' assessments of autonomy in choice of tasks; assessments of the influence of relevant parties toward their allocation of time and effort; perceptions of closeness to deadlines.

- *Controls:* Include demographic characteristics; time on the job; training, and promotion paths.

Results

First we simply looked at the reported levels of trust in the supervisor for different levels of protection from outside pressure, and for different modes of supervision. Table 3.1 presents some of those results.

The cell entries in table 3.1 report the percentage who strongly trust their supervisor for each level of agreement with the question. For example, 40.2 percent of those who strongly agree that their supervisor protects them from the media strongly approve of their supervisor. The percentages are even higher for those who agree that their supervisor protects them from government (60.7 percent) and from other supervisors (40.7 percent).

Similarly, those who strongly agree that the social workers at their department learn by explicit training exercises, 32 percent, are likely to

Table 3.1   Percentage Who Strongly Trust Their Supervisor, Conditional on Level of Agreement with Question

Question	Strongly Disagree	Disagree	Neutral	Agree	Strongly Agree
Protected from media?	37.5	0	18.5	21.9	40.2
Protected from government?	10.0	15.4	22.1	29.4	60.7
Protected from supervisors?	6.3	2.3	22.9	25.1	40.7
Training provided?	5.9	21.2	25.4	29.8	32.0
Classes?	14.3	10.0	25.0	26.4	34.0
Hierarchical?	38.5	32.8	34.1	22.9	12.9
Fired for mistakes?	13.0	21.8	33.8	26.0	23.5
Constantly checked?	28.6	25.1	30.3	21.1	20.0

Source: 2000 survey of North Carolina social workers.

strongly approve of their supervisors. Those who say that they have access to classes to keep up with the field also tend to approve of their supervisor. More coercive aspects of supervision yield the opposite picture. If they say that the organization is quite hierarchical, they are much less likely to report trust in their supervisor. This is also true for feeling constantly checked up on—an echo of our model which assumed that subordinates hate being monitored.

First, we display the sunflower plots[7] for trust in the supervisor as a function of protection from outside pressure (figure 3.4). Quite plainly, the more that the subordinates sense that their supervisor gives them protection from government officials, the media, and other supervisors, the more the subordinates trust their supervisor: all three graphs are populated by large clusters toward the high-protection–high-trust corner.

Next, we present the sunflower plots for trust in the supervisor versus selected measures of supervision (figure 3.5). The upper two plots show the effects of teaching on trust in the supervisor: both graphs are peaked toward the high-protection–high-trust corner. The lower two plots display the effects of more coercive supervision. A sense that the department is hierarchical and that people are fired for their mistakes shifts the clusters away from the high-protection–high-trust corner. Note, however, that despite the differences in levels of trust that the mode is still a relative high degree of trust in the supervisor.

A finer-grained analysis is possible by employing scales that summarize the multiple questions in the study. We have multiple measures for each of the variables in the balloons in figure 3.3. Our approach will be to use principal-components analysis of each set of measures, and to select the first principal component as a scale to represent the measure. This strategy reduces the threat to inference from measurement error, and also provides for a more parsimonious expression of our model. The actual scales appear in appendix A. We produce scales for *protection,*

Figure 3.4   Sunflower Plots of Trust in Supervisor Versus Protection

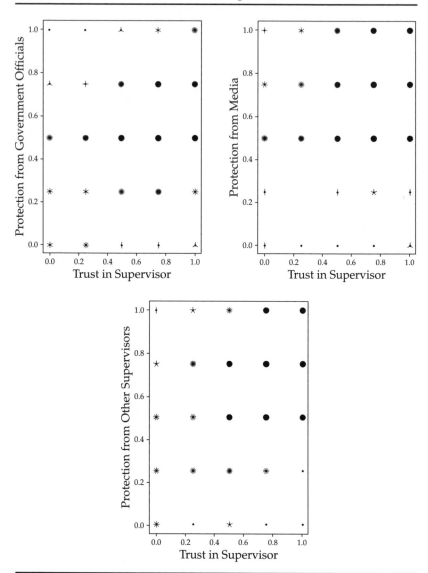

Source: 2000 survey of North Carolina social workers.

discretion, trust in the supervisor, functional preferences, and *solidary preferences.* We also include variables that refer to specific aspects of supervision, in order to assess their relative effects.

Given the subject of the essay, it is particularly worthwhile to highlight our strategy for measurement of trust in the supervisor. We con-

Figure 3.5   Sunflower Plots of Trust in Supervisor Versus Supervision

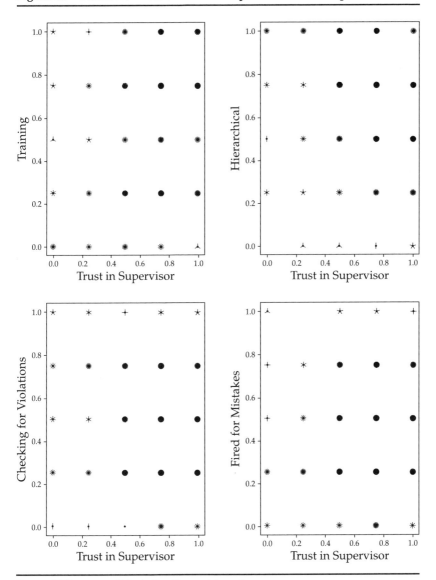

Source: 2000 survey of North Carolina social workers.

tinue to include a direct question: "In general, how much do you trust your immediate supervisor?" In addition, we want to capture ideas of trust involving a belief that the supervisor will follow through on intended decisions and acts with the interests of the subordinate in mind and also the subordinate's expressing comfort in speaking with the supervisor about problems with people in the department or with their clients. As indicated in table 3.2, the eigenvector entries (loadings) are strong, and the eigenvalues break sharply after the first factor, implying a single basic dimension.

Since all the input indicator variables for the principal components analysis are set to the same scale (0 to 1), we can interpret the coefficients on the scales in terms of unit changes (from minimum to maximum) of the indicators.

Working, Shirking, Sabotage, and Trust

Our first multivariate analysis of the effect of trust in the supervisor on allocations of work focuses on three variables:

1. *Work hard:* People in this department generally work pretty hard.

2. *Bend rules:* If you really want to get something done around here, you have to be willing to bend the rules.

3. *Hours:* Total number of hours worked in a given week.

The first item employs a tactic we first used in *Working, Shirking, and Sabotage* to assess the amount of effort the social worker provides. As per contemporary theory of the survey response, the principal object of this oblique reference to "people" is the social worker him- or herself, although the measure imposes a weaker social desirability component (Tourangeau, Rips, and Rasinski 2000). There is also an implicit secondary meaning to the question—are others shirking?

The second item, also from *Working, Shirking, and Sabotage*, attempts to ascertain in an indirect way the respondent's willingness to admit to policy sabotage in a literal sense.

The final item simply assesses the total amount of time a subject spends on the job, as a sum across tasks (paperwork, meetings with supervisor, clients, and coworkers, calls, and travel).

The next stage of the analysis employs three-stage least squares to analyze the implicit system of equations. The estimates appear in table 3.3. The models differ only in their choice of the dependent variable, so the first two panels of coefficients will be identical.

Start with the model for trust in the supervisor. The subordinate's sense of protection from outside interference is a statistically significant and modestly strong predictor of trust. A unit change in sense of protection (for example, a move from strongly disagree to strongly agree) would correspond to an 8 percent increase in reported trust. What is particularly intriguing is that the more subordinates saw training and classes available, the much more likely they were to trust their supervisor. With both training and classes available, they would be nearly 70 percent more

Table 3.2   First Principal Component Scale Construction

Discretion[a]
For the most part, I am in charge of deciding when to complete
the paperwork for my clients' cases.   .37
Employees are expected to follow orders without questioning.   -.08
My supervisor allows me to make what I think is the best decision.   .52
I don't feel that I have as much control over my cases as I would like. .35
My supervisor micromanages everything I do.   -.43
The administration accepts the decisions that I make.   .52

Functional preferences[b]
This job provides me with a sense of accomplishment.   .56
The most rewarding part of this job is that it really makes a difference. .58
It is encouraging to see the high level of idealism that is maintained
by people in this field.   .41
A person enters this profession because he or she likes the work.   .42

Solidary preferences[c]
My coworkers take responsibility for their actions when things go wrong. .43
I feel comfortable in confiding with coworkers about any problems
I have on the job.   .41
My coworkers don't care if they create extra work for other people.   .22
Working hard on my job leads to gaining respect from coworkers.   .35
The environment of the department is one in which coworkers help
each other out.   .44
The department is really very impersonal.   .25
A person gets the chance to develop good friends here.   .40
My coworkers take credit for things that I have done.   .27

Protection[d]
My supervisor does a good job of keeping members of the media
from nosing around in department matters.   .54
My supervisor protects me from government officials from outside
this department.   .65
My supervisor protects me when other supervisors ask me to do things
that take away from my main role here.   .54

Trust in supervisor[e]
In general, how much do you trust your immediate supervisor?   .56
When my supervisor tells me about a decision he intends to make,
he follows through.   .52
I feel that my supervisor generally has my interests in mind when
she makes a decision.   .55
If I have a problem with someone in the department, I feel comfortable
asking my supervisor for help.   .16
If I have a problem concerning a client, I talk with my supervisor
before speaking with anyone else.   .30

Source: 2000 survey of North Carolina social workers.
[a]First two eigenvalues are 1.89 and 1.12.
[b]First two eigenvalues are 1.86 and .88.
[c]First two eigenvalues are 2.67 and 1.21.
[d]First two eigenvalues are 1.59 and .84.
[e]First two eigenvalues are 2.10 and 1.02.

Table 3.3   **Three-Stage Least Squares Estimates of Working and Sabotage as Function of Trust in Supervisor**

	Trust Supervisor	Hours	Break Rules
Work hard			
Protection	0.08**	0.08**	0.08**
Training	0.32**	0.32**	0.32**
Hierarchical	0.06	0.06	0.06
Fired	0.08*	0.08*	0.08*
Classes	0.38**	0.38**	0.38**
Too many cases	0.04	0.04	0.04
Check rules	0.03	0.03	0.03
Trial period	0.20**	0.20**	0.19**
Constant	0.05	0.05	0.05
Discretion			
Trust in supervisor	0.62**	0.62**	0.62**
Functional preferences	0.04*	0.04*	0.04*
Solidary preferences	0.05*	0.05*	0.05*
Privacy	0.04	0.04	0.04
Constant	0.41	0.41	0.41
Work			
Trust in supervisor	0.10**	13.00**	−0.17**
Discretion	−0.09**	−7.44**	0.10**
Trust in supervisor × discretion	0.19**	9.26**	−0.12**
Privacy	0.00	0.59**	0.00
Functional preferences	0.00	0.63**	0.00
Solidary preferences	0.00	0.70**	0.00
Hierarchical	0.03	2.77**	0.03
Fired	0.05	3.98**	0.05
Check rules	0.04	3.40**	−0.04
Constant	0.11	8.66	0.11

Source: 2000 survey of North Carolina social workers.
Note: N = 509. Cell entries are three-stage least squares estimates for the separate structural models.
$*p < .10$ $**p < .05$

trusting in the supervisor. The first inference to draw is that certain institutional aspects of supervision can have a very large and positive effect upon the trust that subordinates have for their supervisors. Clearly, trust is something that supervisors, given the right tools, can use to substantially improve the working relationship.

By contrast, the more coercive tools do not carry nearly as much weight. A sense that the organization is hierarchical, that one can be fired for not doing the right things, a sense of pressure to take on cases, and a sense that the workplace checks on rules all have substantively small—

but statistically significant—effects upon trust in the supervisor. Perhaps what may be more surprising is that all of these effects are positive—one might not, for example, have expected coercive aspects of supervision to engender much in the way of trust.

The next step in the model is to consider the effect of trust in the supervisor upon discretion. The more they report a sense of trust in the supervisor, the more likely they are to report a sense of discretion. Given the scale of the variables, only minor changes in trust of the supervisor can lead toward large changes in sense of trust. By contrast, neither functional nor solidary preferences, nor for that matter a sense of privacy, tends to increase the social worker's sense of discretion.

Finally, what is the effect of trust and discretion on subordinate performance? Subordinates who trust their supervisors report that they work harder, and this effect is the largest in the model. This trust has a secondary effect, since those who trust their supervisor and have a sense of discretion are more likely to report that they work hard, while the unconditioned effect is negative. Strong solidary and functional preferences did not affect work, contrary to our previous work. Again consistent with our prior work, the effect of more coercive aspects of supervision is negligible but positive.

A virtually identical story can be told about the hours on the job. Respondents who report high degrees of trust in their supervisor tend to work thirteen hours more per week than the average. A strong sense of discretion with low trust leads toward nine fewer hours per week than the average. Strong discretion with high trust, on the other hand, increases work by more than seven hours over the average.

Unlike the pattern of results for the coercive aspects of supervision on reports of working hard, there is a small and nontrivial effect of hierarchy, rules, and sensing that one could be fired for malfeasance. Combined, all of these would lead toward an additional ten hours of work per week compared to the average.

As anticipated, the effect of trust and discretion works exactly opposite for willingness to admit to need to break rules, our measure of sabotage. Trusters are less likely to break the rules, whereas those with a strong sense of discretion are more likely to admit to the need to break rules. Interestingly, functional and solidary preferences play little role in the likelihood of a subordinate's breaking the rules, nor do the coercive aspects of supervision. Trust and discretion are what matter most.

Discussion

What have we learned about the importance of trust in public bureaucracies? We identify three specific components of trust.

First, our results clearly suggest that trust between supervisor and subordinate depends upon the availability of opportunities for the supervisor to train the subordinate, not just at the outset but on a continuing basis. Instead of thinking of the supervisor-subordinate relationship in adversarial terms—which principal-agency models take as their starting point—we argue that this relationship is more cooperative. But cooperation still entails uncertainty: What is the mission? What are appropriate boundaries of acceptable client behavior? What are the boundaries of my own behavior? What behavior should I accept in the supervisor? All of these questions raise issues of trust, and our results suggest that clarity of rules and communication are the best ways to achieve such trust.

Like most work in organization theory and public administration, the idea of the cooperative bases of management is far from new. Indeed, Chester Barnard (1938) argued for a conception of management based on exchanges. One could narrowly view the exchange in pecuniary terms, but Barnard clearly also considered subordinate discretion to be an aspect of subordinate authority. The notion of the importance of clarity in rules and in transactions is also not a new one: Charles Perrow (1987) makes a number of subtle points with regard to the purposes of rules within complex organizations. Although some organizations might fancy themselves as ones where behavior of its members is not tightly constrained by rules, Perrow suggests that they simply subject their workforces to unspoken but still enforced rules, resulting in lower morale. Indeed, March and Simon (1958), in their encapsulation of Alvin Gouldner (1954), point to the importance of the use of explicit general and impersonal rules in order to decrease the visibility of power relations.

This research, we think, helps to draw attention away from a not very useful conception of supervision as a problem of "control." To be sure, there is an interest on the part of the supervisor to elicit particular kinds and amounts of effort from his or her subordinates. But narrowly construing this effort as one of constructing strictly defined rules to regulate subordinate performance misses other important dynamics. Like Miller (chapter 5 of this volume), we agree that organizations truly need their component members to contribute beyond the narrow specifications of their jobs. Like Dirks and Skarlicki (chapter 2 of this volume), we agree that such attributes of the supervisor as integrity, fairness, and reliability are as important for maximizing subordinate contributions as perhaps the attributes of the subordinate herself or the nature of the task at hand.

Further, we think that this work has implications for how one conceives of trust itself. Our conception of trust is that an individual trusts another (in this case, the subordinate trusts the supervisor) under a belief that the latter will act in the former's interests, independent of the interests of the other. Like Russell Hardin's (2001) notion of trust as encapsulated self-interest, our conception of trust is contextual and grounded in particular individuals and particular actions: the particular supervisor provides specific resistance or political cover for the subordinate against other authorities. But unlike Hardin's, our conception of trust is not predicated upon a belief in the alignment of interests. It may in fact be quite costly for the supervisor to provide political cover; perhaps it is also a greater long-term gain for the supervisor to stand up for her subordinates. In fact, there might be considerable ambiguity about what is in the interests of the supervisor and whether or not she knows what those are. What matters here are the beliefs about how a supervisor will act with regard to the subordinate's interests.

Trust entails support, and support entails protection. A traditional principal-agency, control-oriented model of supervision in public bureaucracies has recently tended to regard the political principal as something like that where there is a padrone, an official who intervenes at every level of public service. Is the purpose of the "fire alarm" (McCubbins and Schwarz 1985) to have the citizen prod the higher-level political official to intervene in the administration of policy? This may sometimes be necessary, but our results suggest that the ability of the supervisor to protect his or her subordinates cultivates trust of the supervisor. Furthermore, the subordinates tend to see the media, other supervisors, and politicians all in the same light, as belonging to the "opposition." The implication is that the cultivation of trust within a group clearly demarcates those outside the group as the opposition, or at least an obstacle, to functional performance.

And again, perhaps the idea of strict maintenance of a chain of command with demarcated lines of authority, discretion, and autonomy has deep roots within the theory of organizations. Certainly, for Weber a key component of the bureaucratic ideal type was the identification of spheres of authoritative capacity. Likewise, early management scholars (Fayol 1949, Gulick 1937, and Urwick 1956) emphasized the importance of working within scalar chains of command, and holding subordinates accountable to single supervisors. What is perhaps useful to appreciate in this context is how much this notion of the cultivation of trust through protection differs from literal visions of top-down supervision.

Finally, we argue that trust is consequential: subordinates who trust their supervisor behave in fundamentally different ways from those who do not. Trust leads to a greater sense of discretion. Discretion on its own may raise the risk of greater shirking, but discretion accompanied by a sense of trust of the supervisor leads to a higher rate of effort. Trust matters.

We thank the Russell Sage Foundation for providing the funding for the 2000 survey of North Carolina social workers. We also thank Jennifer Merolla, Monique Lyle, and Jason Reifler for research assistance.

Notes

1. See Roderick M. Kramer (1999) for an excellent review of both literatures.

2. Also see Gary Miller (1992, 2001) and Robert Gibbons (2001), who extend Kreps's argument.

3. Research on focal points (or why one equilibrium should be focal) has developed only recently, despite Schelling's pioneering work in the 60s. See Gary Biglaiser (1994) and Barry O'Neill (1999) for reviews of the literature.

4. Obviously there are other options available to a social worker to induce compliance including the ability to remove children from the home, restrain spouses from contact with their family, certify for access to state mental health programs, in addition to the more drastic option explored here whereby the social worker decides whether or not to pull or prolong welfare subsistence checks.

5. This general result is demonstrated by Kreps et al. (1982) and Kreps and Wilson (1982).

6. There was a peculiar pattern of missing data among the questionnaires (item nonresponse), inducing unacceptable and exceptionally low degrees of freedom in the multivariate analysis below. In order to compensate for the missing data, we apply the expectation-maximization importance sampling algorithm advocated by King et al. (2001). In essence, the method imputes for missing data on the basis of the covariance patterns in the observed data, and creates several new (five, by default) data sets. The estimates we report below are averages across the multiply imputed data sets.

7. Sunflower plots are useful for scatterplots where there is a significant overlay, as is the case for the categorical data here. Multiple observations are represented as additional "rays" on the sunflowers.

References

Bacharach, Michael, and Michele Bernasconi. 1997. "The Variable Frame Theory of Focal Points: An Experimental Study." *Games and Economic Behavior* 19(1): 1–45.

Barnard, Chester. 1938. *The Functions of the Executive.* Cambridge, Mass.: Harvard University Press.

Biglaiser, Gary. 1994. "Coordination in Games: A Survey." In *Problems of Coordination in Economic Activity,* edited by James W. Friedman. Boston: Kluwer.

Brehm, John, and Scott Gates. 1993. "When Supervision Fails to Induce Compliance." *Journal of Theoretical Politics* 6(2): 323–44.

———. 1997. *Working, Shirking, and Sabotage: Bureaucratic Response to a Democratic Public.* Ann Arbor: University of Michigan Press.

———. 1999. "The Task Allocation Problem in Public Bureaucracies." Paper presented at the annual meeting of the Midwest Political Science Association, Chicago (April 1999).

Carpenter, Daniel P. 2001. *The Forging of Bureaucratic Autonomy: Reputations, Networks, and Policy Innovation in Executive Agencies, 1862–1928.* Princeton, N.J.: Princeton University Press.

Fayol, Henri. 1949. *General and Industrial Management.* Translated by Constance Storrs. London: Pitman.

Gibbons, Robert. 2001. "Notes on Two Horse Races: Hobbes and Coase Meet Repeated Games." In *Trust in Society,* edited by Karen S. Cook. New York: Russell Sage Foundation.

Gouldner, Alvin W. 1954. *Patterns of Industrial Bureaucracy.* Glencoe, Ill.: Free Press.

Gulick, Luther. 1937. "Notes on the Theory of Organization." In *Papers on the Science of Administration,* edited by Luther Gulick and Luther Urwick. New York: Institute of Public Administration.

Haller, Hans, and Vincent Crawford. 1990. "Learning How to Cooperate: Optimal Play in Repeated Coordination Games." *Econometrica* 58(3): 571–96

Hardin, Russell. 2001. "Conceptions and Explanations of Trust," In *Trust in Society,* edited by Karen S. Cook. New York: Russell Sage Foundation.

Holmstrøm, Bengt. 1982. "Moral Hazard in Teams," *Bell Journal of Economics* 10(2): 324–40.

King, Gary, James Honaker, Anne Joseph, and Kenneth Scheve. 2001. "Analyzing Incomplete Political Science Data: An Alternative Algorithm for Multiple Imputation." *American Political Science Review* 95(1): 49–70.

Kramer, Roderick M. 1999. "Trust and Distrust in Organizations: Emerging Perspectives, Enduring Questions." *Annual Review of Psychology* 50(1): 569–98.

Kreps, David M. 1990. "Corporate Culture and Economic Theory." In *Perspectives on Positive Political Economy,* edited by James E. Alt and Kenneth A. Shepsle. New York: Cambridge University Press.

Kreps, David, Paul Milgrom, John Roberts, and Robert Wilson. 1982. "Rational Cooperation in the Finitely Repeated Prisoner's Dilemma." *Journal of Economic Theory* 27(2): 245–52.

Kreps, David, and Robert Wilson. 1982. "Reputation and Incomplete Information." *Journal of Economic Theory* 27(2): 253–79.

Lipsky, Michael. 1980. *Street Level Bureaucrats: Dilemmas of the Individual in Public Services.* New York: Russell Sage Foundation.

March, James G., and Johan P. Olsen. 1989. *Rediscovering Institutions: The Organizational Basis of Politics.* New York: Free Press.

March, James G., and Herbert Simon. 1958. *Organization.* New York: John Wiley and Son.

McCubbins, Mathew D., and Thomas Schwartz. 1985. "Congressional Oversight Overlooked: Police Patrols Versus Fire Alarms?" *American Journal of Political Science* 28(1): 165–79.

Mehta, Judith, Chris Starmer, and Robert Sugden. 1994. "The Nature of Salience: An Experimental Investigation of of Pure Coordination Games." *American Economic Review* 84(3): 658–73.

Miller, Gary. 1992. *Managerial Dilemmas. The Political Economy of Hierarchy.* New York: Cambridge University Press.

———. 2001. "Why Is Trust Necessary in Organizations? The Moral Hazard of Profit Maximization." In *Trust in Society,* edited by Karen S. Cook. New York: Russell Sage Foundation.

Moe, Terry M. 1984. "The New Economics of Organization." *American Journal of Political Science* 28(4): 739–77.

O'Neill, Barry. 1999. *Honor, Symbols, and War.* Ann Arbor: University of Michigan Press.

Perrow, Charles. 1987. *Complex Organizations: A Critical Essay.* 3rd ed. New York: Random House.

Schelling, Thomas C. 1978. *Micromotives and Macrobehavior.* New York: W. W. Norton & Company.

Simon, Herbert A. 1946. "The Proverbs of Administration." *Public Administration Review* 6: 53–67.

Tourangeau, Roger, Lance J. Rips, and Kenneth Rasinski. 2000. *The Psychology of Survey Response.* Cambridge, U.K.: Cambridge University Press.

Urwick, Luther. 1956. *The Golden Book of Management.* London: Newman, Neame.

Chapter 4

Trust and Distrust in Patient-Physician Relationships: Perceived Determinants of High- and Low-Trust Relationships in Managed-Care Settings

KAREN S. COOK, RODERICK M. KRAMER, DAVID H. THOM,
IRENA STEPANIKOVA, STEFANIE BAILEY MOLLBORN, AND
ROBIN M. COOPER

I think trust is an important part of the doctor-patient relationship.
And, I think it practically defines how successful it will be.
—A physician focus group participant

THE CENTRAL role that trust plays in effective patient-physician relationships[1] has long been recognized and amply documented (see Parsons 1964; Caterinicchio 1979; Barber 1983; Mechanic and Schlesinger 1996; Brody 1992; Pearson and Raeke 2000). Trust has been shown to be a critical factor influencing a variety of important therapeutic processes and outcomes, including acceptance of therapeutic recommendations (Penman et al. 1984; Altice, Mostashari, and Friedland 2001);[2] adherence to physician recommendations (Safran, Taira, et al. 1998);[3] satisfaction with medical care (Thom et al. 1999; Safran, Taira, et al. 1998);[4] symptom improvement following an office visit (Thom et al. 2002); and patient disenrollment (Safran et al. 2001).[5]

Although the importance of trust has been established empirically, there are many essential aspects of trust within patient-physician relationships that are only poorly understood. First, because most research in this area has focused on a patient's trust in the physician (Anderson and Derrick 1990; Safran, Taira, et al. 1998; Thom, Bloch, and Segal 1999; Kao et al. 1998; Thom et al. 1999), we know very little about how physicians actually think about trust in their relationships with their patients. What factors influence physicians' trust of their patients and how does that trust affect, in turn, their behavior when they are treating those patients?

A second area where our understanding remains incomplete concerns the absence of naturalistic accounts of patient and physician trust. Most research on patient-physician trust has relied on survey methods that use standardized instruments. There are many questions concerning the extent to which the most significant features of the psychological aspects of the trust relationship between physicians and patients have been captured by these instruments. Few attempts have been made to ground models of patient-physician trust in more naturalistic, idiographic data that reflect the actual experiences of individual patients and physicians.[6]

Third, there has been relatively little systematic research on the antecedents and consequences of distrust and suspicion in patient-physician relationships. Most research has focused instead on the antecedents of trust and on the process of trust building (Thom, Bloch, and Segal 1999; Thom et al. 1999; Keating et al. 2002; Mainous et al. 2001). These researchers often assume that the absence of trust *is* distrust and therefore hold that the absence of the antecedents of trust breeds distrust. In contrast, we assume that distrust is not merely the absence of trust and therefore the antecedents and effects of distrust are not only distinct from those of trust, but also worthy of our attention.

Fourth, much of the research on patient-physician trust has treated the relationship as sui generis—independent of its particular type or the nature of the setting in which that relationship is embedded. For example, until recently, research on trust in patient-physician relationships has focused primarily on dyadic relations involving one physician and one patient. Increasingly, however, patient care in the United States is provided in managed-care settings. These settings involve multiple physicians who themselves work within a complex system of diffuse, multidisciplinary care provision. Most patient-physician relationships are thus embedded in some type of group practice or larger organizational context, where purchasers, managed-care organizations, providers, and patients participate in a complex system of power relations (Grembowski et al. 1998 and 2002). The proliferation of managed care makes a better understanding of the role of trust and distrust within these settings important.

Recently, a few investigators[7] have begun to conduct research on patient-physician trust within managed-care settings (for example,

Mechanic and Schlesinger 1996; Emanuel and Dubler 1995; Shortell et al. 1998; Hall et al. 2001). Managed-care interventions in the organization and delivery of health services have made issues of establishing and maintaining trust in the patient-physician relationship more problematic. According to one survey, many primary-care physicians are concerned that managed care has negative effects on patient-physician relationships, the quality of care, and physicians' ability to fulfill ethical obligations toward patients (Feldman, Novack, and Gracely 1998). Placing the physician in a gate-keeping role, altering the nature of the incentives to provide low-cost care, imposing constraints on the practice of medicine, and creating reimbursement rules that limit care options—all create potential problems of trust. David Mechanic (1998) also points out that trust in patient-physician relationships may suffer in the new system because of time pressures during the consultations, frequent instances of discontinuity of care, and increased responsibilities of the doctor to advocate for the patient and to allocate care. Mechanic and Mark Schlesinger (1996, 1697) conclude, "In the final analysis, trust will depend more on the quality of the patient-physician relationship than all else. Protecting this relationship from conflicts of interest and suspicion will ultimately best preserve those aspects of trust that are most important to the public and vital to ensuring the quality of their future health care." This recent work on the patient-physician relationship in a managed-care context sets the stage for our research.

A primary aim of our research is to address some gaps in the current research on trust in patient-physician relationships. First, we view the relationship between physicians and patients as reciprocal, and therefore we attend to the patients' reports of their trust in their physicians as well as the physicians' reports of their trust in their patients. We also examine the perspectives of *both* sets of actors as they report on the patient-physician relationship more generally. Second, we adopt a qualitative approach to provide naturalistic accounts of the relationship between patients and physicians to avoid the limits that standardized instruments can impose. Third, we address trust *and* distrust in our study, seeing the two as related but separate concepts. Finally, we conduct our study with a focus on the effects of the organizational context of a managed-care setting on trust and distrust between physicians and patients. This chapter reports some of the preliminary findings from one portion of our research—namely, the perceived determinants of high and low trust in the patient-physician relationship.

Methods and Data: Overview of Procedures

We collected data using both focus groups and individual interviews with patients and physicians in two family practice clinics in the San Francisco

Bay area. Physicians in each clinic were recruited to participate in the focus groups via email contact by the physician investigator on the project. Patients were recruited to participate in the focus groups on the basis of recommendations provided by these physicians.[8] There were separate focus groups for physicians and patients. Focus group moderators used semistructured protocols to elicit patients' and physicians' beliefs about the nature and role of trust in patient-physician relationships and their individual experiences with trust and distrust.

We used data collected in the focus groups primarily to develop and refine our individual interview instruments. Using those instruments, we conducted individual interviews with additional physicians and patients. The physicians were recruited to participate in the individual interviews through their participation in the focus groups and also by email or telephone contact by the physician investigator on the project. We initially contacted them by email and invited them to participate in a forty-to-fifty-minute-long semistructured interview over lunch in their offices. Physician interviews varied in length from thirty to ninety minutes.

The individual patients were recruited in the waiting room of a family practice clinic over several weeks. They completed a short survey while waiting and participated in a ten-to-fifteen-minute semistructured interview following their physician visit.

All focus group meetings and individual interviews were audiotaped and later transcribed. Transcripts were coded thematically and analyzed using QSR NVivo (Qualitative Solutions and Research 1999) software. This software aids researchers in handling, coding, and searching qualitative data. Every effort was made to remove any identifying information from data presented below.

Methods and Data: Overview of Sample Characteristics

We interviewed twenty-one physicians. The largest group among the medical specialties was family medicine (38 percent). Other specialties included cardiology, dermatology, hematology, internal medicine, neurology, ophthalmology, pediatrics, psychiatry, and radiology. Respondents had been in their current practices from one to thirty-five years. Physicians reported that they spent seven to fifty-five minutes with each patient, saw thirty to one hundred and sixty patients a week, and spent twelve to forty-two hours per week with patients and zero to thirty-one hours on administration.

We interviewed thirty-six patients. Patients were also asked to complete a survey containing questions about their sociodemographic characteristics, characteristics of their health care, and trust. Eleven patients

(31 percent of the sample) had been with the physician that they had just seen for less than a year, and nine (25 percent) had never seen this physician. The remaining respondents (n = 16) had seen the physician for more than one year (anywhere from one year to more than five years).

Perceived Determinants of Trust in Patient-Physician Relationships: Some Preliminary Findings

We organize our discussion of the preliminary findings of our study in the following way. First, we discuss the determinants of patient trust in physicians as indicated by the patients themselves in the focus groups and interviews we conducted. Many of their responses closely parallel those found in the emerging survey literature on patient trust and satisfaction (Keating et al. 2002, Mainous et al. 2001, Safran, Kosinski, et al. 1998; Stepanikova, Mollborn, and Cook 2002; Mollborn, Stepanikova, and Cook 2002; Thom et al. 1999, Thom et al. 2002). We provide greater detail concerning the specific link between physician behaviors and patient trust. Second, we look more carefully at the problematic physician behaviors as perceived by the patients that hinder the development of trust (or that create distrust) and that may lead to negative health outcomes or disenrollment, among other things. Third, we move from the analysis of specific behaviors to examine the effect of the social characteristics of both the physicians and the patients on trust in the patient-physician relationship. Specifically, we consider how the gender, age, culture, race-ethnicity, and professional status of the physicians and the patients play a role in the patient-physician relationship. After focusing on both physician and patient reports concerning trust-related phenomena in the patient-physician relationship, we investigate their reactions to the imposition of managed care in the settings in which they receive or deliver health care. We conclude with a discussion of the theoretical implications of this research.

We begin with a focus on the perceptions of the patients of the physicians they encounter. We also present reports from the physicians of their own perceptions of their behaviors which might facilitate (or hinder) the development of a trusting relation.

Factors Contributing to Patient-Physician Trust

Previous research suggests that physician behaviors are important predictors of a patient's trust and other health-care outcomes related to the patient-physician relationship, such as satisfaction and the likelihood of changing physicians (Keating et al. 2002). Patients and physicians in our study mentioned a number of specific behaviors that physicians engage in during their visits that were believed to affect the levels of the patient's trust in his or her physician.

Physician Caring and Empathy   One overarching theme that emerged consistently from both the patient and physician data was that caring and treating a patient in a personal fashion is a critical component of trust development. This theme is consistent with previous research. Scholars have studied verbal and nonverbal behaviors expressing affiliation with the patient (Buller and Buller 1987), concern for the patient (Roberts and Arguete 2000), and treating the patient as a person rather than as a case (Ben-Sira 1980). They argue that these behaviors are irreplaceable in establishing a therapeutic relationship. David Thom and Bruce Campbell (1997) and Carlos Roberts and Mara Arguete (2000) present evidence that establishes a clear link between physicians' socio-emotive behaviors and patients' trust. Still other researchers illustrate that socio-emotive behaviors are related to a patient's satisfaction (Wilson and McNamara 1982, Di Matteo and Hays 1980, Ben-Sira 1980, Buller and Buller 1987), a patient's commitment to the physician (for example, Kasteler, Kane, and Olsen 1976), and the likelihood that the patient will recommend the physician to a friend (Roberts and Arguete 2000).

Physicians who indicate their involvement in the patient's health as well as their care and concern for the patient by using behaviors that ameliorate the power and status differences inherent in the patient-physician relationship engendered more trust. We comment further on aspects of the power difference between physicians and patients and the role it plays in trust building in our concluding discussion.

Many trust-building behaviors of a physician personalize the relationship between a physician and a patient. Patients feel that a physician really cares about them when they are treated as distinct and valuable persons. The following patients emphasize the importance of the physician's genuine interest in the patient's well-being: "Because she cares about me. She cares about my health and I like her and I trust her" (patient 2). Patient 30: "In case you're really interested, it's not always what they do or say. Well, it would be more what they do. If they look at you straight in the eye, if they show that they really care."

Another patient (patient 40) explained "she did seem to be a little more concerned, expressed concerns in terms of specifics. Eye contact. Asked me a variety of questions, more detailed." Another respondent (patient 22) corroborated this view: "You run into some of the doctors who are—the good doctors or the doctors that you feel—oh yeah, this is a good one. I ran into a good one. You know? Hold on to that one. They always fall into the same category about being, like, genuinely caring about others' problems."

Patients expressed that they wanted to be seen as persons, not solely as medical cases. For example, patient 38 stated: "I think it also depends on the doctor . . . on the way they treat you, how they, are they looking at you when they're examining you and how they treat you as a person, not only as a patient. That makes a difference in how much you trust . . . a physician."

Patient 4: "And personal touches that I get from my doctor I think are nice. Like she remembers what I was thinking about doing career-wise the last time I saw her."

Patient 3: "My doctor . . . always remembers who I am, what I do. So it has a personal touch, without being overly nosy or that kind of thing. And always helpful. It's not always what she says, it's the way she is,"

Patient 40 elaborated on these themes of genuine interest and personalization: "[The physician] just talks to you like you're a person; you're not a number. He asks how the family is doing and he makes it very personable, more than okay-next-type, fast-food-type medical treatment. . . . Again, taking the time to have a human interaction rather than a series of rehearsed . . . response behaviors. The thing about a human interaction is that it is an open dialogue and it takes its cues from what's going on rather than from some preset plan that somebody has. . . . That's what a mechanic does with an automobile, not what a person does with another human being. It all comes down really to the level of aloofness, of failing to pay reasonable attention, participate in an exchange. That's something that is very important. . . . It's a matter that he will not give the attention required to bring more of his training to bear on really figuring out what's causing me the problems I have."

At this level, personalization and individualization are fairly abstract constructs. Our data suggest that they can be operationalized in terms of a number of specific nonverbal and verbal behaviors that physicians engage in during their patient interactions. These include eye contact, body language, and the ways physicians manage to receive and give information.

Eye contact. Patient 38 asserted, "I think eye contact is one of the most important things when you're talking to a doctor so that you don't feel like they're ignoring you. If you feel that they are ignoring you, you don't want to continue expressing what you feel." Patient 36 noted, "When she is done, she puts her pen down, and she will make eye contact with me immediately after she's done writing. Her eye contact starts when she enters the door."

Body language. Patients also expressed the belief that physician body language that expressed approachability and attentiveness led to increased trust. Examples of such behaviors included facing the patient, maintaining adequate distance, and refraining from taking notes while speaking. Patient 22 said, "I think the main thing is the body language and the use of language, it was very trusting and very encouraging. And if you sense stuff like the doctor is listening, and not just like—well, go on. You know? It's a very easy and very comfortable situation."

Patient 36, who reported having a high-trust relationship with her physician, stressed the link between her physician's behavior and trust: "Certainly, her bedside manner, or whatever you want to call it in the office. It was very approachable. . . . If I'm in a chair near her desk, or on the bed, or in either case, she will be almost within arm's length of me . . . she does face me. If she needs to jot a note down, she'll jot a note down, and she will stop talking."

Patient 15 emphasized that the physician should not be standing while a patient is sitting: "And he wasn't standing above me, which I know is a big deal, but I've always learned if you stand at the same height or slightly lower, then people are less intimidated. They're more open to talk to you."

Attentive or active listening. Consistent with the previous research finding that a physician's communication style is among the strongest predictors of trust (Keating et al. 2002; Thom 2001; Thom and Campbell 1997), patients and physicians in our study frequently mentioned attentive listening by the physician as a trust-building behavior. Patient 3 stated, "The ones that I trust are the ones that actually will listen to my entire history or listen to what exactly my problem is rather than cutting me off and just making a conclusion of the one thing I've said when they haven't listened to the whole thing."

Patient 10 commented, "Yes, he was definitely listening to what I was saying. Because he knew, he started asking questions." Patient 7 emphasized the importance of nonjudgmental listening: "[W]hen I saw how he reacted to that and sort of just listened and again, nonjudgmental and also somewhat sympathetic and not completely dispassionate. But he listened and said okay I understand you're hurting, you're dealing with stuff."

Physicians also stressed the importance of attentive listening. One physician (physician 14) put it, "[H]aving the space to do that, like walk into a room, sitting down in a relaxed way and saying, so, you know, what's going on? That allows people to feel like they're really listened to, that they're being heard, that they can really open up."

Physician 20 explained, "The best rapport I have with patients is due to two things. The first is being a good listener . . . it's active listening, where you really want to see what really concerns the family . . . so being a good active listener and allowing them—not being judgmental, allowing them to voice their opinion or ask their question, even if it to them is prefaced with something like, this is really confidential." Physician 1 even went so far as to assert, "Low-trust relationships are fairly uncommon if the practitioner was attentive."

Providing and explaining information. Patients indicated that they both expected and appreciated their physicians' efforts to provide them with ample information about their condition and treatment plan. They indicated that open and successful communication of information helped establish a foundation for their trust. Patient 31 put it this way: "She was very helpful. She answered all my questions. She even kind of got on the Web for me real quick to look up a website for me." Patient 32 said of a physician she trusted, "He was very frank, and he used terms that I could understand instead of long, complicated medical terms. He was very down-to-earth, and he was professional, but he was not uptight. He was relaxed and that made me feel relaxed."

Our findings on the importance of explaining and providing information are similar to those of Thom (2001), who reports that explaining, encouraging and answering questions, and checking a patient's understanding are among a physician's behaviors most strongly associated with a patient's trust. Some physicians we interviewed recognized the importance of communicating information and reported taking a proactive role in ensuring the success of the communication process. Physician 10 makes a practice of providing patients with written notes from their conversation: "I sit and write as I talk. So when they leave, they've got in front of them what I explained to them." This physician emphasized, however, that such action requires not only the patient's but also the physician's trust as it makes both parties vulnerable: "And again, it's a trust issue, but you need that in oncology." When a physician such as this one takes the time to write down what transpired during the office visit, both parties are vulnerable due to the potential for incomplete or mistaken information included in the transcripts. If the patient misinterprets something the physician wrote down, the patient might suffer an adverse reaction or worse. Since there is written documentation of the physician's advice, that advice can be more heavily scrutinized and the physician might be at a greater risk for a malpractice suit. Interestingly, this act of risk taking on the part of this physician may contribute to trust building (see Heimer 2000).

The theme of the reciprocal nature of understanding between physicians and patients emerges from the following patient's comment: "So if you communicate with them properly, they can understand you. They can give you more information, and you want a doctor to give us more information about that.... If ... the doctor communicates with me properly, I get confidence that I'm going to do fine" (patient 16).

Physician 12 talked about the importance of being honest and direct in communicating with patients: "[I say] the reason I'm late is because people needed more time than I had and now I'll give you the time you need. And that way I can keep a straight face and look them in the eye." Patient 4 emphasized the physician's direct communication: "It's just more the way that she is. When you first meet her, you see right away that she's just up-front and direct and no blow kind of thing."

Patient Participation in the Decision-Making Process   Scholars examining historical changes in the patient-physician relationship have pointed out that the paternalistic doctor-patient relationship is increasingly yielding to a more consumer-oriented view (Mechanic 1998) in which patients are aware of the available options, behave in response to these options, and evaluate the subsequent health outcomes (Ward 1987). Research suggests that building partnerships between physicians and patients and promoting shared decision making contributes to the achievement of optimal health outcomes (Stevenson et al. 2000). Recently, Nancy Keating and her colleagues (2002) have directly linked shared decision making to trust. Our research corroborates their evidence that patients who are involved in the decision making as much as they would like to be trust their physicians more than those who are not. Patient 22 said, "[The] main thing is someone who is willing to listen and to gather information, put all that information together. And the patient, like me, feeling that I have a say and I'm involved in that decision and I'm a person." Patient 5, in talking about a high-trust relationship with a physician, also stressed active involvement: "He actually offered a number of different suggestions as to what to do about it and how to approach the problem. And basically left it up to me to decide what I felt most comfortable with instead of saying you're going to do this."

Patient 36 shared the following about a trusted doctor: "Not only is that a good time for her to explain what the procedures or tests or what you have are, but it also allows for questions back to her for understanding and compliance. And so, yes, I definitely feel a part of the treatment." Another patient (patient 1) told us, "He took an analytic scholarly approach to the problem he was trying to treat and discussed the problem with me pretty specifically. He expected that I would learn enough that I could engage in a discussion. And I really appreciated that."

Perceived Competence of Physician   A number of patients stated that they consider a physician's competence a crucial condition for developing trust. Patients frequently emphasized the importance of the physician's knowledge and experience. One patient put it this way: "When you say trust, I trust in their knowledge. I really trust in their knowledge and I know that they are really very well prepared doctors" (patient 40). Patient 20 said: "It's crucial that the doctor is well informed.

Patient 23: "Well, when they seem knowledgeable about like what they're talking about and like my problem, or whatever question I have, I don't know if that seems—like that makes you trust somebody more."

Patient 3: "I've had some bad experiences in the past and I think that he seemed very knowledgeable and competent in what he was saying. So no, I think that I pretty much trusted him."

Patient 37 suggested that in the absence of his own medical knowledge, the confidence with which the physician expresses his medical opinion may serve as an important clue about competence: "He's pretty confident about his decisions. So that kind of helps. He seems to know what he's talking about. I'm not a doctor, so I couldn't tell you if what he's telling me is right, but it sounded pretty good."

Physicians also expressed the idea that patients' perceptions of physician competence facilitate trust: "The whole idea that they're not alone and this isn't the only case around and you've managed this before and it may not be a disease that's very treatable. . . . But at least that they're in the hands of somebody who can take care of them in the best way possible" (physician 2).

Physician 14 described negotiating her understanding of competence as the ability and willingness to find the relevant information with the understanding of competence among some patients who expect a priori knowledge: "I think that most important is that we care and if we don't know that we would find out the answer to some problem rather than just knowledge and although I don't know, maybe I'm, knowledge is important. It's pretty important. . . . Some patients are horrified to find out that I don't know what the, if I look something up, they're palpably horrified . . . I'm like, I mean you would not want me to be pulling this out of my brain. Not ever. I look things up all the time."

Physician Availability   Both patients and physicians emphasized the importance of availability and accessibility in maintaining trust in their relationships. Patient 4 said, "She suggested that I email her if I have any troubles before I have a doctor set up. I really appreciate all that."

Physicians mentioned giving patients access to their voice-mail or email and responding to them promptly: "The things that helped build the trust was availability, being available, easily available meaning by phone or by email" (physician 4). The same physician explained why availability is important for trust building: "[I] was just more involved in their life than just seeing them when they come in for a visit, I think, is a key thing in developing trust, because I think people see that you're more interested in them than just the little encounter you have in your office." Physician 5 reflected, "I give most of my patients, certainly those that I feel need my care a lot, my direct voice-mail."

Physician Time Management   Given the perceived importance of availability, it is hardly surprising that perceptions of the physician's time management "style" or habits were also viewed as important in building and maintaining trust by patients and physicians alike. Patient 10 described how a trusted doctor manages not to appear hurried: "She really focused her attention, she focused herself, she looked at me, she looked at my eyes, she responded to what I said, and even though I know she was in a hurry, her manner was not hurried." Patient 9, a foreign national, commented, "In my country, I would say I could trust the doctor when the doctors spend enough time with you, which doesn't mean he spends two hours, just spends the exact time that's needed so you don't feel you are just squeezed between people, but also you don't tell your whole life to the doctor."

Some physicians implied that they actively manage their time to foster trust. One physician reported, "I stop everything, take a big breath so that (and I talk very quickly) but really try to slow down so that they know that even if we've only got ten minutes, it's their ten minutes" (physician 10). In the words of another physician: "I try not to act rushed. I try to be comfortable, I sit down somewhere at the same eye level, I make sure that I shake their hands" (physician 7).

Other physicians explained how they deal with time constraints and use their time management to overcome potential mistrust. One physician reported, "In my sort of day-to-day interactions with patients the ones who are a little mistrustful or I think I try to treat them, I try to foster some trust by spending more time with them" (physician 14). Another physician noted, "The only thing I can do when I get in there if I'm late is say I'm sorry that I'm late and I will try to take care of all your needs. I try to give you all the time you need. The reason I'm late is because people needed more time than I had and now I'll give you the time you need" (physician 12).

Factors Contributing to Distrust or Low Levels of Trust

We believe that distrust is a concept related to yet distinct from trust. Our research supports this view. The data reveal a number of physician behaviors that are perceived as adversely impacting the possibility of relational trust or in fact lead to distrust. In some instances these behaviors are merely the opposite instances of the positive behaviors described above. Negative behaviors not only fail to create the conditions that foster trust, they can actually lead to active distrust. Research in psychology supports the claim that individuals remember negative interactions quite vividly (Fiske 1980). Physicians analyze how the interaction might have gone better or treat the incident as "caused" by some characteristic of the patient. Sometimes physicians see the interactions as a result of the patient's medical condition but more often as a result of the patient's general life circumstances or "who they are." Patients, on the other hand, more often view the negative interaction as a direct indicator of the physician's competence or as the result of the physician's lack of training or interpersonal skills.

Physicians' Trust-Hindering Nonverbal Behavior Patient 36 described in detail several nonverbal behaviors that hindered trust development in her relationship with a physician, mentioning distance, crossed arms, hands in the pockets, and lack of eye contact: "It was the first time I'd seen a surgeon. So, when I was on the table, obviously, in a paper gown of some sort, feeling pretty vulnerable, he comes in, mumbles something, which probably was hello, and stood at the foot of my bed, with his arms crossed. . . . You know, you belong at my bedside, not the foot of my bed. Uncross your arms; get your hands out of your pockets. That's another thing. I don't like hands in pockets. And look me in the eye. . . . He stood at the counter, kind of leaned back on the counter, stood real close to the counter, and I thought, wait a minute. Do I smell? No. There was distance. Granted, you're in a small room, so there's not a whole lot. However, it was noticeable, and, as soon as he walked in the door and stopped at the foot of my bed, that set the tone."

Patient 10 also noted the uninterested attitude a physician communicated nonverbally: "I couldn't see my usual physician here so I came and saw someone who tiredly and dejectedly went through all the usual questions of how long have you had the sore throat, let me look at your nose."

Physicians' Unavailability As physician 4, related, "Things that can make things go away from a good trust relationship would be not being available. So if someone calls and you don't answer them back, either my assistant or me, or they have a concern and you don't get back to them, then I think that definitely starts eroding things. If they can't get through to you, if you're unavailable because your system's so difficult to get through that can be a deficit. . . . Even if someone has a major medical problem and sees a specialist and needs that type of specialty care, if they don't see you as being part of that, then I think that can undermine [trust]."

Perceptions of Physicians as Being Rushed or Hurried Patients are concerned that a rushed physician cannot provide the quality of care they expect. An interviewer asked patient 21, "What did those other physicians do that made it difficult for you to trust them? The ones you had in the past?"

The patient responded, "Very sterile, very—no smile, no sense of humor, just quick, quick, let's get the job done."

Patient 31 said about low trust, "Usually that happened when either the doctor wasn't listening to what I was saying or was rushing me along in the appointment. Or I would make a statement or ask a question and they would either just blow it off or it was clear that their response, they didn't understand what I was trying to get at."

Physicians' Failure to Provide Adequate Explanations   Previous research has shown that patients who feel their physicians do not always give answers that are understandable have lower levels of trust than others (Keating et al. 2002). In our study, patients frequently commented on the physician's failure to provide an adequate explanation. Patient 22 related: "Yes, not explaining themselves and not being very—the body language and so forth. . . . And the intimidating part is all the technical terms that they throw at you."

Patient 1 noted that a patient's lack of understanding can lead to the dissolution of a patient-physician relationship: "In the case of my heart, what exactly, what sort of risks are they trying to address in treating it, which would inform how you would go about treating it. And that's been, with one doctor I've had it's never been clear so I ended up leaving that doctor because I didn't understand why I was being treated the way I was."

Physicians are generally aware of the risks that inadequate communication possesses for trust. As one physician put it, "Another way to decrease trust is if you tell patients no, they can't do something, and then not offer them a good explanation or not give them time to talk about it."

Later, the same physician elaborated: "If someone calls and says they have back pain and they want a referral, you say no, I'm not going to do that. I think if you don't explain to them what your thinking is, then I think that can undermine the trust they have in you, if they don't understand your thinking" (physician 4).

Another physician drew a link between communication, understanding, and compliance: "They are not compliant with whatever the recommendation is because they don't really understand it . . . either because I didn't explain it well enough or [the illness is] not reparable in their culture" (physician 9).

Physicians' Failure to Make Patients Feel Respected   One physician noted that the trust of a patient may be destroyed when the patient feels disrespected and not validated as a person: "I think it's important that you don't talk down to people, that you don't say—oh well that's—here's how it is. Because a physician is not invested with all knowledge and I think that [acting as though they are] goes a long way to destroying trust . . . there's a lot of sophisticated patients and they particularly like not feeling that they're being talked down to and like to be involved in the process" (physician 9).

A similar idea was expressed by patient 22: "This whole thing about trust is very important. I mean, how can you have a good relationship with someone who can't depend on you and trust you if you always make the other party feel like they're idiots?" Patient 20 shared: "I get very frustrated because so many doctors take an authoritative position that's not, I'm going to tell you what to do, I don't have to explain it, I don't have to, you know, pay any attention to your knowledge or your awareness."

Patients' Perceptions of Physician Distrust   When patients perceive that the physician does not trust them, their own trust is undermined. One patient related the following: "I won't go back to the other doctor, because I just didn't feel like she really listened to me and that she really understood what I was saying. It was more like she was questioning my—she was questioning whether I was telling the truth or not" (patient 27). Another patient described how physician behavior that may have indicated a lack of trust completely disrupted the patient's readiness to continue the relationship: "When we were trying to find a dentist, especially for my wife who has had lots of trouble with dentists. I've had experiences with them when we went in and they would say to me, they were going to look at her and I was waiting in the waiting room. I said no, I'm going in with her. And then he started talking and I started taking notes, he says you can't take notes. And that's it. At that point, we said forget it, we're out of here" (patient 7).

Social Category–Based Determinants of Trust and Distrust

In addition to the behaviors that are perceived to be related to mutual trust, both patients and physicians develop conceptions of each other in terms of standard social categories and the inferences they draw from membership in these categories. As recent research makes clear (Abreu 1999; Bogart et al. 2001; Johnson et al. 1986; van Ryn and Burke 2000), physicians, like other individuals, often use socially relevant information in making their judgments about patient characteristics and behaviors. Patients also use this information in making assessments of how competent the physician is and whether the physician *wants* to establish a committed, "meaningful" trust relationship with them. Gender, age, race-ethnicity, social class, occupation, and education are all factors that are as relevant to the patient-physician interaction as to any other class of social interactions. Our data include many references to these factors in both positive and negative ways, that is, as facilitators or inhibitors of a reciprocal trust relationship.

There is a substantial body of theory and empirical research in the social sciences that leads us to expect that social category–based stereotypes should exert considerable influence on how both patients and physicians think about trust and distrust in their relationships (for example, Hegtvedt 1988; Howard 1996; Ridgeway and Walker 1995). So far, research on the relationships between the patient and physician's sociodemographic characteristics and the patient's trust has yielded inconsistent results. Where some authors find weak or no relationships between trust and sociodemographic characteristics (Anderson and Derrick 1990; Thom et al. 1999), others report that trust is related to age, gender, education, and wealth (Wholey and Sommers 2001) as well as race-ethnicity (LaViest, Nickerson, and Bowie 2000; Wholey and Sommers 2001). Accordingly, we were careful when we were coding the data to note any indications of such category-based cues. There were many. Here are our preliminary findings in this regard.

Gender   Gender was mentioned often by both patients and physicians as a significant individual characteristic of the physician. Some felt that gender similarity between patient and physician facilitated trust by creating a more open relationship. One female physician said, "I'm sure that, I'm certain that women, young women and teenagers feel comfortable about coming to me because I enjoy seeing them and I enjoy them more than young men because I understand women better" (physician 14). Possibly gender concordance is more important to female than to male patients. One recent study of emergency-department patients (Derose et al. 2001) found that female patients trusted female physicians more than male physicians and rated female physicians more positively than male physicians on the amount of time spent, the concern shown, and overall. Male patients, on the other hand, trusted and rated male and female physicians similarly on all dimensions of care.

Our data indicate that female physician and male patient relationships may pose special problems for the physician. Two female physicians commented on the difficulties they sometimes encounter when treating older male professionals. One young female physician even terminated a relationship (sending the patient to someone else in her practice) when she felt that the male professional was not willing to see her primarily as a physician, having sexualized their interaction.

Another physician mentioned how gender may affect trust when a history of sexual abuse is present: "I have definitely seen some situations where female patients who have had histories of incest can have a difficult time with a male doctor and especially somebody where, where that element of their past is relevant, you know, to the reasons they're seeing a doctor" (physician 13).

Some doctors talked about the particular importance of gender similarity among some ethnic groups. One doctor noted, "I know many Asian, especially Asian female, patients looking for an Asian female physician. . . . Those female Asians they tend to have some female problems or we have to get details by short histories and probably they think we share the same kind of background, and it's easier to talk about things" (physician 20).

Age One physician reported that age similarity between a physician and patient plays an important role in developing trust. The physician stressed similarities in experiences: "And also someone in the age range of someone I'm familiar with, like my kids are two and five, so kids of that age I really, really feel comfortable" (physician 20).

A similar idea was expressed by patient 35: "I like the fact that he's on the younger side. I probably wouldn't want an older doctor because I think they communicate more, when they were my age that was a long, long time ago as opposed to being not so long ago. And it's nice to have somebody who has kids so they understand . . . their wife has gone through whatever I've gone through or they know."

Different aspects of trust development may be accentuated in childhood, adolescence, middle age, and older age. As one physician noted, "The younger patients are still maybe carrying over from their relationship with pediatricians, where they kind of put themselves in someone else's hands. . . . Older patients might be more in the old model, where there was almost a paternal kind of relationship [where they put themselves in the doctor's hands]. . . . But kind of middle-aged, maybe late thirties, forties, fifties patients, again, this kind of savvy patient group, might see us as an adviser, and take our information similar to information they get from the Internet. . . . [Older patients] might bring something up to me, and if I tell them I don't think it's significant or important, then they'll be more apt to toss it away and say well, this is what the doc thought. Whereas the younger patients might press me a little more, and maybe bring me more stuff from the Internet . . . to make the case. So they might be more seeing all this information as equivalent" (physician 21).

Similarly, patient 37 talked about how trust in a physician develops differently during the different phases of life: "It's gotten a lot easier to talk to them. When I was young, my mom did all the talking. A lot easier to communicate. I trust them a lot more now. I feel like I can tell him pretty much anything."

Culture and Race-Ethnicity Cultural issues emerged as another factor for both the patients and physicians in our study. Physicians frequently commented on the cultural similarities or dissimilarities between the patient and the physician as an important factor in trust building. The theme of the benefits of cultural concordance for patient-physician relationship resonates with recent findings from survey research (Cooper-Patrick et al.

1999; Malat 2001; Saha et al. 1999). As one physician in our study asserted, "I think cultural differences are huge. It's interesting in American medicine because there are so many just white Anglo doctors, that you've got a lot of patients from different cultures trying to access health care from providers that may not understand their cultural differences at all. It makes a difference in how they try to access health care from where they come from. I think in a broader sense in terms of the cultural context just knowing what their perspective is on a disease or disease process, knowing what they think about death or feel about death" (physician 17).

A Japanese female physician noted that many of the patients who had selected her as their family physician were Asian. Another physician noted, "The difficulty for me is that if it's a cultural situation that I'm not aware of or attuned to, then I may not be thinking that way" (physician 9). Yet another physician noted, "But in fact, we are all more comfortable with our own ethnic group. . . . When we're sick or when we're hurting or afraid, [it is] not [just] language but culture" (physician 1).

Physicians also talked about differences in trust building among different ethnic groups of patients. One white physician noticed that African Americans "often distrust the health care system and demand more care" (physician 19). Another white physician, reflecting on his experience with a low-trust patient, commented, "I think that may have something to do with the fact that they're from a Hispanic background, he even speaks with a fairly strong accent, so it tells me a lot about his acculturation which I think speaks to maybe the whole process of just coming to see a doctor especially one who's not Hispanic" (physician 1). The same physician reported the influence of cultural background on trust among those Native American patients who prefer traditional forms of healing: "I worked on an Indian reservation during part of my residency and what was interesting to me there is [that] most of the elders and some of the babies even had been to a medicine man before they came to see us." Such traditional beliefs may set an important context for the formation of patient-physician trust.

Some physicians mentioned special interactions between race-ethnicity and other dimensions of social stratification. One female, nonwhite physician reflected on interactions among age, gender, and race-ethnicity: "In elderly patients, well I guess elderly Caucasian male patients, I feel less trust when I go into the room for the first visit" (physician 8).

Education and Occupation   The patient population at our research sites was on average highly educated. Physicians commented on special issues facing them with this type of patient population. Physician 10 said, "This patient population is so highly educated. And I think the average health education intelligence level is higher. . . . It's also I think because of the educational level. People are used to excellent care in everything, and they're going to put me through my paces a little bit more, and ask more questions, and challenge me a little bit."

Physician 2 speculated on the connection between education level and compliance: "People here are pretty compliant and I don't know that it—it may have something to do with education." Physician 18 made a connection between socioeconomic background and trust, reflecting on its complexities: "People who are in management and marketing tend to trust me more than people with a lower socioeconomic background. . . . It often may have something to do with a person's background and their education, and we have—there are people and they have a lot of degrees and may be very good at one thing, but if they don't understand their body and the biology well enough, and they have their certain mindset, it's difficult to change them. . . . If I know their occupation and their education or social background, that helps me choose the right language to communicate with that individual. You know that . . . a college professor in literature communicates different—in a different language from a physician, communicates different language than somebody who never finished high school."

Thus far, we have discussed both patients' and physicians' reports of the effects of physician behaviors (verbal and nonverbal) as well as the effects of the social categories to which the patients and physicians belong (gender, age, culture, educational level) on trust and distrust between physicians and patients. We have identified how trust can be facilitated or severely hindered as a result of these behaviors or the stereotypes that accompany attention to these social categories. In an effort to expand our focus beyond the dyadic relationship between physicians and patients, we now consider the general impact of managed-care settings on the patient-physician relationship.

Impact of Managed-Care Settings on Patient-Physician Trust

As noted in the introduction, one of the major goals of our research is to provide more insight into the impact of the medical-care setting on the development and maintenance of trust between patients and physicians. Although medical care in the United States is increasingly being delivered in managed-care settings, the impact of that setting on the doctor-patient relationship has received relatively little attention. Indeed, one reason why we adopted a qualitative approach is to generate as much "raw data" as possible about patient and physician perceptions of the impact of this complex setting on trust (and problems of distrust) in their relationships.

Our initial findings seem to validate this approach. We found strong evidence that both patients and physicians in our interviews and focus groups believed that the managed-care setting has had an impact on the development and maintenance of trust in their relationships. Both patients and physicians commented extensively, for example, on the changes in the health-care system that have occurred as a result of the penetration of managed care into all aspects of the delivery system. The most prominent themes associated with the effects of managed care on trust include time constraints, lack of continuity and longevity of the patient-physician relationship, fragmentation of care, and conflict of interests for physicians.

Time Constraints

One important change associated with managed care concerns the time constraints that have emerged with the pressure on physicians for increased productivity. Such constraints reduce the time available for the development of the relationship between the physician and the patient (Sturm 2002; Arnetz 2001). One national study (Linzer et al. 2000) finds that time allotted for physicians to spend with new patients in HMOs (health maintenance organizations) is eight minutes less than in solo practices and thirteen minutes less than in academic practices. Moreover, family physicians in HMOs are more likely to feel they need more time than they are allotted for their new patients (Linzer et al. 2000).

The participants in our study shared the concerns about time pressures and suggested how time constraints may affect the practice of medicine. One family practice physician said: "And there are constraints in the sense that if I spend longer than that [fifteen minutes] with a patient, then I'm getting later and later, and I know I'm going to keep other people waiting. And, I often do spend longer than fifteen minutes with patients but I know there's a cost. Both the patients as well as myself, it affects everything about the way the day goes. So it's a constant tension between trying to respond to the needs that people have and give as much time as necessary but knowing there's never enough time and knowing that it's going to affect everything that happens for the rest of the day" (physician 5).

This physician was also articulate about the breakdown in trust that can occur as a result of managed-care constraints: "I often feel like I'm spending a lot of saved-up goodwill with my patients. Making little withdrawals and spending it . . . so the trust is there . . . but it's as if we're gradually depleting that and I'm not so sure how long that could go on without them, without that trust being so eroded that they would say, 'You're not the same physician I used to know. Or, you're just like all the other physicians.' . . . Just what I see in people's eyes, their behavior when they say, 'Thanks for responding to that issue, I have another question.' They say, 'Well, my wife and I have really had some problems,' and I'll say, 'Make another appointment.' You know people feel that. But here I am, I want to talk about it. Okay, they kind of understand that's not the way it goes anymore. That's not what it's about. I'm here only to address a certain problem."

Patients themselves are aware of the pressure created by the time constraints occurring in managed care. Keating et al. (2002) demonstrate that patients reporting that their physicians do not always give them enough time to explain the reasons for their visit and also do not take enough time to ask the patient questions trust their physicians less than others. Consistent with this research, we find that patients' concerns about time pressures negatively impact trust. Time constraints decrease rapport, make communication more difficult, and create stress. Patient 3 explained: "If they're hurried, I'm not going to automatically trust them because I can't develop any rapport with them in the short amount of time that they have. If they had more time to spend with each patient, I think that automatically you tend to trust someone more that you spent more time with." Patient 5 commented: "I think the interaction between the doctor and the patient is too rushed. There's not enough time to thoroughly communicate and there is a push, not necessarily from the doctor's point, but from outside pressure to make the quick diagnosis and run patients through like cattle through a corral." Patient 5 also said, "That's the biggest thing I've seen, is you just don't have the time with the doctor that you had before. . . . I think from a primary-care perspective, somehow they, I don't know, I know it's the system that kind of bogs it down. They're just so overbooked; they don't have time to take the overall picture." Patient 21 said: "They are put on a heavy, heavy scheduling time constraint, where they have to see so many patients in a certain amount of time. And it's pressure on them; it's pressure on their staff."

Lack of Longevity or Continuity of Care

Because patient-care responsibilities under managed care are often shared by multiple physicians, and because physician turnover in groups may be relatively high, managed care has created conditions under which there is often growing wariness among patients regarding the longevity and continuity of their relationship with a particular physician. Our evidence indicates that this situation has consequences for the development of mutual trust. Both patients and physicians frequently reported that it was easier for patients to develop trust in their doctors in a long-term, personalized relationship with a particular physician than in a short-term, impersonal relationship.

Physician 4 said of long-term relationships with patients: "I think it's something that has to develop over time. It's not something that happens with one single visit." Physician 10 emphasized that in the development of trust relations, "Time is the biggest factor." Physician 14 explained why a long-term, continuous relationship facilitates trust: "[There are] phases in relationships with patients where people are really needy in a certain time, and then they grow out of that, they go through it and then, and if I was present in their needy time, then we can, then they need me less when they sort of trust that I'm going to be there if they need me."

Patients saw a similar connection between trust and the longevity and continuity of the relationship. As one patient put it: "There was a family doctor. I can trust him a lot. Actually, I've had him ever since I was born. I don't know a specific instance, but just over time, built a trust" (patient 37). Patient 38 expressed a similar idea: "You don't develop trust in a single office visit of fifteen minutes. You can get an opinion of the doctor, I think, and you can decide whether or not that you would devote future problems of maybe more significant or private nature, but I don't think on a first visit or even on a fifteen-minute visit that you're going to make a very quick assumption of the doctor trust relationship that you could establish."

Our findings correspond to previous research indicating that length of the patient-physician relationship and the number of visits to the physician are associated with trust (Kao et al. 1998; Safran, Kosinski, et al. 1998; Thom et al. 1999). Unlike previous survey research, however, qualitative data enable us to glean insights into some of the reasons why a long-term relationship is an important factor in the level of a patient's trust in a physician. Patient 21 explains some of the reasons for the importance he places on the continuity and longevity of the relationship: "In fact, we have been coming to him for many, many years, even before he was here. . . . I was very grateful he was available when I had an accident happen a few weeks ago, because I wouldn't want to have to try to explain my history to somebody else. And they wouldn't necessarily understand me. He has a very good memory, he remembers, just bring up a few key words, or he'll remember stuff that I don't remember about my own history."

Continuity of care (or lack thereof) is an especially important issue for patients seeking medical attention for chronic illnesses. As the patients we interviewed who were dealing with chronic conditions stated clearly, mutual trust is essential when confronting a chronic disease because the patient must develop a real partnership with the physician that extends over time. Two-way trust and good communication are critical in the management of the disease. As one patient in a focus group put it, "I'm looking for someone I can collaborate with, and I think that's just my personality. But given the health problems that I've had, I actually don't think I would have made any progress at all if I hadn't had that personality. I think collaboration was my only hope of getting a reasonable diagnosis and trying to resolve treatment problems. I have some chronic health problems, nothing life-threatening. But there are several of them, and they interact, and it's a confusing picture. And nothing but collaboration ever would have worked for me."[9] For these patients especially, the effect of managed care on continuity of care was perceived as often negatively affecting the relationship they have with their physicians and as hindering the potential for the development of mutual trust.

Fragmentation of Care and Diffusion of Responsibility

Another aspect of managed care that concerned a number of patients is the fragmentation of care. Patients were concerned that specialists may not be aware of their overall health. In some instances, these concerns negatively affected their trust. For instance, patient 40 notes, "If the doctor is only looking at this part, it doesn't make any sense for him to ask questions of . . . to see that in context. And not seeing that in context loses their ability to actually make informed decisions." Patient 8 stated: "I get treated by, you know I've had several injuries and things so I'm getting treated by several doctors and I'm never sure whether any one of them has a total picture of my health." Patient 5 commented: "Like I said and I'm seeing an orthopedic surgeon and I don't think she's aware of my overall health. I'm seeing an oncologist. To some extent they're aware. But like I said some of it had to be self-initiated."

Conflicts of Interest Affecting Physicians' Decisions

The conflict of interest created by financial incentives that health plans and insurance companies use to encourage cost consciousness among physicians is frequently discussed by scholars (Emanuel and Dubler 1995; Gould 1998; Kao et al. 1998; Mechanic and Schlesinger 1996; Pearson and Hyams 2002). Both patients and physicians in our study expressed an opinion that the types of payment methods for physicians, as well as the incentives they entail, may create conflict of interest for a physician. Patients felt that a physician's best intentions may sometimes be in conflict with the constraints placed on a physician, such as those concerning insurance and health-care provider rules about tests, treatment, referrals, etc. Patients reported that when a physician's performance is influenced by these constraints, it is difficult for trust to develop.

The patients we interviewed also commented on how the payment methods associated with managed care might affect the relationship with their physician. As Patient 7 put it, "I know a whole lot of people who feel like the whole HMO funding and the pressure to reduce costs is affecting the quality of care that they get." Another patient commented on the practice constraints facing physicians under managed care: "I know it is frustrating for a physician who wants to alleviate someone's fears by running a test, but has to jump through so many hoops and can't get a test approved" (patient 26).

Other patients had the following to say: "I think because of it [constraints by managed care] maybe they get complacent and they can't be bothered with you—they're just processing you [to] get [you] out the door" (patient 24). "The doctors feel like they're strapped because the insurance agencies are taking away their funding. And I think that somewhere it's got to stop. And I think that the patients—the lack of trust that is happening with the patients is a snowball effect from all of these other areas" (patient 31). "They give you the minimum prescriptions. If they can avoid tests, they avoid tests" (patient 9).

Patient 29 related the following view: "I would think that given the public's eye the increasing disparity between the physician being primarily responsible for attending and caring for the patient and also the increasing prevalence of the HMO programs where the doctor has a double responsibility, one to the patient and one to justifying every single penny that goes out, that's a factor which you have to keep in consideration."

Power-Dependence Relations and the Intuitive-Auditor Model of Trust and Distrust in Patient-Physician Relationships

There are many ways in which the findings from this study might be organized conceptually. One framework we have found useful is to construe patients and physicians as interdependent social actors involved in an exchange relationship that is characterized by substantial asymmetries in power and dependence (Cook 1987). Moreover, this hierarchic relationship is itself embedded in a complex institutional setting in which both patients and physicians are influenced by, and are accountable and responsive to, a variety of forces, many of which potentially impinge on the quality of their dyadic relationship. Both patients and physicians see their interactions as embedded in relationships, which are either facilitated or thwarted by the organizational conditions surrounding these interactions. It is clear that our respondents viewed trust in relational terms. They noted the differentials in power, dependence, and vulnerability.

Because individuals in hierarchic relationships are highly motivated to make prudent or intelligent choices when it comes to trust, they monitor a variety of behaviors and the absence of behaviors to determine whether they can trust the other person. They act as "intuitive auditors" (Kramer 1996) who continuously monitor the interactions and exchanges in the relationship. Because of the perceived importance of trust in patient-physician relationships, our model assumes that both patients and physicians act as intuitive auditors who assess the other's trustworthiness. Trustworthiness is operationalized in our model in terms of both intention and competence. Intentional components of trustworthiness judgments relate to the extent to which patients and physicians attribute benign motives and cooperative intentions toward each other. Competence factors include whether the physician has the necessary knowledge to diagnose accurately and to manage the disease or medical condition and whether the patient has the ability to be appropriately assertive and to comply with directives.

Our study identifies a variety of verbal and nonverbal cues that patients track. The cues that seem to foster trust building in the relationship include behaviors that say to the patient she or he is important in the interaction, no matter how brief the visit: active listening as well as attentiveness to details including those that are personal and not directly related to the medical condition (such as information about the patient's family situation or significant others).

Physicians also track patients' verbal and nonverbal behaviors, partially as a means of diagnosis but also as indicators of their patients' trustworthiness. Physicians tend to view patients they can trust as more honest, cooperative, and more likely to follow through with prescribed medical treatment, and hence more compliant. Assessments of the trustworthiness and competence of the patients may in fact affect the nature of the treatment options considered. We have only anecdotal evidence to confirm a relationship between trust and treatment choices, but this is one topic we hope to pursue further in subsequent investigations of reciprocal trust among physicians and patients.

Research in social psychology suggests that vigilance and monitoring decrease as stress and uncertainty about the other's trustworthiness is reduced (Kramer 1996). Vigilance on the part of patients is important in the early stages of establishing a relationship with a physician not only because of patients' vulnerability, but also because patients are attempting to pick up clues about the competence of the physician that aid in their trustworthiness assessment. We recognize, of course, that there also will be substantial individual differences in such vigilance and mindfulness, depending on a variety of dispositional and contextual factors.

Even within our small sample, both patients and physicians varied widely on the complexity of their thinking about trust and distrust. For example, some physicians displayed considerable cognitive sophistication in thinking about how their actions and inactions affect their patients' trust levels. Other physicians displayed less sophistication. In addition, the power differential, while reduced in some relations, was also an important factor in the way participants processed information. As psychologists have noted, power and status differences influence perception. Less powerful actors (and those of lower status) are often more vigilant and thus more aware of the features of the actors in the setting and the situation itself that signal trustworthiness. Often more is at stake for them.

Perceptions Regarding the Reciprocal Nature of Trust in Doctor-Patient Relationships

Only recently have there been attempts to incorporate physicians' views and examine the reciprocal nature of patient-physician trust. One study reports that the fear of patient deception experienced by physicians treating drug users interacts with their patients' concern that they are mistreated and stigmatized, leading to mutual distrust (Merrill et al. 2002). Our evidence confirms the simple expectation that patients as well as physicians often recognize that the development and maintenance of trust is essentially a reciprocal process. Both patients and physicians clearly recognize that physician behaviors facilitate or undermine patient trust. Conversely, there is also some awareness—although it is much less frequently mentioned—that patient behaviors serve as important clues for physician trust in a patient. Part of the asymmetry may derive from the obvious power differences in the relationship, with the actions or inactions of the more powerful actor in the exchange relation being perceived as more important.

Physicians note, for example, that they sometimes have trouble deciphering the purpose of a patient's visit. They become suspicious when they feel as if they are being used primarily for access to controlled drugs or for insurance claims. For example, one participant in a physician focus group commented, "A trust issue would be . . . those times come up with like pain medications or you know, if there is . . . an addiction going on? I mean is [the] pain going on? But that for me is what I probably most often question—you know my trust with the patient. They lose the pills . . . or, they get stolen . . . and then when that happens, then I have a difficult time you know, prescribing the medication at that point."

Physician 8 suggested that some patients' behaviors may undermine the physician's trust in the very beginning: "She seemed from the beginning of my discussions wary of what I thought was going on, and what should be done about it, she seemed, from the moment I began to speak, quite skeptical about what I was saying. And irritated, and interrupted me often to argue with me or present reasons why I might be wrong about what I was saying." If the physician feels she cannot trust the patient, mutual trust is unlikely to develop. It is clear that the trust relation is not one-sided. A physician we interviewed corroborates this finding when he recognizes that both the physician and a patient share responsibility for whether the relationship will be characterized by trust: "If one party starts out being confrontational, then that whole trust is gone" (physician 18).

Like physicians, patients conceive of trust as a primarily relational issue. For example, patient 27 said, "Trust is something that is established early on and it is a two-way thing. I mean, as a patient, I have to go in and have an open mind and not carry my last experiences into the new—into my new appointment or with a new doctor and keep an open mind. And then the other thing is—doctors have to remember they're dealing with human beings despite the pressures from HMOs or the administrators." Patient 31 remarked: "So the doctors need to trust the patient in the fact the patient isn't going to come back and go after the doctor. But if the patient feels like the doctor is trying to solve the problem with them from their experience and trying a number of different things. . . . I think that is more of a partnership type of relationship versus . . . you tell me what to do and I give you just the minimum amount of information to get an answer." Patient 30 was more explicit, saying, "So you have to set up a—which you well know, I'm not telling you anything you don't know—mutual trust. Because with that mutual trust, you can have that kind of rapport." Patient 39 commented, further, "I think the interpersonal relationship has a big impact on trusting the clinical confidence." Thus for both parties to the exchange trust is a kind of glue that makes the relationship work more effectively. When trust is absent the relationship is not likely to last. Either the patient will move on to another health-care practitioner, often initiating a visit for the same condition or problem as the visit to the untrusted doctor, or the physician will try to "dump" the patient if at all possible by putting that patient back into the pool for others to see.

Implications and Conclusions

A primary aim of the present study was to explore some of the perceived determinants of trust and distrust in patient-physician relationships. In contrast with much of the previous research in this area, we focused on eliciting information directly from patients and physicians about their perceptions and beliefs about the factors that increase trust, decrease trust, or lead to active distrust. We expected on the basis of earlier research that asymmetries in the construal of trustworthiness on the part of physicians and patients would be evident. We interpreted these differences as partially determined by power-dependence and status differences between the parties in the relationship. Patients are vulnerable and more likely to feel dependent in the relationship for various reasons. Physicians are typically more powerful, primarily as a result of the competence differential relevant to the interaction, but both parties monitor each other's behavior to determine their relative trustworthiness. According to the intuitive-auditor model, in relationships in which there is such a power difference the less powerful actors engage in more active monitoring of the behaviors that imply trustworthiness. This fact was confirmed in our interviews with both patients and physicians. Not only did patients give much more detailed accounts of physician verbal and nonverbal behaviors that either facilitate or inhibit trust building, they also reported being more vigilant in general concerning their relationships with physicians as well as their organizational context. Patients and physicians alike were quite articulate about the effects of managed care (defined broadly) on their relationships. In particular they cited time constraints and time pressure as affecting trust building. They also referred to potential conflicts of interest created by managed-care incentives to reduce referrals and limit access to specific drugs.

Our data also indicate the importance of social category-based expectancies and stereotypes in patient-physician relationships. There isn't really anything new or surprising about this finding, yet relatively little systematic attention has been given to the cognitions based on social categories in previous research on patient-physician trust. Many of the previous studies have focused only on the perceptions of patients. Few have examined the role trust plays from the perspective of the physician. Most surveys on patient-physician trust do not routinely elicit perceptions from both sets of actors and thus draw an incomplete picture of the relationship between physicians and patients. In our interviews physicians referred to reasons they fail to trust their patients such as low compliance, lack of honesty, or the suspicion that patients are primarily seeking drugs. Physicians also referred to the importance of trust relationships with patients in practicing medicine unencumbered by fears of malpractice suits.

In future research we plan to investigate these behaviors in ongoing patient-physician dyads over time, addressing the concerns of both parties to the relationship. Following a small number of dyads in several different clinics would allow us to provide a more in-depth investigation of the reciprocal nature of trust and to track the effects of different levels of trust on outcomes for both the patients and the physicians. Such outcomes include satisfaction, compliance on the part of the patient, time management for both patients and physicians, and effectiveness of treatment. We also plan to track factors that impede or facilitate the emergence of reciprocal trust in these same patient-physician dyads at the practice level. In addition, we hope to explore more fully what has come to be called in the current research literature in medicine the status concordance between the physician and patient on social characteristics such as race-ethnicity, gender, and, to some extent, age. Our preliminary findings suggest that such concordance (or status consistency) often makes trust more likely to occur. Thus concordance may affect not only the dynamics of the patient-physician relationship but also significant health outcomes. For example, if a critical feature of diagnosis is information about important health-related facts, and status concordance increases the likelihood that such information is conveyed by the patient to the physician, then we will have obtained evidence that is important for both the quality of health care and the eventual cost of health care. Finally, the intuitive-auditor model gives us a window into the cognitive differences—for example, in attentiveness and vigilance—that may help us understand the effects of status or power differences between physicians and their patients. These cognitive factors may also have a significant impact on health care outcomes. Both the patients and the physicians we interviewed provided convincing testimony to the value of trust.

This chapter reports some preliminary findings from a larger ongoing research program on the antecedents and consequences of trust in doctor-patient relationships. This research was supported primarily by a grant from the Russell Sage Foundation. We also gratefully acknowledge funds from the Graduate School of Business and Department of Sociology at Stanford University. We appreciate the assistance of Jennifer van Stelle, Coye Cheshire, and Jeanine Lavender for their help in collecting, coding, and analyzing the data related to this research.

Notes

1. We define the "patient-physician relationship" as a reciprocal relationship between a patient and a physician. Essential parts of this relationship are how the patient relates to the physician as well as how the physician relates to the patient. Similarly, the term "patient-physician trust" is used for the reciprocal trust between a patient and a physician.

2. In a study of 144 cancer patients, Penman et al. (1984) report that out of 16 suggested reasons for accepting therapy, trust in the physician was ranked as most important by 31 percent of the patients, followed by the information provided by the physician and belief in the therapy's effectiveness. Similarly

Altice, Mostashari, and Friedland (2001) found that trust in the physician was the most important predictor of acceptance of retroviral treatment among HIV-positive prisoners.

3. Safran, Taira, et al. (1998) found that patients reporting high trust in their physician were 2.5 times as likely to follow behavioral advice from their physicians (for example, smoking cessation, exercise, safe sex) as patients with low trust.

4. In a study by Thom et al. (1999) trust was a stronger predictor than satisfaction of patients' intention to remain with or to leave their current physicians.

5. Safran et al. (2001) found trust to be the strongest single predictor for patient disenrollment from the physician six months later.

6. Three studies have used qualitative methods to investigate patient trust. In the first, Sally E. Thorne and Carole A. Robinson (1988) interviewed seventy-seven patients with chronic disease. A second study by Thom and Campbell (1997) used four patient focus groups to identify physician and system factors related to patient trust. The third, by Mechanic and Meyer (2001) interviewed ninety patients, thirty from three chronic illness groups (breast cancer, Lyme disease, and mental illness) and found that the three major concepts used by patients in judging trust were interpersonal competence (including caring), technical competence, and agency.

7. Nancy Wyatt (1991) reported that in her search of the medical literature in the early 1990s, only about 1 percent of this literature dealt with the doctor-patient relationship.

8. A list of all patients seen in the past two years for each physician was generated. Each physician was asked to use the list to indicate which patients he or she thought would be appropriate to participate in a focus group. Physicians were asked to exclude patients with cognitive problems, patients who were too ill to participate, and non-English-speaking patients.

9. Another patient said, "I guess I'd change doctors every month if I had to, for a while, yeah. I don't want to be the child in this relationship. I want to be two adults and I suspect I'm not the only person who has a condition that sort of requires that you take that approach. Because if you do, if you have a chronic illness, you do become the expert in your own condition."

References

Abreu, Jose M. 1999. "Conscious and Nonconscious African American Stereotypes: Impact on First Impression and Diagnostic Ratings By Therapists." *Journal of Consulting and Clinical Psychology* 67(3): 387–93.

Altice, Frederick L., Farzad Mostashari, and Gerald H. Friedland. 2001. "Trust and the Acceptance of and Adherence to Antiretroviral Therapy." *Journal of Acquired Immune Deficiency Syndrome* 28(1): 47–58.

Anderson, Lynda A., and Robert F. Derrick. 1990. "Development of the Trust in Physician Scale: A Measure to Assess Interpersonal Trust in Patient-Physician Relationships." *Psychological Reports* 67(3, part 2): 1091–1100.

Arnetz, Bengt B. 2001. "Psychosocial Challenges Facing Physicians of Today." *Social Science and Medicine* 52(2): 203–13.

Barber, Bernard. 1983. "The Logic and Limits of Trust." New Brunswick, N.J.: Rutgers University Press.

Ben-Sira, Zeev. 1980. "Affective and Instrumental Components in the Physician-Patient Relationship: An Additional Dimension of Interaction Theory." *Journal of Health and Social Behavior* 21(2): 170–80.

Bogart, Laura M., Sheryl L. Catz, Jeffrey A. Kelly, and Eric G. Benotsch. 2001. "Factors Influencing Physicians' Judgments of Adherence and Treatment Decisions for Patients with HIV Disease." *Medical Decision Making* 21(1): 28–36.

Brody, Howard. 1992. *The Healer's Power.* New Haven: Yale University Press.

Buller, Mary Klein, and David B. Buller. 1987. "Physicians' Communication Style and Patients' Satisfaction." *Journal of Health and Social Behavior* 28(4): 375–88.

Caterinicchio, Russell Paul. 1979. "Testing Plausible Path Models of Interpersonal Trust in Patient-Physician Treatment Relationships." *Social Science and Medicine* 13A: 81–99.

Cook, Karen S., ed. 1987. *Social Exchange Theory.* Newbury Park, Calif.: Sage.

Cooper-Patrick, Lisa, Joseph J. Gallo, Junius J. Gonzales, Hong Thi Vu, Neil R. Powe, Christine Nelson, and Daniel E. Ford. 1999. "Race, Gender, and Partnership in the Patient-Physician Relationship." *JAMA* 282(6): 583–89.

Derose, Kathryn Pitkin, Ron D. Hays, Daniel F. McCaffrey, and David W. Baker. 2001. "Does Physician Gender Affect Satisfaction of Men and Women Visiting the Emergency Department?" *Journal of General Internal Medicine* 16(4): 218–26.

Di Matteo, Robin M., and Ron Hays. 1980. "The Significance of Patients' Perceptions of Physician's Conduct: A Study of Patient Satisfaction in a Family Practice." *Journal of Community Health* 6(1): 18–34.

Emanuel, Ezekiel J., and Nancy N. Dubler. 1995. "Preserving the Physician-Patient Relationship in the Era of Managed Care." *JAMA* 273(4): 323–29.

Feldman, Debra S., Dennis H. Novack, and Edward Gracely. 1998. "Effects of Managed Care on Physician-Patient Relationships, Quality of Care, and the Ethical Practice of Medicine: A Physician Survey." *Archives of General Internal Medicine* 158(15): 1626–32.

Fiske, Susan T. 1980. "Attention and Weight in Person Perception: The Impact of Negative and Extreme Behavior." *Journal of Personality and Social Psychology* 38: 889–906.

Gould, Susan D. 1998. "Money and Trust: Relationships Between Patients, Physicians, and Health Plans." *Journal of Health Politics, Policy and Law* 23(4): 687–95.

Grembowski, David E., Karen S. Cook, Donald L. Patrick, and Amy Elizabeth Roussell. 1998. "Managed Care and Physician Referral: A Social Exchange Perspective." *Medical Care Research and Review* 55(1): 3–31.

———. 2002. "Managed Care and the U.S. Health Care System: A Social Exchange Perspective." *Social Science and Medicine* 54(8): 1167–80.

Hall, Mark A., Elizabeth Dugan, Beiyao Zheng, and Aneil K. Mishra. 2001. "Trust in Physicians and Medical Institutions: What Is It, Can It Be Measured, and Does It Matter?" *Milbank Quarterly* 79(4): 613–39.

Hegtvedt, Karen A. 1988. "Social Determinants of Perception: Power, Equity, and Status Effects in an Exchange Situation." *Social Psychology Quarterly* 51(2): 141–53.

Heimer, Carol. 2000. "Solving the Problem of Trust." In *Trust in Society*, edited by Karen S. Cook. New York: Russell Sage Foundation.

Howard, Judith A. 1996. "Social Cognition." In *Sociological Perspectives on Social Psychology*, edited by Karen S. Cook, Gary A. Fine, and James S. House. Boston: Allyn & Bacon.

Johnson, Shirley M., Margot E. Kurtz, Thomas Tomlinson, and Kenneth R. Howe. 1986. "Students' Stereotypes of Patients as Barriers to Clinical Decision-Making." *Journal of Medical Education* 61(9, part 1): 727–35.

Kao, Audley C., Diane C. Green, Alan M. Zaslavsky, Jeffrey P. Koplan, and P. D. Cleary. 1998. "The Relationship Between Method of Physician Payment and Patient Trust." *JAMA* 280(19): 1708–14.

Kasteler, Josephine, Robert L. Kane, and Donna M. Olsen. 1976. "Issues Underlying Prevalence of Doctor-Shopping Behavior." *Journal of Health and Social Behavior* 17(4): 328–39.

Keating, Nancy L., Diane C. Green, Audley C. Kao, Julie A. Gazmararian, Vivian Y. Wu, and Paul D. Cleary. 2002. "How Are Patients' Specific Ambulatory Care Experiences Related to Trust, Satisfaction, and Considering Changing Physicians?" *Journal of General Internal Medicine* 17(1): 20–39.

Kramer, Roderick M. 1996. "Divergent Realities and Convergent Disappointments in the Hierarchic Relation: Trust and the Intuitive Auditor at Work." In *Trust in Organizations: Frontiers of Theory and Research*, edited by Roderick M. Kramer and Tom R. Tyler. Thousand Oaks, Calif.: Sage.

LaViest, Thomas A., Kim J. Nickerson, and Janice V. Bowie. 2000. "Attitudes About Racism, Medical Mistrust, and Satisfaction with Care Among African American and White Cardiac Patients." *Medical Care Research and Review* 75, supplement 1: 146–61.

Linzer, Mark, Thomas R. Konrad, Jeffrcy Douglas, Julia E. McMurray, Donald E. Pathman, Eric S. Williams, Mark D. Schwartz, Martha Gerrity, William Scheckler, Judy Ann Bigby, and Elnora Rhodes. 2000. "Managed Care, Time Pressure, and Physician Job Satisfaction: Results from the Physician Worklife Study." *Journal of General Internal Medicine* 15(7): 441–50.

Mainous, Arch G., III, Richard Baker, Margaret M. Love, Denis P. Gray, and James M. Gill. 2001. "Continuity of Care and Trust in One's Physician: Evidence from Primary Care in the United States and the United Kingdom." *Family Medicine* 22(January): 22–27.

Malat, Jennifer. 2001. "Social Distance and Patients' Rating of Healthcare Providers." *Journal of Health and Social Behavior* 42(4): 360–72.

Mechanic, David. 1998. "Public Trust and Initiatives for New Health-Care Partnership." *The Milbank Quarterly* 76(2): 281–302.

Mechanic, David, and Sara Meyer. 2001. "Concepts of Trust Among Patients with Serious Illness." *Social Science and Medicine* 51(5): 657–68.

Mechanic, David, and Mark Schlesinger. 1996. "The Impact of Managed Care on Patients' Trust in Medical Care and Their Physicians." *JAMA* 275(21): 1693–97.

Merrill, Joseph O., Lorna A. Rhodes, Richard A. Deyo, Alan Marlatt, and Katharine A. Bradley. 2002. "Mutual Mistrust in the Medical Care of Drug Users." *Journal of General Internal Medicine* 17(5): 327–33.

Mollborn, Stefanie Bailey, Irena Stepanikova, and Karen S. Cook. 2002. "Patients' Trust in a Physician." Paper presented at the International Sociological Association Meeting. Brisbane (July).

Parsons, Talcott. 1964. *The Social System*. Glencoe, Ill.: Free Press.

Pearson, Steven D., and Tracey Hyams. 2002. "Talking About Money: How Primary Care Physicians Respond to a Patient's Question About Financial Incentives." *Journal of General Internal Medicine* 17(1): 75–79.

Pearson, Steven D., and Lisa H. Raeke. 2000. "Patients' Trust in Physicians: Many Theories, Few Measures, and Little Data." *Journal of General Medicine* 15(7): 509–513.

Penman, Doris T., Jimmie C. Holland, Geraldine F. Bahna, Gary Morrow, Arthur H. Schmale, Leonard R. Derogatis, Charles L. Carnike, and Roxanne Cherry. 1984. "Informed Consent for Investigational Chemotherapy: Patients' and Physicians' Perspectives." *Journal of Clinical Oncology* 1984(2): 849–55.

Qualitative Solutions and Research. 1999. QSR NVivo. Melbourne, Australia: Qualitative Solutions and Research.

Ridgeway, Cecilia, and Henry Walker. 1995. "Status Structures." In *Sociological Perspectives on Social Psychology*, edited by Karen S. Cook, Gary A. Fine, and James S. House. Boston: Allyn & Bacon.

Roberts, Carlos A., and Mara S. Arguete. 2000. "Task and Socioemotional Behaviors of Physicians: A Test of Reciprocity and Social Interaction Theories in Analogue Physician-Patient Encounters." *Social Science and Medicine* 50(3): 309–15.

Safran, Dana Gelb, Mark Kosinski, Alvin R. Tarlov, William H. Rogers, Deborah A. Taira, Naomi Lieberman, and John E. Ware. 1998. "The Primary Care Assessment Survey: Tests of Data Quality and Measurement Performance." *Medical Care* 36(5): 728–39.

Safran, Dana Gelb, Jana E. Montgomery, Hong Chang, Julia Murphy, and William H. Rogers. 2001. "Switching Doctors: Predictors of Voluntary Disenrollment from a Primary Physician's Practice." *Journal of Family Practice* 50(2): 130–36.

Safran, Dana Gelb, Deborah A. Taira, William H. Rogers, Mark Kosinski, John Ware, and Alvin R. Tarlov. 1998. "Linking Primary Care Performance to Outcomes of Care." *Journal of Family Practice* 47(3): 213–20.

Saha, Somnath, Miriam Komaromy, Thomas D. Koepsell, and Andrew B. Bindman. 1999. "Patient-Physician Racial Concordance and the Perceived Quality and Use of Health Care." *Archives of Internal Medicine* 159(9): 997–1004.

Shortell, Stephen M., Teresa M. Waters, Kenneth W. B. Clarke, and Peter P. Budetti. 1998. "Physicians as Double Agents: Maintaining Trust in an Era of Multiple Accountabilities." *JAMA* 280(12): 1102–8.

Stepanikova, Irena, Stefanie Bailey Mollborn, and Karen S. Cook. 2002. "Patient-Physician Trust and Obtaining Medical Care." Paper presented at the Pacific Sociological Association Annual Meeting. Vancouver (April).

Stevenson, Fiona A., Christine A. Barry, Nicky Britten, Nick Barber, and Colin P. Bradley. 2000. "Doctor-Patient Communication About Drugs: The Evidence for Shared Decision-Making." *Social Science and Medicine* 50(6): 829–40.

Sturm, Roland. 2002. "Effect of Managed Care and Financing on Practice Constraints and Career Satisfaction in Primary Care." *Journal of American Board of Family Practice* 15(5): 367–77.

Thom, David H. 2001. "Physician Behaviors That Predict Patient Trust." *Journal of Family Practice* 50(4): 323–28.

Thom, David H., David A. Bloch, and Eleanor S. Segal. 1999. "An Intervention to Increase Patients' Trust in Their Physicians." *Academic Medicine* 74(2): 195–98.

Thom, David H., and Bruce Campbell. 1997. "Patient-Physician Trust: An Exploratory Study." *Journal of Family Practice* 44(2): 169–76.

Thom, David H., Richard L. Kravitz, Robert A. Bell, Edward Krupat, and Rahman Azari. 2002. "Patient Trust in the Physician: Relationship to Patient Requests." *Family Practice* 19(5): 476–83.

Thom, David H., Kurt M. Ribisl, Anita L. Stewart, and Douglas A. Luke. 1999. "Validation of a Measure of Patients' Trust in Their Physician: The Trust in Physician Scale." *Medical Care* 37(5): 510–17.

Thorne, Sally E., and Carole A. Robinson. 1988. "Reciprocal Trust in Health Care Relationships." *Journal of Advanced Nursing* 13(6): 782–89.

van Ryn, Michelle, and Jane Burke. 2000. "The Effect of Patient Race and Socio-Economic Status on Physicians' Perceptions of Patients." *Social Science and Medicine* 50(6, March): 813–28.

Ward, Russell A. 1987. "HMO Satisfaction and Understanding Among Recent Medicare Enrollees." *Journal of Health and Social Behavior* 28(4): 401–12.

Wholey, Douglas R., and Andrew R. Sommers. 2001. "The Effect of Preferences, Choices, Markets, and Managed Care on Satisfaction with Choice and Trust." Working paper, available at: www.hsr.umn.edu/mcc/Research/Papers/Wholey_and_Sommers_Trust.pdf.

Wilson, Pamela, and Regis J. McNamara. 1982. "How Perceptions of a Simulated Physician-Patient Interaction Influence Intended Satisfaction and Compliance." *Social Science and Medicine* 16(19): 1699–1704.

Wyatt, Nancy. 1991. "Physician-Patient Relationships: What Do Doctors Say?" *Health Communication* 3(3): 157–74.

Chapter 5

Monitoring, Rules, and the Control Paradox: Can the Good Soldier Švejk Be Trusted?

GARY J. MILLER

O NE OF the most fascinating and revealing forms of organizational sabotage is "working to rule"—precisely following rules while providing no voluntary effort beyond that required by the rules. An especially destructive form of "working to rule" involves applying the rules most carefully where they are least appropriate to the situation. This technique was perfected by Private Josef Švejk, a leading Czech cultural hero and the eponym of Jaroslav Hašek's satirical novel *The Good Soldier Švejk* (Hašek [1920–23] 1974). In World War I, the Czechs were formally on the same side as their Austrian rulers. Many Czechs deserted and went over to the culturally similar Russians that they had been sent to fight. Švejk, a peaceful beer drinker drafted into the Austrian imperial army, chose a simpler way—he just obeyed orders. But in obeying them, he managed to confound every military goal of his Austrian officers.

For example, Švejk worked as an assistant for the chaplain, who sent him to buy communion wine "from Voslau in Lower Austria." Švejk took that to mean he was to travel to Lower Austria itself, a journey that took days and left the chaplain assuming he had deserted. Any ambiguity in orders left Švejk ample room to instigate disaster. But any attempt to make orders absolutely explicit simply defined better the minimum effort Švejk could get away with. Švejk's next boss, Lieutenant Lukas, ordered Švejk to do nothing except on his express orders. Consequently, when the lieutenant's mistress showed up, Švejk refused to give her any assistance with her baggage or any information

99

about the lieutenant—claiming lack of explicit orders. When she complained to the lieutenant, he gave Švejk new orders regarding his mistress: "to fulfill all her wishes, which you must regard as a command. You must behave gallantly, and serve her decently." The lieutenant left Švejk with money to buy her wine and cigarettes. With the aid of the wine, Švejk seduced her and reported back to the lieutenant that he had obeyed her slightest whim and fulfilled all her wishes—"about six" in number. Throughout his "career," Švejk was able to wreak havoc in a way that was technically consistent with the rules and mandates of superiors.

Švejk was taking advantage of a basic fact known to members of most organizations: it is simply impossible to specify in advance all the behaviors that the organization will require from its employees if it is to survive and thrive. This is the organizational manifestation of the phenomenon known as "contractual incompleteness" in economics (Coase 1937). There are behaviors that cannot be routinized, explicitly specified beforehand, or rewarded afterwards: Sales staff must watch customer body language for signals that indicate what sales arguments will be most persuasive. Teachers learn to be alert for "teaching moments" when students are especially receptive to particular lessons. Effective police officers learn to watch for subtle cues that indicate suspicious behavior. Such desirable behaviors cannot be contractualized.

In short, efficient behaviors generally cannot be mechanically elicited from unmotivated officials. Unmotivated teachers can learn how to get through the school year with a minimum of fuss—and a minimum of impact on their students. Police officers can easily figure out strategies consistent with any set of standard operating procedures that keep them safely out of danger—and render them useless to the community. As a result, virtually any public organization would grind to a halt if its members did nothing more than provide minimal compliance with rules and orders. Hence, as a way of applying pressure on management, "working to rule" may be as effective as going on strike.

The first section of this paper establishes that there are monitoring situations in which efficient contracting, either on outcomes or behaviors, is impossible. When this is true, the pursuit of self-interest by public bureaucrats and their superiors is insufficient to guarantee an efficient outcome. The result is a situation characterized by David Kreps (1990) as a "trust game": both bureaucrats and their superiors would be better off if bureaucrats could be trusted not to pursue their short-term self-interest. In such a situation, members of the organization will not set aside short-term self-interest unless they are convinced that other members of the organization are acting the same way and that the distribution of benefits from cooperation will make them, as well as other members, better off in the long run. As Chester Barnard (1938) has written, the function of the executive is to develop cooperation among organizational members.

I take the term "trust" to refer to these beliefs about the cooperative intentions of others in the organization. I argue that, in the presence of incomplete contracts, effective management requires inducing this form of trust in organizational members. Otherwise, members will see the advantage of "working to rule," rendering the organization rigid and dysfunctional.

Specifying Tasks Versus Specifying Outcomes

Contractual incentives can be linked either to outcomes or behavior. "Working to rule" is potentially a problem only if contracts based on outcomes are prohibitively expensive. Otherwise, outcome-based bonuses can be used to motivate enthusiastic effort. In this section, I will review the conditions under which outcome-based contracts fail. This will lead to an examination of contracts that are based on specification of behavior.

An example of incentives linked to outcomes is a sales commission. Consider a car salesman who is paid a commission for each car he sells. The sales director's monitoring task is relatively simple: she must simply keep track of how many cars are sold, and write a paycheck that reflects the salesman's accomplishments.

The advantage of such outcome-based contracts is clear. The sales director does not have to write elaborate rules specifying required sales behaviors, such as, "Always tell the customer about your children in college and the high cost of tuition," or "Mention the manufacturer's rebate within the first minute and a half of conversation." The salesman will adopt such tricks if they are effective, and will have every incentive to use them, flexibly, when they enhance sales.

With a commission system, the cost of monitoring is negligible. The sales director does not have to spend scarce resources monitoring and enforcing rules. The sales director does not have to eavesdrop on the salesman's conversations with clients, or keep track of the subordinate's facial mannerisms. The incentives built into the commission-based employment contract align the subordinate's goals—earning money—with the company's goals—selling cars. As a result of this alignment, the firm is able to economize dramatically on the resources dedicated to monitoring and supervision of the sales staff. The firm does not have to prepare a manual of rules to be followed by the sales staff, nor hire supervisors who closely watch the activities of the staff, and sanction them when the rules are broken. And not the least, the organization is immune to any threat of "working to rule" as an employee technique of sabotage.

On the other hand, the same automobile company may have a service staff who have a thick manual of rules to follow. When an automobile is brought in for a tune-up at sixty thousand miles, the company may not leave it to the mechanic to decide whether or not to check the brakes, or examine the transmission fluid. The mechanic will normally have a long checklist of required behaviors and a backup manual specifying how to perform each behavior. Furthermore, the organization must hire supervisors, each of whom will monitor a relatively small number of mechanics and try to make sure that the rules are followed, sanctioning mechanics who omit any of the required behaviors or perform them inappropriately. Because the mechanic's output, a safe and effective tune-up, is more difficult to observe and contract on than the salesman's output, a customer who has signed a sales contract, the firm must deal with the consequences of incomplete contracting. In short, the firm is *forced* to spend money and other resources on specifying exact behaviors for the mechanic and hiring supervisors to monitor and sanction the work rules.

Clearly, the sales position is one in a class of positions that we can characterize as "outcome-based contracting." Other examples would be skilled craftsmen or computer programmers, who produce an output that can be presented to a hierarchical superior. The requirements of the job are to produce the output according to certain specifications, but the superior does not attempt to specify the behavioral inputs that lead to the desired product. The programmer's boss will not specify what kind of solution to a programming problem the programmer should attempt. Nor does the supervisor try to tell a skilled welder or carpenter how to go about his job. The knowledge in both cases, like the knowledge of how to close a deal, is "implicit," or inside the employee's head, and the supervisor does not have be a programmer, welder, or saleswoman herself in order to recognize whether the product in fact meets the desired specifications.

Hierarchies do well to use outcome-based incentives when they can be cheaply and easily imposed. The conditions for doing so are roughly the following:

1. The outcome is easily measurable in all important (value-determining) aspects.

2. The outcome is produced by the individual, without an exogenous component to the production function.

3. The outcome is produced by an individual, not a complex team.

If any of these conditions is violated, outcome-based contracting will be increasingly difficult, costly, or impossible. For example, if the number of sales is primarily determined by macroeconomic variables beyond the control of the salesman, then a risk-averse agent will be reluctant to accept an outcome-based compensation contract. The same is true for a craftsman whose raw materials are of variable quality and determinative of the value of the craftsman's product. As a result, there will be significant "agency costs" associated with inducing risk-averse agents to accept such positions (Miller 1992, 124–27). In general, it can be shown that the smaller the agent's impact on the desirable outcome, the *larger* must be the outcome-based bonus if it is to incentivize the agent adequately. An agent with only a 10 percent impact on the final outcome must have a bonus ten times that of an agent who has a 100 percent impact on the final outcome. As a result, the agency costs may be so high as to deter the use of outcome-based contracting (Miller and Whitford 2002).

Similarly, if it takes an entire team to produce the measurable outcome, then an outcome-based bonus simply creates a prisoner's dilemma problem within the team—each member of the team would be best off if the other team members work hard while the individual shirks (Miller 1992, 143–58). As a result, any one member of the team can claim that the team's low productivity is the result of someone else's failed efforts. In such situations, the classic solution is to invest in sufficient supervisory staff to specify the value-maximizing actions of individuals in the team and monitor whether their behavior meets the standards.

As a result, many organizational tasks simply do not lend themselves to outcome-based incentives. The rest of this paper discusses the alternative: close specification of desired behaviors by means of rules and commands, and sanctions to enforce those behaviors.

In particular, I will argue that built-in inefficiencies may plague management by monitoring. The inefficiencies may be understood by picturing the monitoring relationship as a one-shot game with a Pareto-suboptimal equilibrium. The paper begins with a simple model that captures the essence of management by monitoring. As in most such situations, the inefficiencies may be ameliorated by the establishment of *long-term trust.* That is, if both manager and employee value a long-term relationship, then cooperation may sustain more efficient outcomes than are obtainable in one-time play.

This paper will examine the nature of the "tit-for-tat" exchange that is capable of Pareto improvements in organizations in which labor contracts are based on monitoring of individual actions rather than measurement of individual outcomes. Furthermore, cooperation requires *trust* in that hierarchical superiors must yield some of their capacity for discovering and punishing shirking by subordinates. The paper discusses a variety of cases of both noncooperation and cooperation in monitoring games, and the political and policy implications of the model.

A Model of Monitoring and Control

Most public bureaucracies are organizations in which individual members are unlikely to produce an *individual* outcome that is measurable and rewardable. A fireman may be the most valued and energetic member of the fire team, but nevertheless the valued product, the capacity to put out fires, is not the result of the efforts of that individual or any other individual on the team. A public school third-grade teacher may be incompetent, but some of her students may perform well on standardized tests because of the effects of heredity, family environment, and talented first- and second-grade teachers. A rifleman in an infantry squad may be talented and heroic, but all the tactics taught to the squad are based on the interdependence of all the members of the squad, not heroic John Wayne qualities by any one member. As a result, compensation based on individual productivity is, in general, impossible in most public bureaucracies.

For this reason, most public bureaucracies are associated with a high level of hierarchy and rules. The fireman, the public school teacher, the infantryman are provided with a set of operating procedures, rules, and hierarchical dictates. Here we examine a model involving such an employee who is part of a large, integrated operation, such as an infantry soldier, a fireman, or an assembly-line worker. His activities are valued only so far as they are productive of an overall organizational purpose or product. We will call the employee Švejk (pronounced "Schweik").

As is typical of employment contracts, Švejk's contract specifies that he will work for a flat wage (W), which he will receive in exchange for accepting the direction of the organization, in the form of supervisor's commands and fixed operating rules. If he fails to follow the directives, he will receive a sanction in the form of a penalty that is subtracted from his wage. We can operationalize the penalty as a parameter K, which equals either a fixed positive number or zero in any time period, depending on whether or not he is discovered to be in violation of organizational directives.

Švejk's expected compensation is $E(V) = (1-p)W + p(W-K)$, where p is the probability that he is discovered violating an organizational directive and therefore receives the penalty K. This simplifies to $W - pK$. Švejk experiences a cost C from exerting effort (e) to obey organizational directives. The cost function $C(e)$ has a positive first and second derivative, indicating increasing marginal costs of effort. We assume that Švejk, as a rational actor, works only up to the effort level at which his marginal cost of effort equals his marginal gain.

If his effort has no effect on the probability that he will be caught in violation, then he will exert no effort. However, in general, we assume that p is a monotonically decreasing function of Švejk's effort: the harder he works, the less likely it is that he will be found in violation of the rules and punished. But the supervisor also has an impact on the probability of catching Švejk in violation of the rules—by spending costly resources in monitoring him. We can express this as $p = P(e,m)$, where m is the monitoring effort of the supervisor. (The decision variables for the two players in the game are shown in italics.) Substituting this function for p in his compensation equation and taking the derivative allows us to conclude that Švejk will provide effort up to the point at which the marginal cost of effort equals K times the marginal impact of effort on the probability of being caught.

This leads to three simple conclusions about Švejk's effort: he will work *less* hard at onerous tasks (where the marginal cost of effort rises more steeply); he will provide *more* effort when his effort has a bigger impact on reducing the probability of being caught; and he will provide *more* effort if failing to do so would lead to a stiffer punishment K. It also leads to a fourth conclusion: since the marginal impact of effort on the probability of being caught is itself a function of m, the supervisor's monitoring efforts will also induce *more effort* from Švejk. This last relationship is shown in figure 5.1, which shows what we will term Švejk's effort response curve in m.

The effort response curve of an employee who is paid a flat wage to follow hierarchical directives is therefore positively sloped. The exact nature of the relationship depends on several things, such as whether the marginal impact of Švejk's effort on his probability of getting caught is increasing or decreasing. If it is decreasing fast enough, then at some point extra effort is more costly than it is beneficial to him, and his effort response curve becomes more vertical, indicating that it will be virtually impossible to induce him to supply more effort beyond a certain point. If the probability of catching Švejk in noncompliance is zero when $m = 0$ (as would be the case when P is a multiplicative function of m and e), and if the marginal cost of the first bit of effort is positive, then Švejk will provide *no effort* when the manager provides no monitoring. This is shown by having Švejk's effort response curve start at the origin.

The manager monitors Švejk's activities. Her decision variable is m: how many resources to devote to monitoring Švejk. She receives rewards from Švejk's compliance efforts and realizes that zero monitoring will result in zero effort; but the resources devoted to monitoring are costly. She will monitor until the point at which the marginal cost of monitoring equals the marginal benefit of induced effort. Clearly, if monitoring were sufficiently cheap, then she would devote an infinite amount of resources to it and induce perfect compliance from Švejk. The more costly the monitoring technology, the less resources she will devote to it, holding the value of Švejk's efforts constant.

Figure 5.1   More Monitoring Results in More Effort (in One-Shot Game)

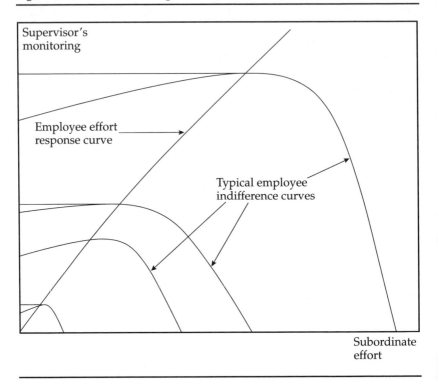

Source: Author's compilation.

Thus, Švejk and his superior are playing a game in the two-dimensional space in figure 5.1, in which the horizontal axis is Švejk's effort and the vertical axis is the amount of monitoring by the manager. The sequencing of the game is simple: the superior sets a level of monitoring, and Švejk then selects the level of effort that maximizes his gain given that level of monitoring.

Clearly, Švejk is best off at the origin ($m = 0$, $e = 0$): he supplies zero effort, and he cannot be punished because there is no possibility of being discovered in violation of the rules. We may assume that with a "typical" utility function, he has convex indifference curves around that ideal point. For any given level of rule monitoring m, Švejk's best response is a particular level of effort that is given by a tangency point between one of his indifference curves and the horizontal line associated with that level of monitoring. Several such tangency points are shown in figure 5.1.

His effort response curve is an upwardly sloping line consisting of the set of such tangency points, as in Figure 1, indicating that more rule-monitoring induces more effort from Švejk. For every point on the upward-sloping reaction function, Švejk's indifference curve at that point has slope 0.

The superior's ideal point is at 100 percent effort by Švejk, with no rule monitoring (since rule monitoring is costly). The superior has indifference curves that are convex around that point. Their exact shape depends on the relative value of Švejk's effort and the costliness of rule monitoring. As long as both are costly, however, the slope of the superior's indifference curves will be positive, as shown in figure 5.2.

Clearly, the superior has one best choice, given Švejk's response function, shown in figure 5.2. It is a point of tangency between Švejk's response function and the superior's highest possible indifference curve, as shown. This is the subgame-perfect Nash equilibrium of the game. If the monitoring is relatively inexpensive and effective, then this equilibrium will invoke a high level of effort; if monitoring is relatively expensive and ineffective, then it will invoke a low level of effort.

What do we know for sure about the equilibrium outcome E? Unless it is at the origin, then it is Pareto-suboptimal. Both the manager and Švejk could agree that there is some outcome that is better for both of them.

The reason for this is that at the point E, Švejk has an indifference curve with slope 0, whereas the superior has an indifference curve with a positive slope (equal to Švejk's response function at that point). The indifference curves are not themselves tangent—they cross. This means that there is a region (shown in figure 5.2), which gives *both players* greater utility than the point E. All of the Pareto-preferred region involves *less monitoring* than at the point E. Many of these points involve *more effort* by Švejk than the point E. In other words, a trade should be possible in which Švejk supplies extra effort in return for reduced monitoring. Thus, in this game we know exactly what cooperation would look like: a trade of employee effort for employer trust, where "trust" means the employer reduces her ability to monitor Švejk, while hoping Švejk will supply more effort than Švejk has a self-interested reason to supply. Given the simple assumptions of the monitoring model, this is the only form of cooperation that will make both Švejk and his supervisor better off.

In fact, given assumptions about their indifference curves, then some of the Pareto-preferred outcomes involve no monitoring whatsoever, but a complete delegation from the manager to Švejk. Assuming that there is always a trade-off between monitoring costs and compliance for the superior and that there is always a trade-off between effort and loss of autonomy for Švejk, the only Pareto-optimal points will be along the horizontal axis itself, including points T, C, and U.

Unfortunately, the Pareto-optimal outcomes (like C) are not equilibrium outcomes. An absence of trust makes them unavailable. The

Figure 5.2   Stackelberg Equilibrium (E) and Pareto-Preferred Region

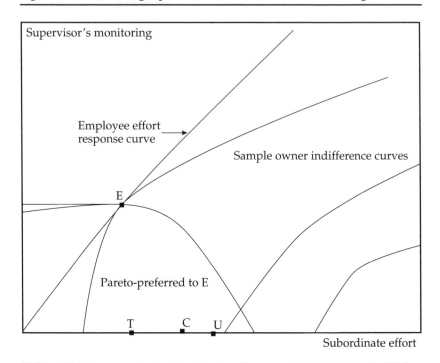

Source: Author's compilation.

manager would like to say, "I will spend no resources on monitoring if I can trust you to work at a level of effort that will yield C—and we will both be happier than at the equilibrium outcome E." But without monitoring, the optimal thing for Švejk to do is to provide zero effort, not outcome C. Even if Švejk agreed ahead of time not to loaf, the statement would be contrary to his self-interest, and not credible to the manager. The same thing could be said for everything else in the Pareto-preferred region, since all such points are off the effort-reaction function.

However, attaining outcomes *off* of this reaction function is precisely what this essay is about. How might Švejk and his manager attain a nonequilibrium that makes them both better off? What would cooperation look like in a real-world setting, and how might it be achieved?

"Gift Exchange": Autonomy for Effort

One early suggestive analysis, called "The Cash Posters," is by the sociologist George Homans (1954). These employees were assigned the routine (not to say monotonous) task of registering cash payments against the accounts of utility company customers. The company had supervisors who had the capacity to monitor the employees' behavior closely. There were work rules to be enforced, such as no conversation among cash posters, that were intended to encourage both accuracy and productivity. The company's standard was three hundred postings per hour, with a high degree of accuracy. The cash posters were paid a flat wage, with no bonus for exceeding the standard. Cash posters could move to a different job, but the other jobs available paid the same wage. If they failed to meet the standard they would be rebuked, with the possibility of course of being fired for any employee who consistently could not meet the standard.

Since there was no compensation for work beyond the standard, the economist George Akerlof (1982), in his analysis of the cash posters, notes that "the standard economic model of contract would predict that workers set their work habits to meet the company's minimum standards of performance" (547). Surprisingly, however, cash posters exceeded the minimum by an average of 17.7 percentage points, with a range from 2 percent to 46 percent. Akerlof interprets this extra effort as a "gift" to the firm. The firm could reciprocate this gift in a variety of ways. One is by paying more than a market-clearing wage, or what has been called an "efficiency wage"; under certain assumptions, both the firm and the employees could be better off than they were with the firm's getting minimum effort from a market-clearing wage.

More relevant for our purposes is the possibility that the firm reciprocates the employees' extra effort with what Akerlof calls "leniency." Leniency, interpreted here as a weakening of monitoring (m), can be valued by employees both instrumentally and for its own right. Instrumentally, it is valued because it means a reduction in the possibility of punishment. Leniency is also directly valued as "freedom" or "autonomy." Employees experience a utility cost from "having someone breath down their necks." A "good" employer is one who will allow the employees the flexibility to arrive late occasionally when the children are slow to get ready for school, will allow changes in work rates to correspond to varying energy levels during the day, and will turn a blind eye to minor rule violations, like conversing on the job, that relieve tedium.

This exchange of leniency for unrewarded effort was observed among the cash posters. Indeed, Homans documents that this was to some extent a conscious strategy among the managers at the utility company: "The fact is that cash posting looked to an outsider like a hard and dull job. A number of girls who were offered it had turned it down. The supervisors wisely felt that they would have a still harder time getting recruits and getting out production if they tried to bear down on a group of young girls like this one" (Homans 1954, 726). The management realized that "a group of young girls like this one" would have resented a managerial style of "bearing down" on them. As a result, a variety of work "rules" were not enforced—notably the work rule forbidding conversation among the employees: "They were convinced they could do their work without concentrating on it—they could work and talk at the same time. In theory, talking was discouraged. In practice, the supervisors made little effort to stop it" (Homans 1954, 727).

There was a great deal of variation among the cash posters, and some of them felt that the really hard workers were foolish for working as hard as they did. They feared that management would simply increase the expected effort level. But this concern did not manifest itself in group norms to restrict output and work to rule:

> The attitudes characteristic of restriction of output were present in the group; the thing itself was not, certainly not as an organized group practice. But neither did the girls feel under any pressure to work particularly fast. Indeed, *the lack of pressure may have been the very thing that helped some of them to work, in fact, very fast indeed.* (Homans 1954, 728; emphasis added)

I believe that Homans is correct in implying that it is tighter control efforts that trigger contrary work-restriction norms among employees. In fact, the voluntary "gift exchange" that Homans saw among the cash posters had not always been present. The girls who had been there longer remembered when work restriction (working to rule) was standard. The worst producer among the cash posters was critical of the best producers: "They try to get four or five hundred and walk their legs off. I tell them they don't know how we had to fight to get things the way they are now" (Homans 1954, 732). However, for most of the girls in the room, there had to be a delicate balance in which extra effort rewarded and *sustained* the leniency of the managers, just as the leniency of the managers rewarded and sustained the extra effort by the cash posters.

The bargain thus struck was (like C in figure 5.2) off the effort-response curve, and therefore theoretically not sustainable. How can such a bargain be negotiated and sustained? The simplest model has to do with repeated games.

Cooperation Through Repeated Games

The advantage of most organizations is that both sides recognize they are in this for the long haul. In Robert Axelrod's (1985) apt phrase, the future casts a long "shadow" in public bureaucracies. What would cooperation look like in such an organization, and what role would "trust" play in a cooperative outcome?

Laxness would not be rational for an employer in a one-shot game; remember that zero monitoring by the superior will induce zero effort by Švejk. However, in the context of a *repeated* game, laxness would be one part of a "tit-for-tat" strategy that could support cooperation as an equilibrium. Leniency in monitoring is the reward for extra effort (to the right of the employee-response curve), while a return to more intense monitoring is the threat against shirking.

Imagine that the game described in figures 5.1 and 5.2 is repeated a number of times. In each period of this game, the superior sets a monitoring level, the subordinate picks an effort level, and both sides receive a payoff. If this game were repeated exactly k times, Švejk would have no incentive to provide any effort level off of the effort-response curve. The effort-response curve is by definition Švejk's most self-serving effort level given any level of monitoring. Since the supervisor knows that Švejk will respond with a point on the effort-response curve, the supervisor has no reason to monitor any less aggressively than that at level m_E.

But knowing that the final outcome will be E, there is no reason to cooperate in the penultimate period. By backward induction, the outcome will consistently be E for any finitely repeated game.

However, suppose that the game does not terminate at a particular time. Like an ongoing organization, there is in any time period a probability d that the game will be repeated another time. This is the familiar scenario in which cooperation is sustainable.

Suppose the supervisor were to play the following trigger strategy: "I will supply zero monitoring as long as I find that you supply effort levels equal to e_C or greater. If I ever discover that you have supplied less effort than that, then I will revert to monitoring levels of m_E." To this repeated game strategy, it is rational for Švejk to respond with the following trigger strategy of his own: "I will supply effort equal to e_C as long as you in fact provide zero monitoring. But if I ever find you supplying more monitoring than that, then I will respond by a point on my effort-response curve forever after that." Each of these strategies is a best response to the other's strategy, as long as the probability of repeated play is sufficiently high. In other words, rational, self-interested individuals can agree to cooperate (play the given trigger strategy) as long as the other does.

Each has a threat that "enforces" the other's cooperation. The supervisor's threat is to increase monitoring if Švejk does not put out high levels of effort; Švejk's threat is minimal compliance—working to rule—if the supervisor increases monitoring. What looks like a "gift exchange" could simply be the rational response of supervisor and employee to the other's implicit threats.

With this repeated game perspective, it is possible to explain what might be called the "control paradox."

Explaining the "Control Paradox"

This value placed on lenient, or "soft," oversight is present in most sociological studies of employee relationships. In Alvin Gouldner (1954), for example, employees at the gypsum plant express appreciation of the original management team for letting them take care of errands on personal time, "borrow" modest amounts of firm materials for personal purposes, and be flexible about arriving and departing on time. In return, employees were willing to work overtime when the company really needed it; they also gave a greater effort than the level of monitoring or consequences for shirking really warranted.

This all changed when a strict new management came in. The new managers heightened the awareness of hierarchical authority, clamped down on rule enforcement, and put in a time-clock so that they could monitor and sanction tardiness and absenteeism. The net effect of this was to create a workforce of "good soldiers," like Švejk. As Gouldner notes, the strict enforcement of rules heightened the awareness of the workforce on the *minimum* effort they could offer without being fired. Less voluntary compliance resulted in a tightening of the rules and increased monitoring by hierarchical superiors, which in turn resulted in even less willing compliance. The net result, Gouldner suggests, was decreased performance. The case is a compelling example of the "control paradox," whereby stricter attempts to control subordinates result in less effort by subordinates.

The idea that more monitoring and supervision could result in less control seems paradoxical, especially in light of the effort-response function in figure 5.2. Along the effort-response curve, stricter monitoring results in more effort. But the key to understanding the control paradox is that the relevant points of comparison are E (on the effort-response curve) and C (off it). The cooperative outcome C in figure 5.2 is a delicate equilibrium of a repeated game—*off* the employee's control-response curve—enforced by something like a trigger strategy. What Gouldner documented at the gypsum plant is a collapse of the cooperative equilibrium from C to E—implying more monitoring and less effort.

Notice that this does not mean that the monitoring and control are irrelevant—even when not used. In the cooperative equilibrium of the repeated game, it is the credible threat of tightened monitoring that encourages the employee to provide high levels of effort "voluntarily."

Other Examples of the Control Paradox

Notice that Homans documented an awareness of the control paradox among the managers of the cash posters: the managers believed that an attempt to "crack down" on the cash posters would induce a loss of the voluntary effort. In other words, they were lenient precisely because they expected that *more* monitoring would result in *less* effort!

The same thing can be seen in numerous other settings. One of the most striking examples was in the Hovey & Beard Company's toy-painting operation (Strauss 1955). Management had reengineered the painting task so that eight workers sat at an endless chain of hooks, on which toys were to be carried off after being spray-painted. Every hook was supposed to carry a toy. The new system involved a certain investment in new machinery and the management expected a return on the investment. However, the women who had this job were learning the new system more slowly than planned, and their morale was low. They complained that the engineers had set the speed of the hooks hopelessly fast, and that there was no chance they would ever be able to keep up the intended rate. They claimed further that the ventilation was bad, and it was too hot. Output was low.

After some time, the supervisor took it upon himself to get a few minor concessions from management, including some ventilation fans. The workers were "jubilant"; one of the things they seemed to enjoy most was deciding among themselves about the best possible placement of the fans. The supervisor sensed that this represented an increase in the workers' autonomy—an aspect of the work environment that they controlled. After more discussion with the workers, he forwarded an even more drastic concession of worker autonomy: he proposed that management allow the workers to set the speed of the hooks by themselves. The employees promised to improve production if they could set the rate of the hooks "faster or slower depending on how we feel" at a given point during the day (Strauss 1955, 93). Over the objection of the time-study engineers, who claimed that they had scientifically determined the optimal rate for the hooks, management agreed to install a speed control at the work station of the work leader.

Once again, the workers were overjoyed. They discussed changes in timing—settling on "low" before and after lunch, "high" during most of the rest of the afternoon. Morale jumped, and production increased sharply. The workers earned a "learning bonus" that had been agreed on when the new technology went into place. The workers had agreed to an explicit bargain of the sort described in figure 5.2: increased effort in exchange for more lenient supervision and autonomy. Both sides were better off.

Ironically, however, the situation did not last, owing to forces outside the workroom. Skilled workers in other parts of the plant were jealous of the paint girls' autonomy and their earning of the learning bonus. The engineers continued to insist that the girls were operating the hooks at the improper pace, despite the fact that productivity had gone up. Suddenly, and without discussion, the superintendent revoked the learning bonus and returned the pace of the hooks to the time-studied constant speed. This triggered the appropriate punishment strategy on the part of the girls—production dropped sharply. Within a month all but two of the girls had quit, followed by the supervisor. Thus, this case provides illustrations—occurring within a short time span—of both sides of the control paradox: increased effort for more lenient supervision, and then decreased effort as a response to stricter management.

Protecting the Cooperative Equilibrium

The Hovey & Beard case illustrates that other forces may impinge on the establishment of a cooperative equilibrium between supervisor and employees. Another case shows how the cooperative equilibrium was maintained by misrepresenting the situation to all those outside of the workroom—including upper management.

In the Homans's Western Electric studies, management felt they had a strong set of rules (against chatting, sharing tasks, mutual assistance, etc.) and a supervisor to monitor and enforce the rules. The supervisor was also supposed to keep an accurate account of electrical connections wired and soldered by his workers. However, the reality in the bank-wiring room turned out to be that the rules were never enforced. Nor did the supervisor even monitor output levels as he was supposed to do. "Instead he let the wire men themselves report their output to him" (Homans 1950, 61). In fact,

> There were a good many other things going on in the Observation Room, as in the department as a whole, of which higher management would not have approved. The group chief (supervisor) knew this, but there was little he could do about it. To enforce the rules would have required his standing over the men all day, and by so doing he would have sacrificed all hope of establishing good relations with them. He would have lost even that minimum of influence that he needed if he was to do any kind of a job at all. Under these circumstances he chose to side with the group and wink at much of what was going on, especially as he was in a position to protect himself. Output was considered good. (Homans 1950, 63)

What the supervisor was protecting was a bargain that had been struck in which the work group enforced a high level of group productivity by encouraging precisely those activities—job sharing, mutual assistance, chatting and socializing—that the rules were meant to prohibit. The men reported—and the supervisor recorded—output that was an accurate per-work long-run average, although individuals might deviate from that average in any given day. The members of the work group actively caused trouble for anyone in the workroom who tried to invoke hierarchical authority of any kind, and it seems clear that the supervisor's relaxation of authority and total failure to enforce work rules were part of the "social contract" in the workroom, which were reciprocated by honest and satisfactory effort on the part of the employees.

The most telling incident occurred with Mazmanian, the most disliked person in the workroom. Mazmanian was an inspector, whose job was to test the quality of the electrical connections made by the other men. He did not take part in the group's social activities, and he tended to set himself above the others because of his college education. He was disliked precisely because he systematically violated work-group norms, especially the prohibition against claiming hierarchical authority. When he eventually "squealed" to the personnel division about conditions in the workroom, it created a dilemma for the supervisor. Clearly, if the supervisor backed Mazmanian's version of the story, he would both lose his support with the men and implicate himself in the habitual violation of work rules that took place in the room. Therefore the supervisor denied Mazmanian's revelation of his laxity, and Mazmanian was transferred out of the room. This incident reveals the dependence of the supervisor on the willing cooperation of the men and reinforces the message that the price of willing cooperation is the leniency of those in the room with managerial authority.

Control in Street-Level Bureaucracy

Many bureaucratic tasks are ones (teaching, police work, social service) for which the ability of supervisors to monitor subordinate behavior is limited and the costs of monitoring individual behavior are large. The effort-response curve may rise steeply in the vertical dimension, meaning that increased monitoring has limited impact on the individual's level of effort, which remains low. The equilibrium behavior in such situations may involve a great deal of monitoring and little subordinate effort. Such an organization is likely to be perceived as "bureaucratic" in the fullest pejorative sense of the word: bureaucrats will be seen as rigid and inflexible, obsessed with following procedures rather than serving their public clientele, determined to use organizational rules and routines both as excuse for inaction and defense against external criticism.

At the same time, the gains from cooperation—extra effort for less coercive monitoring—may be large. Peter Blau's excellent in-depth analysis of a state employment agency (1963) provides a compelling contrast between two sections, section A and section B, performing nearly identical tasks of trying to connect out-of-work clients with employment opportunities. Employees in both sections were closely monitored, although imperfectly. Statistics were kept on several measurable behaviors, such as the number of interviews resulting in referrals, etc. Other activities that were also crucial to serving the clients were more costly to gather and were therefore ignored. These included whether placement counselors, on receiving promising employment leads from employers, shared those leads broadly with the entire section or "hoarded" them for the clients they saw personally. Blau (but not the agency) gathered data on the proportion of job leads received by a bureaucrat that were eventually filled by that bureaucrat's clients; a disproportionately high number indicated that the employee had found ways to "hoard" those job openings, and was labeled by Blau as "competitive" behavior.

Section A had a strict supervisor who based performance evaluations on the statistics available, saying, "Here, in the production figures, is the answer to the question, How good are you?" (Blau 1963, 65). This supervisor's attitude induced (intentionally or not) a high level of competitiveness among many of the section A interviewers. Within section A there was a strong correlation between competitiveness and productivity (Blau 1963) and performance evaluations. The most competitive employment counselors (those who hoarded information most often) got the highest productivity figures and benefited in their performance evaluations.

In section B, however, the supervisor was perceived as being much less reliant on the productivity statistics. By monitoring the placement statistics less closely, the supervisor rewarded such competitive behaviors as "hoarding" less. "Since their ratings were not primarily based on performance records, members of Section B were less anxious about productivity, and this encouraged the development and persistence of co-operative norms" (Blau 1963, 65). In particular, the cooperative norms included much more sharing of employment opportunity information among employment counselors. As a result, there was no correlation between competitiveness and productivity.

This led to an aggregation paradox: "[T]he group much concerned with productivity [section A] was less productive than the group unconcerned with it [section B]" (Blau 1963, 69). By sharing employment opportunities more widely, section B was able to fill 67 percent of job openings, compared to 59 percent for section A. The supervisor's use of hierarchical monitoring and performance evaluations apparently triggered a manifestation of the control paradox: more monitoring and less productive behavior. Comparative success in section B was due to the ability of the supervisor to deemphasize the overt use of control mechanisms, which was reciprocated with more non-monitored cooperation in the behaviors that really counted—the sharing of placement opportunities.

Both section A and section B were in equilibrium—the behavior of both kinds of supervisors was rational *given the response of their subordi-*

nates. I suggest that section A and section B were at points E and C, respectively, in figure 5.2. It was rational for the employees in section A to "hoard" placement information that made possible the productivity records that supported positive performance evaluations; but it was just as "rational" for employees in section B to reciprocate a more flexible supervision style with more voluntary and cooperative effort. It was rational for the supervisor of section A to provide close monitoring and to link performance evaluation with performance, when that managerial style was so obviously efficacious in motivating strong performance figures; but it was also rational for the supervisor in section B to provide more lax monitoring and flexible performance evaluations when that managerial style was reciprocated by stronger section performance as a whole. Each actor's style was a "best response" to the respective partner, as is definitionally true of equilibrium behavior. The difference was that the actors were coordinating on quite different equilibria in the two sections.

Implications: Congressional Oversight and the Control Paradox

The paradoxical possibility of more control inducing less organizational success has ominous implications for congressional oversight, for the purpose of congressional oversight is to increase the level of monitoring and control. Donald Warwick's (1975) account of the State Department provides yet another example in which tightened control results in inferior outcomes.

The State Department's Area O served its administrative functions: personnel, materials, office space allocation, etc. It was, like the rest of the State Department, known for being bound by red tape and the need for hierarchical clearances. In an attempt to make the organization more responsive and efficient, the director of Area O eliminated many of the procedural rules that restricted individual behavior, and eliminated many of the levels of hierarchy in the chain of command beneath him. With a flatter hierarchy, every subordinate would find it difficult to turn to her superior for directions—they would have to take initiative and make decisions for themselves more often. The elimination of rules requiring clearances would have the same effect. The net effect was to drastically reduce the level of monitoring experienced by each subordinate in Area O.

The changes resulted in more work being done by a smaller staff, improved the section director's information level about the organization, and thus his ability to make effective decisions. Despite early signs of success, the changes were not greeted with a great deal of enthusiasm from either the managers or the employees. The officials at the

State Department knew that they were in a hostile political environment; they had few interest group supporters working for them in Congress. And in fact, the State Department had been a favorite scapegoat with Congress since at least the fall of China in 1949. The department was known for its elitist, Ivy League orientation to foreign policy. Senator Joe McCarthy was the most prominent in a long string of members of Congress who were hostile to the department. At the time of the Area O reforms, Congressman John J. Rooney (New York), of the House Appropriations Committee, was known for his close scrutiny of State Department programs, searching for both waste and signs of un-Americanism.

As a result of this hostile external environment, State Department managers felt a strong need for close control of their subordinates. They never knew when some anonymous subordinate would take some action that would make them liable to ridicule or worse in front of Congressman Rooney. Consequently, they felt the need for more assistants to decrease the span of control, and more rules that would ensure safe decisions by subordinates. Both hierarchy and rules were regarded favorably by superiors, because they would help ensure that no subordinate would take some action that would threaten their careers.

Similarly, subordinates at Area O knew that the reduction of monitoring by their own superiors did not mean that they were free from punishment. Warwick recounts stories of individuals brought from the depths of the State Department to account for decisions that Congressman Rooney did not like (Warwick 1975, 74–75). Consequently, a reduction in departmental monitoring did not decrease employee exposure; it *increased* the risk of exposure to Congress itself.

The personnel system at the State Department further encouraged rigid, rule-following behavior. Employees knew that the surest way to be "selected out" of the Foreign Service was to stand out of the crowd. Consequently, they felt a need to be able to justify each of their actions. Justification came through two routes: hierarchy and rules. Each officer wanted to be able to say, "My behavior was authorized by my immediate superior," or "My behavior resulted from a simple application of standard operating procedure."

The Area O experiment provides two important warnings about implementing a cooperative solution in order to improve efficiency in an organization. The first is that decreasing monitoring is not likely to result automatically in reciprocated voluntary effort if the reward system continues to punish risk-taking behavior, as the Foreign Service was known to do. Second, decreasing monitoring at a lower level is not going to invoke reciprocated voluntary effort if the threat of punishment from higher levels in the hierarchy (that is, Congress) persists or increases.

Both superiors and subordinates, therefore, could agree on the need for hierarchy and rules. In the case of the Area O reforms, Warwick reports that essentially all of the eliminated levels of hierarchy and rules were reestablished within a few short years. In the presence of a hostile environment and vague performance criteria, a high level of hierarchy and rules becomes an equilibrium in the bureaucratic game. No rational Foreign Service officer would be anything other than a "good soldier" like Švejk. The net effect is that congressional attempts to increase control of the State Department were instrumental in the creation of the bureaucratic characteristics that Congress disliked. The irony is that Congress's actions were crucial to the process that resulted in the evolution of a State Department that Congress loved to hate.

Policy Implications: Public Versus Private Schools

The State Department is not the only case in which external control can decrease the performance of the controlled agency. While one might think that the goal of a public school is a great deal clearer than the goal of the State Department, that is evidently not the case. Research by John Chubb and Terry Moe (1988) has found that democratic political processes impose multiple conflicting goals on our school districts. In some places prayer in schools is a large issue; in others, it is creationism. Schools are simultaneously to teach patriotic values, reduce teenage pregnancy, and fight the war against drugs. On top of this are the goals of teachers themselves. Teachers, students, and parents in public schools are much more confused about their schools' goals than the same constituencies of private schools. With a shared, clear vision for the school, parents, students and educators in private schools find it easier to generate satisfactory results without a great deal of hierarchy or rule monitoring.

In public schools, goals are more ambiguous, and monitoring by principals and school boards is more threatening. Private schools are much less likely to be monitored by outside administrators than public schools, and the school board is significantly less intrusive in matters of disciplinary and personnel policy (Chubb and Moe 1988, 1073). In public schools, principals are less likely to have teaching experience, more likely to be motivated by a preference for administration, and less successful in demonstrating leadership in the eyes of the teachers (1078). Public school teachers experience more monitoring and less autonomy in curriculum design, text selection, techniques, discipline, etc. As a result, teachers in private schools are more likely to agree that "success is not beyond their personal control," and their job satisfaction is higher (1083).

The picture that emerges is one in which public school teachers are more rule-bound and monitored, and feel less in control and less satisfied.

In the least effective schools, rules and hierarchy become the means for protecting teachers and school administrators from political flak (as in the State Department). To some degree at least, school board members get what they want (reelection), bureaucrats get what they want (security), and the only losers are the students and their parents.

The central point is that the successes of private schools occur without the strict overhead control associated with public schools. The control that parents have in private schools is through the market mechanism of choice, not through the hierarchical lines of principal-agency theory. The more school boards try to "control" teachers—by creating ever-elongated monitoring hierarchies, by proliferating rules that limit teacher autonomy—the more clearly they create the conditions for rigid, uninspired teaching and decrease the overall effectiveness of their own schools. In successful schools (public or private), clarity of shared goals motivates more successful educational experiences than bureaucratic control can ever hope to do.

Policy Implications: Regulation

John Scholz (1991) provides an interesting example of the control paradox in his analysis of regulatory agencies. We may think of a regulatory agency as the "supervisor" in the Švejk game, and the regulated firm as Švejk. Absent any monitoring effort, the firm will do just as it pleases. More monitoring results in a higher probability of being caught in a violation and sanctioned—and therefore more effort to comply. The regulatory agency picks the optimal level of monitoring effort by equating marginal benefit and marginal costs in the normal way.

As Scholz carefully points out, there are short-run forces that produce unsatisfactory outcomes. The firm would like for the agency to overlook minor technical violations while helping the firm discover how to comply with minimal cost and disruption—but if the agency does so, then the firm has every incentive to take advantage by means of "minimal compliance." The agency wants the firm to share information, but if the firm does so, the agency has every incentive to take advantage of this by turning that information into quick and easy convictions and penalties. Thus, the short-term equilibrium of this game (what he calls the "deterrence equilibrium") is a combination of maximal enforcement and minimal compliance, and is not particularly satisfactory to either the regulated firm or to the regulatory agency.

Scholz carefully describes how both sides are made better off by a "flexible" enforcement regime combined with "voluntary" compliance, even though that outcome is unstable in the short run. It is only sustainable, as we have reviewed earlier in this paper, as a long-term equilibrium when both sides implicitly threaten maximal enforcement and minimal compliance in order to induce voluntary compliance and flexible enforcement from the other side. Using empirical data from state-level occupational safety and health agencies, Scholz is able to show a regulatory manifestation of the control paradox: those agencies that engage in maximal (coercive) enforcement have higher injury rates among covered employees than those that engage in cooperative, flexible enforcement strategies. Evidently, in the long-run equilibrium, regulatory agencies are able to induce a more cooperative response from regulated firms, and the social benefits of this are observable in more effective efforts to enhance worker safety.

One might well ask why any state would pursue a maximal enforcement strategy that is less effective than a cooperative approach. The answer that Scholz suggests evokes the relationship between the State Department and Congress. External political figures beholden to labor groups feel that supporting a "cooperative" relationship between firms and agencies is suggestive of "softness" or being "co-opted" by business. Therefore, they find it politically advantageous to push a tough regulatory stance that is in fact less effective.

At the heart of this result is the control paradox. Because tighter and tougher monitoring seems, on the face of it, more likely to produce beneficial results than a more flexible approach, the benefits of the latter are not available without a long-term cooperative approach. In the hierarchical chain of control, state politicians are not known for their long-term outlook; reelection needs are immediate, and therefore the short-term advantages of control are preferred to the long-run (but politically risky) benefits of relaxing the legislature's hold on the regulatory bureaucracy.

Getting to Cooperation: The Role of Trust

This paper has tried to establish that in a monitoring relationship, both sides may gain from a "gift exchange" of autonomy (laxer monitoring) for voluntary effort. I have also argued that this exchange is sustainable as one of the cooperative equilibria to the repeated game. This implies that the "shadow of the future"—the shared knowledge of the benefits to be received from a long-term, committed relationship—is crucial to establishing and maintaining this cooperative equilibrium (see Axelrod 1985).

But what else is necessary? We know from the Folk Theorem that there are a number of equilibria to the repeated game, in which different levels of effort are displayed by Švejk. The point T, on the horizontal axis, is sustainable as an equilibrium of a slightly different repeated game equilibrium than that which sustains point C. The same is true for U. Each player would prefer either T or U to the point C, but they would be likely to have sharp differences in opinion about T versus U. And of course, the point E is also an equilibrium to the repeated game.

The implication is that a long "shadow of the future," and a shared desire to cooperate away from E, is not sufficient to guarantee a cooperative outcome. Another requirement is a solution to the coordination problem created by the multiplicity of viable outcomes from cooperation. What would it take to coordinate on a single, Pareto-optimal equilibrium such as T, U, or C?

I would argue that solving the coordination problem requires a leadership that is capable of generating a high level of confidence on the part of the players that everyone is converging on a particular cooperative outcome, and that everyone (especially the leader) can be trusted to implement the cooperative strategies that support that equilibrium. Notice that once an equilibrium is reached, then self-interest on all parts should be sufficient to sustain it. But coordinating on that equilibrium requires trust.

An example is supplied by Barbara Koremenos (2004), who studied a leadership change at Illinois's Department of Aging. The department's inspectors were required to investigate and evaluate nursing homes. Under the previous director, Jan Otwell, the written manuals specifying the required actions of these evaluators had become enormously thick. Her replacement as director, Victor Wirth, had been a professional in the department until leaving a few years earlier. When he returned as director, he said, "I'd been gone from the department six and a half years. I came back and looked at the paperwork in that program and I called my staff in and said, 'My God! How did we get here?' Just unreal!" (Koremenos 2004, 41). Wirth believed that the amount of paperwork that resulted from this fixation on monitoring was a distraction from the real job of the organization—which was ambiguous and subject to contractual incompleteness. Instead, Wirth tried to place emphasis on "providing quality services" (7). He believed that, ultimately, providing quality services would only be accomplished if the knowledge and motivation of the professionals were unleashed, noting:

> These nonprofits, these social workers, these providers: they're in it for the right reasons. It's a small minority that isn't. But the whole measuring system was aimed at that minority rather than giving everyone the benefit of the doubt, involving them more. The system that was built had one basic assumption: people were basically dishonest and they would try to falsify paperwork. This is not the case—ninety-nine percent. If you've ever spent time in the field, in nonprofits in the state, you'll find very, very dedicated people, very client-oriented people. (Koremenos 2004, 14)

Wirth spent much more time than his predecessor communicating with subordinates up and down the hierarchy. This included an unusual open-door policy, and "management by walking around." He felt that this was necessary in order both to communicate the goals of the organization and to decrease the emphasis on monitoring and sanctions. Wirth felt that he had to create the expectation on the part of employees that someone who made a mistake while honestly trying to serve organizational goals was protected from sanctions—in other words, he had to create trust. The new approach was quickly communicated throughout the organization. One bureau chief said, "We've relaxed somewhat on specifics. There's more flexibility on what can be accepted; this gives the case management level more discretion and autonomy. For social services, we were too rigid in the past" (Koremenos 2004, 14).

A bureau chief subordinate recognized that an emphasis on close monitoring could only do so much anyhow. The subordinate recognized the Švejk-like ability of employees to strategize over rules: "Audits only catch those who don't know how to play the game, get around the rules. You all know how to do that; you could write a book on it! *You won't need to do that anymore*" (Koremenos 2004, 14; emphasis added).

By Koremenos's account, the less control-oriented style had the desired impact of improving organizational performance. Service quality not only improved, but it did so while budget cuts went into effect. The department was able to cut $5.4 million in Wirth's first year and $10 million in the second year (Koremenos 2004, 1). Much of this saving may be attributed to decreased monitoring and paperwork costs.

I would argue that "trust" clearly plays a role in "switching" equilibria—from E to C. The problem is one of coordination—creating common knowledge by all relevant players that each person can expect the appropriate behaviors for C from all other relevant players. The employees, notably, have to trust that the supervisor is in fact *not* going to monitor employees closely in order to be able to affix blame in the case of external hostility. It is reasonable to believe that the supervisor is going to take this course only if the supervisor is a particular kind of bureaucratic leader—one who is committed to succeeding by making the organization work well, not by using the organization as a stepping stone to higher office in a different organization. The bureaucratic leaders who inspired the most loyalty and confidence in their subordinates were careful both to create a shared commitment to a set of organizational goals and to find ways to convince employees that they were protected from external threats as long as they took risks in furtherance of those organizational goals. As one official at the Illinois Department of Aging said of Wirth, "It's a whole different thing of trust. . . . They knew if Vic said he was going to do something he would. And if he said he wasn't going to do something, he wasn't" (Koremenos 2004, 31).

But supervisors also need to have some trust in their employees. In offering outcome C instead E as the coordinated equilibrium, they are offering a deal: autonomy for voluntary effort. They have to believe that their employees value autonomy and are willing to make and honor the proposed deal.

Conclusion: The Control Paradox and "Crowding Out"

As Bruno Frey (1999) has pointed out, if agents voluntarily supply a level of effort equal to X, then normal economic analysis would suggest that financial compensation should result in a larger amount X + Y. However, Frey points out that this commonsense conclusion is not always empirically borne out. In the area of donating blood, financial compensation may induce some volunteers to stop donating blood, perhaps concluding that since their donations were not based on a financial incentive, a cash inducement in effect relieves them of a moral obligation to donate further (see Titmuss 1971). In Frey's terminology, cash inducements "crowd out" voluntary donations, which can result in fewer total donations.

On the basis of the model in this paper, the same thing could be said of negative sanctions. If voluntary contributions result in a level of effort equal to X, then common sense would tell us that negative sanctions for failing to contribute should raise the total contributions to X + Y. As the gangster Al Capone is supposed to have said, "You can get more cooperation with a smile and a gun than a smile alone." But not always; sanctions may "crowd out" voluntary contributions. It remains an open question, given the monitoring technology, whether the level of effort induced by sanctions is greater or less than that induced by a more flexible supervisory style. Švejk's commanders found that the capacity to administer beatings and detention nevertheless got them very little valuable effort from Švejk.

Frey's interpretation is that people have some level of intrinsic motivation that generates a significant level of nonsanctioned effort. A second assumption is that sanctions, positive or negative, decrease the intrinsic motivation. This paper has supplied an alternative explanation for "crowding out" that is based on the model in figure 5.2 and repeated-game theory.

In this story, the difference in effort levels between outcome C and outcome E has nothing (necessarily) to do with intrinsic motivation or its crowding out. The difference is simply the equilibrium that is being played. Both C and E are rational, given the appropriate expectations about others' play. If subordinates expect superiors to play a trigger strategy, in which they supply decreased monitoring until they observe subordinates shirking, then they may rationally supply high levels of voluntary effort so as not to set off the trigger. Voluntary compliance averts close monitoring, and thus the threat of the negative sanction. The higher effort level with less monitoring is not necessarily due to intrinsic interest in the task but may be due to the coordination on an efficient equilibrium in which the threats are implicit rather than explicit.

This paper has supplied numerous examples of the control paradox. In some cases, tighter control results in worse outcomes (as in the State Department) and in some cases more lenient control results in better outcomes (as in the Illinois Department of Aging). As in so many aspects of social life, bureaucratic behavior offers the intriguing prospect of counterintuitive results and challenging insights.

Reciprocity-based trust is not equally available in every principal-agent relationship. This quality is no doubt hard to generate in distant, impersonal relationships among people who have no ongoing relationships or, worse, a relationship already characterized by mistrust and suspicion. It is easiest to generate in face-to-face relationships among people who already have a basis of understanding and perhaps an ongoing relationship of trust. Generating trust carries with it its own costs, perhaps in the form of establishing face-to-face relationships of the sort that managers such as Victor Wirth of the Department of Aging are known for.

The choice among various motivational and control techniques is therefore a major decision for a leader in a bureaucracy. But for those leaders in technological settings in which it is difficult and costly to monitor effort or reward outcomes, creating an "autonomy for effort" trade may be the best of several imperfect options.

References

Akerlof, George. 1982. "Labor Contracts as Partial Gift Exchange." *Quarterly Journal of Economics* 97(2): 543–69.

Axelrod, Robert. 1985. *Evolution of Cooperation*. New York: Basic Books.

Barnard, Chester I. 1938. *The Functions of the Executive*. Cambridge, Mass.: Harvard University Press.

Blau, Peter. 1963. *The Dynamics of Bureaucracy*. 2nd ed. Chicago: University of Chicago Press.

Chubb, John, and Terry Moe. 1988. "Politics, Markets, and the Organization of Schools." *American Political Science Review* 82(4): 1065–87.

Coase, Ronald. 1937. "The Nature of the Firm." *Economica* 4: 386–405.

Frey, Bruno S. 1999. "Institutions and Morale: The Crowding Out Effect." In *Economics, Values, and Organization*, edited by Avner Ben-Ner and Louis Putterman. New York: Cambridge University Press.

Gouldner, Alvin. 1954. *Patterns of Industrial Bureaucracy: A Case Study of Modern Factory Administration*. New York: Free Press.

Hašek, Jaroslav. [1920–23] 1974. *Good Soldier Švejk and His Fortunes in the World War*, translated by Josef Lada. New York: Crowell.

Homans, George C. 1950. *The Human Group.* San Diego: Harcourt Brace Jovanovich.

———. 1954. "The Cash Posters: A Study of a Group of Working Girls." *American Sociological Review* 19: 724–33.

Koremenos, Barbara. 2004. "Leadership and Bureaucracy: The Folk Theorem and Real Folks." *Rationality and Society.*

Kreps, David M. 1990. "Corporate Culture and Economic Theory." In *Perspectives on Positive Political Economy,* edited by James Alt and Kenneth Shepsle. New York: Cambridge University Press.

Miller, Gary J. 1992. *Managerial Dilemmas: The Political Economy of Hierarchy.* Cambridge, New York, and Melbourne: Cambridge University Press.

Miller, Gary J., and Andrew B. Whitford. 2002. "Trust and Incentives in Principal-Agent Negotiations." *Journal of Theoretical Politics* 14(2, April): 231–67.

Scholz, John T. 1991. "Cooperative Regulatory Enforcement and the Politics of Administrative Effectiveness." *American Political Science Review* 85(1): 115–36.

Strauss, George. 1955. "Group Dynamics and Intergroup Relations." In *Money and Motivation: An Analysis of Incentives in Industry,* edited by William F. Whyte. New York: Free Press.

Titmuss, Richard Morris. 1971. *The Gift Relationship: From Human Blood to Social Policy.* New York: Pantheon Books.

Warwick, Donald. 1975. *A Theory of Public Bureaucracy: Politics, Personality, and Organization in the State Department.* Cambridge, Mass.: Harvard University Press.

Chapter 6

Commitment, Trust, and Worker Effort Expenditure in Organizations

JOHN M. DARLEY

FOR MANY organizations, all that is necessary for organizational success is that the workers follow directions, and all that is necessary for that to happen is that they be adequately compensated for following directions and successfully producing product. Managers can observe both what the workers are doing behaviorally and the products that the workers produce. James Wilson (1989, 159) refers to organizations where these conditions obtain as "production organizations." In this sort of organization, it is understood by all that the trade-off involves "an honest day's work for an honest day's wage."

In other sorts of organizations, for the organization to succeed the members of that organization must intelligently and energetically do what they can to contribute to the organization's goals. In these organizations, it is often the case that the workers have knowledge and skills that managers lack, and the firm's success depends on the workers' contributing those skills and knowledge when the management cannot specify exactly what it is they need the workers to do, and thus cannot build a compensation system around task measurements. While it is possible to see that the joint product of the organization's efforts achieve success (or occasional failure), it is essentially impossible to subdivide the group's contributions to the final product into contributions by individuals. This sort of organization often adopts a management-by-objectives stance. It then faces the difficult problem of setting up a system to compensate workers in ways that will moti-

127

vate the workers to contribute in ways that the management cannot exactly specify in advance. One solution sees that the compensation is delivered at the level of the organizational unit producing the joint product.

The organizations on which I focus in this chapter are the latter sort and I will comment on two aspects of those organizations: first, the balance of financial and nonfinancial incentives that optimally motivate the workers in such organizations; second, the ways that these motivational systems eventually implicate the concept of "worker trust in management," a concept that has recently commanded a meteoric rise in attention from organizational theorists. More will be said about this later, but for now note that the workers must trust that they will be fairly compensated for the efforts they put in, without the management having a very close sense of what those efforts entailed, and exactly what those efforts contributed to the eventual success of the project.

Let us borrow Jeffrey Pfeffer's (1998) term, "high-involvement organizations," for the subset of organizations that seem to design effective compensation systems—effective in the sense that they seem to elicit smart, hard work from employees. Let us also remember his demonstration that high-involvement organizations are remarkably successful in the marketplace: their stock values rise above those of same-industry firms that do not use high-involvement strategies (Pfeffer 1998, chapter 2). First, what exactly do we need the organization's members to do in order for the organization to succeed? As the above discussion suggests, the workers need to function with some independence, seeing what needs to be done and mustering their skills to do it, in coordination with the other workers. Tom Tyler and Steven Blader (2000) suggest that there are four things that organization members do that matter in this process: (1) The organization's members generally follow the explicit rules, directives, and practices of the organization, meaning in practice that they obey the directives that specify what one should do. (2) They obey the directives that specify what one should not do, such as the prohibitions against employee pilfering. The third and fourth categories of behaviors are perhaps more important to the success of the organization than the first two. (3) The members voluntarily take on tasks that are needed for the completion of their work group tasks, even if those tasks are "not in their job description." (4) They use their powers of reasoning to realize that there are some activities that they should not do, even if the rules are silent about not doing these activities. Later we will have more to say about the management practices of such organizations, but as Pfeffer points out, workers in these organizations work harder because they have increased commitment to the organization and they work smarter because the organization encourages them to apply their knowledge and energies to their work.

Motivating Workers

Next, how do we bring the workers to do these things, to do what Tyler and others have suggested the organization needs them to do in order to succeed? How, in terms of the vocabulary of organizational theory, do we motivate the workers to work hard and smart? This question has been answered in two principal ways.

Pay for performance. The classic answer, drawn loosely from rational-choice considerations, is that we must provide incentives to the workers to work hard. That is, people are generally motivated by considerations of self-interest, and the motivational designer succeeds by connecting incentives that appeal to the self-interested individual to the performance of tasks that the organization needs done. The conception of incentives has been defined broadly and narrowly in various theories, but in a capitalist society the core incentive is seen to be money. Money is the maximally efficient incentive, in that recipients can deploy the money to maximize their own satisfactions.

Promotions can figure as incentives within this system, but largely because they imply higher salaries. If recognition programs such as "the employee of the month" are motivating, this is so only because they signal the coming of future bonuses, or increased job security, or some other concrete benefit.

Complex compensation systems. The other principal answer to the question of how people can be motivated is less clear in focus. The core definition offered by advocates of this type of motivational definition often seems to be a negative one. I would characterize the definition as follows: There are human motivations other than greed (their term for incentive-driven motives) and organizations must fill these motivations to provide maximal worker satisfaction and output (see, for instance, Fincham and Rhodes 1999, chapter 5, for a review of some of these theories). Many theorists writing about these motives refer, either directly or in spirit, to Abraham Maslow's famous hierarchy of needs, which he outlined in his classic 1954 work, *Motivation and Personality* (Maslow 1954).

Social psychologists would divide these nonfinancial motivations into two classes: those that are largely internal to the individual, and others that are intrinsically interpersonal in nature. An internal motivation would be the pride a craftsperson takes in her work product; an interpersonal motive would be the sense of belongingness or identity that an individual gets out of participating in a smoothly functioning problem-solving group. A useful omnibus term for the interpersonal-motivation theories is "social-identification" theories, although those theories also can include internal motivations such as pride.

The Group-Value Theory: A Social-Identification Theory

Tyler's (Tyler and Blader 2000) group-value theory is a useful version of a social-identification theory, since the motivating procedures that it identifies as important have been empirically shown to be effective in the workplace. The general finding is that in groups whose members are treated with various markers of respect, group members are willing to work hard for group interests without being specifically incentivized for their exact contributions.

What are these specific markers of respect manifested by organizations that show respect? Tyler has suggested many such markers, though they vary somewhat across organizational contexts. The most common markers are giving the individual voice, listening carefully to the employee's concerns, and hearing her or his side of the story. Second, the organizational authorities are benevolent toward the organization members. Finally, in conflicts between organizational members, they are neutral and try to arrive at principled decisions instead of playing favorites. Over the years the group-value model has evolved conceptually (Smith and Tyler 1996). Perceptions of trust, neutrality, and standing (Tyler 1994) have sometimes been identified as the major antecedents to willingness to engage in group-benefiting activities. At other times, pride (in the group or the work) and respect (from the group) have been identified as the main reasons why people will devote efforts to group projects (Tyler 1999). Whatever the specific formulation, proponents of the group-value model, like similar models of interactional justice (Bies and Tripp 1987; Greenberg 1996), claim that the reasons most people care about being treated in these ways are expressive, and not just instrumental. These treatments matter beyond their implications for implied future gratifications of self-interest. (This of course in not to deny that they do have implications for future financial incentives; the worker trusts the organization to provide adequate compensation for his past history of above-and-beyond-the-call-of-duty efforts on the completed project.) What I am suggesting is that people who are the recipients of these treatments interpret them as signaling a commitment to them and this in turn invites them to place trust in the employer.

Returning to Pfeffer's list of the practices of what he calls "high-commitment management practices," they seem to me to indicate why it is that these practices invite the workers to feel that they can place unconditional trust in the organization that uses those practices.[1] These practices (Pfeffer 1998, 64–65; see also all of chapter 3) include employment security, reduced status distinctions, self-managed teams, decentralization of decision making, and sharing of financial and performance information throughout the organization. Compensation in the high-commitment organizations is high as compared to that of similar organizations, and contingent on whole-organization performance. For the moment we return to the question of what mix of financial and other incentives the organization uses for compensating its workers. (Why it is that these practices are likely to produce unconditional trust in workers will be discussed in a later section.)

Compensation Systems and Organizational Structures

The compensation systems in most organizations involve a mix of financial and nonfinancial motivations, but sometimes one or another element of the mix takes a leading role: financial, pay-for-performance, or social-identity incentives. The question of where the emphasis can be predicted to lie in different organizations is, I think, answered by an examination of "the organization of the organization" in question.

Project Organizations

Project organizations are temporary, they exist for only a limited term. Such project organizations are pulled together for the solution of a single problem or to carry out a single project and are dissolved following the completion of the project. In such organizations it makes sense that the members be recruited for the financial incentives they receive for participating and that they be further financially incentivized by bonus payments for completion of the project, on the basis of agreed-upon measures of the success of the project's final product. This does not mean that a significant source of satisfaction to the project workers can't lie elsewhere, that financial compensation is the only reward. An example of nonfinancial compensations, although it is quite extreme, can be found in Tracy Kidder's *The Soul of a New Machine* (1982). The book describes the lives of a group of computer designers who were challenged to design and build a groundbreaking computer. What stands out is how little the financial compensation, once it was established at a fairly high level, meant to the workers in their day-to-day work, compared to two other things: first, the intellectual joys of solving the various design problems that arose, and designing components that would live up to the apparently impossible requirements that the project required; second, the recognition received from other group members when the group created a beautiful solution to a roadblock problem. Recognition of one's own talents from a group of highly talented individuals was a great reward.

An interesting conclusion emerges. To motivate workers to join a project team, financial incentives are necessary, although many will be drawn to work on the project because of the intellectual challenges it raises. Once the team is formed, it probably would be a mistake to attempt to create financial incentives for individual members of the project team, since that might lead to competition among a group of people who will succeed largely by being cooperative. Incentives delivered at the level of the group will further motivate successful completion of the project. However, once the project is under way, a good deal of the motivation of the project members is nonfinancial and comes from the challenges of solving the problems that the project presents, and by the esprit de corps that the challenges develop.[2]

Continuing Organizations

More commonly, organizations are ongoing and exist for the purpose of performing continuous tasks rather than one-shot projects. Manufacturing organizations, stock brokerage houses, government agencies, and most other organizations are of this sort. They may occasionally form teams designed to solve a particular organizational problem, or to create a new invention to manufacture, but permanent organizational members, temporarily seconded to the project team, staff these projects.

In these organizations the question of what motivates members becomes more complex. Somewhat different issues arise in motivating them to consistently perform in the interests of the organization. These workers will likely be brought into the organization on the basis of both their predictions about long-term future financial compensation and about whether the organization will fulfill their social-identity motivations. For instance, many organizational members are to some extent motivated by the pride that they would take in working for their organizations and the esteem in which they are held by other individuals for working in that organization. Some years ago, to say that one worked for IBM engendered this kind of pride and this kind of admiration. More recently working for a well-known dot-com had the same effect. This pride was certainly one reason that many accepted employment offers in those organizations.[3]

The organization that Tyler and Blader (2000) studied was a continuing, for-profit organization that consistently led workers to perform in beyond-the-call-of-duty ways by showing them respect. Organizations that give the individual voice, listen carefully to the employee's concerns, and have employees' best interests at heart have employees who are more willing to do what the company needs them to do in order for the company to prosper. That is, if workers perceive that the organizational authorities are benevolent toward them, if the authorities remain neutral in conflicts between organizational members, and try to arrive at principled decisions instead of playing favorites, then the workers generate high output. The importance of being treated with markers of respect will be even higher for workers in nonprofit organizations, since they are likely to have traded off some financial benefits to work in a lower paid environment because of their identification with the organization's goals.

Recall that we are considering the meaning of treatments of respect to persons who are in long-term relationships, rather than short-term project employments, with their organizations. Those long-term employees are concerned with how they will be treated in the future by the organizations. Will there be long-term jobs for them? Will they be fairly compensated in the future for the hard work they are putting in now? These are questions workers have regarding the organizations' long-term commitment to them.

They are, in other words, questions about the degree to which workers can place trust in the organizations. Current signals of respect from the organizations lead workers to believe that they can count on the organizations' respect in the future. The trust that the individual has in the organizational authorities centers on the premise that the organization really does care about the individual's future well-being. This is an acute question for workers who are being asked to make high-effort contributions toward producing a group product for which no explicit system has been contracted for the future compensation of the workers for these already-made contributions.

Trust and Organizational Performance

Let us pose the question simply. How can an organization member trust someone in the organizational authority structure to deal with these compensation considerations fairly?[4] Two somewhat different answers are suggested in the literature and, more important, exist in the minds of all who think about trust. First, I can trust you because you will be damaged if you fail to fulfill my trust. Perhaps your reputation in the organization of which we are both a part will be ruined if you fail to live up to my trust. Perhaps I can have recourse to the court system if you treat me in certain unfair or harassing ways. Perhaps, if I feel that you have violated my trust by inadequately paying me for my important contributions in the past, I will withhold my best-effort contributions in the future. In any event, I can count on you because it is in your self-interest to be counted on. This we will call calculational trust. I will trust you when (and perhaps only when) something reasonably ugly will happen to you if you fail to produce what I trusted you to produce. Or alternately you produce, but do so in the enforceable expectation of future benefits from me.

The kind of trust signaled by statements like "I trust you" proves to reference a rather different meaning of trust. This meaning can be elucidated roughly as "I trust you to have my best interests at heart." I trust then that you will think carefully about my needs and my wants, and work to fulfill them. The key to the trust that I place in you is that you hold a particular attitude of regard for me that motivates you to focus on my concerns. No external rewards or punishments are necessary for you to do what is right for me.

These two kinds of trust differ sharply in their essential character. The questions as to which kind exists in a particular setting—or even whether both kinds do exist—is the central one in trust research. Why do we, why can we, trust? Whom can we trust, in what ways, and when? Trust proves to be a battlefield on which a number of theories of human motivation confront each other. One central issue is whether there is a "calculational component" to all instances of trust when the trust exists between individual workers and the organizations for which they work.

Concerning the varieties of trust that exist between organizations and workers, the aspect of the topic we are here concerned with, in many instances the relationship that exists between worker and organization is one of calculational trust. This is characteristically the case when workers understand that they are being paid for the product they produce, and both the worker and the organization have clear perceptions of how the product will be evaluated. This is easier to achieve when the worker's production is largely under her own control, and becomes more complicated in situations in which groups of workers are the unit of production rather than individuals. So for reasons documented below, the typical problem with a calculational trust relationship is that the worker sometimes will perceive that the organization has not quite kept its side of the bargain. At other times, the worker is led to perceive that the organization has formed a bond with the worker that is noncalculational in nature. "We all here are one big family, committed and caring for each other." If is often useful for an organization to promote these perceptions on the part of the workers, because these are the conditions that cause the workers to expend a good deal of time, intelligence, and effort on the organization's behalf. The problem arises when the organization fails to sustain the behaviors that the worker has come to expect from a noncalculational trust relationship. The workers' reactions to the discovery that the organization did not in fact have a continuing commitment to worker well-being can be quite explosive.

Calculational Trust Theories

A number of theories are read as suggesting that trust, or "trust" is possible only when constraints exist within the system that enforce actions that live up to a person's trust, or punish untrustworthy ones. The banner under which adherents to these theories march carries the motto "I trust because I keep my powder dry." That is, I make sure that sanctioning mechanisms are in place that enforce trustworthy actions. The underlying assumption concerning human motivation in these theories is that it is self-benefiting, in an opportunistic way, and will capitalize on the opportunity of claiming gains that need not be reciprocated.

This is the assumption that most social scientists associate with economics, and economists are often kind enough to live up to the stereotype. Persons searching for this assumption about trust's viability will find it reflected both in the theory of rational choice and transaction-cost economics. Other areas of social science contribute theories that reflect this dismal, or "realist," view of trust. The classic scientific theory of management notoriously assumed that the worker was motivated only by external reinforcements, would loaf when he could, and required supervision. In other words, the worker was untrustworthy as far as the goals of management were concerned. Agency theory (Milgrom and Roberts 1992), although much more sophisticated in its analytic structure, makes similar assumptions about the motivation of the worker, and attempts to produce motivational systems that carefully tie financial incentives to measures of individual performance. The essential component of these theories is that one cannot trust workers to perform what the company needs unless financial incentives are attached to concrete measures of worker performance. One can, of course, treat workers with dignity and recognize their achievements, but it is in their linkage with the financial rewards that these more indirect expressions have meaning.

Compensation schemes that are structured to deliver financial compensation proportional to the inputs that the worker makes to the completion of the project or to the high-level performance of her job tasks have been the topic of many empirical studies and theoretical reviews. A good deal is known about how to design these systems, although those who write on the topic do acknowledge the complexities centering on worker trust in these systems (see Lawler 2000 for a recent example).

Several recent authors have insightfully commented on some of the problems in such systems that are likely to leave the worker feeling habitually undercompensated. Denise Rousseau and Violet Ho (2000, 276–87) have stressed the importance of the "psychological contract" existing between worker and the organization, pointing out that it is subjective. From the worker's perspective, the contract reflects the worker's beliefs regarding the terms of the exchange agreement binding him or her and the compensation and respect commitments made in return by the organizational structure and the individuals who administer it. In a similar way, probably in the mind of the supervisor of the worker, there exists a perception of the employment contract as perceived by the organizational representative. One way of thinking about this is that there exists somewhere the real form of the contract between worker and organization, but over time the real contract recedes in memory, and becomes overlaid with each side's perceptions of the contract. This probably creates a "reality" that did not exist in the first place, given the transaction-cost theorists' realization that for any reasonably complicated principal-agent arrangement, no complete contract can be created.

Like any understanding between individuals, a worker-employer contract is likely to be subject to certain all-too-human misunderstandings, many of which are driven by what is called the "self-serving bias." When a group of people produces a product, or a married couple has shared doing various household chores, group members perceive reasonably accurately the contributions that each group member has made and at the same time a systematic distortion is superimposed by each ego on the accounting. For example, in a traditional household, both the husband and the wife are aware that the wife does the largest percentage of the chores, but the total contribution the pair accounts for adds up to more than 100 percent. In other words, one, and more likely both, exaggerate their own contributions (Ross and Sicoly 1979). The generalization to contributions to a work team's success is obvious; to the degree that the compensation is expected to be based on individual contributions, each group member is in for disappointment when the compensation is delivered because each member will have exaggerated his or her own contributions.

Another reason for the accounting distortion is that people retain stronger impressions of their own successes and others' failures. Thus, both workers and managers are likely to think that they have fulfilled their obligations, forgetting a few that they did poorly on and that the other side did well on. These and similar processes will lead the workers to have expectations for compensation that are higher than will be delivered. (The extensive literature in equity theory deals with the actions that persons who feel unfairly under-compensated are likely to take. See, for example, numerous references to discussions of "equity" in the subject index of Rynes and Gerhart 2000.)

Noncalculational Trust Theories

Researchers studying human relationships in families, romantically involved couples, and other instances of communal rather than exchange relationships have documented the existence of interactional patterns that might suggest that the interactants have what we could call noncalculational trust in each other (Clark and Mills 1993). In these relationships, one is expected to give to the other according to what that other needs as soon as those needs become apparent, rather than treat the other as a partner in an exchange relationship.

We can concede that these noncalculational instances of trust exist in personal and kinship relationships and even are preconditions for these relationships to exist, while asking whether they occur in more conventional organizational settings. But anthropologists (Fiske 1990) remind us that this skepticism may be a perception that arises from our own cultural perspective, in which the vocabulary of self-interest is held to be the true explanation of a person's actions. In other cultures, actions undertaken for the good of the collective are routinely expected and routinely occur. Dale Miller (1999) has pointed out that self-interest is the perspective that dominates in the explanatory vocabularies of our culture, and has experimentally demonstrated that it is mobilized by respondents to explain activities that actually were done for other than self-interested reasons.

Other scholars have pointed out that there are other arenas of our society in which the relationships seem to be non-exchange-based and apparently noncalculational in nature. In our own culture, the best-supported theories as to why men fight in wartime (McPherson 1997; Marshall 1947) are that the motive for actions that risk one's own life is to live up to the expectations of the small group of fellow warriors with whom the individual has bonded. Although an elaborate calculational story could be told about this, scholars are clearly more disposed to the noncalculational interpretation.

Still, it is sensible to ask whether a noncalculational kind of trust has any important rule to play in relationships within workplace organizations. The answer, for many theorists and researchers, is yes. They do not deny that financial incentives, which are generally calculational in nature, are a central concern to workers. But some organizational theorists thinking about trust in organizations seem to suggest that both kinds of trust are found in these settings and, furthermore, that organizations in which considerable elements of noncalculational trust exist are disproportionately high-functioning organizations. For instance, "human relations" theories of human behavior in organizations assert the existence and importance of noncalculational trust. Or at least one constant pole of the dialectic that seems to routinely take place in theories of worker management in organizations emphasizes a human relations, human resources, human capital outlook that generally seeks to engage employee loyalty to bring those employees to be intrinsically committed to the goals of the organization. These theories tend to at least sketch the duties that the organization owes to the worker in return. Pfeffer (1998, 66–68) points out that his high-commitment organizations work very hard to give employees job security, doing all they can to avoid layoffs or downsizing during slower work periods, and this creates considerable worker loyalty.

Loyalty is characteristically a reciprocal relationship and the notion of reciprocal loyalty is certainly susceptible to being conceptualized as a relationship of trust of the noncalculational kind and workers are likely to conceive of it on those terms.

Robert L. Heneman, Gerald E. Ledford, Jr., and Maria T. Gresham (2000) have an insightful discussion of the utility of the organization's contract with the worker being one of "investment in" the worker. When the organization and the worker have what Anne S. Tsui and colleagues (1997) call a "mutual investment contract," production is high. Heneman, Ledford, and Gresham (2000, 198) define a mutual investment contract as one

> where there are broad, unspecified, and open employer inducements and employee contributions. Forms of compensation that may be appropriate here include skill-based pay as an investment in human capital, stock as an incentive for long term participation, and benefits (such as dependent care and concierge services) to allow the employee to make a high commitment to work.

Heneman, Ledford, and Gresham (2000, 198) call another common management-worker "contract" the "underinvestment contract," in which the employer expects broad and open-ended contributions from the workers, such as cooperating with other workers, but provides pay only for short-term outcomes achieved by the individual. An example would be compensation based largely on sales commissions for sales that the individual salesperson achieves. The underinvestment contract characteristically produces the worst results.

The Evidence for Noncalculational Trust in Organizations

Over the years, social scientists have examined the evidence that this noncalculational kind of trust exists in organizations and motivates individuals to behave in ways that further organizational goals. On my reading of their thinking, at least many of them assert its existence. One observation is that in organizations in which this kind of trust exists, it has been developed over time. Roderick M. Kramer (1996) has given us the useful notion of an individual in interpersonal situations as an "intuitive auditor," one who mentally keeps score of past occasions on which the organizational hierarchy has been trustworthy or untrustworthy. "Judgments about others' trustworthiness (or lack of it) are largely history-dependent processes. . . . Trust thickens or thins as a function of the cumulative history of interaction between interdependent parties" (218).

Blair H. Sheppard and Marla Tuchinsky (1996) suggest a sequence in which trust develops between organizational members, or between an individual and an organization, and this sequence may allow us to conceptualize the shifting tasks of Kramer's intuitive auditor as well as a possible transition between the two kinds of trust. "Deterrence-based trust," the common first stage of trust, is possible when there are negative sanctions for failing to act in a trustworthy fashion and the other party will not risk being penalized by those sanctions. It is obviously highly calculational. "Knowledge-based trust" becomes possible when, generally following repeated and multifaceted interactions, one can predict the other's trustworthy behavior. This seems to be a level of trust that is intermediate between calculational and noncalculational trust. Finally, in "identification-based trust," the other identifies with my goals. If this kind of relationship has been established, one can allow the other to act as one's agent, knowing that the decisions made are ones we would make for ourselves. This seems to me to be an example of noncalculational trust. Robert Lewicki and Barbara Bunker (1996) array these levels of trust into a developmental sequence and focus on the transitions between these stages of trust. If after a series of deterrence-based trust encounters, my internal auditing function learns that the other party is consistent in producing trustworthy behavior and threats are not required for this consistency, then I move to begin to develop knowledge about the other's "needs, preferences, and priorities," which allows a transition to knowledge-based trust. While knowledge-based trust is developing, the task of the intuitive auditor moves away from monitoring outcomes and instead searches for the underlying disposition of the other person.

The attributional task of the interacting individual changes with changes in the stage of trust: for instance, in the transition from knowledge- to identification-based trust, the task moves from developing a knowledge of the other's perspective to an identification with the other's perspective. What one is doing here is "taking the perspective of the other." Reasonable amounts of research in social psychology suggest that this step also includes an empathetic identification with the other person's goals.

When one feels that the goals of the other interactors include identification with one's own goals, the internal auditor can "take a vacation." However—and this is perhaps a friendly amendment to Kramer's concept—the auditor can quite unexpectedly get called back from vacation. Some rapid mental adjustments occur if the relationship has reached the stage of noncalculational trust and then evidence arrives that the noncalculational trust is not warranted.

Betrayal: The Consequence of Violation of Noncalculational Trust

A violation of noncalculational, identification-based trust has the potential to shatter relationships; it is experienced as a moral violation. This occurs because the realization dawns that the other individual really does not identify with one's aspirations and needs. Instead, depending on the violation, other interpretations are forced into mind: "She was just in it for the money"; "He only wanted me to exploit my talents, he didn't care about my development"; or classically, "I thought he loved me but he only wanted to have sexual intercourse with me."

Oliver Williamson (1993, 482) is the author of a famous paper on varieties of trust, in which the distinctions between calculational and "almost non-calculational trust" are made. With what seems to me to be acute psychological wisdom, he remarks, "I would reserve [the term] betrayal for [a violation of] personal trust and would use breach of contract to describe [a violation of] calculative relations. As hitherto remarked, breach of contract is sometimes efficient; . . . by contrast, betrayal of a personal trust can never be efficient. Betrayal is demoralizing."

If we accept this psychological insight that feelings of betrayal are reactions to trust violations in which the trust was perceived to be noncalculational, then we have a way of knowing whether an employee's presumption about the employer is that the employer has noncalculational regard for the employee. So the clue that at least some of these organizational relationships involve noncalculational sorts of trust lies in the fact that those are exactly the relationships in which trust can be demonstrated to be "betrayed" by an act of the employer—the act signifying that the other does not reciprocate the concern for the well-being of the one who trusted in this passionate way, who now feels certainly diminished, rejected, cast aside, destroyed by the other.

There are a number of ways in which organizations signal that their commitment to workers is calculational in nature. Sometimes the economic climate for the organization shifts in a disastrous direction, as it did for information technology companies at the end of the 1990s. Desperate attempts to shift corporate strategies, wave after wave of layoffs as the companies "downsized" or "delayered," salary cuts for the remaining workers, and other employee-shedding tactics came into play in the ensuing years. The more thoughtful compensation experts recognize this and attempt to suggest a new employment contract, in which the employees understand the temporary nature of their employment, take responsibility for the development of their skills and knowledge, and generally act as do free agents in the world of sports. Edward Lawler (2000, 8) has suggested, "[A]s the idea of lifetime careers, secure jobs, and loyalty to a single company has disappeared, highly talented individuals increasingly are looking for the best financial deals."

This is, I suspect, good advice for individuals, but it may be hard advice for the worker to take. As I have suggested before, the intelligent company seeks to have its workers engage with corporate projects in the wholehearted way suggested by Tyler, Pfeffer, and others. Such a company certainly would not wish for an employee who at one stage in the project becomes the key player in its success to take the rational action of the free agent and negotiate for a salary raise to continue working. In fact, as those who study corporate culture and the role of continuing employees as the repositories of corporate tacit knowledge point out, continuity of personnel is an underrecognized but critical component of corporate success. So the corporation will give various types of signals to the employees implying that if the employees continue with the organization they will have a bright future.

What may be pivotal here is the conflicted role of middle levels of management in proffering noncalculational commitments to the workers when they are, in some sense, not "authorized" by the real workings of the organization to do so. Believing, as they do, in the will of the organization to have loyalty toward themselves, they in turn signal this type of loyalty to their subordinate workers. By doing so, probably in less than completely conscious ways, they elicit greater efforts from the workers, and higher outputs. But they cannot insulate the workers from the conditions that cause upper management to take actions that are breaches of the loyalty that they have encouraged the workers to show.

As suggested, we respond explosively to occasions in which noncalculational trust seems to have been violated. Given the frequent demonstrations of this kind of reaction on the part of workers in organizations, we have evidence that workers have placed noncalculational trust—now betrayed—in their work organizations.[5] For most of us, ample evidence of this has been revealed in newspaper, magazine, and television interviews with workers and middle level managers who have been "downsized" in recent reorganizations. And it is not only loss of jobs that provoke this reaction. Sim B. Sitkin and Darryl Stickel (1996, chapter 10) show the coruscating reaction that is generated when a control system is imposed on research scientists and the scientists see that system as misdirected. The scientists feel that what is signaled is a lack of trust by the administration in the principle that the scientists will do what is best for the company absent a system that monitors that they do so. Their reactions are highly negative; they are, in a word, demoralized. Later we will examine the often-violent sequels to this reaction.

A good deal of organizational-theory writings turn out to focus on one aspect of noncalculational trust, namely, does or should an organization trust its workers to do what is right for the company or the community? It depends on one's theory of human motivation. Whether an organization trusts its employees depends on the prevailing image of the employee built into what W. E. Douglas Creed and Raymond E. Miles (1996, chapter 2) call the organization's "managerial philosophy." The philosophy centers on assumptions about the trustworthiness of subordinates as well as their competence and their ability to exercise self-direction and self-control. As noted earlier, the philosophy embedded in scientific-management theories was that workers were neither trustworthy, capable, nor reliable. Later theories of management, human relations– or human resources–oriented theories, have rejected one or more of those rather pessimistic assumptions, and regard it as appropriate for the organization to trust its employees, in both senses of trust. But one point being made here is that an organization that treats its workers as trustworthy may be signaling to the workers that the workers can have unconditional trust in the organization, and that may not be a side of the relationship that the organization can commit itself to sustaining.

Tom R. Tyler and Peter Degoey (1996) seem to be making this point (chapter 16) in that they consider organizations other than corporations and consider the reciprocal development of trust between organizations and members. They argue that in all organizations, the psychological dynamics of trust allow for what we have been calling a noncalculational kind of trust relationship, which grows out of the way an organization treats its individual members. If the organization treats members in a generally respectful way, this leads to members' developing trust in the authority. These organizations are able to count on self-sacrificing, group interest–advancing actions from their group members. An organization gains attributions of trustworthiness from its member by signals they give that they respect the status and dignity of individuals, are well-disposed to them, and will be fair rather than biased in taking decisions that involve them. They present some evidence that suggests that these considerations matter more to organization members than the variables that would be suggested by a more instrumental account of trust, such as favorableness of past decision outcomes.

Drawing on social-identity theory, Kramer, Maralynn B. Brewer, and Benjamin A. Hanna (1996, chapter 17) suggest a similar notion of "identity-based trust." When an individual identifies with a group, in the sense suggested by social-identity theory, the individual expects others in the group to behave in a trustworthy fashion, and the individual's identity is tied to the success of the organization for which they have made sacrifices. Interestingly enough, they suggest that this kind of trust will, at least for an interval, persevere past its betrayal: "I will act in a trustworthy way regardless of what others do."

The notion of identifying with an organization as long as that organization treats one in a respectful manner reminds us that some of the antecedents of this perspective lie in the procedural-justice area. Joel Brockner and Phyllis Siegel (1996, chapter 18) contribute a theoretical integration of procedural and distributive justice notions and trust. They suggest that treating individuals in what seems a fair and respectful way—procedural propriety—leads the person to make certain attributions to the authority, namely, that the authority intends to behave properly toward that person. It produces attributions that the authority is concerned with one's well-being. Brockner and Siegel then make an interesting further point: it still remains to be seen whether the authority is competent and reliable. Thus, an organization may make a bad decision, one that may have highly negative consequences for individuals, but may do so not because it is disrespectful of individuals but because the decision maker is unreliable, or the organizational coordination processes are unreliable. Decision outcomes, plans, work allocations, and other outcomes provide evidence for the competence and reliability of the authority. Therefore a distributively bad outcome, following an apparently procedurally fair process, should raise questions about the competence of the authority; in fact, attributing the outcome to incompetence can preserve the attribution of a motive for fairness to the authority, even if the outcome was not fair. Eventually, one's reaction to a stupid set of organizational authorities will be a different sort of mistrust, a mistrust in the correctness of their decisions, but may not have all of the consequences of the discovery that the authorities are badly disposed toward the workers or violate standards of fairness in dealing with the workers.

The central theme so far is that it seems useful for the organization to encourage the workers to experience unconditional trust in the organization, but this trust cannot always be sustained because current analyses suggest that the organization cannot always reciprocate it, and unconditional trust by one party demands that they believe that unconditional trust can be placed in the other party.

It can be easily shown that there are very negative consequences for the organization of the workers' discovery that they misplaced their trust in the organization. This becomes obvious when one examines the consequences of an organization's "betrayal" of the trust of individuals. The validity of the use of the emotionally loaded word "betrayal" turns out to be a clue that noncalculational trust can exist between an individual and an organization because betrayal is the emotion felt when an individual who trusts an organization in a noncalculational way is let down by the organization that the individual trusted.[6]

What is the standard reaction to betrayal? A desire for revenge. Robert J. Bies and Thomas M. Tripp (1996, chapter 12) use this fact—the desire for revenge—as an ingenious entry point to examine trust in organizations. Thus we could say that if an organization member expresses a desire for revenge, this is a proof that the member feels betrayed. Betrayal in turn is the emotion engendered by being let down by someone with whom one thought one had a relationship of noncalculational trust. Therefore, desires for revenge demonstrate the prior existence of noncalculational trust, now destroyed.

When our internal intuitive auditor provides us with the conclusion that we have been betrayed by someone in whom we trusted in an organization, we often seek revenge. Betrayals of trust within an organization can first include acts that harm the assumed moral order of the corporation. The point here is that the organization is the initiator of the betrayal sequence by taking actions that violate its own rule structure. These include organizational rule violations such as promoting people who have not met the formal requirements for the promotion; violating the general "codes of honor" that govern relationships between all people, a category that would include shirking job responsibilities or claiming credit for another's ideas; and acts of an abusive authority, such as demanding access to subordinates at all hours of the day and night. A second category of betrayals of trust involves damaging the identity of a subordinate by, for instance, giving personal criticism in public. If we attribute these actions to the character of the violator, as opposed to the violator's "blowing off steam" under high situational pressures to do so, then the implications are major; the superior is in personal violation of ethical standards, has violated the responsibilities that are inherent in the role of superior. The attributions can also spread to the organizational management, who has failed to constrain the harm doer.

The results of these sorts of attributions to superiors and the organizations can be far-reaching. They have the potential of creating an organizational member who hopes for bad outcomes for the organization, and occasionally works to bring those bad outcomes about. In other words, the person seeks revenge, first from the superior who inflicted these wounds on the member, but soon from the organization that rewarded or at least tolerated the superior's so doing. Depending on the relative play of forces, these attributions can lead to exit, either literally quitting the job or withdrawing one's efforts from achieving organizational goals, or attempts to change the organization, or attempts to extract from the organization compensation for the harm done. If, later, a crisis occurs for the organization (and it will), prior lack of trust can lessen the efforts individuals are willing to put in to cope with the crisis, make individuals less likely to make the decisions that might save the organization, and less likely to engage in the often high-effort-requiring collaborations that are necessary to get the organization through the crisis.

Can Trust Be Rebuilt?

Instances in which workers are going to feel that the organization has violated the trust relationship are likely to occur for any number of reasons. Therefore it is critical to ask whether the damage done to the workers' relationship with the organization is permanent. Because if so, the damage that the workers will seek to do to the organization will be continuing. Lewicki and Bunker (1996) articulate the steps that would need to be taken to restore trust if an individual or organization has violated the noncalculational trust of another: there has to be an acknowledgment that a violation has occurred; an admission that one was the true cause of the violation; an admission that the act was destructive; and an acceptance of responsibility for the destructive effects. This last requirement often brings action consequences with it: first, to remedy the situation as much as is possible and, second, to steer well clear of actions in the future that would erode the foundations of the tentatively restored trust.

These admissions are hard for an individual to make; intuitively, they are likely to be harder for an organization to make, given the diffusion processes that go on within organizations. The requirement here, Williamson suggests (1993, 483), is that the unit that betrayed must " 'reform,' rather than merely 'do better.' "

The Organizational Dilemma: Trust Misconstruals

A theme has emerged from this analysis, and it is one that warrants careful examination. For several reasons, the wise corporation at a minimum provides an institutional environment that, in Williamson's terms, "provides general purpose safeguards that relieve the need for added transaction-specific supports" (Williamson 1993, 476). To express it less laconically, the wise corporation provides an environment in which the individual worker is able to vest trust in the organization, and in the other workers with whom he or she forms temporary work groups. The corporation avoids rewarding individuals who take credit for others' work, or who act in other ways that would produce an organizational climate of dishonesty being rewarded. One reason why the organization does this is because it increases productivity; promoting trust can be in the service of enlightened organizational self-interest. Williamson (1993, 486) makes an interesting remark about this sort of institutional or hyphenated trust: "In the degree to which the relevant institutional features are exogenous, institutional trust has the appearance of being noncalculative. In fact, however, transactions are always organized [governed] with reference to the institutional context [environment] of which they are a part. Calculativeness thus always reappears."

But to whom does this calculativeness reappear? And when and with what effect? It is the thesis of this chapter that there is a natural tendency for workers in a setting in which long-term trust in the organization is possible to perceive that the organization is in a noncalculational relationship with them. (We ought to note that organizations often do a good deal to foster this belief with various communications about the "value of our excellent workforce" to the organization, implying that they do indeed see intrinsic value in the workers.) There are, of course, great benefits to organizations in bringing the workers to the conclusion that the bonds between worker and organization are symmetric and deep: organizations that engage the trust and loyalty of their organization members reap rich benefits for doing so. Specifically, if the trust given by the members to the organization is of the deepest, least calculational sort, the evidence we have examined suggests that they identify with the organization, gain self-esteem from its successes, work hard at their jobs, and struggle to avert the threats from crises that befall the organization.

Therefore, for the individual who has vested this kind of trust in an organization, it is not the case that the calculational, institutional trust "always reappears." However, it may reappear for the worker when certain kinds of organizational crises appear. These crises seem to suggest that the survival of the organization requires inflicting harm on the worker. And of course, organizations are quite free to do so in our country: analysts have observed that, as compared to other Western countries, the legal system of the United States gives the employers a great deal of leeway to abruptly sever employment of workers or to materially alter the conditions of their employment, job description, and compensation. The spectacular instances of these occasions involve "downsizing," "redundancies," "your skills are no longer needed." The fact that worker employment is at the discretion of the employer as opposed to some sort of protected entitlement of the worker often can be forgotten in times of rising employment but becomes painfully evident to workers when the economy is generating "layoffs."

"Calculativeness," then, reappears in the minds of the powerful, and so thereafter is forced into the minds of the workers. The organization members discover that calculational trust was the kind of trust management felt. But the worker felt noncalculational trust in the organization, and as we said earlier, this sort of trust is one of those relationships that must be bilateral to succeed. This worker, for whom "betrayed" is not too strong a word, is altered by this betrayal, and is at least temporarily not available for future relationships of noncalculational trust. If the individual has at hand the means of harming the organization, she or he is likely to do so.

Further, there are moral issues that need to be faced, ethical questions that arise when a powerful entity encourages those less powerful to enter a relationship of noncalculational trust with it, without making a symmetrical commitment in return.

This leads to the question as to whether it could be useful for the organization to take actions not in its best interests in order to maintain the possibilities of individuals' bonding in a noncalculational way to the organization. Certainly, some organizations have found it so: the Marine Corps, even in retreat, goes to incredible efforts to take their wounded out with them, in fact they go to incredible efforts to take their dead out with them. But what an odd idea that a corporation in a capitalistic economy should do the same! Then we recall the story about the behavior of the owner of the Malden Mill in Methuen, Massachusetts, Aaron Feuerstein, after the mill was ruined by fire in December 1995. The owner could have used that as a reason to close the plant and move future manufacturing to a lower-wage region. He didn't do so; he paid the salaries of the workers while the plant was being rebuilt, and rehired them when the new plant opened.[7]

Much was made of this in newspapers and television reports. This is perhaps an indication of a national disquiet with what is sensed to be a moral imbalance between corporations, apparently asking for the highly committed efforts from workers that may only stem from a noncalculational attitude toward the corporation, while in the last analysis not reciprocating with the same kind of loyalty. (We should note that the story has an ambiguous ending, reminding us of the limits of what is possible. The corporation went into bankruptcy some years later, to some extent as a function of the payments made to the loyal workers during the factory downtime.) Some analysts feel that the central task facing the modern corporation is to work out ways of creating the conditions that honestly let the workers experience noncalculational trust in the organization, without resorting to false claims of "security" or "lifetime employment." I am somewhat skeptical as to whether this is possible, given the tendency I have noted for people to gravitate toward the perception that their relationship with the organization of which they are long term-members is noncalculational. And we also need to remember that the evidence of Tyler and others suggests that the organization reaps great benefits from showing respect for its employees; they work harder. But the markers of respect look to this writer as though they imply a symmetrical noncalculational relationship between organization and workers. This analysis is pessimistic for the possibility of reciprocal trust between workers and organizations in a world of limited-term employment.

Summary

The modern organization requires not only mechanical rule-following actions from its members, but an enthusiastic application of their intelligence and commitment to take actions that they see will accomplish what the organization needs. Organizations that treat their members with "respect" are likely to elicit such actions from their members and benefit greatly from doing so.

However, there are complex consequences of this show of respect. It seems likely that the organization that treats its members in a "respectful" fashion convinces the members that the organization has a commitment to the well-being and the future of the individual. The member believes that the organization will keep this commitment even at some cost to the organization. This set of beliefs is inferred from the respectful treatment the member receives, and reciprocally enables the member to have a similar, noncalculational, trusting relationship with the organization. This in turn leads the member to permit himself to expend energies and make personal sacrifices for the organization.

Unfortunately, sometimes the organization takes actions that signal to its members that the organization does not really have the noncalculational commitment to its members that they came to assume was in existence. Downsizing workers while giving bonuses to CEOs can have this effect, as can violations of standards of fairness or of decent treatment of workers.

The reactions of members to this disconfirming discovery are both theoretically informative and deeply consequential for their relation to the organization. The reaction is an emotional one, and a major component of it is a feeling of betrayal. On the theoretical side, the fact that the emotion felt is betrayal provides support for my contention that the workers were feeling that they could noncalculatingly trust the organization. The action consequences of this feeling of betrayal are that they feel that they had been tricked into "giving their all" to the organization, and are now justified in, say, extracting compensation under the table from the organization's resources in recompense for the injury done them. Second, they have feelings of anger that provide the moral justification for acts that are intended as retaliation on the organization that betrayed them.

Notes

1. "Unconditional trust," and the related concept of "conditional trust" have been best articulated by Oliver Williamson (1993) in a much cited article.

2. There is a transitional case to consider here, in which one takes a job that is defined as having a set lifespan, but one hopes to be retained by that organization past the life span of the defined project. In this instance, some of the issues that we raise below become relevant; and the uncertainty about the duration of the contract adds complexity to the employee's side of the considerations.

3. Stock options were briefly a preferred mode of employee compensation. In most organizations, they were largely given to top management and were often manipulated in ways that separated the compensation of top management from increased stockholder value. In those organizations who extended stock options, or more generally, shares in the company, more widely among workers, these were important to the workers for a number of reasons. The options were both a hope of huge future compensations, thus binding talented workers to companies that were not paying high com-

pensation in the present. So an option was both an external marker of individuals' value to the companies and a source of social comparison envy that contributed greatly to the self-esteem of the workers who could talk about "their options or shares."

4. Whether one trusts a particular member of the organizational authority structure is a question that can be separated from the question of whether one trusts the authority structure. Generally, for the exposition I am going to do here, I am going to blur the distinction between the two, normally referring to trust in the impersonal authority structure. When it is necessary to distinguish the two questions, I will make that clear.

5. Workers may also respond explosively to the loss of an entitlement that, on reflection, they knew was not one in which they were entitled to trust would continue to be there. The appropriate suggestion probably is that workers will always react to violations of what they feel they have earned as their noncalculational rights and will sometimes react in similar ways to violations of expectations that reflection tells them were not unconditionally there for them.

6. The assertion here is that betrayal is an emotion uniquely provoked by the violation of noncalculational trust and thus an infallible indicator of occasions when noncalculational trust has been experienced by one but not both sides of a relationship. This is not a circular argument, but it is an empirically falsifiable one.

7. It should also be pointed out that since the inspiring aspect of this story has been publicized, the plant has gone in and out of bankruptcy. Thus the complete story points to the genuine dilemma faced by organizations that experience financial crises.

References

Bies, Robert J., and Thomas M. Tripp. 1987. "The Predicament of Injustice: The Management of Moral Outrage." In *Research in Organizational Behavior*, edited by Barry M. Staw and Larry L. Cummings. Volume 9. Greenwich, Conn.: JAI.

———. 1996. "Beyond Distrust: 'Getting Even' and the Need for Revenge." In *Trust in Organizations: Frontiers of the Theory and Research*, edited by Roderick M. Kramer and Tom R. Tyler. Thousand Oaks, Calif.: Sage.

Brockner, Joel, and Phyllis Siegel. 1996. "Understanding the Interaction Between Procedural and Distributive Justice: The Role of Trust." In *Trust in Organizations: Frontiers of the Theory and Research*, edited by Roderick M. Kramer and Tom R. Tyler. Thousand Oaks, Calif.: Sage.

Clark, Margaret, and Judson Mills. 1993. "The Difference Between Communal and Exchange Relationships: What It Is and Is Not." *Personality and Social Psychology Bulletin* 19(6): 684–91.

Creed, W. E. Douglas, and Raymond E. Miles. 1996. "A Conceptual Framework Linking Organizational Forms, Managerial Philosophies, and the Opportunity Costs of Controls." In *Trust in Organizations: Frontiers of the Theory and Research*, edited by Roderick M. Kramer and Tom R. Tyler. Thousand Oaks, Calif.: Sage.

Fincham, Robin, and Peter Rhodes. 1999. *Principles of Organizational Behavior.* 3rd ed. Oxford and New York: Oxford University Press.

Fiske, Alan Page. 1990. *Structures of Social Life: The Four Elementary Forms of Human Relations: Communal Sharing, Authority Ranking, Equality Matching, Market Pricing.* New York: Free Press.

Greenberg, Jerald. 1996. *The Quest for Justice on the Job: Essays and Experiments.* Thousand Oaks, Calif.: Sage.

Heneman, Robert L., Gerald E. Ledford, Jr., and Maria T. Gresham. 2000. "The Changing Nature of Work and Its Effects on Compensation Design and Delivery." In *Compensation in Organizations: Current Research and Practice,* edited by Sara L. Rynes and Barry Gerhart. San Francisco: Jossey-Bass.

Kidder, Tracy. 1982. *The Soul of a New Machine.* New York: Avon Books.

Kramer, Roderick M. 1996. "Divergent Realities and Convergent Disappointments in the Hierarchic Relation. Trust and the Intuitive Auditor at Work." In *Trust in Organizations: Frontiers of the Theory and Research,* edited by Roderick M. Kramer and Tom R. Tyler. Thousand Oaks, Calif.: Sage.

Kramer, Roderick M., Maralynn B. Brewer, and Benjamin A. Hanna. 1996. "Collective Trust and Collective Action: The Decision to Trust as a Social Decision." In *Trust in Organizations: Frontiers of the Theory and Research,* edited by Roderick M. Kramer and Tom R. Tyler. Thousand Oaks, Calif.: Sage.

Lawler, Edward E. 2000. *Rewarding Excellence: Pay Strategies for the New Economy.* San Francisco: Jossey-Bass.

Lewicki, Robert, and Barbara Bunker. 1996. "Developing and Maintaining Trust in Work Relationships." In *Trust in Organizations: Frontiers of the Theory and Research,* edited by Roderick M. Kramer and Tom R. Tyler. Thousand Oaks, Calif.: Sage.

Marshall, S. L. A. 1947. *Men Against War: The Problem of Battle Command in Future War.* Washington, D.C.: Combat Forces Press.

Maslow, Abraham. 1954. *Motivation and Personality.* New York: Harper & Row.

McPherson, James M. 1997. *For Cause and Comrades: Why Men Fought in the Civil War.* New York: Oxford University Press.

Miller, Dale. 1999. "The Norm of Self-Interest." *American Psychologist* 54(12): 1053–60.

Milgrom, Paul R., and John Roberts. 1992. *Economics, Organization, and Management.* Englewood Cliffs, N.J.: Prentice-Hall.

Pfeffer, Jeffrey. 1998. *The Human Equation: Building Profits by Putting People First.* Boston: Harvard Business School Press.

Ross, Michael, and Fiore Sicoly. 1979. "Egocentric Biases in Availability and Attribution." *Journal of Personality and Social Psychology* 37(3): 322–36.

Rousseau, Denise, and Violet Ho. 2000. "Psychological Contract Issues in Compensation." In *Compensation in Organizations: Current Research and Practice,* edited by Sara L. Rynes and Barry Gerhart. San Francisco: Jossey-Bass.

Rynes, Sara L., and Barry Gerhart, eds. 2000. *Compensation in Organizations: Current Research and Practice.* San Francisco: Jossey-Bass.

Sheppard, Blair H., and Marla Tuchinsky. 1996. "Micro-OB and the Network Organization." In *Trust in Organizations: Frontiers of the Theory and Research,* edited by Roderick M. Kramer and Tom R. Tyler. Thousand Oaks, Calif.: Sage.

Sitkin, Sim B., and Darryl Stickel. 1996. "The Road to Hell: The Dynamics of Distrust in an Era of Quality." In *Trust in Organizations: Frontiers of the Theory and Research*, edited by Roderick M. Kramer and Tom R. Tyler. Thousand Oaks, Calif.: Sage.

Smith, Heather J., and Tom R. Tyler. 1996. "Justice and Power: Can Justice Motivations and Superordinate Categorizations Encourage the Advantaged to Support Policies Which Redistribute Economic Resources and Encourage the Disadvantaged to Willingly Obey the Law." *European Journal of Social Psychology* 26(2): 171–200.

Tsui, Anne S., Jone L. Pearce, Lyman W. Porter, and Angela M. Tripoli. 1997. "Alternative Approaches to the Employee-Organization Relationship: Does Investment in Employees Pay Off?" *Academy of Management Journal* 40(5): 1089–1121.

Tyler, Tom R. 1994. "Psychological Models of the Justice Motive: Antecedents of Distributive and Procedural Justice." *Journal of Personality and Social Psychology* 67(5): 850–63.

———. 1999. "Why People Cooperate with Organizations: An Identity-Based Perspective." In *Research in Organizational Behavior*, edited by Robert I. Sutton and Barry M. Staw. Greenwich, Conn.: JAI.

Tyler, Tom R., and Steven Blader. 2000. *Cooperation in Groups*. Philadelphia: Psychology Press.

Tyler, Tom R., and Peter Degoey. 1996. "Trust in Organization Authorities: The Influence of Motive Attributions on Willingness to Accept Decisions." In *Trust in Organizations: Frontiers of the Theory and Research*, edited by Roderick M. Kramer and Tom R. Tyler. Thousand Oaks, Calif.: Sage.

Williamson, Oliver E. 1993. "Calculativeness, Trust and Economic Organization." *Journal of Law and Economics* 36(1): 453–86.

Wilson, James Q. 1989. *Bureaucracy: What Government Agencies Do and Why They Do It*. New York: Basic Books.

PART II

TRUST AND DISTRUST IN TEAMS AND NETWORKS

Chapter 7

Will Security Enhance Trust Online, or Supplant It?

HELEN NISSENBAUM

P ROMOTERS OF the Internet and other digital media cite many and diverse benefits of these advances to humanity, from wide-ranging access to information and communication to enhancement of community and politics to stimulation of commerce and scientific collaboration. As the digital infrastructure has grown in size and complexity, however, even the most enthusiastic proponents acknowledge that the benefits are not inevitable but rest on a number of contingencies. Key among them is trust. Just as in conventional settings where trust improves the lives, prospects, and prosperity of individuals, relationships, and communities, so would it online, and just as distrust can degrade many dimensions of life, so can it online.[1] Because of its importance to a flourishing online world and because trust online poses distinctive challenges, it has attracted the attention of a number of scholars, researchers, and practitioners in technical as well as nontechnical fields, which has yielded an extensive literature in scholarly and trade publications, the popular media, and government reports, and an active showing at conferences.[2]

Much of this work on trust online is devoted either to empirical investigation of key variables relevant to trust online or to developing technical models, mechanisms, and designs for encouraging and supporting trust online. While acknowledging the practical contributions of both these lines of work, this paper questions the conceptual assumptions behind them, arguing that the successful end-point of these efforts will not be trust at all but something else, something closer to surety, or the certainty that one is secure, particularly through technically imposed constraints.

155

Background

The impetus for studying trust online has emerged primarily from two sources: concerns of technical experts over computer and network security, and concerns of proponents of ecommerce over possible pitfalls of the new medium. By the late 1990s, computer scientists and engineers had come to discuss goals of the technical field of computer and network security in terms of trust, seeking to build "trusted" or, rather, trustworthy, systems.[3] Trust came to be viewed as an aggregate or higher-order property of systems manifesting a constellation of other valued properties, including integrity, availability, survivability, and so on (Schneider 1999). These experts worried that our vast networked information system—the network of networks that includes local private systems as well as public systems like the Internet, the Web, cyberspace—is vulnerable to technical failure as well as malicious attack.[4] Those whose interest in trust stemmed from an interest in ecommerce understood that consumers would balk if they were fearful of being harmed in any of a variety of ways, such as being defrauded, having their credit card numbers stolen, or receiving poor-quality goods. Businesses, too, would stay away if they anticipated costly losses from failure to pay, repudiation of customer commitments, technical failures, and so on.[5]

Although the sources of concern over trust are distinct, there is significant overlap in the nature of the solution envisioned—namely, a suite of technical security mechanisms aimed at inducing users in various roles to trust networked information systems and one another. Mechanisms that would ensure trustworthy systems would in turn induce consumers to trust providers of goods and services; providers, to trust consumers; and both of these, to trust the vendors of underlying technical systems and in general would engender a climate of trust online.[6] So conspicuous has been the vision of trust through security portrayed by these two groups that it currently occupies the mainstream—in part because there are no equally persistent, competing interpretations, and in part because talk of trust online is relatively new and in the mainstream view, relatively uncontested. Later in this chapter, I shall say more about these mechanisms, but here I would like to label this common vision with a slogan: trustworthiness as security, or *trust through security*.[7]

This chapter articulates a skeptical position on the vision of trust through security; instead I contend that the ideal endpoint of trust through security is surety and not, in fact, trust. This contention draws on a commonsense conception of trust elucidated in a number of important philosophical and other theoretical works. It does not challenge the value of surety itself but argues that striving for surety online is different and sometimes even inimical to striving for trust; conflating the two misconstrues the nature of trust and misses the point of why we care about it. Accepting this claim, however, means that we will need to make an explicit normative (or policy) commitment either to the value of an online environment grounded in surety, or to one grounded in trust.

Conceptual and Technical Scope

Before elaborating on key themes and contrasts, it is necessary to delineate the scope of this paper. The conceptual domain of trust is immensely broad and not always internally consistent; the realm of computing and information and communications media is itself large and varied. We need, therefore, to make certain simplifying assumptions and qualify the scope of our investigation in order to make a meaningful contribution even within this more limited domain.

In its broadest sense, the online world we speak of could cover the entire technological system, vast and powerful, that sits at the hub of almost all other parts of the critical infrastructures of society, controlling—and in some cases conjoining—energy, commerce, finance, transportation, education, communication, and more, and in so doing affecting almost all modes of social, community, cultural, and political life.[8] This essay does not address the system as a whole—the vast and powerful grid that connects and controls satellites, nuclear devices, energy, the stock exchange, and so forth. Instead, it focuses on the parts of the system directly experienced by ordinary people, who in increasing numbers use it to talk, conduct business transactions, work, seek information, play games, and transact with public and private institutions. At present, this realm comprises the World Wide Web (the Web) and the various servers (computers), conjoined networks, people, and institutions that constitute it. It also comprises the realm that at times interacts with the realities of the offline world and at other times fragments into an apparently independent and separate reality that some writers and participants have taken to calling cyberspace, or the "virtual" world.

Neither does this essay cover everything that the word "trust" could mean. Trust is an extraordinarily rich concept covering a variety of relationships, conjoining a variety of objects. One can trust (or distrust) persons, institutions, governments, information, deities, physical things, systems, and more. Here, I am concerned with two ways that "trust" is used. One is as a term describing a relationship between one person (a trustor) and another (the trustee). Although, in practice, the trustee position could be filled by almost anything, here I limit consideration to cases where the trustee is a being to which we are willing to attribute intentions, motivations, interests, or reasons, and might also refer to as "agent." Central in this category are people—individually and in groups; I would also be willing to include organizations, communities, and institutions. However, in my discussion I exclude from the "trustee" category at least one quite common referent for trust in the online context: the networked, digital information systems themselves, the layered hardware and software that individually constitute the microsystems and the macrosystem that is formed by these. This is not because of any deep-seated disagreement with those who write about trust in relation to networked information systems or information and communications technology and worry about the dependability of these systems, their resilience to various forms of failure and attack, and their capacity to protect the integrity of online interactions and transactions. My reasons are pragmatic. These cases are sufficiently distinct from one another that they deserve separate (but equal) treatment. Following others, I use the term "confidence" to refer to trust in systems, recognizing that trust in the online world begins with confidence in systems, but does not end there.[9]

Conditions of Trust

At the same time that proponents of the Internet acknowledge the key role of trust in enlivening activity, interaction, participation, and institutional growth, they recognize the distinctive challenges to trust building posed by the online realm. To see how these challenges arise, it is useful to consider, first, conditions that have been associated with the formation of trust generally, and then the ways that online mediation affects them; determine mechanisms governing trust, namely factors that systematically affect tendencies to trust (or not to trust) other people, groups, and institutions; and how features of online interaction affect them.

It is worth noting that for the purpose of this discussion, it does not matter whether trust is a species of belief (or expectation)—a cognitive stance—or is a noncognitive attitude, even though this is a matter of some disagreement among theorists and social scientists. Some, such as the philosopher Annette Baier (1986), who assert a version of the former view would probably frame the inquiry into mechanisms in terms of reasons that systematically undergird trust, and may even subject such reasons to judgments of rationality or irrationality.[10] Those, such as the philosopher Lawrence Becker (1996), who defend a noncognitive account of trust would probably frame theirs as an inquiry into factors to which the formation of trust is systematically responsive as cause to effect.[11] Most important, agnosticism on this matter should not block access to empirical and analytic results that link trust with the variety of phenomena that are widely perceived to function as cues, clues, or triggers, whether as reasons or merely causes.

A caveat: The factors listed below should not be understood as a complete account of causes of or reasons for trust formation but should be understood to be selective, reflecting a particular concern for trust in the online context. Furthermore, I acknowledge that my efforts are conceivably incompatible with views on trust—such as those of Adam Seligman (1997)—that reserve the concept of trust for an even more qualified subcategory of attitudes than the one I have articulated above. Seligman would probably say of many of the cases I mention below, where trust is induced by perceived similarity, roles, and other structured relationships, that these are instances of confidence and not trust.[12] To engage further on this point of disagreement—interesting as it is—would deflect us too far from the main subject here. It is important, though, to acknowledge the difference between my more ample and Seligman's more austere concepts. One way to reconcile the difference would be to suggest that followers of Seligman's usage recast the concern of this chapter as being one of trust, faith, confidence, and familiarity online.

History and Reputation

One of the most convincing forms of evidence that others merit trust is their past behavior. If they have behaved well in the past, protected our interests, have not cheated or betrayed us, and in general have acted in a trustworthy manner, they are likely to elicit trust in the future. If they have disappointed us in the past, then we will tend not to trust them. Where we have not built a history of direct interaction with others, we may refer to the experiences of others—we may be influenced by reputations.

Inferences Based on Personal Characteristics

A trusting attitude may be triggered by the presence of perceived qualities in the other. Philip Pettit identifies four: virtue, loyalty, prudence,[13] and a desire for the good opinion of others,[14] all qualities that influence whether a person will trust those who are seen to have them. Pettit writes: "To be loyal or virtuous or even prudent is, in an obvious sense of the term, to be trustworthy. It is to be reliable under trust and to be reliable, in particular, because of possessing a desirable trait" (Pettit 1995, 211). The fourth quality, namely a desire for the good opinion of others, although less deserving of our admiration, is nevertheless a powerful mechanism for preventing betrayals of trust.[15] Accordingly, Pettit recommends against calling the person who chases good reputation trust*worthy*, preferring a more modest commendation of trust-*responsive*, or trust-*reliant*.[16] Though not in direct disagreement with Pettit's characterization, Adam Seligman offers a different perspective, drawing attention to the importance of familiarity, similarity, and shared values as triggers of trusting attitudes.[17] What we know about someone, what we may infer on the basis of "their clothing, behavior, general demeanor," (Seligman 1997, 69) may lead us to judgments about their values and moral commitments, especially telling if we judge these to be similar to ours. A common religious background, high school, neighborhood, or traumatic experience (for example, having fought in the same war) affects our level of confidence in predicting what others will do and how inclined we are to rely on them. Though related to loyalty, these considerations are not identical. When one depends on a loyal cousin, for example, one counts on the family relationship to induce trust-reliance in one's cousin. Where trust is triggered by familiarity and, perhaps, a perception of shared values, a trustor does not necessarily count on these qualities to cause trustworthy behavior; the trustor merely forms expectations regarding the likely actions of these others.

Relationships: Mutuality and Reciprocity

Aside from personal qualities, the relationship in which one stands to another may bear on the formation of trust. The presence of common ends can stimulate trust. Such cases of mutual ends occur when a person is "in the same boat" as another. When I fly in an airplane, for example, I place trust in the pilot partly because he is in the plane with me and I presume that we have common, or confluent, ends; our fates are entwined for the few hours during which we fly together.

Reciprocity is slightly different, but it, too, can be grounds for trust. In a reciprocal relationship, we trust others not because we have common ends but because each of us holds the fate of others in our hands in a tit-for-tat manner. This may occur, for example, when people are taking turns. The agent whose turn is first deals fairly, reliably, or responsibly with the other because soon the tables will be turned. The relationship of reciprocity admits of great variability. In some cases there is a clear and imminent reversal of roles (this year I am chair of our department, next year you take over); in others it is more generalized (I might donate money to cancer research hoping that when I become ill, these funds will somehow help me). Reciprocity is evident in communities that are blessed with a climate of trust, its members helping those in need and trusting that when they themselves are in need, others will help them.[18]

Role Fulfillment

There is another, perhaps more compelling reason for trusting the pilot of my airplane. After all, the pilot would not trust me, in spite of our common interest in staying alive. Crucial to my trusting the pilot is that he is a pilot, and being a pilot within the framework of a familiar system has a well-articulated meaning. I know what pilots are supposed to do; I am aware of the rigorous training they undergo, the stringent requirements for accreditation, and the status of airlines within a larger social, political, and legal system. Several of the authors already mentioned have discussed the importance of roles to the formation of trust.[19]

Contextual Factors

One of the most intriguing factors to affect our readiness to trust, beyond those that are tied to what we know about the other, is the nature of the setting in which we act.[20] Such settings can be construed quite locally as families, communities, and towns or can extend to such large and diffuse entities as nations and countries.

Four elements seem relevant. The first is publicity: a setting in which betrayal and fidelity are routinely publicized is likely to be more conducive to trust-reliance, and consequently trust, than a setting in which people can effectively hide their deeds—especially their misdeeds. The second is reward and punishment: settings in which rewards and sanctions follow trustworthiness and betrayal, respectively, are likely to induce trustworthiness and trust. Third, where reward and punishment for fidelity and betrayal are not systematically available, promulgation of norms through other means can effectively shape behaviors and establish a climate of one sort or another. Norms are conveyed through parables, education, local lore, songs, fables, and local appraisal structures. What do these norms convey? Do they condemn betrayal and celebrate fidelity or do they mock gullible marks of confidence tricks and disdain cuckolded spouses while proffering admiration to the perpetrators?[21] Finally, a society can nurture a trusting climate by setting in place, through public policy or other means, various forms of "trust insurance" to provide safety nets for those whose trust is betrayed.[22] A simple example of such a policy is the current arrangement of liability for credit card fraud, which must surely increase people's willingness to engage in credit transactions.

Obstacles to Trust Online

It must be the case that at least some uneasiness comes from the novelty or unfamiliarity of online interaction, which by itself can slow the formation of trust. Citing novelty is not all that informative because even if novelty is a key factor, it is important to investigate why it should produce particular outcomes and whether one particular aspect of the new experience is more material to the outcome than others. We must, therefore, look beyond novelty for those features specific to online interaction that bear on trust. Those that we list below—flexible identity, disembodiment, and inscrutable contexts—cloak aspects of character and personality, the nature of relationships, and settings that normally function as triggers of trust or as reasons for deciding to trust (or distrust).

Flexible Identity

The medium's initial design allowed for agents to obscure identity quite easily, and this status holds, to some extent, into the present.[23] In many online transactions, agents are not compelled to relinquish the identities of their offline selves. Although the capacity for anonymity online is beneficial in a number of ways, it shrinks the range of cues that typically trigger trust. If identity is conceived as a thread upon which interactions with others are strung, then without identity, we lose the capacity to thread together a history of interactions and predict outcomes on the basis of past experiences of either vindicated trust or betrayal. Lacking knowledge of sustained identity also deprives us of a means to learn from the experiences of others whether an agent is trust-reliant, since the construction of reputation is hampered—even if not precluded altogether.

Lacking knowledge of an agent's sustained identity also deprives us of knowledge about the relationships in which we stand to others, for example, whether these are reciprocal or cooperative. Finally, because identity is bound up with accountability, people might presume that anonymous agents are less likely to act responsibly. As a result, people would be less inclined to trust.

Disembodiment

Online there is an opacity not only with respect to others' identities but also with respect to many of the personal characteristics that affect (heighten or diminish) attitudes of trust. We are separated from others in time and space; we lack cues giving evidence of similarity, familiarity, or shared value systems. We may not know the other's gender (male, female, or "other"), age, race, socioeconomic status, occupation, mode of dress, or geographic origins. We lack the bodily signals of face-to-face interaction (see Herz 1995). Are we communicating with a fourteen-year-old girl or a fifty-seven-year-old man posing as a fourteen-year-old girl? Are we selling a priceless painting to an adolescent boy or to a reputable art dealer?[24] Are we sharing a virtual room with an intriguing avatar (in the online world a graphical icon representing a person, frequently in the context of a game or community discussion) or a virtual rapist?[25] We must conduct transactions and depend on others who are separated not only by distance but also by time, who are disembodied in many of the ways in which the nature of their concrete presences typically contributes to our sense of their trustworthiness.

Inscrutable Contexts

The settings of online interactions are frequently inscrutable (sometimes self-consciously so) in ways that affect readiness or inclination to trust.

One casualty is role definition, likely to persist until we develop mechanisms for articulating and supporting social, professional, and other roles. Even with roles that appear equivalent to offline counterparts—for example, "shopkeeper"—we lack explicit frameworks of assurances that support them. Online these institutional expectations are not yet as completely formed. For example, in the typical retail experience of buying an automobile in the United States, the role of "used car salesman" has a quite different connotation for trust formation from that of a salesman representing a high-end vehicle such as Mercedes. As for the roles and terms for them that have emerged in cyberspace (like "sysops," avatars, bulletin board moderators, and so on) that do not have obvious counterparts offline, their duties and responsibilities are even less clearly defined and understood.

Just as roles are still relatively unformulated, so are background constraints and social norms regarding qualities like fidelity, virtue, loyalty, guile, duplicity, and trickery. Are we sure that betrayal will be checked, that safety nets exist to limit the scope of hurts and harms, and so on? Although there is evidence of various groups—social groups, interest groups, cultural groups, hackers—vying to promote their respective norms, the territory remains relatively uncharted, a situation whose complexity is further compounded by the territory's global reach. Participants, especially the majority who are not strongly identified with any one of these groups, can rightly be confused. For them, the most rational stance may be one of caution and reserve.

It is important to note that what I call inscrutability of contexts has a double edge. Many people have observed that it is precisely this quality of cyberspace that is so liberating, enticing, promising. Enthusiasts invite you to participate *because* it is new, different, better, seamless, immediate, unstuffy, truly democratic, and so forth. I am not sure, therefore, that the immediate solution to the problem of inscrutability is a wholesale transfer of existing norms, even if we could bring that about.

Security and Trust

It is not surprising that the task of stimulating trust would fall to computer security experts, security-minded systems managers, and government oversight bodies concerned with computer security. Of course, computer security is not a new concern, but has developed alongside computing itself, responding to changes in the technology and the needs of its rapidly expanding range of applications. Promoters of the new medium see yet another role for security technology. They believe it holds promise for engendering trust online because the very mechanisms developed to fulfill general computer and network security needs also, as a matter of fact, seem to supply some of the elements critical to trust that are perceived to be missing in the online environment—the missing cues, clues, and triggers that affect the formation of trustful (or distrustful) attitudes and beliefs.

What follows is a brief overview of security mechanisms that have been suggested as ways to achieve a more secure and trustworthy online environment, either by restoring relevant triggers or constraining the possibilities for harm. I have simplified the picture by organizing these mechanisms into three rough categories: (1) access control, (2) transparency of identity, and (3) surveillance. The categories, which largely are my own construction, are an obvious simplification of the broad range of work in computer and network security. My intent is not to describe categories explicitly adopted by computer security experts themselves, nor to suggest that there is a monolithic effort of people and projects, but to provide explanatory clarity relevant to the purposes of discussing trust. The categories reflect functionality, not underlying structural similarities, and, as we shall soon see, are highly interrelated.

Access Control

One of the earliest worries of computer security, from the time when computers were stand-alone calculators and repositories of information, was to guard against unwanted access to the computer and its stored information, to maintain the integrity of the information, and to control distribution of the valuable and limited resource of computational power. Early on, the security mechanisms developed to prevent illegitimate and damaging access involved everything from passwords to locked doors.[26] The demands on computer security mechanisms expanded and became more complicated as networks and interactivity evolved. Vulnerability to intrusion increased because networks opened new means of infiltration—email, file transfer, and remote access—that could not be blocked by locked doors. The infamous Morris worm, which received widespread national attention in 1999, jolted all users into noticing what security experts must certainly have feared: that it was merely a matter of time before vulnerabilities in theory would be exploited in practice.[27]

The Internet, and in particular the Web, has further expanded the modes and extent of interactivity while at the same time exposing participants to new forms of unwanted access and attack. The old fears remain: namely, infiltration by unauthorized persons (hackers, crackers, and so on), damage to information and systems, disruptive software flowing across the Net, information "stolen" as it traverses the networks, terrorists and criminals invading the infrastructure and bringing down critical systems. And new fears emerge: "evil" websites that harm unsuspecting visitors, Web links diverted from intended destinations to others, and disruptive applets—mini applications that visitors to websites can download onto their own systems to enable them to enjoy more extensive services from that site. Rohit Khare and Adam Rifkin note, "While [you are] doing nothing more serious than surfing to some random Web page, your browser might take the opportunity to download, install, and execute objects and scripts from unknown sources" (Khare and Rifkin 1997, paragraph 4). For example, to view a video clip visitors might need to download a player program in addition to the video files themselves; or to view and interact with financial information provided by a financial services company they may download a mini-spreadsheet program. In the process of downloading the appropriate application, however, the user's computer system is infected with a harmful and often devastating applet. Greater interactivity spells greater vulnerability and a need for more extensive protections. Bruce Schneier, a computer security expert, comments on the almost unavoidable vulnerability of the Internet to attack:

> One problem is the permissive nature of the Internet and the computers attached to it. As long as a program has the ability to do anything on the computer it is running on, malware[28] will be incredibly dangerous.
>
> And anti-virus software can't help much. If a virus can infect 1.2 million computers (one estimate of Melissa infections) in the hours before a fix is released, that's a lot of damage. . . .
>
> It's impossible to push the problem off onto users with "do you trust this message/macro/application" messages. . . . Users can't make good security decisions under ideal conditions; they don't stand a chance against a virus capable of social engineering. . . .
>
> What we're seeing here is the convergence of several problems: the permissiveness of networks, interconnections between applications on modern operating systems, email as a vector to tunnel through network defenses as a means to spread extremely rapidly, and the traditional naïveté of users. Simple patches won't fix this. . . . A large distributed system that communicates at the speed of light is going to have to accept the reality of viral infections at the speed of light. Unless security is designed into the system from the bottom up, we're constantly going to be fighting a holding action (Schneier 1999, paragraphs 1, 6, 9, 11, 12, 13).

Working within the constraints of current network and system architectures, security experts have developed a tool kit of mechanisms to protect people and systems against unwanted and dangerous access. One reason why demands on such a tool kit are considerable is because the agents of unwanted access may be not only people but also bits of code, like applets. Standard techniques like passwords remain in use, fortified where needed by such mechanisms as "firewalls," which are software barriers built around systems in order to make them impermeable except to people or code that is "authorized."[29] Cryptographic techniques are used to protect the integrity and privacy of information stored in computers; such techniques also protect against theft and manipulation as information travels across networks. Some protection is offered against treacherous applets—for example, one that might reformat a user's hard drive or leak private information to the world—through security features built into Java (a computer language that greatly enhanced the range of possible Web-based engagements) that limit what applets can do. There are, however, regular announcements of flaws in this security.[30] There is fundamentally no known technical means of differentiating "good" from "bad" applets. How could there be, except in some possible future when computers would be able to discern categories of human values?

Fixing Identity

The people and institutions of the online world have diverse tastes when it comes to identification. Some are happy to link themselves to their full-blown offline identities, while others prefer to remain virtual selves. Among the second group, some are happy to maintain consistent identities represented by "handles" or pseudonyms, while others prefer full anonymity. The goal of security efforts in this category is to give more transparent access to online agents in order to stave off at least some of the threats and worries that follow from not knowing with whom one is dealing. Identifiability is considered particularly useful for recognizing malevolent or mischievous agents. And in general, it helps answer some of the questions that trust inspires us to ask: Is there a recognizable and persistent identity to the institutions and individuals behind the myriad websites one might visit? Can we count on agents online to keep their promises? For the sake of ecommerce, how do we prevent malicious agents from posing as legitimate customers or service providers and conducting bogus transactions, tricking and defrauding legitimate participants? In other words, we strive to reintroduce identifying information, at least as much as is needed to create a history, establish a reputation, hold agents accountable, and so on.[31]

Security efforts have focused on the task of making identity sufficiently transparent to protect against these and other betrayals and harms in an effort to build what the information law expert Lawrence Lessig has called "architectures of identification."[32] Mostly, they are interested in developing a strong link between a virtual agent and a physical person through a constellation of information that is commonly seen as proving identity even offline.[33] Security experts are investigating the promise for identification of biometrics—for example, fingerprints, DNA profiles, and retinal images. Furthermore, cryptographic techniques are deployed to authenticate users, computers, and sources of information by means of digital signatures and digital certificates working within a socially constructed system of certification authorities, trusted third parties who vouch for the binding of cryptographic keys to particular identities—particular persons and institutions. These same mechanisms are intended to prevent repudiation by agents of commitments or promises they may have made. A long chain of research and development focuses on various dimensions of so-called "trust management" such as these (Blaze, Feigenbaum, and Lacy 1996).

Schemes of identification, even the attenuated forms, work hand in hand with access control, because controlling access almost always means distinguishing the sanctioned, legitimate users from the illegitimate ones, not preventing everyone from using a system or the information in a system. In the case of applets, because direct examination of the applet can provide only imperfect evidence, we may rely on what is known about who sent them for another source of discrimination between "good" and "bad" applets.[34] "Trust management systems" are offered as integrated mechanisms for identifying and authenticating the identity of those people, information, and code that affect us, and they are also supposed to authenticate an applet's origins. The Snow White fairy tale offers an irresistible comparison: if Snow White had known the true identity of the bearer of the apple, she could have avoided the fateful bite.

Security experts seem to be engaged in a Sisyphean battle as they ward off attacks, repair system flaws, close up loopholes and "backdoors," and devise new layers of protection—a process that is suspended only until the next attack occurs. Outspoken security experts accept that this is an inevitable consequence of the "open" architecture of the Internet and Web, which many consider to be fundamentally insecure.[35] As a result, we live with an unstable equilibrium of relative comfort until the latest, more devastating intrusion is made public; there is a flurry of reaction, followed by relative comfort, and so the cycle continues.

Surveillance

A third layer overlaid upon the security offered through access control and transparency of identity is surveillance: we keep an eye on things in order both to prevent harms and to apprehend perpetrators after harm has been done. Surveillance can involve active watching and tracking, which can be fairly fine-grained, as demonstrated by the monitoring software that many business organizations have installed on their computer systems. Or it can be relatively coarse-grained, as are some "intrusion detection" systems, where real-time monitoring issues an alarm in response to suspicious or unusual activity, to be further investigated if necessary.[36] Surveillance can also involve passive recording (reifying) of digital trails. Popular means include logging and auditing, which creates records of activity which authorities can sift through at a later time. Logging and auditing helped authorities identify David Smith as the creator of the Melissa virus.[37]

Can Trust Be Secured?

The question is whether the array of security mechanisms—firewalls, biometrics, digital signatures, intrusion detection, auditing, and so forth—will bring about trust online. It is useful to give this question a somewhat harder edge: If we could reach an ideal end state with all three categories of security mechanisms—perfectly valid and reliable access control, identifiability, and surveillance—converging on perfection, will we have secured trust?

There is prima facie reason to answer yes because the mechanisms in question appear to address the missing triggers of trust and, failing that, to provide direct protection against some of the harms users might fear, which caused them to be distrustful in the first place. Transparent identity, for example, makes it easier to judge whether others are trustworthy— "safe bets"—or disreputable and worthy of suspicion. Mechanisms of nonrepudiation would restore accountability and restrain those inclined to dishonesty. Strong and smart walls, limits on the flow of information, and constraints on the actions that are possible, would establish safe zones by allowing in only authorized (vetted) individuals and institutions and allowing only nonhazardous actions.

Nevertheless, I will argue, in spite of its prima facie attractiveness, security—or rather the particular vision of security occupying the mainstream—will not bring about trust but, rather, surety. I argue this not because I think security is unimportant but because the ends of trust online are not well served by this mainstream vision of security. The rhetoric is misguided because when the proponents of security and ecommerce try to bind trust too closely to security, they threaten to usurp a concept as rich and complex, as intensely social, cultural, and moral as trust for one slim part of it. The mistake is not merely semantic; it has a weighty practical edge. Pursuing trust online by pursuing the complete fulfillment of the three goals of security would no more achieve trust and trustworthiness online—in the full-blown sense of these qualities—than prison bars, surveillance cameras, airport X-ray conveyor belts, body frisks, and padlocks could achieve it offline. This is the case because the very ends envisioned by the proponents of security and ecommerce are contrary to core meanings and mechanisms of trust. Security misses the mark in two ways: it undershoots trust, and it overshoots it.

Security Is No Panacea

Let us begin with the first critique of the idea of creating trust online through security—namely, that even a perfect embodiment of the three principles of security does not go far enough for trust, in significant and

systematic ways. To clarify, it will be useful to set in place a simplification, framing what is at stake in terms of "insiders" and "outsiders."
Experts in computer security are worried about outsiders: malicious,
avaricious, incompetent, or simply unauthorized outsiders who may
break into our online space, damage or steal information, and destroy
or compromise our systems. Security mechanisms are developed to
keep outsiders where they belong—outside—and to help spot or identify outsiders who might be attempting to break in, in order to prevent
or punish them.

This approach pays far less systematic attention to the threat of insiders, those agents—individuals and organizations—who by degrees have
gained sanctioned access to our space. Some may even count among the
respectable, socially sanctioned, reputable members of online society, yet
they engage in actions that many citizens of the online world dislike,
resent, or even consider harmful. They track our Web activities, they collect and use personal information without our permission, they plant
"cookies" on our hard drives, they hijack our browsers while they download ads, they fill our mailboxes with spam, and they engage in relentless
commercialism. Some of these insiders—perhaps not the "respectable"
ones—"troll" our discussion groups, afflict us with hateful, inflamma-
tory, mean-spirited emails ("flame" us), send us threatening chain mail,
and even attack our virtual selves.[38] In other words, even if the walls of
security keep outsiders outside, they do not curtail the agents and activities that, behind the veil of respectability and legal sanction, make online
citizens skittish, cautious, and resentful. Such security barriers do not
address various forms of activity that are fully capable of engendering a
climate of suspicion and distrust online even if we are successful in our
projects to secure the online world from "outsiders."

Even in the physical world, attention only to the threats of outsiders
leaves us vulnerable to a host of dangers. In the familiar case of physical safety, some of us go to great lengths trying to protect ourselves from
bodily harm, staying clear of dangerous parts of town, affixing padlocks
to our doors, installing burglar alarms in our homes, accepting the ever-
increasing use of video surveillance in public spaces. Homicide statistics, however, tell a curious story: when the relationship of the killer to
victim is known, we find that only 22 percent of killers are strangers—
the proverbial outsiders.[39] Seventy-eight percent are spouses, friends,
and acquaintances. Betrayal comes from those who are allowed within
our spheres of safety, within our safe zones.

My intention is not to launch into paranoid realms of suspicion and
universal distrust. It is to illustrate that keeping outsiders out does not
necessarily ensure safety. A wall of defense against malicious outsiders
does not defend against the threats posed by sanctioned insiders, who
energetically defend their "right" to exercise online freedoms—by means

of cookies, misleading registrations, matching, mining, and so on. They are, arguably, chipping away at trust just as surely as amoral hackers are. They are just as capable as hackers of causing a dangerous ebb in the abundant social capital we currently enjoy in life online.

Because it is in the nature of trust to be conservative—slow both to ebb and to grow—the results of these transgressions may not be immediately evident.[40] That the transgressions I speak of are capable of undermining trust, however, is implied by several of the works that have shaped this essay. One example is found in a long-term study of ecommerce, which shows that consumers' trust is related to their understanding of how information about them is treated; it wanes if they think that it will not be held in confidence.[41]

Another important insight that explains why interventions like the familiar suite of security mechanisms cannot fully induce trust is that trust is as sensitive to motives and intentions as it is to actions and outcomes, if not more so. It is in the goodwill of others, the philosopher Lawrence Becker has argued, that we trust or fail to trust, not necessarily in their actions.[42] As long as we believe that others are well intentioned toward us, our trusting attitude toward them will survive a great deal of bad news: "incompetence, mendacity, greed, and so forth" (Becker 1996, 51). This holds for the relation of citizens to government as well as among persons. According to Becker, only when citizens begin to attribute the poor performance of governments to deviant motivations— e.g., corruption or inappropriate power seeking—will they "respond in ways that are . . . volatile and disruptive" (Becker 1996, 59). Citizens' trust, it seems, is able to survive incompetence, at least for a while. In a similar vein, Paul Slovic (1993), an expert on risk assessment, reports that the extent to which citizens are willing to accept societal risk resulting from technological innovation is related to their degree of confidence in the motives of those in charge.[43]

Similar ideas emerge in Tom Tyler's research on public trust of police and the courts. Tyler is interested in variables that affect citizens' confidence in legal authorities, their readiness to accept outcomes, and their evaluation of the quality of decision making and fairness of procedures.[44] He finds that the most important variable for trust is the motives of authorities,[45] which he calls motive-based trust: "Motive-based trust is distinct from judgments about whether or not authorities behave as anticipated. It involves an inference about the 'spirit' or 'motive' that will shape behavior, not what specific behavior will occur" (Tyler 2001). One of Tyler's somewhat surprising findings is that in brushes with law enforcement and legal authorities, people's positive reactions are tied more strongly to inferred motives than even to whether or not the outcomes of their cases were favorable to them.[46]

The significance of these ideas to the purposes of this section is to emphasize that the behavior of many sanctioned, established, powerful individuals and organizations is capable of undermining trust when their motives are unclear, even when the actions they undertake, such as Web tracking, for example, are not immediately aggressive or harmful. In these cases, when we learn of such activities we may find them ambiguous. What would matter to us for purposes of trust would be the motivations behind the behaviors. As long as we are not able to read people's minds, it is difficult, often impossible, to assess motives and intentions directly. So we usually find ourselves drawing on as many indirect sources as possible, sometimes resorting to subtle detection and artfulness.

One important indirect source of others' intentions is their interests. When, for example, a politician seeking office expresses concern for a particular situation, voters might attribute the expression not to genuine feeling but to an interest in being elected. In a case of this type, as much as we welcome and praise the action, it may not serve as grounds for trust as long as we see it emanating from a motive of vote seeking. In the case of Web tracking—and, more generally, information gathering and commercialism—we might initially be willing to read positive meaning into such practices. As time goes by, and we take measure of the distance between our own interests and those of the trackers (profit and potency), we begin to reinterpret those same actions as forms of betrayal. Actions that at first seem neutral or even friendly can come to be seen as sinister when interpreted in light of reasonably inferred plausible negative motives and intentions.

We all need to interact, even cooperate, with others whose interests are not consistent with our own and may even conflict with ours. In such cases, we transact cautiously, ever on the lookout for betrayal, sometimes seeking protections from the most egregious harms, betrayals, and exploitation. So trust remains elusive.

If we choose not to pursue policies for the online world that aim to contain the pursuit of avaricious interests that are contrary to those of the citizens of the Net, we are, I fear, planting the seeds of general distrust. People may continue to participate in this arena, but will do so with caution and a sense of wariness—wisely so, in interactions with those whose interests run contrary to our own, and whose actions may be annoying, bothersome, intrusive, or even threatening. Guardedness will be the norm.

Those who would pursue *security* in the name of trust do us this disservice. They focus on the outsider, the aberrant individual or organization, the trickster, the evil hacker, and the scam artist. These are the villains from whom security would protect us. In proportion to actual harm done to individuals online, too much attention is paid to the aberrant individual, the trickster, and the evil hackers lurking outside the borders of civilized online society. The media play up dramatic cases: the Melissa virus, spies who infiltrate systems and sell secrets to our enemies, or hackers who distribute unauthorized copies of intellectual works. But these techniques to guard against malicious outsiders do nothing against agents acting behind the veil of respectability who invade our privacy and offend us by turning cyberspace to their own interests, which are not ours.

We should take greater heed of the sanctioned harms of respectable insiders; we should question the systemic imbalances between the individual citizens of the online world and the organizations that create it with little sense of the interests of the individuals. For the vast majority of Net users, it is the second group and not the first that is the significant danger; it is the second, at least as much as the first, that affects our attitudes of trust online. Powerful security mechanisms may keep us safe from malicious outsiders at the cost of our online experience, but such mechanisms still leave us vulnerable to those inside agents. We can keep out the aberrant individuals, but we remain powerless against parties that are poised systematically to exploit their positions. If we care about developing a climate of trust online—full-blown trust, not a thin substitute—we must address these conditions of imbalance between individuals and institutions. Evil hackers are not the only, nor are they the most important, barriers to trust online. If we do not address the systemic problems, trust will erode and we will not easily recover from a sense of wholesale exploitation.

Securing Trust Versus Nourishing Trust

If the earlier criticism was that security does not go far enough, this one is that security, as envisioned in the three categories, overshoots the mark and might quash trust by creating an environment in which trust is not allowed to take root and flourish. Here, an excursion back to theoretical and empirical studies of trust is useful. Trust, we learn, is an attitude. It is almost always a relational attitude involving at least a trustor and a trustee. In this relation of trust, those who trust accept their vulnerability to those in whom they place trust. They realize that those they trust may exercise their power to harm, disappoint, or betray; yet at the same time they regard those others "as if" they mean well, or at least mean no harm. Trust, then, is a form of confidence in another, confidence that the other, despite a capacity to do harm, will do the right thing in relation to the trustor. For the philosopher Annette Baier, trust is "accepted vulnerability to another's possible but not expected ill will (or lack of good will) toward one" (Baier 1986, 235); trust is the "reliance on others' competence and willingness to look after, rather than harm, things one cares about which are entrusted to their care" (Baier 1986, 259). For Russell Hardin, "[T]rust involves giving discretion to another to affect one's interests" (Hardin 1993, 507). In a similar vein, Adam Seligman holds trust to be "some sort of belief in the goodwill of the other, given the opaqueness of other's intentions and calculations" (Seligman 1997, 43). Francis Fukuyama adds a social dimension to his account, describing trust as the "expectation that arises within a community of regular, honest, and cooperative behavior, based on commonly shared norms, on the part of other members of that community" (Fukuyama 1995, 26).

Usually trust involves more than the trustor and trustee; there is almost always an object with respect to which the trustor trusts the trustee.[47] For Annette Baier, this is demonstrated in her example of trusting the plumber to take care of the pipes in her home but not to take care of her daughter—and trusting a baby-sitter to take care of her daughter but not to take care of the pipes.[48] A person might entrust even her life to a friend, but not her heart. In the online world, there is similar discretion about not only whom one is prepared to trust but what one is prepared to entrust to them; for example, many consumers have learned that they can trust Amazon.com to deliver their orders but not trust it with their personal information.[49]

The theories of trust that I have studied differ from one another in many ways; cutting across these differences, however, is a common theme linking trust with vulnerability. When people trust, they expose themselves to risk. Although trust may be based on something—past experience, the nature of one's relationships, and so on—it involves no guarantees. As Hardin writes, trust is "inherently subject to the risk that the other will abuse the power of discretion" (Hardin 1993, 507). In trusting, we are acknowledging the other as a free agent, and this is part of the exhilaration of both trusting and being trusted. Where people are guaranteed safety, where they are protected from harm via assurances—if the other person acted under coercion, for example—trust is redundant; it is unnecessary. What we have is certainty, security, and safety—not trust. The evidence, the signs, the cues and clues that ground the formation, that give evidence of the reasonableness of, trust must always fall short of certainty; trust is an attitude without guarantees, without a complete warranty.[50] When we constrain variables in ways that make things certain—that is, safe—we are usurping trust's function. Trust is squeezed out of the picture.

No loss, some, like Richard Posner, would say: "But trust, rather than being something valued for itself and therefore missed where full information makes it unnecessary, is, I should think, merely an imperfect substitute for information" (Posner 1978). According to Posner's position, if we must choose between trust—and, consequently, vulnerability—on the one hand and certainty on the other, then certainty must win.

In practice, however, such a choice has significant consequences, which are as evident online as off. In a world that is complex and rich, the price of safety and certainty is limitation. Online as off, we do not have the means at our disposal for assuring safety and certainty without paying this price: streamlining and constraining the scope and nature of inter actions, relationships, and community; limiting the range and nature of allowable activity; needing to make a priori judgments about those with whom one will or will not interact; having to accept increasing levels of monitoring and surveillance.[51] In general, the cost of surety—certainty and security—is freedom and wide-ranging opportunity.

The link between trust and vulnerability seems to be both conceptual and empirical. The conceptual claim is that whatever the feeling or attitude one experiences when acting and anticipating in a context of certainty and safety, it cannot be trust; this is not what trust means. The empirical conjecture, which has occupied the work of several scholars, is that in a context of complete certainty, the material conditions needed to induce and nourish trust are absent.[52] Trust does not flourish in a perfectly secure environment for reasons that are very different from the reasons for which trust does not flourish in a hostile, threatening environment. For trust to develop between an individual and either another individual or an organization, the trustor must somehow have had the opportunity to test the other agent and have had that agent pass the test. Luhmann explains the crucial role of uncertainty in the process of building trust:

> First of all there has to be some cause for displaying trust. There has to be defined some situation in which the person trusting is dependent on his partner; otherwise the problem does not arise. His behaviour must then commit him to this situation and make him run the risk of his trust being betrayed. In other words he must invest in what we called earlier a "risky investment." One fundamental condition is that it must be possible for the partner to abuse the trust. (Luhmann 1979/1988, 42)

When we are placed in a context in which we depend on others for our well-being and are assured, guaranteed by whatever means, that these others are prevented and restrained and therefore incapable of harming us, then the context, though safe and secure, is not one that nourishes trust. No test has been given; none has been passed. The variables that theorists and empirical scientists have identified as trust-inducing may signal the reasonableness of trust in a particular setting, but when grounds are transformed into guarantees of good behavior, trust disappears, replaced not by distrust but perhaps by certainty. In the presence of a violent psychopath whose limbs are shackled, one feels not trust but, at best, safety.

Another empirical basis for doubting the efficacy of security to deliver trust is that boxing people in is a notoriously bad strategy for inducing trustworthiness or even trust-reliance. Constraining freedom directly or indirectly through, say, surveillance may backfire and have the opposite effect. Roderick Kramer, in reviewing empirical work in the social sciences, notes:

> Ironically, there is increasing evidence that such systems [based on sanctions] can actually undermine trust and may even elicit the very behaviors they are intended to suppress or eliminate. In a recent discussion of this evidence, Cialdini identified several reasons why monitoring and surveillance can diminish trust within an organization. First, there is evidence that when people think their behavior is under the control of extrinsic motivators, intrinsic motivation may be reduced. Thus, surveillance may undermine individuals' motivation to engage in the very behaviors such monitoring is intended to induce or ensure. (Kramer 1999, 591)

Philip Pettit's observations reinforce this view: "[C]ertain intrusive forms of regulation can be counter-productive and can reduce the level of performance in the very area they are supposed to affect. . . . If heavy regulation is capable of eradicating overtures of trust, and of driving out opportunities for trusting relationships, then it is capable of doing great harm" (Pettit 1995, 225).

Inducements available to individuals and institutions to encourage trustworthiness are most effective when they operate indirectly. Above all, people need to perceive that they have a choice. By means of these inducements, including sanctions and rewards, clearly articulated norms, education, character development, and so on, we may increase the incidence of trust as well as trust-reliance. If, however, we go too far and deny the possibility of choice, we deny what is fundamental to trusting relationships and climates of trust. Symbols of trust can be exhibited in small but clear ways, as illustrated at the service counter of a popular downtown cafe. A discreet sign says, "At our busy times, please be respectful of those waiting for tables." We do not coerce the good etiquette of standing in a queue, we merely make known our norms and our trust in others to behave decently.

These considerations lead me to posit two conceptions of trust. In both, trust involves placing one's fate in another's hands expecting but not being certain of the other's good will. In one conception, however, trust is understood as merely instrumental—in Richard Posner's words, "an imperfect substitute for information." Trust still has enormous value because in most cases in which we must act and make decisions, online and off, we do not have assurances; trust acts as a bridge between uncertainty and action. Yet because the ideal of these circumstances is one of assurance and certainty, we will continually work to close the gap of uncertainty, to limit and possibly eradicate the vulnerability. When buying goods online, banking, downloading information and entertainment, and so on, we welcome movement toward greater surety. Trust is the bitter pill we must swallow in order to achieve the primary purposes of these transactions.

The other conception of trust regards it as being an overriding value, valuable in itself. When trust is so conceived, trust-based relationships would not be better if the scope of trust were minimized; rather the opposite holds. In traditional realms, trust among family members exemplifies this conception. Consider the case of parents trusting their daughter. Although they could achieve greater surety by placing their daughter under surveillance, reading her diary, checking up on her at school, and so on, most of us would agree that a trust-based relationship is better, is closer to the ideal of a parent-child relationship. The other version might provide certainty, but at a great cost to quality. In the online environment, a similar conception operates but in spheres some-what disconnected from those we have mainly been discussing. Although no easy definition captures these spheres, they can be characterized by means of a set of typical features: they tend to reside in the not-for-profit sectors, are peer- and community-based, and are self-organizing rather than commercial, hierarchical or authority-based. They extend across a wide variety of substantive interests from political to recreational to technical, including the myriad online communities that consolidate around grassroots political interests (for example, e-thepeople and Institute for Applied Autonomy),[53] and cultural, gender, environmental, and even technology-related issues.

Reviewing specific cases, Lee Sproull and Sara Kiesler draw attention to more than six hundred volunteer health-support groups (which have been used by more than 6.5 million Americans); fifty thousand net-based volunteer technical-support user groups; software development and dis-cussion groups (including open-source and Slashdot); mentoring and tutoring groups; political concern and advocacy communities; geograph-ically bounded communities; peer-to-peer file-sharing communities; groups cohering around recreational online games—MUDs (Multi-User Dungeons), MOOs (Multi-User Object-Oriented Domains)—and more (Sproull 2003; Sproull and Kiesler 2003). Yochai Benkler has identified numerous highly productive efforts in what he has called commons-based peer-production, in which individuals devote time and effort to produce impressive intellectual goods online, not because a boss or manager so commands them, nor because they wish to sell the product in the marketplace, but because they choose to invest in a community-based effort (see Benkler 2002). The activities in which all these groups engage is highly diverse—the planning of civic action, promotion of political and humanitarian causes, discussion, organization, game play-ing, information production, protest, voting, and more. Of course, not all are directed to generally beneficial ends, including groups espousing racist, neo-Nazi, and violent anti-abortion themes.

These cases are relevant to trust because they define a realm in which we are likely to find inherently, rather than instrumentally, trust-based interactions and relationships. Unlike the relationships discussed earlier, where individuals settle for trust when they would rather have surety and safety, these relationships are valued because they are trust-based. To explore this idea a little further, consider the case of the art site TeleGarden.[54] TeleGarden is a collaborative art project and community cohering around a website and a "real" garden—roughly six square feet—which was on exhibition in Linz, Austria, at the Ars Electronica Center until November 2002. The garden is cultivated by a robot (with occasional help from museum staff) which carries out commands of TeleGarden website participants. The robot plants seeds in specified locations, waters, and provides visual feedback to the site. Created in 1995 by a team of computer scientists and engineers on the faculty of the University of Southern California, TeleGarden is now self-governed by its participants, who frequently "visit" the garden, perform maintenance, and mingle with friends on the website's discussion boards. Every few months, when the garden overfills with plants, members of the museum staff clear and replace it with fresh soil, and a new growing season is declared.

The TeleGarden project holds many dimensions of interest—its technical features, aesthetic qualities, nature of the community, why participants derive joy and satisfaction, and so on. Relevant to our discussion, however, is a particular aspect of the site's governance. Technical design features as well as explicit norms impose few constraints on participants' behaviors. Besides the rule that participants must serve conscientiously for a while, helping water the garden and participating in chat-room discussions, before they are allowed full privileges like being allowed to plant seeds, there are few restrictions. This leaves the garden vulnerable to sabotage and the community chat rooms vulnerable to offensive postings. As a matter of fact, there have been rare occasions when members have intentionally ruined the garden by overwatering and planting seeds on top of those planted by others, and have posted pornography to chat rooms. On those occasions, the organizers discussed the possibility of altering the underlying mechanisms to impose technical constraints on these forms of sabotage. They decided not to.

According to the two-conception schema, this decision indicates a commitment to trust as a defining value of the TeleGarden community. In a different version of TeleGarden, organizers might have decided to alter system software to impose watering, planting, and censorship guidelines forcibly. This would have protected the garden plot against those harms, but the community, too, would have been altered. The point is not to judge one of these alternatives to be better or worse than the other, it is to suggest that they are different. Some might prefer the safer, more predictable version, others might find the trust-based Tele-Garden more interesting, challenging, compelling, or exhilarating. In the trust-based version, part of the value and pleasure of membership is enjoying the opportunity to interact with others who behave well even though they have the freedom to act otherwise.

Although TeleGarden is only a small and somewhat obscure instance of online community, it represents a particular mode of action and relationship not uncommon online as well as off. In traditional, more widely experienced arenas, we find in ideals of human relationships, such as friendship, citizenship, community, camaraderie, family, and more, that trust is embodied not instrumentally but as an essential element. In this same way, I would argue, replacing trust with surety in many of the community, peer-based, political activities online would be to extract from them something that lies at their very hearts. How, then, does this lead us to answer the motivating questions of this article: Does surety enhance or supplant trust online? If it does, are we better off for it?

Conclusion: Struggle for the Soul of Cyberspace

I am not opposed to computer security. The basic mechanisms underlying it are diverse and capable of being shaped in an enormous variety of ways, and in turn shape the online world and the experiences possible within it. Security technology does not, in general, necessarily result in the trajectory we have just examined, in other words, does not necessarily lead to limitations on the complexity, richness, intensity, and variety of experience to be had online while not assuring protection from sanctioned predatory activities. Developed wisely, security technologies could produce a measure of safety with sufficient degrees of freedom to nourish trust. Cryptography is a good example: it can be used in the service of transparent identification, but may also be used to protect individual interests in privacy, freedom of association, and free speech.

Yet even the security mechanisms discussed and challenged here, namely, those that enable surveillance, sustain identifiability, and form selectively permeable fortresses—let us call this "high security"—are not in themselves objectionable. High security, or surety, can be good; it is even necessary for a great many settings: airplane flights, military compounds, national secrets, nuclear power plants, banks, prisons, and more are all settings where we welcome Richard Posner's vaunted certainty.[55] Nevertheless, if the arguments of this article have succeeded, they will have convinced readers that the pursuit of trust must be decoupled from the pursuit of high security; trust will not ride in on the coattails of security. Even so, these arguments do not in themselves provide an answer to the further question of what course of action we—the virtual agents, people, institutions—who populate the online world or they, influential parties involved in building and governing the technical infrastructures, ought to pursue. That question is about what we envision for the online world, what kind of medium it is, what kind of environment it should be good for, and what values it ought to embody, trust or surety.

The social theorist Niklas Luhmann, whose profound work on trust has been widely influential, characterized trust as a mechanism for reducing complexity, enabling people to cope with the high levels of uncertainty and complexity of contemporary life (Luhmann 1979/1988). Trust makes uncertainty and complexity tolerable, enabling us to focus on few alternatives without being frozen in the mire of all possible alternatives, unable to act and decide in situations that call for action and decisiveness. In trusting, Luhmann writes, "[O]ne engages in an action as though there were only certain possibilities in the future" (1979/1988, 20).[56] Trust enables "co-operative action and individual but coordinated action: trust, by the reduction of complexity, discloses possibilities for action which would have remained improbable and unattractive without trust—which would not, in other words, have been pursued" (25).

A highly secured cyberspace provides a good climate for activities like commerce and banking, and for established commercial, public, and governmental institutions. The interests and modes of interactions that would *not* flourish in a highly secured cyberspace are likely to include the creative, political, unusual, freewheeling, subversive, possibly profane, possibly risky modes and activities of individuals. For airplane flights, we may welcome security checks, but for these other kinds of activities and interactions, for the virtual hustle and bustle that has come to resemble (and in some cases replace) much of our common experience, people avoid brightly lit scrutiny. To express the trade-off in Luhmann's terms, we may say that while both trust and security are mechanisms for reducing complexity and making life more manageable, trust enables people to act in a richly complex world, whereas security reduces the richness and complexity. Which one of these alternatives we would like to take hold online should be a matter for full and deliberate consideration and should not follow merely as an accidental consequence of immediate technological imperatives and hasty policy choices.

My own preference would be for a progressive social vision of cyberspace that preserves the degrees of freedom that trust needs. At the same time, we ought to develop technologies of security that might make possible pockets of high security for the kinds of transactions that call for it, without making that the dominant norm throughout. Outside of these pockets, we could maintain minimal protections—perhaps safety nets to prevent catastrophic harms. If we set these to be our goals, then we will have set the stage for trust. But we will *only* have set the stage. The work of nourishing trust and trustworthiness remains as deep and complex a social challenge as ever, calling for a familiar range of diverse responses, including the promulgation of norms, moral and character education, and, ultimately, comfort for the hurt.

Notes

1. This article is an outgrowth of a collaborative project with Edward Felten and Batya Friedman, and owes much to them. It was supported by grants from the National Science Foundation, SBR-9729447 and SBR-9806234. I am grateful to my colleagues Tamar Frankel, Jeroen van den Hoven, Rob Kling, Harry Frankfurt, and Mark Poster for their probing questions and suggestions; and to Beth Kolko, Helen Moffett, Michael Cohen, and Hyeseung Song, Sayumi Takahashi, Robert Young, and Erich Deitrich for editorial and research assistance. Earlier versions of the paper were presented at the New York University School of Law Conference on a Free Information Ecology, Computer Ethics: Philosophical Enquiry 2000, in New York City in April 2000, and the Boston University School of Law Conference on Trust Relationships in Boston from September 22–23, 2003. It builds on an earlier paper, Nissenbaum (2001).

2. For a sense of the robustness of the field of research that interest in trust online has spawned, see, for example, the many and diverse projects and directions represented at the First International Conference on Trust Management (2003).

3. A misuse of language persists within the technical computer security community: proponents of a particular security device invariably use the term "trusted" to signal their faith that the system in question is trustworthy. This usage is misleading, as it suggests a general acceptance of the device in question when in fact it is the duty of the proponents to argue or prove that it is indeed worthy of this acceptance.

4. See, for example, Schneider (1999, 1): "The widespread interconnection of networked information systems allows outages and disruptions to spread from one system to others; it enables attacks to be waged anonymously and from a safe distance."

5. See, for example, Backhouse (1998, 28), discussing security issues in ecommerce; Hoffman, Novak, and Peralta (1999, 80), addressing the trust issues between consumers and businesses in ecommerce; Moskowitz (1998, paragraph 1), discussing the doubts that plague ecommerce; Ratnasingham (1999, paragraph 1), arguing that trust is an "important antecedent" for successful business relationships; Salnoske (1998, 24), commenting that both businesses and consumers regard transaction security as their biggest concern; Steinauer, Wakid, and Rasberry (1997, 118), exploring "technology or other processes that can help increase the level of confidence . . . in electronic commerce"; Woolford (1999, 18), arguing that electronic deals suffer from the problems of "authenticity and integrity"; and Camp (2000).

6. See, for example, Abdul-Rahman and Hailes (1998, 48–60), discussing the weaknesses of current security approaches for managing trust; U.S. Department of Defense (1999), classifying computer systems into four divisions of enhanced security protection; Khare and Rifkin (1997), "develop[ing] a taxonomy for how trust assertions can be specified, justified and validated"; Reiter (1996, 71), describing group communication protocols that distribute trust among a group.

7. Although I will not be discussing their work explicitly, I must acknowledge another community of researchers that has built an area of research and practice around trust, within the field of computer-human interaction. See, for example, Schneiderman (2000, 58–59), outlining certain steps, such as disclosing patterns of past performance and enforcing privacy and security policies, that designers can take to encourage trust in online relationships; Cassell and Bickmore (2000, 50–56); Corritore, Kracher, and Wiedenbeck (2001); Fogg et al. (2002); Friedman, Kahn, and Howe (2000).

8. See Schneider (1999, 12–23), evaluating whether and to what degree we can rely on existing networked information systems that support our critical infrastructures. This report urged a set of actions to increase trustworthiness and limit our vulnerability to harm, even catastrophe, that might result from failures due to malfunction or malicious attack. See also 240–55, outlining the commission's conclusions and recommendations.

9. See Seligman (1997, 19), arguing that trust in systems entails confidence in a set of institutions.

10. See Baier (1986, 259), arguing that in some instances it is more prudent to distrust rather than to trust.

11. See Becker (1996, 58), noting that a "proper sense of security is a balance of cognitive control and noncognitive stability."

12. See Seligman (1997, 16–21), explaining the difference between trust and confidence.

13. See Pettit (1995, 210), arguing that the mechanisms of trust can explain why "trust builds on trust."

14. Pettit (1995, 203), commenting that many are not proud of this trait.

15. See Pettit (1995, 203), arguing that people regard their desire for the good opinion of others as a disposition that is hard to shed.

16. See Pettit (1995, 207), arguing that "where trust of this kind materializes and survives, people will take that as a token of proof of their being well disposed toward one another, so that the success of the trust should prove to be fruitful in other regards."

17. Seligman (1997, 69), arguing that familiarity relates to the "human bond" rooted in identity.

18. See Putnam (1993, 172), arguing that reciprocity undergirds social trust, which facilitates cooperation in communities.

19. See, for example, Seligman (1997, 22), arguing that the concept of social role has been "fundamental to modern sociological analysis"; Baier (1986, 256),

arguing that people trust others to perform their roles in society; Pettit (1995, 221), arguing that divisions among people in a community are likely to reduce the chances of people from different sides trusting one another.

20. See Luhmann (1979/1988, 78–85), discussing the conditions necessary for trust to be formed; Hardin (1993, 514), asserting that the "terrible vision of a permanent underclass in American city ghettos may have its grounding in the lesson that the children of the ghetto are taught . . . that they cannot trust others"; Pettit (1995, 222), arguing that a society in which trust is found only in small family groups might become very cynical; Weinstock (1999).

21. See Luhmann (1979/1988, 84), commenting on how "complex and richly varied the social conditions for the formation of trust are."

22. See Hardin (1993, 522), discussing social mechanisms that generate trust; Pettit (1995, 220), arguing that the "trust-responsiveness mechanism" has implications for institutional design; and Weinstock (1999).

23. There is far more complexity to this issue than I need, or am able, to show here. See, for example, Nissenbaum (1999, 141), discussing anonymity and what it means to protect it; Wallace (1999, 23), offering a definition of anonymity.

24. In 1999 a thirteen-year-old boy from Haddonfield, N.J., who was participating in eBay auctions bid away $3.2 million on items like a van Gogh sketch and a 1971 Corvette convertible. His parents were successful in freeing themselves from responsibility for these transactions. See "Boy Bids $3M at Online Site," available at Associated Press Online, Haddonfield (April 30, 1999).

25. See Dibbell (1994), describing a fictional virtual rape in an online multiuser domain.

26. This is what I mean by organizing according to functionality. Structurally, a password is a very different device than a locked door, but in relation to this aspect of computer security, access control, the two are effectively the same.

27. See Ashley Dunn, "Computer World Battles Faster-Moving Viruses Technology," *Los Angeles Times,* October 4, 1999 (reflecting on the "notorious" outbreak of the Morris worm and explaining that an Internet security clearinghouse was created in response to the damage done by the worm).

28. Malware is a term used generally to refer to the varieties of computer codes produced with the intention of bothering or harming recipients or victims.

29. See, for example, Schneider (1999), defining firewalls and identifying them as one of the mechanisms used to prevent unwanted access to computer systems.

30. See, for example, McGraw and Felten (1997), reporting that a "code-signing hole" had been found in Java software; King (1996), noting that "several security flaws have been reported since Sun [Microsystems, Inc.] announced Java."

31. An interesting alternative tack is explored in work on online reputational systems that do not necessarily relay an agent's true identity. See Resnick et al. (2000).

32. See Lessig (1999, 34–35), identifying three common architectures of identity used on the Internet: passwords, "cookies," and digital certificates.

33. But see Nissenbaum (1999, 143), arguing that the capacity in the information age to aggregate and analyze the data necessary to identify an individual even without access to a name presents a new challenge to protecting anonymity, where society desires to do so.

34. The security of Microsoft's browser, Internet Explorer, is based on this principle.

35. See Schneier (1999, paragraph 9): "One problem is the permissive nature of the Internet."

36. This seems to be the form of the Federal Intrusion Detection Network (FIDNet) system proposed by the National Security Council and endorsed by the Clinton administration to protect government computers. See Marc Lacey, "Clinton Outlines Plan and Money to Tighten Computer Security" (*New York Times*, January 8, 2000), in which FIDNet is identified as part of the Clinton administration's larger computer security plan. See also "White House Fact Sheet: Cyber Security Budget Initiatives" (*U.S. Newswire*, February 15, 2000), outlining the Clinton administration's budget initiatives related to cybersecurity for fiscal year 2001; White House (2000), discussing various government intrusion detection systems. The FIDNet proposal has met with significant opposition from various civil liberties groups. See, for example, John Markoff, "The Strength of the Internet Proves to Be Its Weakness" (*New York Times*, February 10, 2000), noting that FIDNet caused alarm among civil libertarians, who said it would be used to curtail privacy on the Internet; Patrick Thibodeau (2000) reporting on privacy group's testimony before the U.S. Senate Judiciary Subcommittee on Technology, Terrorism, and Government Information.

37. See John Leyden (1999, 7), reporting that America Online assisted federal and state law enforcement agents in identifying David Smith as the creator of the Melissa virus; Lee Copeland (1999), noting that America Online tracked Smith down by tracing the virus to a list server in New Jersey; Hiawatha Bray, "N.J. Man Charged in Computer Virus Case" (*Boston Globe*, April 3, 1999), noting that America Online assisted the government agents in identifying Smith.

38. See Dibbell (1994), describing a fictional virtual rape in an online multiuser domain.

39. See U.S. Department of Justice (1994), reporting that "in murders where the relationship between the victim and the offender was known, 44% of the victims were killed by an acquaintance, 22% by a stranger, and 20% by a family member."

40. See Becker (1996, 50), noting that "ordinary life" provides substantial anec-dotal evidence that most people have personal relationships in which they remain "trustful despite the known untrustworthiness of others"; cf. Slovic (1993, 677), describing trust as fragile and identifying "the asymmetry principle," whereby trust is usually created slowly but destroyed in an instant, often by a single event.

41. See Hoffman, Novak, and Peralta (1999, 82), concluding that the primary barriers to consumers' providing demographic data to websites are related to trust and noting that more than 72 percent of Web users indicated they would provide demographic data if the websites would provide information about how the collected data would be used.

42. See Becker (1996, 59), arguing that a person's loss of confidence in another person's motivations does more harm to the relationship than when the other person proves to be "merely unreliable or not credible."

43. See Slovic (1993, 680), contrasting the reactions of French and American citizens to risks associated with nuclear power and noting that the French public's acceptance of the risks is partly related to the public trust in the state-run nuclear program, which has a reputation for emphasizing public service over profits.

44. See Tyler (2001), advocating a "proactive model of social regulation" that is based upon encouraging and maintaining public trust in the "character and motives of legal authorities."

45. Tyler (2001), "Motive based trust is central to situations in which people rely upon fiduciary authorities" (366) and summary of results of an empirical study concluding that trust is an important factor in shaping people's reactions to their experience with legal authorities because "people who trust the motives of the authority with whom they are dealing are more willing to defer to that authority" and "trust leads to more positive feelings about the legal authority involved" (376).

46. Tyler (2001), "In the context of a specific personal experience with a legal authority, people are willing to voluntarily defer based upon their belief that the authorities are acting in a trustworthy manner. They infer trustworthiness from the justice of the actions of the authorities" (396), and discussion of the opportunities police officers and judges have to develop public goodwill by justifying outcomes by reference to the public's moral values, in the outcome context, and treating people fairly in the procedural context (398).

47. See Baier (1986, 236), analyzing trust as a relationship in which "A trusts B with valued thing C," and in which B is given discretionary powers with respect to C; Hardin (1993, 506): "To say 'I trust you' seems almost always to be elliptical, as though we can assume some such phrase as 'to do X' or 'in matters Y' "; Weinstock (1999).

48. Baier (1986, 245): "We take it for granted that people will perform their role-related duties and trust any individual worker to look after whatever her job requires her to. The very existence of that job, as a standard occupation, creates a climate of some trust in those with that job."

49. See Goldberg, Hill, and Shostack (2001), discussing changes to Amazon.com's privacy agreement protecting customer information that resulted in reduced protections.

50. See Luhmann (1979/1988, 20), noting that trust is based in part on familiarity, history, and past experiences, and (24), arguing that trust always

involves the risk that the harm resulting from a breach of trust may be greater than the benefit to be gained by trusting; Pettit (1995, 208), arguing that irrespective of how one defines risk taking, trust always involves putting oneself in a position of vulnerability whereby it is possible for the other person to do harm to the trustor; Weinstock (1999).

51. There has been discussion in the media about the Clinton administration's proposals to monitor both governmental and private networks for signs of terrorist and criminal activity. See, for example, Robert O'Harrow, "Computer Security Proposal Is Revised: Critics Had Raised Online Privacy Fears" (*Washington Post*, September 22, 1999), reporting that civil liberties groups welcomed changes to the Clinton administration's original proposals, in particular limitations on automatic data collection; see also Tyler (2001), discussing the Clinton administration's proposal for, and reaction to, enhanced computer network security programs.

52. See Luhmann (1979/1988, 15), noting that "trust increases the 'tolerance of uncertainty' " and explaining that "mastery of events" [that is, knowledge] can replace trust.

53. See: www.e-thepeople.org and www.appliedautonomy.com/.

54. I am grateful to Gaia Bernstein for sharing the results of her research on TeleGarden, which is part of a larger book project (in progress) with Yochai Benkler, Greg Pomerantz, and Alan Toner, on commons-based productions by peers.

55. See note 56.

56. See Luhmann (1979/1988, 20), noting that trust evolves from past experiences that can guide future actions.

References

Abdul-Rahman, Alfarez, and Stephen Hailes. 1998. "A Distributed Trust Model." *New Security Paradigms Workshop* 48: 48–60.

Backhouse, James P. 1998. "Security: The Achilles Heel of Electronic Commerce." *Society* 35(4): 28.

Baier, Annette. 1986. "Trust and Antitrust." *Ethics* 96: 231–60.

Becker, Lawrence. 1996. "Trust as Noncognitive Security About Motives." *Ethics* 107(1): 43–61.

Benkler, Yochai. 2002. "Coase's Penguin, or Linux and the Nature of the Firm." *Yale Law Journal* 112(3): 369–446.

Blaze, Matt, Joan Feigenbaum, and Jack Lacy. 1996. "Decentralized Trust Management." In *Proceedings, 1996 IEEE Symposium on Security and Privacy.* Available at: http://citeseer.nj.nec.com/blaze96decentralized.html.

Camp, L. Jean. 2000. *Trust and Risk in Internet Commerce.* Cambridge, Mass.: MIT Press.

Cassell, Justine, and Timothy Bickmore. 2000. "External Manifestations of Trustworthiness in the Interface." *Communications of the ACM* 43(12): 50–56.

Copeland, Lee. 1999. "Virus Creator Fesses Up—Admits to Originating and Disseminating Melissa." *Computer Reseller News* (September 6).

Corritore, Cynthia L., Beverly Kracher, and Susan Wiedenbeck. 2001. "Trust in the Online Environment." In *Usability Evaluation and Interface Design Cognitive Engineering: Intelligent Agents and Virtual Reality*, edited by Michael J. Smith, Gavriel Salvendy, Don Harris, and Richard J. Koubek. Mahwah, N.J.: Erlbaum.

Dibbell, Julian. 1994. "A Rape in Cyberspace; or, How an Evil Clown, a Haitian Trickster Spirit, Two Wizards, and a Cast of Dozens Turned a Database into a Society." In *Flame Wars: The Discourse of Cyberculture*, edited by Mark Dery. Durham: Duke University Press.

First International Conference on Trust Management. 2003. Crete, Greece (May). Available at: www.itrust.uoc.gr/.

Fogg, B. J., Cathy Soohoo, David Danielsen, Leslie Marable, Julianne Stanford, and Ellen R. Tauber. 2002. *How Do People Evaluate a Web Site's Credibility? Results from a Large Study*. Palo Alto: Stanford Persuasive Technology Lab, Stanford University. Available at: http://www.consumerwebwatch.org/news/report3_credibilityresearch/stanfordPTL_TOC.htm.

Friedman, Batya, Peter Kahn, and Daniel Howe. 2000. "Trust Online." *Communications of the ACM* 43(12): 34–40.

Fukuyama, Francis. 1995. *Trust*. New York: Free Press Paperbacks.

Goldberg, Ian, Austin Hill, and Adam Shostack. 2001. "Trust Ethics and Privacy." *Boston University Law Review* 81(2): 407–22.

Hardin, Russell. 1993. "The Street-Level Epistemology of Trust." *Politics and Society* 21(December): 407–22.

Herz, J. C. 1995. "Cross-dressing in Cyberspace." In *Surfing on the Internet*. New York: Little, Brown.

Hoffman, Donna L., Thomas P. Novak, and Marcos Peralta. 1999. "Building Consumer Trust Online." *Communications of the ACM* 42(4): 80–85.

Khare, Rohit, and Adam Rifkin. 1997. "Weaving a Web of Trust." Available at: www.w3journal.com/7/s3.rifkin.wrap.html (accessed on November 21, 2003).

King, Richard. 1996. "Java Sun's Language Is Scoring Some Early Points with Operators and Suppliers." *Tele.Com* (May 1).

Kramer, Roderick M. 1999. "Trust and Distrust in Organizations: Emerging Perspectives, Enduring Questions." *Annual Review of Psychology* 50(17): 569–98.

Lessig, Lawrence. 1999. *Code and Other Laws of Cyberspace*. New York: Basic Books.

Leyden, John. 1999. "Melissa's Creator Faces 'Hard Time.' " *Network News* (April 14): 7.

Luhmann, Niklas. 1979/1988. "Trust: A Mechanism for the Reduction of Social Complexity." In *Trust and Power: Two Works by Niklas Luhmann*. Reprint, New York: John Wiley & Sons.

McGraw, Gary, and Edward Felten. 1997. "Understanding the Keys to Java Security." *Javaworld* (May 1). Available at: http://www.javaworld.com/javaworld/jw-05-1997/jw-05-security.html.

Moskowitz, Robert. 1998. "Ask Yourself: In Whom Can You Really Trust?" *Network Computing* (June 15). Available at: www.networkcomputing.com/911/911colmoskowitz.html.

Nissenbaum, Helen. 1999. "The Meaning of Anonymity in an Information Age." *Information Society* 15: 141–44.

———. 2001. "Securing Trust Online: Wisdom or Oxymoron." *Boston University Law Review* 81(3): 635–64.

Pettit, Philip. 1995. "The Cunning of Trust." *Philosophy and Public Affairs* 24(3): 202–25.

Posner, Richard. 1978. "The Right of Privacy." *Georgia Law Review* 12(3): 393–422.

Putnam, Robert D. 1993. *Making Democracy Work.* Princeton, N.J.: Princeton University Press.

Ratnasingham, Pauline. 1999. "Implicit Trust Levels in EDI Security." *Journal of Internet Security* 2(1). Available at: www.addsecure.net/jisec/1999-02.htm.

Reiter, Michael K. 1996. "Distributing Trust with the Rampart Toolkit." *Communications of the ACM* 39(4): 71–74.

Resnick, Paul, Ko Kuwabara, Richard Zeckhauser, and Eric Friedman. 2000. "Reputation Systems." *Communications of the ACM* 43(12): 45–48.

Salnoske, Karl. 1998. "Building Trust in Electronic Commerce." *Business Credit* 100(1): 24. Available at: www.nacm.org/bcmag/bcarchives/1998/articles 1998/jan/jan98art2.html.

Schneider, Fred B., ed. 1999. *Trust in Cyberspace.* Washington, D.C.: Commission on Information Systems' Trustworthiness, National Research Council.

Schneiderman, Ben. 2000. "Designing Trust into Online Experiences." *Communications of the ACM* 43(12): 57–59.

Schneier, Bruce. 1999. "Risks of E-mail Borne Viruses, Worms, and Trojan Horses." *Risks Digest* 20(2). Accessed June 17, 1999, at: http://catless.ncl.ac.uk/ Risks/20.45.html.

Seligman, Adam B. 1997. *The Problem of Trust.* Princeton, N.J.: Princeton University Press.

Slovic, Paul. 1993. "Perceived Risk, Trust, and Democracy." *Risk Analysis* 13(6): 675–82.

Sproull, Lee. 2003. "Online Communities." In *The Internet Encyclopedia,* edited by Hossein Bidgoli. New York: John Wiley.

Sproull, Lee, and Sara Kiesler. 2003. "Transforming Public Volunteer Work." Paper presented at conference of the U.S. Department of Commerce, Transforming Enterprise: First International Conference on the Economic and Societal Implications of Information Technology. Washington (January 27–28, 2003).

Steinauer, Dennis D., Shukri A. Wakid, and Stanley Rasberry. 1997. "Trust and Traceability in Electronic Commerce." *Standard View* 5(3): 118–24.

Thibodeau, Patrick. 2000. "Senate Hears Objections to 'Cyberalarm.' " *Computerworld* (February 7). Available at: http://www.computerworld.com/news/ 2000/story/0,11280,41224,00.html.

Tyler, Tom R. 2001. "Trust and Law Abidingness: A Proactive Model of Social Regulation." *Boston University Law Review* 81(3): 361–406.

U.S. Department of Defense. 1999. "Department of Defense Trusted Computer System Evaluation Criteria." Accessed July 1, 1999, at: www.all.net/books/ orange.

U.S. Department of Justice. 1994. *Bureau of Justice Statistics: Selected Findings, Violent Crime.* Volume 3. Washington: Government Printing Office.

Wallace, Kathleen. 1999. "Anonymity." *Ethics and Information Technology* 1(1): 21–31.

Weinstock, Daniel M. 1999. "Building Trust in Divided Societies." *Political Philosophy* 7(3): 287–307.

White House. 2000. "Defending America's Cyberspace: National Plan for Information Systems Protection, Version 1.0: An Invitation to Dialogue." *Executive Summary* 15.

Woolford, David. 1999. "Electronic Commerce: It's All a Matter of Trust." *Computing Canada* 25(18, May 7): 13. Available at: www.plesman.com/Archives/cc/1999/May/2518/cc251813b.html.

Chapter 8

Architects of Trust: The Role of Network Facilitators in Geographical Clusters

BILL MCEVILY AND AKBAR ZAHEER

C AN TRUST be purposively designed and constructed? Trust is often treated as a dyadic phenomenon that unfolds between two parties according to a fairly well defined evolutionary path. We seek to broaden our understanding of the developmental logic of trust by proposing that trust can be intentionally shaped and further that certain actors are skilled in the art and craft of building trust among others. Such architects of trust play a vital role as network facilitators in geographical clusters where firms simultaneously collaborate and compete. Our theory is based on a grounded case study of the office furniture manufacturing industry clustered in the western Michigan region. The case demonstrates that network facilitators create trust by taking deliberate actions that include identifying shared interests, developing common expectations, leveraging a critical mass of influence, and compressing networks in physical space and time. By defining and identifying the active network role played by network facilitators, we provide a theoretical framework for explaining why and how trust emerges in networks of firms to enable collaborative competition in geographical clusters.

Geographical clusters have captivated the attention of a diverse array of social scientists from political science (Sabel 1993; Saxenian 1994), sociology (Powell 1990; Kanter 1995), strategic and international management (Porter 1990; Nohria 1992), and economic geography

189

(Krugman 1991; Scott 1992; Storper 1992). What is most striking about this form of economic activity is that firms in geographical clusters often simultaneously collaborate while competing in downstream product markets. Among the explanations advanced for such cooperative competition is the novel forms of network organization—typically characterized as dense and overlapping webs of social, professional, and exchange ties (Powell 1990)—observed in geographical clusters. The ongoing patterns of interaction in a region encourage the development of shared understandings, collective identities, and, most important, mutual trust among firms, which enable levels of collaboration that otherwise would be difficult to achieve and sustain. However, what is less clear is how these intense patterns of interaction and supporting norms emerge in the first place and evolve over time. Rather, network forms of organization and high levels of trust among firms are often taken as given, their presence treated as a starting assumption for analyses of geographical clusters. Viewed this way, the distinctive social context of geographical clusters spontaneously arises and naturally develops on its own, independent of any guiding forces. Our purpose in this paper is to question this perspective and inquire into the origin and development of the interfirm trust underlying the network patterns and cooperative behavior characteristic of many geographical clusters.

To explore this question we take an inductive approach by presenting an in-depth case study that focuses on the office furniture manufacturing industry clustered in western Michigan.[1] The case study is particularly appropriate for our purposes since it provides a fine-grained illustration of the developmental path of interorganizational trust that serves as the foundation for collaboration among competing firms.

Our analysis of the case study reveals a number of unique and surprising insights. Chief among these is the critical role that regional institutions play in supporting firms in geographical clusters by performing what we call a *network facilitator* role. We observe that regional institutions are central to the creation and maintenance of regular patterns of interaction and the development of trust among firms in the cluster. We also note that the influence of regional institutions on the development and maintenance of interfirm trust is the result of specific *actions* taken by these network facilitators. Rather than arising and developing spontaneously, we present a view of interorganizational trust as being actively and purposively shaped and "engineered" by network facilitators. Taken together, these findings suggest a novel perspective on the origins and evolution of interfirm trust in geographical clusters.

Michigan's Office Furniture Industry Council

Many economic development programs, as everyone knows, are either well-intentioned failures or publicity-minded frauds. This one is indubitably neither.[2]

Charles F. Sabel,
"Studied Trust: Building New Forms of
Cooperation in a Volatile Economy"

In 1991 Michigan was one of the first seven states to receive federal funding for its industrial extension activities. The Western Michigan Manufacturing Technology Center (WMMTC) sought to enhance the competitiveness of the western Michigan region through offering a variety of outreach and technical assistance services to the region's manufacturers, particularly the smaller ones, in order to help them modernize their facilities and improve their overall performance. In pursuit of this mission the WMMTC allied with other economic development organizations in the region. The Office Furniture Industry Council (OFIC) is the outcome of one such effort.

Like many other municipalities and economic development organizations around the country, the WMMTC had become dissatisfied with "smokestack chasing"—the use of tax incentives to lure large manufacturing companies to a region (Osborne 1988). The rationale for this shift in emphasis in economic development policy away from large manufacturers was noted by one economic development official whom we interviewed: "Well, all of a sudden it was clear that being bigger was not going to be the answer in the future. We were just beginning to see some of the potential of this whole flexibility, responsiveness, customer satisfaction, etc."

Interestingly, this changed orientation was inspired in part by learning from the experience of geographical clusters located in northern Italy. Economic development officials from Michigan traveled to the Emilia-Romagna region, where they observed firsthand how networks of small specialist producers relied on a different model for organizing and coordinating economic activity than what is typically observed in the United States. As this official recalled in our interview:

> An important thing, even early on . . . was what we'd learned over in Northern Italy. . . . [T]his group of small shoe manufacturers worked together as a network, and by working together were able to capture a significant part of the world market in high-fashion women's shoes. And even though they were independent businesses, they knew that by sharing, by off-loading work to others, by having a network of suppliers and producers, that in fact they could act like a very big business, but still maintain their flexibility.

On the basis of these observations, officials at the WMMTC decided to adapt the northern Italy model to western Michigan and work with a entire industry sector. The office furniture manufacturing industry, with its related supplier base, presented an attractive opportunity to implement such a model. Furniture companies with headquarters in the Grand Rapids and surrounding area represent 45 percent of the output of their $8.5 billion industry ("Furniture Makers Standardize," *Plastics News*, April 11, 1994, p. 1). As a WMMTC official we interviewed noted, this concentration of firms made the regional industry an ideal candidate: "In western Michigan, and I mean within literally about a seventy-mile radius [of Grand Rapids], almost 50 percent of the total volume of office furniture manufactured in the United States is produced. It's quite astounding when you think about it. In one form or another all seven out of the eight manufacturers that are a part of this council, and this specific supplier development initiative, are located in that perimeter."

In the early 1990s the office furniture industry faced an increasingly competitive global environment and recessionary conditions. In October 1991, the OFIC was established by the WMMTC in conjunction with manufacturers and suppliers in the office furniture industry to serve as an advisory panel that would promote supplier development in the industry. By directing the WMMTC's institutional resources toward improving performance at the supplier level the OFIC sought to "produce a 'multiplier' effect in the regional economy because the benefits would work their way up to the furniture assemblers" ("Furniture Makers Standardize," *Plastics News*, April 11, 1994, p. 1).

Membership in the OFIC consisted of representatives from seven office furniture manufacturers, nine suppliers, and the WMMTC, in addition to other regional economic development officials. The OFIC decided to focus on opportunities for improvement that affected all firms in the industry—opportunities, as it turned out, that required a high level of trust and cooperation among firms for the potential gains sought to be realized. In particular, the OFIC targeted four areas for improvement and standardization: packaging, quality assurance, electronic data interchange (EDI), and color (see table 8.1).

Although the creation of standard practices in these four areas could make all firms better off by reducing redundancies and inefficiencies, these benefits would only accrue if each individual firm committed to, and actually carried out, a common course of action. Standard practices for managing manufacturer-supplier exchanges represent public goods (Dybvig and Spatt 1983; Katz and Shapiro 1985) in the sense that they make a group of firms better off overall, but no one firm alone has the incentive to incur the costs and risks associated with their creation and dissemination. The market structure of the office furniture industry is oligopolistic, meaning that no single manufacturer dominates the industry

Table 8.1   Industry Standards Created by the OFIC

Standard	Description
Packaging	Prior to the packaging standard, each of the manufacturers had different requirements for packaging, labeling, and delivering products. As a result of the inherent diseconomies of operating several packaging operations at relatively low scale, rather than a single packaging system, the opportunities for suppliers to improve delivery performance and to reduce lead times were limited.
Quality assurance	Similar efficiencies were attained by standardizing supplier quality assurance. Each manufacturer had its own separate auditing system and each would individually qualify a supplier on the basis of different criteria. For a supplier, this meant incurring the costs of being certified many times each year, maintaining separate sets of inspection records, and having multiple procedures manuals and other documentation demonstrating adherence to different interpretations of quality manufacturing principles. With only one set of expectations, suppliers would find the process less burdensome than before, and would be more likely to meet the standards (see "Area Furniture Industry Lauds Streamlining," *Grand Rapids Press*, May 27, 1994, p. 64).
Electronic data interchange	Although many of the manufacturers had been using EDI with suppliers for years, broadly following the ANSI X.12 standard, each company had developed its own unique, customized, transaction conventions. This meant that each time a supplier acquired a new trading partner, new software would have to be purchased or existing software modified. Consequently, many suppliers kept separate terminals for each customer and would print out new orders and then re-key them into their own computer system. The OFIC developed a standard set of transaction conventions, each with a single format, that would allow manufacturers and suppliers to exchange all stages of procurement information from request for quotes to payment orders, thus allowing suppliers to dispense with multiple terminals for each customer ("Information Interchange Builds Path for Suppliers," *Grand Rapids Business Journal*, May 1994, p. 81).
Color	The most recent effort undertaken by the OFIC was to create a common method for documenting and measuring color. A subcommittee of representatives from manufacturers and suppliers developed standards that would minimize redundancy, establish a common language for describing color, and reduce color ordering time.

Source: Authors' compilation.

(unlike the Microsoft-dominated software industry) in a way that allows it to impose its will. Consequently, in order for a manufacturer to establish its own standards, it would have to offer suppliers financial inducements or even absorb the costs of suppliers' investments, which would pose the risk of being incompatible with a future standard. Most important, individual firms face the risk that other firms, both competitors and suppliers, would be reluctant to invest in the dedicated assets required to implement the proposed standard. For instance, suppliers may be reluctant to incur the costs of adopting the standard of any one particular manufacturer for fear of being incompatible with the systems or practices of other manufacturers or of having to incur additional costs in the future should a different standard emerge. Under these circumstances, where the provision of standards is not feasible by individual firms for both coordination and strategic reasons, network facilitators are critical for collective action to emerge.

Given its short history, the achievements of the OFIC have been considerable and have in fact received national attention. The OFIC has been recognized for helping participating firms realize greater efficiencies by streamlining their processes and modernizing their operations. Specifically, by standardizing various aspects of the buyer-supplier exchange relationship, suppliers have been able to eliminate duplicate systems and processes that were maintained for dealing with different manufacturers. Although the OFIC initiatives produced successful collaboration among firms on the development of standards that greatly enhanced the efficiency of manufacturer-supplier exchange relations, these outcomes did not occur merely as a result of establishing the OFIC.

The case study illustrates how interfirm collaboration was induced by directed actions taken by the WMMTC acting as a network facilitator, namely: (1) identifying shared interests; (2) developing common expectations; (3) leveraging a critical mass of influence; and (4) compressing networks. The case study that follows illustrates how a network facilitator performed these actions and enabled collective action among firms in the office furniture industry. Figure 8.1 presents a model summarizing the theory of network facilitation that we inductively derive from the case.

Identifying Shared Interests

A fundamental challenge in getting the OFIC off the ground was persuading the participating firms to work together to identify shared interests. Initially, when individuals from the WMMTC approached the manufacturers with the idea of forming the council, manufacturer executives were decidedly ambivalent and displayed a marked lack of commitment to the proposal. While the manufacturers realized that the

Figure 8.1   Theoretical Model of Network Facilitation

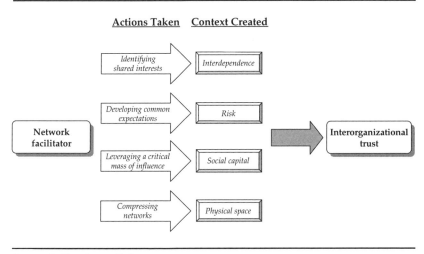

Actions Taken   Context Created

Identifying shared interests → Interdependence

Developing common expectations → Risk

Network facilitator

Leveraging a critical mass of influence → Social capital

Compressing networks → Physical space

→ Interorganizational trust

Source: Authors' compilation.

council represented an opportunity to collectively improve their supply chains more than they could individually, they were reluctant to sit down with their direct competitors for fear of revealing competitive information and attracting antitrust scrutiny. We spoke with the director of purchasing for one of the participating manufacturers who described the difficulties of getting the council started:

> As a member of the council, our company was hesitant to disclose our practices with our competitors. The first meetings were not productive, but gave us a chance to talk to each other. Later we were able to find common ground to work together. . . . It was a real slow process. I remember the first meeting that we had, sitting around that table, looking at everyone—I mean, we were all competitors. First of all, there was a concern, are we violating any kind of Robinson Patman Act, or whatever it might be, that stifles competitiveness. And once we were assured that that wasn't the case, then it was well, we're gonna be very guarded with the information that we share, simply because we are competitors.

In order to address concerns about revealing proprietary information to competitors, the WMMTC established ground rules, like agreeing that no information on sensitive topics such as pricing, product design, or marketing strategy would be discussed during the meetings. Even with these safeguards in place, though, the fact that the firms did eventually discover common ground was hardly a foregone conclusion. The WMMTC was able to guide the participating firms in this direction through a series of meetings, which allowed them to explore avenues of shared interest. Two separate meetings were initially held, one with the furniture manufacturers and a second with the suppliers. The two groups were then brought together at a third meeting to discuss shared interests and to prioritize projects. The outcome of these three meetings with the manufacturers and suppliers was a joint priority list which established the agenda of the OFIC for the next couple of years focusing on the creation of industry standards in the area of packaging, quality assurance, EDI, and color. The decision to concentrate on standards for governing upstream exchange can be attributed to the fact that through these meetings the manufacturers eventually came to appreciate the extent of their interdependence when it came to improving supplier performance.

The discovery of this interdependence was possibly the most important outcome of the initial meetings. The WMMTC representatives highlighted the fact that the manufacturers not only had similar goals when it came to improving supplier performance, but that they also shared many of the same suppliers. What was perhaps more of a revelation for manufacturers than the degree of overlap in supply chains was the fact that each of them was pursuing independent approaches to supplier development. This meant that manufacturers were placing conflicting demands on suppliers, who consequently were unsure about which, if any, set of improvement programs to invest in. At the same time, the widespread adoption of common standards by the suppliers for governing exchange relations would only occur if the manufacturers collectively agreed to them. A representative of the WMMTC, whom we interviewed, described the significance of this realization by saying, "It was just as powerful for the furniture makers themselves to see that they were sharing so many of the same suppliers that they themselves could agree on a common agenda to improve the industry at large."

Prior to the formation of the OFIC, nobody had a clear picture of the structure of the network of exchange relationships among manufacturers and suppliers. By revealing the extent of overlap in supplier channels to the manufacturers, the WMMTC helped the participating firms recognize opportunities for eliminating duplication through collaboration. Further, the early OFIC meetings surfaced promising avenues for pursuing these joint goals. As one of the WMMTC representatives we interviewed explained, "It was the suppliers who flat-out said, we'll tell you where there's duplication and waste. If you can get the furniture makers to listen to this agenda and prioritize for them what they can collaborate on, then you've got it."

One important reason why the WMMTC was able to gain access to proprietary and competitive information was the director's social capital—his network of social and professional ties. The director has deep roots in the region. He is part of a well-known family that has worked in the office furniture industry for three generations. In addition, he has personal relationships with many of the managers and executives in the industry stretching back to when they grew up together in the area. More important, the director had extensive experience working in the industry: eight years for one of the manufacturers and another seven leading an industry trade association. As a result of his past experience in the industry he not only was well known but brought with him to the WMMTC established social and professional relationships with the seven manufacturers and many of the supplier firms. His well-established reputation as a trusted and credible individual meant that the director could "speak their language" and appreciate their concerns. It also meant that participating firms knew he would respect the sensitivity of the information he was gaining access to. Managers and owners were confident that the director would not use the information he was entrusted with in a way that would be detrimental to the interests of their firms. Along these lines, a colleague of the director whom we spoke to explained,

> Unless you have a higher-level relationship you don't get into those kind of discussions. . . . It is sensitive [information] and it's only because of [the director's] sort of position in the region and the respect he has gained, do they entrust him with that kind of information. The director's position is very different [from] somebody else who does not have his background or relationship with the presidents, because he can walk into a company president's office as well as he can [into the office of] the director of corporate purchasing.

These comments also highlight the point that the role of the WMMTC was not simply to bring together formerly antagonistic groups. Instead, the WMMTC was actively involved in coordinating the discussions that were taking place and helped to manage the give-and-take that was needed to usher the firms through this process. By redefining the nature of their exchange relationships in a way that exposed shared interests, the participating firms were able to discover mutually beneficial collaborative opportunities that had previously gone unnoticed. One of the individuals from the WMMTC we spoke with said of the firms' role, "I think we are facilitators of the way these firms approach their buyer-seller relationship. I'm not sure that any third party is going to get in there and restructure the way they manage them, but I do believe we've had a pretty significant influence on the way they approach it."

This notion of an actor that is actively involved in organizing and guiding interaction and dialogue among firms but at the same time is not an actual player in the interchange taking place captures the essence of the network facilitator role. In effect, the network facilitator is a catalyst that initiates interfirm collaboration and creates the enabling conditions for collective action to unfold. The high level of trust in the WMMTC was a crucial factor underlying its capacity to act as a network facilitator. Indeed, it is difficult to envision how shared interests would have been identified and cooperation would have emerged among firms in the western Michigan office furniture industry without the active involvement of the WMMTC.

Developing Common Expectations

Recognizing the opportunity to benefit from a set of common standards was not, by itself, enough to cause those standards to become a reality. Since standards are most beneficial if they are widely diffused and adhered to, each firm was reluctant to take action and implement the standards until it became apparent that others were doing the same. Consequently, firms had to trust that their competitors and their exchange partners were serious about developing and following a common course of action, rather than exclusively promoting their own interests, possibly at the expense of others. At the same time, each firm had to act on the standards in order to signal trustworthy behavior to its competitors and exchange partners.

It took a year and a half for the manufacturers to agree to create a joint quality-assurance standard, and it was their second attempt at creating an industry standard ("Area Furniture Industry Lauds Streamlining," *Grand Rapids Press*, May 27, 1994, p. C4). Despite the first unsuccessful attempt at creating a common packaging standard, the effort proved to be a valuable learning experience for the firms participating in the OFIC. Firms realized that simply agreeing to standards was not enough to bring about their widespread adoption. Rather, the public-goods nature of the standards required that each firm contribute to their dissemination by committing to and actually adopting the standards. The *expectation* that participating firms would follow through on their commitment to implement the standards was perhaps the most important precursor to the initiation of the standards' adoption.

One of the WMMTC officials who helped coordinate the OFIC described to us the dynamics of initiating the adoption of standards in the following way: "[The firms] had to find something, they had to find an action or a behavior that they were committing themselves to take that would be different than prior behavior. And that one specific thing was agreeing on this standard supplier quality audit." The supplier quality audit was an area in which cooperation held clear, unambiguous benefits for the firms. However, since participation in the OFIC was completely voluntary, there was little in the way of enforcement mechanisms to ensure that stated promises to take action would be upheld at various points throughout the process of developing and implementing the standard. Consequently, the participating firms were essentially trusting that other participants would keep their word at each stage.

Rather than simply leave to chance whether participating firms would carry out their promises to take action, the WMMTC took a number of steps to create a context highly conducive to the development of common expectations. One such measure was carefully selecting the membership of the OFIC. The individuals at the WMMTC were able to use their network of social and professional ties to forge a coalition of firms that were well suited for engaging in collective action. In particular, from their past experience in the industry the WMMTC officials knew which firms were most predisposed toward helping advance public, rather than parochial, interests. The guiding philosophy for the composition of the OFIC was to select participants who were more likely to take the lead in working together as a means of establishing trust among themselves. One representative of a participating firm described to us the WMMTC's approach in constructing the OFIC as follows:

> Well, there certainly was some hesitation from the manufacturers. They were a little skeptical and said look, how can I sit down with my competitors and talk about my suppliers? They were very skeptical. Many of the suppliers were very skeptical of sitting down with a group of their customers. There's always the—you know, gee it was a lack of trust all the way around. And so it took some negotiating and took some diplomacy. . . . [The director] selected a few other companies around the area that we felt were good companies, that were diverse, would be neutral, at the same time would be candid and forthright in their opinions.

While the problems of collaborating with competitors were obvious, there were less-obvious difficulties in collaborating up and down the supply chain. In particular, prior to the formation of the OFIC, buyer-supplier relationships were somewhat adversarial in nature. Furniture manufacturers typically sourced the same component from multiple suppliers and the best combination of good, fast, and cheap determined the supplier of the day. Suppliers had little or no input into design, and customers had even less input into production. Consequently, it was critical that the representatives selected to participate in the OFIC be able to see beyond their historical differences and reconceptualize their business relationships to envision how working in conjunction with former adversaries was not only feasible, but also pragmatic. For these reasons, the WMMTC enlisted as company representatives on the council the key individuals responsible for managing buyer-supplier relationships, who stood to benefit most from common standards. As a representative from the community college that helped the WMMTC organize the OFIC explained to us:

> To form the Office Furniture Industry Council, we did not necessarily get company CEOs. . . . We didn't have the people who had to bring their ego on their sleeve. What we got were purchasing agents, we got some middle managers. But these are the people that actually do things. And so it's the people who regularly interact with the suppliers whose job was going to be easier. . . . There was something in it for them.

In addition to selecting representatives who stood to benefit directly from the initiatives of the OFIC, the WMMTC was able to help these individuals see how their *firms* would gain from participating. Beyond getting the right people together, it was vital that these individuals comprehend the direct and tangible ways that working on a cooperative effort would affect their own firms. Being able to make this link between the collective undertaking and the individual firms' benefits enabled the representative to make a compelling case to others in their own firms for taking action on implementing the standards and trusting that other firms would do the same. The WMMTC helped the participants translate the objectives of the OFIC into meaningful firm-level outcomes—in effect demonstrating how large payoffs made the risk of a possible breach of trust still worthwhile. As one of the officials involved in initiating the OFIC stated to us:

> You've gotta facilitate this communication and facilitate this relationship and you've got to be able to do it, though, in a context and with a vision. So it's key that you've got people involved that are able to see and artic-ulate the vision that says we need you to stay involved for this reason, and here's how eventually you'll be better off . . . and then we draw a big dollar sign on a piece of paper, you know.

The WMMTC was able to show the participating firms that the OFIC initiatives were connected to and aligned with their own individual interests because of the WMMTC's own extensive history as a trust-worthy network facilitator working with organizations in the area. The WMMTC enlisted the support of other economic development organi-zations such as Grand Rapids Community College, which had estab-lished working relationships with individual firms that were built up over a number of years. As a result of these relationships, organizations like the community college had a strong track record of delivering valu-able services and a detailed awareness of how businesses in the area operated. This network of ongoing relationships proved to be invalu-able to keeping the participating firms involved in the OFIC projects, as one representative from the community college noted to us:

> What we were able to do is go back and get people to the table with whom we have previously worked. [We] were able to call many people that we had built a relationship with over a number of years, and had

built trust, by being out there particularly in training of their employees. We were able to call these people and say, "Look, we've delivered help and services to you over the last several years. . . . Please come. Trust us." [T]he people who invited the businesses were people who had actually worked with them.

Mutual trust among firms developed incrementally as they directly observed other firms making and upholding small initial promises, beginning with the agreement on the supplier quality audit alluded to earlier, which eventually expanded into more significant commitments and ultimately led to the implementation of standards. These ideas are reflected in the comments of one participating supplier representative we interviewed:

> [T]here was some skepticism, but we began to break the ice and we had a good meeting the first time, and people said maybe we're on to something. Let's carry this ball a little bit further. And within a few months, you know, we were meeting on a regular basis. Trying to get to know each other and everybody expressing really what their company's needs were.

The WMMTC also put its own reputation and credibility on the line by persuading firms that their continued participation and involvement would pay off down the road. More important, the WMMTC assured the individual participants that they could trust each other to uphold their commitments to implement the standards. If the "pledges" made by the WMMTC on behalf of the participants proved inaccurate, the trustworthiness of the WMMTC, its principal stock in trade, would be damaged. A representative of the community college echoed this point to us by stating:

> What I think made it work is really a fairly long—certainly over a number of years—series of activities in the community with businesses that built the foundation and the ability and the trust. . . . Because in my experience the key to working with businesses is that there has to be a trust built. And the trust is around the motive of anybody in any kind of public-sector program, whether it's WMMTC . . . or whether it's the community college. . . . Because you're asking them to come together, trust each other, do some things differently, and they're saying well, can we trust you? Is this, you know, just a flavor of the week or is this something that has some substance?

The ability of a network facilitator to act as a trustee in this way is integral to the development of common expectations among firms. Trust in the WMMTC by the participating firms was crucial to their initial involvement since it enabled firms to overcome their initial hesitation to collaborate with rivals and suppliers. Trust in the WMMTC was also important for firms' continuing participation in the OFIC, which served as a signal of their commitment to develop and implement the standards. By referencing its history of working relationships with firms the WMMTC tilted the balance in favor of the development of mutual trust.

Leveraging a Critical Mass of Influence

The mutual trust that developed among firms participating in the OFIC was an enabling condition for them to commit to and implement the standards. The commitment and actions of these firms as a group, which represented a large and influential segment of the industry, sent a powerful message to the broader industry. In particular, having seven of the largest manufacturers agree on standards for governing exchanges reduced the uncertainty confronted by suppliers. The agreement by these seven manufacturers on standard approaches for governing buyer-supplier exchanges had a potent effect on the willingness of suppliers to make the investments necessary to implement the standards at their end. In this regard, the OFIC represented a conduit through which the separate influence of the seven manufacturers could be amassed and channeled. As the director's comments to us indicate, the WMMTC made a concerted effort to take advantage of this critical mass of influence:

> We had these seven big firms that represented this enormous critical mass of sales and that commercial influence helped us immensely to get the suppliers to pay attention. Any time seven of their largest customers, or even one or two of their largest customers, any time they can be articulate about some general needs, and some specific needs, obviously the supplier, out of respect to his commercial well being, is going to pay attention. And they're even going to pay more attention if there are three or more talking about the same thing.

Despite the fact that the manufacturers' influence held the potential of increasing the diffusion of standards among suppliers, there was also the possibility that the "subtle arm twisting" would backfire and be viewed as excessively coercive. What was perhaps more compelling to the suppliers was to hear from the suppliers who were members of the OFIC that they were favorably disposed toward adopting the standards. As mentioned earlier, the WMMTC carefully selected firms that were willing to take the lead and engage in collective action. An additional benefit derived from this selection process was the word-of-mouth endorsements provided by the supplier firms participating on the OFIC that helped diffuse and promote the adoption of the standards to the widest possible audience. A supplier representative participating on the council described to us his role in disseminating the standards as follows:

> There's a lot of other people in the supply based community here that I consider to be personal friends as well as business associates. And there's always a little bit of them versus us. I'm one of us, and the manufacturers were them. So you know, I'd get phone calls saying, "Look, tell me about this packaging standard. What's this all about? Is this somebody trying to ram something down our throat or is there something in it for us?" And so, there were times that I had to take the role of a cheerleader, if you will, and promoter and say, "Yeah, this is gonna be good for our company. And it's gonna be good for your company, too. Get on board."

The combined influence of the seven manufacturers and supplier firms participating on the OFIC were powerful devices in the campaign to disseminate the standards throughout the office furniture industry. However, these tools could not be productively employed by just anyone. For instance, if the manufacturers as a group had attempted to undertake the standards initiative themselves, the suppliers would have questioned their motives. A representative of a supplier firm echoed this point to us:

> Whether it had been two or more manufacturers who got together or two or more suppliers—just as an example, if I'd gotten together with three or four other suppliers and said, "Look, let's go talk to the manufacturers, let's join up together on some things to help save some money, let's go talk to a director of purchasing and tell them that if we all get together and do A, B and C we're gonna jointly reduce our costs and it's gonna save them money," I'm sure the director of purchasing would have said, "All right, what are these guys up to?" And at the same time, if you know, three buyers all show up and say they want to sit down and have a meeting with me as a supplier, I'd say, "Whoa— what's going on here?"

At the same time, the participating firms were wary of a competitor taking the lead role in the standard-setting process for fear that this firm would attempt to sway the standards in a way that was most beneficial to itself. This notion that the competitive dynamics within the OFIC could be at cross-purposes with the creation of a common standard was expressed by a representative of a manufacturer who recalled the difficulty encountered with designing the standards: "I chaired [the packaging] endeavor. And let me tell you, it was taxing, it was tedious, it was a very difficult thing to pull together because of the competitive nature in the industry. Everyone had their own specifications and they thought that's what should be adopted."

Given the inherently parochial outlook of the individual firms, it was critical that the OFIC initiatives be headed up by an actor without a vested interest in the precise form that standards assumed. From the standpoint of the suppliers, there was concern about manufacturers promoting a standard that required extensive investments on the supplier's part, given the possibility that the returns would be largely appropriated by manufacturers demanding lower prices. At the same time, the manufacturers were concerned that the eventual standards would benefit a competitor disproportionately if that firm assumed the leadership role. What became clear is that a neutral third party without a direct stake in the outcome was needed to guide the standard-setting process. In this regard, the WMMTC was seen as impartial, given its sector-wide charter, which implied that it could mediate divergent interests in a way that served the region at large without favoring one firm or group of firms. A participating manufacturer representative aptly articulated this point to us:

> I do not believe that this would have ever happened without the WMMTC. . . . Someone not in the industry had to provide leadership to bring everyone together. Because if a company in the industry had done it, then I'm sure—I would assume the level of cooperation would not have been as great. But, the WMMTC, well, it was a neutral party, with meetings at a neutral location. So that as much as anything, I think, tended to allow companies to say okay, we will get involved in this thing.

From this statement one can see how the WMMTC created a context that encouraged the development of collaboration among firms. The role of the WMMTC as an impartial third party went beyond providing a structure for interaction to actually mediating the process by reconciling conflicting positions and defusing misunderstandings that arose among the firms. One supplier representative noted to us how the impartiality of the WMMTC helped to smooth the process:

> To make this kind of a program successful, anyplace, you have to have a neutral third party. And you've gotta have a sponsor, if you will. Somebody that can be the intermediary or the mediator, if you will. It's gotta be somebody that can help neutralize, you know, the misconceptions that can come up or that are in existence in the beginning.

As these and other interviewees emphasized, being impartial is integral to the effectiveness of network facilitators. Impartiality permits the network facilitator to overcome inherent suspicions among firms and to launch collaborative endeavors that would be difficult for the firms to initiate themselves.

Compressing Networks

Perhaps the most critical action taken by the WMMTC was organizing and coordinating forums where firms had the opportunity to interact on a regular basis, thereby increasing the density of the regional network. These forums took a number of different forms. The OFIC itself met on a monthly basis. Further, for each of the four standards, the WMMTC organized subcommittees composed of representatives from manufacturers and suppliers to develop standards and to oversee their dissemination and implementation. The subcommittees typically met weekly for a period of a year or more. In addition to the subcommittees, the WMMTC also formed approximately twenty user groups that brought together small groups of five to eight managers from supplier companies to jointly pursue continuous improvement issues on a regular basis. By far the largest and most significant event hosted by the WMMTC was the biannual Office Furniture Manufacturers and Suppliers Forum conference, where the subcommittees made progress reports and presented finalized standards to the broader office furniture industry.

Through the biannual conferences the WMMTC was able to have a direct effect on firms' commitments to collective action by publicizing their intentions and actions, thereby signaling the direction they were going. The biannual conferences served as a forum where the manufacturers could make public pronouncements and go on record about the standards they were preparing to adopt and preferred that their suppliers use. One important result of making such pronouncements publicly was to credibly commit firms to pursuing a course of action. Since the announcement to adopt a standard was made in front of other suppliers and manufacturers, if a firm did not follow through on its commitment it risked tarnishing its reputation. In effect, the biannual conferences provided a medium for signaling commitments and transmitting intentions to the broader industry. The biannual conferences were also occasions where the WMMTC announced the number of suppliers who had implemented a certain standard, thereby creating a bandwagon effect. A manufacturer representative described to us the function of the biannual conferences most succinctly:

> There are two basic elements of importance when you look at the forums that we have. One is a communication to the supplier community. Activities that are taking place, that have taken place. It's more of an update as to this is what we've been doing. Secondly, and equally important, is to share new opportunities. . . . [T]here's definitely an opportunity to meet people in other companies and industries. So there is some interface that can be developed. There are some relationships that can be established. . . . It's networking.

ividual suggests, the biannual conferences were not only
communicating the progress of the standards but also an
ving existing ties and creating new ones. These periodic
ated forums that allowed and facilitated novel patterns
_teractions by recombining networks among firms in the
region. In particular, firms attending the conferences were exposed to
many more contacts in one place than they would be otherwise. The
flow of information among firms was accelerated and firms and individuals could benefit from the richer interaction that occurs through
face-to-face dialogue with one or more people. An important result of
these interactions was the vicarious learning from other manufacturer
and supplier firms that were engaged in evaluating and implementing
the standards. In particular, comparing notes from discussions with several industry colleagues gave firms a better appreciation of the costs and
benefits of adopting the standards.

The forums that the WMMTC organized also provided a vehicle for
ensuring that individual firms remained on board and upheld their
commitments to the OFIC and other participating firms. The compres-
sion of the network that occurred at the forums increased the density of
ties, which enhanced monitoring and the formation of deterrence-based
trust. By making it more apparent which firms were pulling their weight
and which were not, the forums made it easier to detect and discourage
shirking and encouraged the continued participation, long-term commitment, and equitable contribution by individual firms to the collective endeavor. The difficulties encountered with ensuring that each firm
contributed its fair share were summarized by a representative of a participating supplier firm whom we spoke to:

> There have been some times that I personally—as well as other members
> of the council—had some frustration in that we have not always been able
> to gain and have 100 percent participation on a company by company
> basis. . . . So there's a perception that, you know, not every company's
> pulling their weight and supporting the process equally.

While the sanctions available to the firms participating in the OFIC
were somewhat limited, given the voluntary nature of the initiatives, the
forums organized by the WMMTC represented the most feasible means
of discouraging firms from failing to do their part in the collective undertaking. Establishing clear and unambiguous rules of participation, disseminating them widely, and making noncompliance patently obvious
held the most promise for enforcing firms' equitable contributions. In
effect, the forums allowed the participants to easily identify firms that
were not doing their part and collectively sanction the shirkers by the
threat of disapproval from industry colleagues, customers, and suppli-

ers. The quote from a representative of a participating supplier firm we interviewed captures how the rules in the forums were put into effect:

[W]e actually put together some written guidelines as to what and how we wanted to see the—how the council is to operate. And among the guidelines we put in there is that each company will have a member representative, and a designated alternate. And the implication is we expect every member company of the council to have someone at every meeting. And if you're the primary and you can't make it, we want you to have your alternate.

In this regard, it was less the WMMTC that disciplined errant firms than the firms themselves, acting with the backing of the OFIC. The legitimacy of the forums organized by the WMMTC was considerably enhanced by its reputation as a trustworthy and impartial entity.

The case of the western Michigan office furniture industry represents a successful collaboration among competitors, buyers, and suppliers. In this respect, the case tells a story similar to others about collaboration among competitors in geographical clusters. But this case is unique in that it provides insight into the role of a network facilitator and the actions it took that contributed to the realization of successful collaboration. More specifically, by identifying shared interests, developing common expectations, leveraging a critical mass of influence, and compressing networks, the WMMTC acted as a network facilitator and nudged firms toward levels of interfirm trust and collaboration that otherwise would have been difficult to achieve and sustain. What are the broader implications of the network facilitator role for understanding interfirm trust and collaboration? We discuss these next.

Discussion

Can trust be deliberately designed and constructed? The case of the western Michigan office furniture industry forces us to grapple with this question. What makes the question so intriguing is that we typically think of trust as an inherently relational phenomenon. Trust necessarily requires two parties—a trustor and a trustee. But is trust merely a dyadic, relational phenomenon, or are there other parties outside the relationship that influence the formation of trust between two parties? A growing body of research is beginning to advance the idea that context is a powerful force acting on the dynamics of trust (Rousseau et al. 1998). An exemplar of this emerging perspective is the compelling evidence reported by Ronald S. Burt and Marc Knez (1995) demonstrating how third-party gossip acts as a sort of ambient heat on trust formation that can accelerate the tendency toward, or away from, trust in a relationship. Third-party contacts that are strongly tied to one or both individuals in a

ιip tend to amplify trust predispositions in the relationship.
 an effort to solidify their own relationship to ego, a third
rm ego's preliminary assessment of alter as trustworthy,
 ego more certain of his or her belief in alter's trustwor-
 ιently, when ego is inclined to trust (distrust) alter, she or
... will be even more likely to do so in the presence of a third-party contact. The key insight we glean from this research is that network structure is a critical aspect of the context surrounding trust formation.

The case presented here is consistent with an emphasis on network structure, but adds another critical element to the mix: *network action.* The context surrounding trust formation consists of not only the pattern of relationships among actors but also the ways in which those actors engage, or disengage, themselves and each other around specific events, initiatives, and projects. The focus on action provides a useful vantage point from which to consider the contextual conditions conducive to the formation of trust. From this perspective, the formation of trust is indeed embedded in a context populated by third parties; third parties that we call network facilitators to emphasize their deliberate and intentional acts to promote and sustain trust (or alternatively, impede and derail it).

The actions taken by network facilitators that we have identified appear to operate on four different "pressure points" of the context surrounding trust formation by stimulating responses, releasing energy, and bypassing blockages. The network facilitator described in the case seemed to provide an initial charge at each pressure point and set off subsequent interactions that eventually gained sufficient momentum to become self-sustaining.[3]

The first pressure point that the network facilitator manipulated was salience of *interdependence* among firms that emerged in the course of identifying a set of shared interests. This realization prompted firms to recognize that they would have to rely on each other to fulfill their collective interests and it provided the impetus to further pursue the initiatives they had identified. Interdependence is widely recognized as a key condition for trust (Rousseau et al. 1998). Interestingly, the network facilitator in the case was able to use interdependence as a tool for fostering trust by first getting firms to recognize the extent of their mutual dependence. The network facilitator brought about the realization of interdependence by helping the firms to see their network structure more clearly (by identifying common suppliers), suggesting that the degree to which network structure is accurately perceived (Bondonio 1998; Casciaro 1998; Krackhardt 1987) plays an important role in trust formation. The network facilitator was also able to make the interdependence among firms more salient by accessing sensitive and proprietary information that the firms were not willing to share directly with each other. Here, the added value of a third party acting as a network facilitator is perhaps most visible. Without the involvement of the network facilitator it is doubtful that the firms would have been willing to share the information required to realize their degree of interdependence.

A second pressure point that the network facilitator zeroed in on was *risk*, which has also been identified as a key feature of the context within which trust develops (Rousseau et al. 1998). Once again, the network facilitator managed to employ risk as a tool that engaged certain actors, set in motion ongoing interactions, and bypassed various obstacles. In particular, the network facilitator carefully selected firms to lead the industry initiatives that were known to be risk takers and willing to take a chance, rather than adopting a wait-and-see attitude. This highlights the fact that rather than viewing risk as exogenous, the network facilitator saw it as something to be manipulated and used to the network's advantage. The network facilitator also sought to mitigate the risk these firms faced by keying in on the individuals within those firms who stood to gain the most from the project and helping them understand in very concrete terms the rewards attached to the risks. These actions associated with managing risk were vital because they helped overcome the chicken-and-egg problem of who moves first and takes the initial steps toward developing trust. Once one firm demonstrates its good-faith intentions by taking some action, other firms will find it easier to follow and act on their own inclination. Obviously, if all firms waited for somebody else to move first, nobody would have taken a risk. Selecting risk takers and influencing their perception of risk are actions that helped resolve the problem of who moves first.

A third pressure point the network facilitator used to help overcome the problem of who moves first was its own *social capital*—its network of social and professional ties. More specifically, one of the ways the network facilitator was able to increase firms' confidence in each other was to put its own credibility on the line and vouch for the trustworthiness of the other participating firms. Because of its history of successful interactions with businesses in the community, the support it enlisted from other credible economic development organizations, and the personal reputation of the director, the WMMTC was trusted by the firms participating in the OFIC. Moreover, by saying "trust us" the WMMTC as a network facilitator was redirecting the placement of trust and at the same time transforming dyadic trust relationships into triadic relationships. For instance firm A was more willing to trust firm B's integrity because firm A trusted the network facilitator's judgment about firm B, and because the network facilitator trusted firm B's integrity. In this way, the network facilitator was able to transfer trust (McEvily, Zaheer, and Perrone 2003; Stewart 2003) by acting as an advisory intermediary (Coleman 1990). Brokering trust in this way requires the network facilitator to invest its social capital. Such an investment entails risk because the network facilitator's reputation as a competent adviser is at stake. At the same time, if the network facilitator invests its social capital soundly it can enjoy a healthy return in the form of increased trust throughout the network—an example of how investing social capital can produce a multiplier effect. At the same time, the network facilitator's impartiality was another valuable feature of its social capital that permitted it to sponsor the industry initiatives in a way that avoided suspicion and concerns about parochial, rather than collective, interests being served.

The final pressure point that the network facilitator employed was *physical space*. The forums organized provided a venue for firms to meet, interact, exchange information and advice, and remain up-to-date with the latest developments. Even more important, they reconfigured and compressed the network in a way that increased density. As a result of the increased density the forums enhanced the credibility of commitments. At the same time, the greater density of the network provided the firms with a more effective means of detecting shirking and enforcing norms (Coleman 1990). This sort of deterrence-based trust (Burt and Knez 1995) can be an effective means of sustaining the initial momentum created in the trust formation process.

Interdependence, risk, social capital, and physical space are some of the most vital organs in the anatomy of the trust formation process. We have discussed these as pressure points to emphasize the idea that network facilitators act on these elements in ways that engage, energize, and ease interactions among others. The job of the network facilitator is to create and shape a context conducive to trust formation, and to set the process in motion. What happens next is in large part determined by how the members of a network respond to the network facilitator's actions and by how the network facilitator continues to guide the process. While it is ultimately the members of a network that determine whether and to what extent trust is constructed, network facilitators can play an important role by serving as the architects of trust, who design and organize a supportive social context.

Not only is our concept of a network facilitator relevant to the office furniture industry in western Michigan, but it also appears to fit well with examples of collective action in other geographical clusters. For instance, we venture that the Semiconductor Equipment and Materials Institute (SEMI) in Silicon Valley (Saxenian 1994) embodies attributes of a network facilitator. Like the WMMTC, SEMI convened forums that provided opportunities for industry colleagues to interact and compressed "social and professional networks in time and space" (Saxenian 1994, 49). By fostering the development of common expectations and mutual trust, SEMI was instrumental in the development of industry standards. Similarly, the Manufacturing Innovation Networks in Pennsylvania (MAIN) brought together formerly antagonistic parties and helped them to develop mutual trust (Sabel 1993). By surfacing long-held assumptions that acted as barriers to cooperation, the MAIN project facilitated the identification of shared interests among the participants. In this way, MAIN performed the role of a network facilitator to a considerable degree.

Although network facilitators appear to play an active role in other geographical clusters, there are some boundary conditions that limit the generalizability of our theory. In particular, the applicability of our network facilitator model may be limited in clustered industries with a dominant firm. For instance, in the garment industry clustered in northern Italy, Benetton is not only the lead firm but also the coordinating hub in a network of specialist producers and subcontractors that do not have direct access to downstream markets (Heskett and Signorelli 1982). Consequently, Benetton is by itself able to exert influence over its supply chain to bring about collective action. We also recognize that our network facilitator model may not apply in cases where there is a legitimate regulatory body enforcing cooperative agreements. For example, in the Champagne district in France, the industry association Comité Interprofessionel du Vin de Champagne (CIVC) is vested with formal regulatory authority by the state (Cool and Henderson 1996). In both of these cases, the authority of a dominant firm or a state regulatory body is unquestioned and the entity is able to enforce rules and sanctions to limit free riding and achieve cooperation and collective action without the need for an external network facilitator or, for that matter, for much trust. In contrast, in the office furniture industry of western Michigan there is a large number of manufacturers rather than a single dominant firm, and there is no regulatory body to oversee the enforcement of cooperative agreements. In such a setting, a network facilitator becomes necessary to create the context for the creation of network trust and for collective action to take place.

Summary

We propose that the role of a network facilitator in a network is a critical feature of the economic success of geographical clusters. Network facilitators allow and encourage firms to surmount the problems inherent in the provision of public goods by acting on "pressure points" and taking actions that capitalize on their embeddedness in regional networks to actively engineer networks of trust.

We thank Joe Galaskiewicz, Stefanie Lenway, Susan McEvily, Pri Shah, Andy Van de Ven, and Sri Zaheer for their thoughtful comments and useful suggestions on earlier versions of this paper. We would also like to gratefully acknowledge the generosity and valuable insights of the individuals from the western Michigan area who participated in the case study.

Notes

1. This case study draws on semistructured interviews conducted between May 1995 and November 1996 with current and former officials of Michigan's economic development agencies and with representatives of participating supplier and manufacturer firms. The length of the interviews varied from thirty minutes to two hours. All interviews were tape-recorded and transcribed. Unless otherwise noted, all quotations in the case study come from interviews. We also drew on various articles appearing in the business press between 1993 and 1995 discussing the cooperative arrangements in the office furniture industry of western Michigan. We analyzed these data following the guidelines for theory building from case study research (Eisenhardt 1989). The field interviews and archival materials were first examined in an exploratory fashion to identify consistent patterns in the data (Miles and Huberman, 1984). Next, we compared similarities and differences across interviews to derive a preliminary set of constructs and theoretical relationships. We then iteratively refined the constructs and relationships by applying them to each of the interviews, and by relating them to similar theoretical concepts and relationships in the extant literature, until there was theoretical saturation (Glaser and Strauss 1967; Strauss and Corbin 1998).

2. This comment was made in reference to the MAIN program in Pennsylvania.

3. In this respect, the actions of network facilitators are analogous to those of the federal government when it provides stimulus packages to "prime the economic pump" during downturns.

References

Bondonio, Danielle. 1998. "Predictors of Accuracy in Perceiving Informal Social Networks." *Social Networks* 20: 301–30.

Burt, Ronald S., and Marc Knez. 1995. "Kinds of Third-Party Effects on Trust." *Rationality and Society* 7(3): 255–92.

Casciaro, Tiziana. 1998. "Seeing Things Clearly: Social Structure, Personality, and Accuracy in Social Network Perception." *Social Networks* 20(4): 331–51.

Coleman, James S. 1990. *Foundations of Social Theory*. Cambridge, Mass.: Harvard University Press.

Cool, Karel, and James Henderson. 1996. "Establishing and Maintaining Industry Cooperation: The Case of the Champagne Industry." Working paper. Cedex, France: INSEAD.

Dybvig, Philip H., and Chester S. Spatt. 1983. "Adoption Externalities as Public Goods." *Journal of Public Economics* 20: 231–47.

Eisenhardt, Kathleen. 1989. "Building Theories from Case Study Research." *Academy of Management Review* 14(4): 532–50.

Glaser, Barney G., and Anselm L. Strauss. 1967. *The Discovery of Grounded Theory: Strategies for Qualitative Research*. Chicago: Aldine.

Heskett, James L., and Sergio Signorelli. 1982. "Benetton (A)." Case study, number 9-685-014. Boston: Harvard Business School.

Kanter, Rasabeth M. 1995. *World Class: Thriving Locally in the Global Economy.* New York: Simon & Schuster.

Katz, Michael L., and Carl Shapiro. 1985. "Network Externalities, Competition, and Compatibility." *American Economic Review* 75(3): 424–40.

Krackhardt, David. 1987. "Cognitive Social Structure." *Social Networks* 9: 109–34.

Krugman, Paul. 1991. *Geography and Trade.* Cambridge, Mass.: MIT Press.

McEvily, Bill, Akbar Zaheer, and Vincenzo Perrone. 2003. "Trust as an Organizing Principle." *Organization Science* 14(1): 91–103.

Miles, Matthew B., and A. Michael Huberman. 1984. *Qualitative Data Analysis.* Beverly Hills: Sage.

Nohria, Nitin. 1992. "Information and Search in the Creation of New Business Ventures: The Case of the 128 Venture Group." In *Networks and Organizations,* edited by Nitin Nohria and Robert G. Eccles. Boston: Harvard Business School Press.

Osborne, David E. 1988. *Laboratories of Democracy.* Boston: Harvard Business School Press.

Porter, Michael E. 1990. *The Competitive Advantage of Nations.* New York: Free Press.

Powell, Walter W. 1990. "Neither Market nor Hierarchy: Network Forms of Organization." *Research in Organizational Behavior* 12: 295–336.

Rousseau, Denise M., Sim B. Sitkin, Ronald S. Burt, and Colin Camerer. 1998. "Not So Different After All: A Cross-Discipline View of Trust." *Academy of Management Review* 23(3): 393–404.

Sabel, Charles F. 1993. "Studied Trust: Building New Forms of Cooperation in a Volatile Economy." *Human Relations* 46(9): 1133–70.

Saxenian, Anna Lee. 1994. *Regional Advantage: Culture and Competition in Silicon Valley and Route 128.* Cambridge, Mass.: Harvard University Press.

Scott, Allen J. 1992. "The Roepke Lecture in Economic Geography: The Collective Order of Flexible Production Agglomerations: Lessons for Local Economic Development Policy and Strategic Choice." *Economic Geography* 68(3): 219–33.

Stewart, Katherine J. 2003. "Trust Transfer on the World Wide Web." *Organization Science* 14(1): 5–17.

Storper, Michael. 1992. "The Limits to Globalization—Technology Districts and International Trade." *Economic Geography* 68(1): 60–93.

Strauss, Anselm L., and Juliet Corbin. 1998. *Basics of Qualitative Research: Techniques and Procedures for Developing Grounded Theory.* Thousand Oaks, Calif.: Sage.

Chapter 9

Trust in Context: The Development of Interpersonal Trust in Geographically Distributed Work

ROXANNE ZOLIN AND PAMELA J. HINDS

WITH THE help of Internet technologies such as email and computer-based collaboration tools, the number of geographically distributed cross-functional teams, the number of sites at which team members work (Armstrong and Cole 2002), and the interdependence of the tasks undertaken by distributed teams are increasing. Although remote work groups have existed for a very long time (see King and Frost 2002), historically, remote operations undertook more independent activities, such as the sourcing and transportation of goods (O'Leary, Orlikowski, and Yates 2002). Today's distributed teams perform highly interdependent tasks such as creative design and problem solving. Such strong interdependence, however, requires trust (Sheppard and Sherman 1998; Shapiro 1987).

In this chapter we explore the relationship between geographic distribution and trust among distributed and collocated members of global teams. We examine the development of trust between members of these teams as well as the effect of trust on individual performance.

Trust has been defined as "a psychological state comprising the intention to accept vulnerability based on positive expectations of the intentions or behavior of another irrespective of the ability to monitor or control that other party" (Rousseau et al. 1998, 395; see also Mayer,

Davis, and Schoorman 1995). Trust, however, is only meaningful within a particular context or situation (see Gambetta 1988). Russell Hardin (2000) offers the trust equation "A trusts B about X." The trustor, person A, trusts the trustee, person B, about X, the object of trust, which is the task or behavior that the trustor expects. We add "Z" to the equation to create "A trusts B about X when Z," where Z is the context of trust or the situation in which the trustor and trustee are embedded. We believe that examining the object and context of trust are particularly important in the work environment, where trust may be narrowly construed to encompass performance of a particular task and one's ability to act may be largely determined by the characteristics of the context in which one works.

Trust Development

In their model of organizational trust, Roger C. Mayer, James H. Davis, and F. David Schoorman (1995) argue that trust develops as a function of the trustor's propensity to trust, the extent to which the trustee perceives the trustor as trustworthy, and the trustor's perception of situational risk. They argue that perceived trustworthiness is a function of how capable (ability), how benevolent, and how honorable (integrity) the trustor perceives the trustee to be. They add that risk will moderate the relationship between the trustor's attitude and his or her willingness to act in a trusting way such that higher levels of trust will be required when higher levels of risk are present. Roxanne Zolin and her colleagues (2004) add several components to the Mayer, Davis, and Schoorman (1995) model. They argue that the trustor's assessment of the rewards possible from the situation also come into play in determining the trustor's behavior, more completely capturing the situational determinants of trust. They also add the trustor's perception of the trustee's performance, arguing that perceived trustworthiness will be updated to reflect the extent to which trustees are perceived as following through on commitments.

The model of trust development presented above may not, however, obtain for all situations. In particular, we consider the situation in which coworkers are geographically distant from one another and must rely heavily on technology to mediate their interaction. In these situations, trust may be particularly important because monitoring is more difficult. Ironically, trust also may be more difficult to develop because coworkers have fewer opportunities to interact face-to-face, have less unplanned interaction, rely more heavily on technology to mediate their interactions, and often are more heterogeneous because they inhabit different cultural contexts.

Trust in Geographically Distributed Dyads

The trend toward distributed work is growing (Armstrong and Cole 2002). In a recent study, respondent firms reported that 63 percent of their new product development teams would be geographically distributed within the next few years, and 22 percent of these would be globally distributed (McDonough, Kahn, and Barczak 2001). Although distributed work is becoming increasingly prevalent, little is known about the social dynamics that result for distributed workers (see Maznevski and Chudoba 2000). For the purposes of this paper, we define a geographically distributed team as one in which some team members are located in different cities or countries. Similarly, geographically distributed dyads are pairs of coworkers who are located in different cities or countries. Hence, in many geographically distributed teams some dyads are distributed and some are collocated.

Geographical distribution of coworkers means that they spend less time in the presence of one another, often have different physical and cultural contexts, and rely more heavily on technologies such as telephone, email, video and teleconferencing, Internet chat, and facsimile to mediate their interactions. Because distant coworkers generally spend less time in the presence of one another, they are less likely to develop rapport and trust (Kiesler and Cummings 2002). With distance, spontaneous interaction is more difficult, which contributes to reduced information sharing and interpersonal attraction between members (Kiesler and Cummings 2002). Simply being present with others also increases feelings of familiarity (Zajonc 1968), which has been linked to the development of trust on work teams (Wilson 2001).

In addition to reduced physical proximity, distributed coworkers often inhabit different physical, organizational, and cultural contexts. Members in different locations may use different technologies, have different work processes, conform to different interaction norms, be paid according to different reward and compensation systems, have different vacation schedules, confront different stressors (such as economic or political issues), and have different cultural perspectives. For example, David J. Armstrong and Paul Cole (2002) describe a situation in which "the two sites had different definitions of completed product quality and tested their work with different procedures. These differences caused unexpected conflicts and delays and were taken by either side as signs of bad faith and political maneuvering" (200). In addition to creating or fueling conflict, occupying different contexts can detract from mutual understanding (Clark and Brennan 1996; Fussell and Kreuz 1992; Olson and Olson 2000). Catherine D. Cramton (2001) describes five problems that result from differences in context: (1) failure to communicate contextual information, (2) uneven distribution of information, (3) differences in speed of access to information, (4) difficulty in communicating and understanding the salience of information, and (5) difficulty in interpreting the meaning of silence. Because the development of trust is in part based upon information about the trustee and the situation, reduced or inaccurate information about the trustee is likely to negatively affect the development of trust. Ronald S. Burt and Marc Knez (1996) also offer evidence that the probability of trust will increase with indirect connections that are likely to provide gossip and rumor. When embedded in different social contexts, indirect connections are less prevalent and consequently trust may be inhibited.

Distributed coworkers also must rely more heavily on technology to mediate their interaction. Reliance on communication technologies has been associated with less social interaction (Sproull and Kiesler 1991; see also Olson and Olson 2000), more time pressure, less information sharing (Hollingshead 1996), more misunderstandings (Armstrong and Cole 2002; Cramton 2001), and more conflict (Hinds and Bailey 2003). Communication technologies, in comparison to face-to-face interaction, make it more difficult to convey many of the social cues (touch, gestures, voice intonation, facial expressions, and so forth) that are helpful for interpreting feedback and negotiating understanding.

We believe that gathering the information required to assess the extent to which someone is a caring and honorable person, and to assess their competence vis-à-vis the task that must be accomplished will be difficult when coworkers are distant, occupy a different context, and are reliant upon technologies for interaction. Because the development of trust is based largely upon information that the trustor has about the trustee and the situation, such a reduction in information is likely to inhibit the development of trust. For example, Rebecca E. Grinter, James D. Herbsleb, and Dewayne E. Perry (1999, 312) reported that team members on distributed teams had more difficulty assessing the competence of others—they did not trust that those at remote sites could "handle the work assigned to them."

Hypothesis 1: Trust will be lower in distributed dyads than in collocated dyads.

There is evidence that trust changes over time as people gather more information and update their perceptions (Kramer 1999; Rousseau et al. 1998; Lewicki and Bunker 1996). In our model, we assume that perceived trustworthiness will be updated as coworkers observe the performance of their colleagues and evaluate the extent to which they follow through on commitments. However, individuals rarely seek disconfirming information and may actually try to avoid it (Good 2000).

Therefore, trust may be resistant to change once established and thus more stable over time than predicted (see Ring and van de Ven 1994). This may be particularly true in distributed work because disconfirming information may be less visible (see Cramton 2002). Thus, distributed coworkers may be able to avoid disconfirming information and sustain their initial (and perhaps inaccurate) impressions of trustworthiness for an extended period of time. This is consistent with the findings of Sirkka L. Jarvenpaa and Dorothy E. Leidner (1999) that distributed teams that establish trust from the beginning are more likely to sustain high levels of trust.

We do, however, expect some development of trust between distributed workers over time. Although distance and reliance on mediating technologies may prove challenging, there is evidence that people adapt to media (for example, Markus 1994; Orlikowski 2000; Zack and McKenney 1995) and develop close interpersonal relationships over time (Walther 1997).

Hypothesis 2: Distributed coworkers modify their trust of one another over time, but less so than collocated coworkers.

In their model, Mayer, Davis, and Schoorman (1995) propose that risk will moderate the relationship between trust and trust behavior. They suggest that trust will more likely result in trust behavior when risk is perceived to be low and that greater levels of trust will be required when risk is high. Zolin et al. (2004) extend and modify this aspect of Mayer and colleagues' model by adding perceived reward—the extent to which the trustor stands to benefit from the interaction. For example, if the task has the potential to result in great value and reliance on the trustee is the best way to attain that value, then the potential reward is great and trust is likely to increase.

Normally, one would suppose that high levels of risk would make trust more difficult whereas generous rewards would motivate coworkers to trust one another so that the reward could be achieved. However, we posit that risk will loom larger in geographically distributed dyads than in collocated dyads, for two reasons. First, we anticipate that coworkers will experience work with distant coworkers as inherently more risky. Regardless of the reality of the situation, people enjoy distributed work less and report that they find success more elusive in distributed situations (for example, McDonough, Kahn, and Barczak 2001). Thus, any amount of risk will be more salient and more likely to inhibit the development of trust. We anticipate that this effect will be particularly strong when the rewards of the task are perceived as weak.

Hypothesis 3: Coworkers' trust will be predicted by perceived risk more in distributed dyads than in collocated dyads.

Trust and Performance

Trust between coworkers can have a positive effect on performance (see Hughes, Rosenbach, and Clover 1983; Klimoski and Karol 1976), although this effect may be moderated by motivation (Dirks 1999). In geographically distributed settings, we expect the trust-performance relationship to be even stronger. As discussed earlier, distributed coworkers have more opportunities for miscommunications and misinterpretations. They also have less opportunity to talk through issues, gain clarification, and resolve misunderstandings. Thus, distributed coworkers may be called upon more frequently to give their coworkers "the benefit of the doubt" when the others' actions are not visible and are subject to misinterpretation. Distributed coworkers may need to rely on trust to avoid a downward cycle of blame and faulty attributions, which could result in withholding of information, competition between group members, and an unwillingness to coordinate work. In a recent study of firms with new product-development teams, behavioral challenges were reported to have a significant effect on the performance of distributed teams and "generating trust between team members" was seen as one of the top three behavioral challenges for these teams (McDonough, Kahn, and Barczak 2001).

We predict two effects of trust on individual performance. First, we predict that *being trusted* will translate to better performance. When trusted, coworkers are more likely to share information (Clegg et al. 2002; Klimoski and Karol 1976) and to give their colleagues the benefit of the doubt. Chris Clegg and colleagues (2002), for example, found that organizational trust increased the level of idea suggestion and implementation among aerospace design engineers. When trusted, coworkers are likely to feel more psychological safety and experience a stronger sense of commitment to the work. Second, we predict that working with others one trusts will improve performance. We reason that *trusting others* will result in increased psychological safety and a stronger sense of commitment. Akbar Zaheer, Bill McEvily, and Vicenzo Perrone (1998), for instance, found that interpersonal trust plays a direct role, in conjunction with organizational trust, in lowering negotiation costs in interorganizational exchange. Similar results were found in Jeffrey H. Dyer and Wujin Chu's (2003) study of Japanese, U.S., and Korean car manufacturers, in which perceived trustworthiness was associated with greater information sharing and lower transaction costs. In sum, we argue that trusting and being trusted by coworkers will be associated with better performance.

Hypothesis 4a: Being trusted by coworkers will be associated with better performance.

Hypothesis 4b: Having more trust in one's coworkers will be associated with better performance.

Method

To evaluate the development of trust in geographically distributed dyads, we studied student construction design teams that each included an architect, a structural engineer, and a construction manager. Students reported on average eight months of full-time work experience in their field and twelve academic courses in the relevant disciplines. We observed the teams over three consecutive years; the survey data we present was collected in the last year.

Over a period of three years, we studied student teams to understand the development of interpersonal trust between distributed and collocated coworkers. Student teams were chosen for three main reasons. First, student teams replicate a work environment more closely than other forms of research methodology, such as a laboratory experiment. Second, student teams can be studied more closely than industry teams by means of surveys and interviews. Students provide higher response rates to questionnaires and allow the more frequent surveys required for longitudinal studies. Third, student teams form at the same time, work on the same task, and operate in the same organizational environment. By holding constant these factors, we have a more controlled setting in which to examine our variables of interest.

Participants

As described in Zolin et al. (2004), the participants for this study were students in the seventh and eighth generation of a computer integrated architecture-engineering-construction (A-E-C) class organized by Stanford University (Fruchter 1999). Master's degree candidates attending American, European, and Asian universities and drawn from three different disciplines—architecture, engineering, and construction management—worked in globally distributed teams for four months to design a five-million-dollar building according to a client's specifications. The graduate students were assisted by undergraduate "apprentices" and mentored by globally distributed professionals working in each discipline.

To facilitate assignment to groups, students were randomly assigned a skill profile (for example, experience working in an earthquake zone) during an initial face-to-face meeting attended by all students. Each project had a specific characteristic, such as being located in an earthquake zone. In an ice-breaking exercise, students identified and joined the project that best suited their randomly assigned skill profile (for example, those with experience working in earthquake zones were likely to join projects with a building to be located in an earthquake zone). By chance, each team included at least one member who was not collocated. By necessity, each team had to have at least one team member from each of the three disciplines. After the two-day project launch, teams did not meet again face-to-face until the final presentation four months later. Distributed coworkers communicated mainly through computer-based Internet applications. Internet meeting applications allowed audio and video communication and desktop file sharing. Internet message applications allowed synchronous message transfer between two or more parties. Collocated dyads also used face-to-face meetings as needed.

Data Collection

We provided online surveys and conducted structured interviews with forty-five participants in twelve teams composed of three to four team members each, distributed among ten locations in six countries: the United States, Switzerland, Holland, Germany, Slovenia, and Japan. All team members participated in the research, and we received a 100 percent response rate on both surveys. During the first week of the project we gathered information about the number of courses taken, work experience in each discipline, and the students' perceptions of their own risks and rewards associated with the project. Approximately one month later and again three months later, we distributed dyadic surveys in which we asked each team member to rate each of his or her other team members on trustworthiness (benevolence, ability, and integrity) and follow-through and to indicate the extent to which they checked on the work of each other team member (our measure of trust). This survey yielded 108 usable dyadic responses, responses from A about B.

Dependent Variables

The primary dependent variables of interest in this study are trust and performance.

Trust. Zolin and her colleagues (2004) describe a measurable behavior that indicates trust: monitoring or checking on the work of the trustee. Numerous authors note the inverse correlation between trust and monitoring or checking (Strickland 1958; Gambetta 1988; Kramer 1999). To create a measure of checking, we averaged across four items from the dyadic survey (see table 9.1). The scale reliability for the four items was acceptable (alpha = .77). Each item was rated on a five-point scale with 5 equating to high levels of checking. By reverse-coding our checking variable, we created a measure of trust.

Table 9.1   Survey Questions

Trust
1. How often have you needed to check or ask to see if this team member had completed her or his commitments?[a]
2. How often have you counted or compared to see if this team member was contributing to the group?[a]
3. How often have you worried about this team member's performance?[a]
4. How often have you checked on this team member's progress on the deliverables promised?[a]

Risk
1. How much is at stake for you (what do you have to lose) if one team member does not do his or her job?

Reward
1. What goals do you hope to achieve with this project? (Not directly used)
2. How important are those goals?

Perceived trustworthiness
Care
1. How often has this team member made an extra effort to make your job easier?
2. How often has this team member listened carefully to hear your problems or concerns?
3. How often has this team member notified you when she could not meet a commitment?
4. How often has this team member passed on new information or ideas that may be helpful to you or the group?
5. How often does this team member check to make sure that communication was received or understood?
Ability
1. How often has this team member exhibited technical or project competence?
2. How often have you noticed that team member exhibit professional behavior?
Integrity
1. To what extent is this team member honest or dishonest?[a]
2. To what extent is this team member virtuous or sinful?[a]

Follow-through
1. How often did this team member follow through on work commitments?
2. How often did this team member fail to follow through on work commitments?[a]
3. How often did this team member complete work commitments on time?
4. How often did this team member fail to complete work commitments on time without good reason?[a]

Source: Based on Zolin et al. 2004.
[a]These items were reverse-coded.

Performance. To create a measure of individual performance, we used the student's final grade. A portion of the grade was determined on the basis of the students' contributions to the project in their own disciplinary areas (architecture, engineering, or construction management), which they presented at the end of the project. Another significant portion of the grade was based on the overall team project. A multidisciplinary team of faculty and industry experts assessed the individual and team presentations. Thus, we considered the grade to be a reasonable measure of the student's performance on the project.

Independent Variables

The primary independent variables of interest in this study are geographic distribution; the trustor's perception of the trustworthiness of the trustee; the trustor's perception of the follow-through of the trustee; and the trustor's perception of risk and reward.

Geographic distribution. This is a dichotomous variable in which dyads are either located on the same campus (collocated = 0) or split between two distant campuses (distributed = 1). Distributed dyads could be separated by just fifty miles or could be as far apart as different continents. We examined the effect of time zones but saw little difference, so we collapsed distribution into a single dichotomous variable.

Perceived trustworthiness. This independent variable was measured in the dyadic surveys by asking the trustor questions about perceptions of the perceived trustworthiness of the trustee. Consistent with Mayer, Davis, and Schoorman (1995), we conceptualized perceived trustworthiness as being composed of benevolence, ability, and integrity. Each of the items (see table 9.1) was measured on a five-point scale with 5 equal to high and 1 equal to low perceived trustworthiness. The items were averaged to compute the value for perceived trustworthiness. We confirmed that the scale for perceived trustworthiness was reliable as a single factor in both month 1 and month 3 (alpha = .84 and .84, respectively).

Perceived risk and reward. This was assessed from questions administered the first week of the project (see table 9.1). The scale for these items was 1 to 5 where 5 was equal to high levels of risk or reward.

Perceived follow-through. This was a measure of the trustor's perception of the extent to which the trustee followed through on commitments and delivered work on schedule (Zolin et al. 2004, see table 9.1). Four items were measured on a five-point scale with 5 equivalent to high levels of follow-through. To create a measure of perceived follow-through, we averaged across the four items. The scale had a reliability of .89 (month 1) and .88 (month 3).

Analysis

We tested our hypotheses using linear regression models and structural equation modeling. Because our data were dyadic, we tested the assumption that the trustor's trust is independent of the trustee's trust, in other words, that reciprocal trust does not exist. To test this assumption we conducted a test for autocorrelation. However, the Durbon-Watson

(Hamilton 1992) test statistic was higher than the upper limit (d = 2.14), suggesting that reciprocation of trust was not strong in the dyads we studied.

We conducted structural equation modeling using the estimation procedure of AMOS (Hoyle 1995; Byrne 2001) to observe the effects of variables over time. Our goal was to test our hypotheses about trust development in distributed dyads as compared with collocated dyads. Hence, we adopted a strictly comparative analysis approach. We also used Bollen-Stine bootstrapping to adjust for the small sample size and non-normal distributions of variables (which can overestimate the χ^2 statistic and lead to rejection of acceptable models) thus improving our ability to assess model fit (Byrne 2001).

Results

We collected data at three points in time to enable us to conduct longitudinal analyses. The descriptive statistics for and correlations between our variables are provided in table 9.2. On the whole, participants reported a moderate level of trust with the average being 3.49 (SD = .87) on a five-point scale at month 1 and 3.58 (SD = .70) at month 3. As expected, the correlation between trust at month 1 and trust at month 3 (r = .32, p < .001) was positive and significant, suggesting that initial trust predicted later trust. Perceived trustworthiness at month 1 also predicted trust at month 3 (r = –.44, p < .001) indicating that perceived trustworthiness may have contributed to later trust.

In hypothesis 1, we argued that trustors in distributed dyads, as compared with those in collected dyads, will trust their coworkers less. We therefore expected a negative relationship between geographic distribution and trust. We compared the mean level of trust of distributed and collocated dyads in month 1 and month 3 (see figure 9.1). In an ANOVA (analysis of variance) analysis comparing distributed and collocated dyads, we found no significant difference at month 1 (F[1, 106] = .04, p < .85) or at month 3 (F[1, 106] = .69, p < .41). Although we found that collocated dyads experienced greater perceived trustworthiness than distributed dyads, these differences were not significant. In ANOVA analyses comparing perceived trustworthiness in distributed and collocated dyads, we found that distributed dyads reported higher perceived trustworthiness at month 3 (F[1, 105] = 5.26, p < .02), although not at month 1 (F[1, 106] = 2.40, p < .12). Thus, although trust did not vary significantly between distributed and collocated dyads, perceived trustworthiness was significantly greater among collocated dyads, providing some support for hypothesis 1.

Hypothesis 2 was that distributed dyads will update their trust less over time than will collocated dyads. A quick look at figure 9.1 reveals

Table 9.2 Descriptive Statistics and Correlations for Variables

	Mean	Standard Deviation	1.	2.	3.	4.	5.	6.	7.	8.	9.	10.	11.
1. Trust (month 1)	3.49	.87											
2. Geographic distribution	.71	.45	-.02										
3. Risk	3.68	.71	.12	.06									
4. Reward	4.19	.91	.13	.16	-.08								
5. First-quarter grade	3.71	.50	.02	.02	-.17+	-.08							
6. Perceived trustworthiness (month 1)	3.58	.75	.22*	-.15	-.26**	.13	-.23*						
7. Perceived follow-through (month 1)	3.94	.82	.47***	-.13	-.18+	.23*	-.05	.59***					
8. Trust (month 3)	3.58	.70	.32***	-.08	-.17+	.16+	-.02	.44***	.44***				
9. Perceived trustworthiness (month 3) Second-quarter grade	3.80	.46	-.07	-.11	-.13	-.11	.79***	-.12	-.01	.03			
10. Perceived trustworthiness (month 3)	3.93	.68	.16+	-.22*	-.38***	.05	.01	.55***	.46***	.60***	-.01		
11. Perceived follow-through (month 3)	3.99	.67	.04	-.17+	-.30**	.17+	-.03	.50***	.50***	.66***	.07	.76***	
12. Courses taken	11.49	5.41	-.22*	-.05	-.33***	-.13	.04	.27**	.11	.15	.18+	.18+	.13

Source: Authors' compilation.
Note: N = 108.
+p < .10 *p < .05 **p < .01 ***p < .001

Figure 9.1   Comparisons of Mean Levels of Trust for Distributed and Collocated Dyads for Months 1 and 3 on Scale of 1 to 5

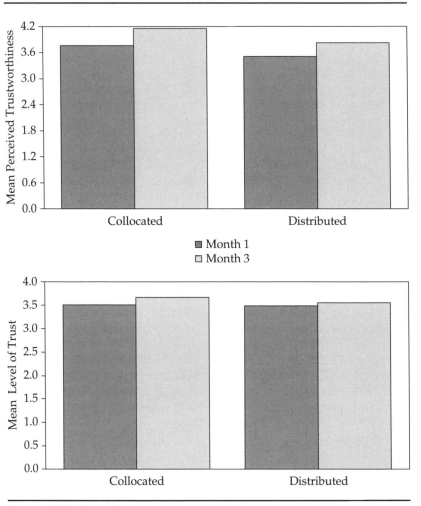

Source: Authors' compilation.
Note: N = 108.

that members of collocated dyads did not change their level of trust from month 1 to month 3 any more than the members of distributed dyads. A one-way ANOVA confirms no significant difference between distributed and collocated dyads in the change in trust between month 1 and month 3 ($F[1, 106] = .20$, $p < .66$). These analyses, however, merely suggest that average levels of trust did not change. It is possible that trust changed more in collocated dyads but that the averages obscure increases and decreases in trust. We therefore examined more closely the changes in trust. An examination of absolute difference in trust between month 1 and month 3 indicates that distributed dyads exhibited significantly less change than collocated dyads (F[1, 107] = 4.09, p < .05). Over 19 percent of the collocated dyads experienced increased trust in their coworkers, whereas only 9 percent of distributed dyads increased trust from month 1 to month 3. Further, over 16 percent of the collocated dyads decreased trust for their coworkers whereas only 10 percent of distributed dyads decreased trust from month 1 to month 3. These analyses provide some support for hypothesis 2, indicating that trust may increase less but that it also may deteriorate less in distributed as compared with collocated dyads.

In our logic leading up to hypothesis 2, we argued that participants will use performance information—perceived follow-through—to update their perception of the trustworthiness of their coworkers. To the extent that coworkers are perceived to have delivered on commitments, perceived trustworthiness should increase. To the extent that coworkers are not perceived as delivering on commitments, perceived trustworthiness should decrease. We expected this effect to be stronger in collocated dyads because they are able to gather data about their coworkers' performance more easily than members of distributed dyads. To investigate this we created a structural equation model (AMOS) that reflected the predicted relationships (see model 1, figure 9.2). In model 1, we analyzed only collocated dyads and found that perceived follow-through at month 1 predicts perceived trustworthiness at month 1 and ultimately trust at month 3. When using the data from collocated dyads, this model fit well (χ^2 [1, N = 31] = .023, p = .88). When testing the same model with data from the distributed dyads, however, model 2 fit poorly (χ^2 [1, N = 77] = 8.92, p < .003), providing support for our arguments that distributed coworkers use performance data less to update their perceptions than do collocated coworkers. In fact, a better fit with the data from the distributed dyads is a model in which perceived follow-through mediates the relationship between perceived trustworthiness at month 1 and trust at month 3 (χ^2 [1, N = 77] = 3.30, p < .07, see model 3, figure 9.2). To determine model fit, we used several standard fit indexes. B. M. Byrne (2001) reports that a value above .95 in the RFI index indicates superior fit. The RFI of model 2 for distributed dyads is below .95 (.931) whereas the RFI of model 3 is above .95 (.974), indicating that model 3 has a more acceptable fit than model 2 for our sample of distributed dyads.

To further test hypothesis 2, that trust is more stable over time in distributed dyads, we constructed two structural equation models showing the change in our variables over time in collocated and distributed dyads (see figure 9.3). Model 4 includes only our sample of collocated dyads and reveals no significant relationships between perceived follow-through, perceived trustworthiness, or trust at month 1 or month 3; con-

Figure 9.2   Structural Equation Models Predicting Perceived Trustworthiness and Trust

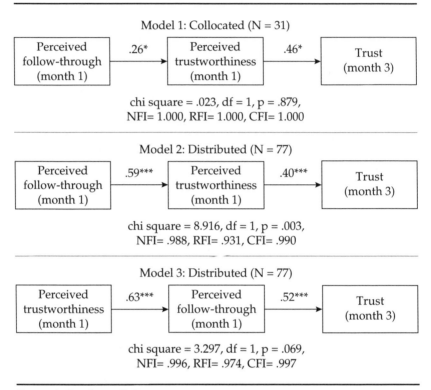

Model 1: Collocated (N = 31)

| Perceived follow-through (month 1) | .26* → | Perceived trustworthiness (month 1) | .46* → | Trust (month 3) |

chi square = .023, df = 1, p = .879,
NFI= 1.000, RFI= 1.000, CFI= 1.000

Model 2: Distributed (N = 77)

| Perceived follow-through (month 1) | .59*** → | Perceived trustworthiness (month 1) | .40*** → | Trust (month 3) |

chi square = 8.916, df = 1, p = .003,
NFI= .988, RFI= .931, CFI= .990

Model 3: Distributed (N = 77)

| Perceived trustworthiness (month 1) | .63*** → | Perceived follow-through (month 1) | .52*** → | Trust (month 3) |

chi square = 3.297, df = 1, p = .069,
NFI= .996, RFI= .974, CFI= .997

Source: Authors' compilation.
$+p < .10$ $*p < .05$, $**p < .01$, $***p < .001$

sequently the model has a very poor fit (χ^2 [8, N = 31] = 38.677, p = .000, with NFI = .947, RFI = .860 and CFI = .957). Model 5, which includes only our sample of distributed dyads, indicates significant relationships between perceived trustworthiness at month 1 and month 3, perceived follow-through at month 1 and month 3, and trust at month 1 and month 3. The model has an acceptable fit ((χ^2 [8, N = 77] = 18.8, p = .016), with NFI = .989, RFI = .971 and CFI = .994), suggesting that perceived trustworthiness, perceived follow-through, and trust are all fairly stable across time in these teams. These analyses provide additional support for hypothesis 2.

Hypothesis 3 is that members of distributed dyads will use risk as a basis for trust more than members of collocated dyads. We used ordinary least square (OLS) regression models to test this hypothesis (see table 9.3). When only risk and reward were used to predict trust they were not significant for either collocated or distributed dyads (see models 6a and

Figure 9.3   Structural Equation Models Predicting Trust Development

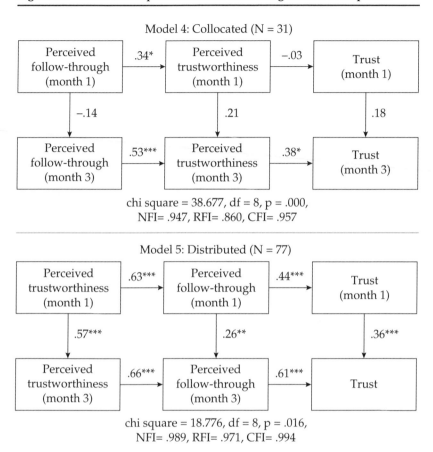

Model 4: Collocated (N = 31)

chi square = 38.677, df = 8, p = .000,
NFI= .947, RFI= .860, CFI= .957

Model 5: Distributed (N = 77)

chi square = 18.776, df = 8, p = .016,
NFI= .989, RFI= .971, CFI= .994

Source: Authors' compilation.
+*p* < .10 **p* < .05, ***p* < .01, ****p* < .001

6b, table 9.3). We theorized that the effect of risk on trust would be moderated by the reward perceived in the situation, such that high risk would reduce trust unless rewards also were high. Therefore we reversed the risk term to represent low risk and multiplied it by reward to create a term representing the interaction between low risk and reward. When this interaction term was added to the model for collocated dyads (model 7a), risk (β = 2.96, p < .01), reward (β = 3.22, p < .001) and the interaction term (β = –4.15, p < .01) were significant. With distributed dyads, when the interaction term was added to model 7b, none of the terms were significant, although risk (β = .96, p < .10) and reward (β = .65, p < .10) were more strongly predictive than the interaction term (β = –.99, n.s.). This

Table 9.3   OLS Estimation of Trust in Month 3 for Collocated and
             Distributed Dyads

	Collocated		Distributed	
Independent Variables	6a	7a	6b	7b
Intercept	***	*	***	
Low-risk	.18	2.96**	.18	.96+
Reward	.05	3.22***	.15	.65+
Low-risk X reward		−4.15**		−.99
Adjusted R-squared	−.03	.26	.04	.05
Model F	.49	4.49*	2.53+	2.39+
Degrees of freedom	2, 28	3, 27	2, 74	3, 73

Source: Authors' compilation.
Note: For models 6a and 7a, N = 31. For models 6b and 7b, N = 77.
$+p < .10$, $*p < .05$, $**p < .01$, $***p < .001$

evidence provides no support for hypothesis 3, that risk would be stronger in distributed dyads. In fact, these analyses suggest that risk and rewards may be more salient in collocated than distributed dyads.

Hypotheses 4a and 4b are that trust will be important to individual performance, both to those who are trusted by and those who are able to trust their coworkers. To test this we constructed two structural equation models of the proposed relationships between trust and individual performance (see figure 9.4, models 8 and 9). Because performance is measured at the individual level, we used the individual as our unit of analysis for this test and therefore our sample size was reduced to 41. We included four variables in the models. In the model predicting the effect of being trusted by one's coworkers (model 8), we included the extent to which the coworker was perceived as trustworthy by all of her team members (averaged across team members), the extent to which the coworker was trusted by all of her team members, and the coworker's grade at month 2 and month 4. In the model predicting the effect of trusting one's coworkers (model 9), we included the extent to which the coworker perceived his team members to be trustworthy (averaged across team members), the extent to which the coworker trusted his team members, and the coworker's grade at month 2 and month 4. Although the models are a good fit to the data, neither model suggests a strong relationship between trust and performance. However, the model predicting the effect of being trusted (model 8) resulted in a more significant relationship between trust and performance (p = .13 versus p = .50). Although these analyses do not provide support for hypothesis 4a or 4b, the results of model 8 suggest that future research on the effect of being trusted by one's team members may be warranted.

Figure 9.4   Structural Equation Model Predicting Performance

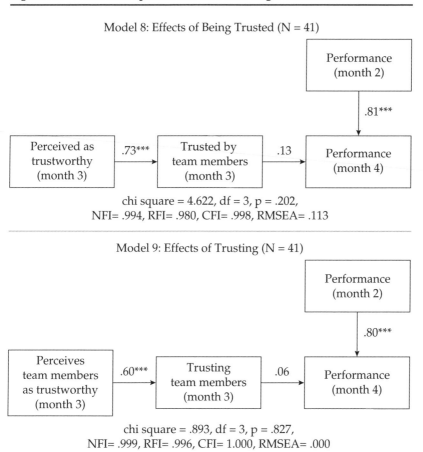

Model 8: Effects of Being Trusted (N = 41)

chi square = 4.622, df = 3, p = .202,
NFI= .994, RFI= .980, CFI= .998, RMSEA= .113

Model 9: Effects of Trusting (N = 41)

chi square = .893, df = 3, p = .827,
NFI= .999, RFI= .996, CFI= 1.000, RMSEA= .000

Source: Authors' compilation.
+$p < .10$, *$p < .05$, **$p < .01$, ***$p < .001$

Discussion

In this chapter we examine the effect of geographic distribution on the development of trust. Although we expected to find less trust between team members who were geographically distant, we found no evidence of this. We did, however, find that perceived trustworthiness was lower in distributed than in collocated dyads. We also found that trust was more stable and may develop differently in geographically distributed than in collocated dyads. In the collocated dyads we studied, trust was more volatile—both increasing and decreasing more over time than in distributed dyads. Collocated team members also updated trust on the basis of their perceptions of their team members' follow-through on commitments, although distributed team members appeared to use their initial perceptions of trustworthiness to evaluate follow-through. These data suggest that first impressions can be particularly powerful and enduring on geographically distributed teams.

Our data also provide some support for the argument that distributed teams will invoke "swift trust"—trust that is conferred on the basis of the role the trustee occupies (Meyerson, Weick, and Kramer 1996; Jarvenpaa and Leidner 1999). "Swift trust" can provide the basis for impersonal trust when trust is necessary and there is not adequate time to develop it. Sirkka L. Jarvenpaa and Dorothy E. Leidner (1999) reported that some distributed teams they studied developed "swift trust"—establishing trust early on and maintaining it throughout a six-week project—but that others had difficulty developing trust if it was not established from the beginning. Our results also indicate that trust between distributed workers was relatively stable over time. If it started out high, then it tended to remain high throughout the project. These findings suggest that trust may be difficult to develop in distributed teams, but that "swift trust" could be a desirable alternative.

It is, however, important to consider that the teams in our sample met at the beginning of the project for at least two days of ice-breaking exercises and project planning. This allowed the partners in distributed dyads to form rich first impressions of one another. Many distributed team members do not have this opportunity and in fact may never meet face-to-face. We believe that team members who do not meet face-to-face early in the project will not establish such high levels of trust and may not be able to maintain high levels of trust over an extended project. Therefore, it is important that future research examine the development of trust in distributed teams that do not have the opportunity to meet face-to-face or teams that meet for the first time at a later stage in the project.

It is also important to note that trust *did* change over time in distributed dyads even though it did not change as much as it did in collocated dyads. There is ample evidence that distributed team members adapt to distance and to the technologies on which they rely (see, for example, Zack and McKenney 1995) and learn to develop strong interpersonal relationships with distant colleagues (see Walther 1997). Distributed team members in our sample increased trust (9 percent) as nearly much as they decreased it (10 percent), although collocated team members increase trust (19 percent) more than they decreased it (16 percent). These data suggest that trust may be more difficult to create and may deteriorate more at a distance, but more research is needed to evaluate this claim.

Contrary to our expectations, we did not find that trust between members of distributed dyads was more sensitive to perceived risk than it was for those in collocated dyads. In fact, we found the opposite—that trust between members of collocated dyads was more sensitive to perceived risk. There are several possible explanations for these results. First, given our measure of trust (checking), these results effectively mean that those in collocated, high-risk situations feel the need to check more frequently on their coworkers. Those who are distributed from their coworkers, however, may feel that checking on them is too difficult or time consuming, so they elect to not do so. Thus, distributed workers, even though they perceive the situation to be high-risk, may be compelled to trust their team members because it is an easier option. Second, risk may be more salient for collocated workers because they are regularly reminded of the interdependence between themselves and their coworkers while distributed workers may be lulled into forgetting the interdependence they share (see Grinter, Herbsleb, and Perry 1999). Thus, fears about project success may manifest themselves in reduced trust between collocated coworkers. Unfortunately, we do not have the data to evaluate this conjecture, but hope that future research will more deeply explore the complex relationship between risk and trust.

As predicted, collocated coworkers used their evaluation of follow-through to update perceived trustworthiness. In contrast, distributed coworkers used their assessment of perceived trustworthiness to evaluate follow-through. In addition to affecting the development of trust in distributed dyads, this could have implications for the ability of coworkers to accurately assess the quality of work produced by their distant colleagues. With the data we have, it is difficult to ascertain whether or not the impressions of coworkers were sound. It is possible, for example, that distributed coworkers are less influenced by factors unrelated to performance such as attractiveness, friendliness, or ethnicity than are collocated coworkers. Closer examination of the relationship between interpersonal impressions and perceived performance in distributed work seems to be a fruitful direction for future research.

There are several limitations to the study we present here. First, all of the dyads that we studied were embedded in distributed teams. Our comparisons were not between collocated and distributed teams, but between collocated and distributed members of distributed teams. Although this is not necessarily an issue when examining interpersonal trust, it does weaken our ability to generalize the results to collocated teams or to collocated dyads that are members of collocated teams. This issue is complicated by the fact that many distributed teams have some collocated and some distributed dyads, as our teams did. Our sample of teams was small (n = 12), so it was not possible to conduct analyses to understand the dynamics of team-level trust on distributed teams. We believe that this is an important avenue for future research. Our sample of collocated dyads also was small (n = 31). Such a small sample may have obscured differences that existed. Therefore, we caution the reader to look at the patterns that we uncovered and not at the differences we neglected to find.

Another possible limitation to this work is the scale we used to measure trust: the trustor's desire to check on the trustee. Many writers highlight the close relationship between trust and checking, or monitoring (Strickland 1958; Gambetta 1988; Kramer 1999). Although this measure is consistent with our definition of trust, it is an indirect measure. Unfortunately, reliable alternatives have yet to be developed. We believe that the development of more direct behavioral measures of trust is an important area for future research.

This work also was conducted with student teams. Although this enabled us to examine dyads that were similar on many dimensions, to better isolate the factors in which we were interested, and to conduct longitudinal research with a reasonably high response rate (and minimal turnover), we assume that trust and the development of trust between members of cross-functional, distributed teams in an industry setting are more complex than we were able to observe. With a better understanding of how trust may develop differently in distributed dyads, we are armed to conduct future research in teams that are embedded in a more complex organizational environment.

With the caveats above, we offer several recommendations for members and managers of distributed teams. First, it appears from this and other work that first impressions are particularly important for distributed work. It may therefore be important that coworkers meet face-to-face early in the life of the project, getting to know one another and discussing project goals (Armstrong and Cole 2002; Kraut et al. 1992). Although trust did not appear to vary between collocated and distributed dyads, perceived trustworthiness did, suggesting that distant coworkers may benefit from receiving more information and assurance about their coworkers' capabilities, benevolence, and integrity. Given the power of first impressions, this information should be shared as early as possible in the project or relationship. Finally, our study suggests that distributed dyads may have difficulty observing others' performance and gathering performance information. Facilitating the sharing of this information is an important role for leaders of distributed work (see also Weisband 2002). Formal procedures (reports, meetings, and so forth) also may alleviate the need to monitor the work of distant colleagues (see O'Leary, Orlikowski, and Yates 2002). In sum, early face-to-face meetings, more information about the abilities and character of distant colleagues, and more explicit sharing of performance information between coworkers might facilitate the development of trust among geographically distributed workers, laying the groundwork for better performance.

The authors would like to thank the students, faculty, and mentors of Stanford University's CEE222 class for their participation in the "Trust in Global Teams" research project.

This research was supported in part by National Science Foundation grant IIS-9872996 to the second author.[1]

Notes

1. Correspondence concerning this article should be addressed to Roxanne Zolin, Graduate School of Business and Public Policy, Naval Postgraduate School, P.O. Box 433, Marina, Calif. 93933, phone: (831) 865-1700, email: rvzolin@nps.navy.mil.

References

Armstrong, David J., and Paul Cole. 2002. "Managing Distances and Differences in Geographically Distributed Work Groups." In *Distributed Work*, edited by Pamela J. Hinds and Sara Kiesler. Cambridge, Mass.: MIT Press.

Burt, Ronald S., and Marc Knez. 1996. "Trust and Third-Party Gossip." In *Trust in Organizations: Frontiers of Theory and Research*, edited by Roderick M. Kramer and Tom R. Tyler. Thousand Oaks, Calif.: Sage.

Byrne, Barbara M. 2001. *Structural Equation Modeling with AMOS: Basic Concepts, Applications, and Programming*. Mahwah, N.J.: Erlbaum.

Clark, Herbert H., and Susan E. Brennan. 1996. "Grounding in Communication." In *Perspectives on Socially Shared Cognition*, edited by Lauren B. Resnick, John M. Levine, and Stephanie D. Teasley. Washington, D.C.: American Psychological Association.

Clegg, Chris, Kerrie Unsworth, Olga Epitropaki, and Giselle Parker. 2002. "Implicating Trust in the Innovation Process." *Journal of Occupational and Organizational Psychology* 75(4): 409.

Cramton, Catherine D. 2001. "The Mutual Knowledge Problem and Its Consequences in Geographically Dispersed Teams." *Organization Science* 12(3): 346–71.

———. 2002. "Attributions in Distributed Work Groups." In *Distributed Work*, edited by Pamela J. Hinds and Sara Kiesler. Cambridge, Mass.: MIT Press.

Dirks, Kurt T. 1999. "The Effects of Interpersonal Trust on Work Group Performance." *Journal of Applied Psychology* 84(3): 445–55.

Dyer, Jeffrey H., and Wujin Chu. 2003. "The Role of Trustworthiness in Reducing Transaction Costs and Improving Performance." *Organizational Science* 14(1): 57–68.

Fruchter, Renate. 1999. "Architecture/Engineering/Construction Teamwork: A Collaborative Design and Learning Space." *ASCE Journal of Computing in Civil Engineering* 13(4): 261–70.

Fussell, Susan R., and R. J. Kreuz. 1992. "Coordination of Knowledge in Communication: Effects of Speakers' Assumptions About What Others Know." *Journal of Personality and Social Psychology* 62(3): 378–91.

Gambetta, Diego. 1988. *Trust: Making and Breaking Cooperative Relations.* Oxford: Blackwell.

Good, David. 2000. "Individuals, Interpersonal Relations, and Trust." In *Trust: Making and Breaking Cooperative Relations,* edited by Diego Gambetta. Available at www.sociology.ox.ac.uk/papers/good31–48.doc.

Grinter, Rebecca E., James D. Herbsleb, and Dewayne E. Perry. 1999. "The Geography of Coordination: Dealing with Distance in R & D Work." Paper presented at the 1999 SIGGROUP conference, Phoenix (November 14–17).

Hamilton, Lawrence C. 1992. *Regression with Graphics: A Second Course in Applied Statistics.* Belmont, Canada: Duxbury Press.

Hardin, Russell. 2000. *Trust and Trustworthiness.* New York: Russell Sage Foundation.

Hinds, Pamela J., and Diane E. Bailey. 2003. "Out of Sight, Out of Synch: Understanding Conflict on Distributed Teams." *Organization Science* 14(6): 615–32.

Hollingshead, Andrea. 1996. "Information Suppression and Status Persistence in Group Decision Making." *Human Communication Research* 23(2): 193–219.

Hoyle, Rick H. 1995. *Structural Equation Modeling: Concepts, Issues, and Applications.* Thousand Oaks, Calif.: Sage.

Hughes, Richard L., William E. Rosenbach, and William H. Clover. 1983. "Team Development in an Intact, Ongoing Work Group: A Quasi-Field Experiment." *Group and Organizational Studies* 8: 161–86.

Jarvenpaa, Sirkka L., and Dorothy E. Leidner. 1999. "Communication and Trust in Global Virtual Teams." *Organization Science* 10(6): 791–815.

Kiesler, Sara, and Jonathan C. Cummings. 2002. "What Do We Know About Proximity and Distance in Work Groups? A Legacy of Research." In *Distributed Work,* edited by Pamela J. Hinds and Sara Kiesler. Cambridge, Mass.: MIT Press.

King, John L., and Robert L. Frost. 2002. "Managing Distance over Time: The Evolution of Technologies of Dis/Ambiguation." In *Distributed Work,* edited by Pamela J. Hinds and Sara Kiesler. Cambridge, Mass.: MIT Press.

Klimoski, Richard J., and Barbara L. Karol. 1976. "The Impact of Trust on Creative Problem Solving Groups." *Journal of Applied Psychology* 61: 630–33.

Kramer, Roderick M. 1999. "Trust and Distrust in Organizations: Emerging Perspectives, Enduring Questions." *Annual Review of Psychology* 50: 569–98.

Kraut, Robert, Jolene Galegher, Robert Fish, and Barbara Chalfonte. 1992. "Task Requirements and Media Choice in Collaborative Writing." *Human Computer Interaction* 7(4): 375–407.

Lewicki, Roy J., and Barbara B. Bunker. 1996. "Developing and Maintaining Trust in Work Relationships." In *Trust in Organizations: Frontiers of Theory and Research,* edited by Roderick M. Kramer and Tom R. Tyler. Thousand Oaks, Calif.: Sage.

Markus, M. Lynne. 1994. "Finding a Happy Medium: Explaining the Negative Effects of Electronic Communication on Social Life and Work." *ACM Transactions on Information Systems* 12(2): 119–49.

Mayer, Roger C., James H. Davis, F. David Schoorman. 1995. "An Integrative Model of Organizational Trust." *Academy of Management Review* 20(3): 709–34.

Maznevski, Martha L., and Katherine M. Chudoba. 2000. "Bridging Space over Time: Global Virtual Team Dynamics and Effectiveness." *Organization Science* 11(5): 473–92.

McDonough, Edward F., Kenneth B. Kahn, and Gloria Barczak. 2001. "An Investigation of the Use of Global, Virtual, and Collocated New Product Development Teams." *Journal of Product Innovation Management* 18(ER2): 110–20.

Meyerson, Debra, Karl E. Weick, and Roderick M. Kramer. 1996. "Swift Trust in Temporary Groups." In *Trust in Organizations: Frontiers of Theory and Research,* edited by Roderick M. Kramer and Tom R. Tyler. Thousand Oaks, Calif.: Sage.

O'Leary, Michael, Wanda Orlikowski, and JoAnne Yates. 2002. "Distributed Work over the Centuries: Trust and Control in the Hudson's Bay Company." In *Distributed Work,* edited by Pamela J. Hinds and Sara Kiesler. Cambridge, Mass.: MIT Press.

Olson, Gary, and Judith Olson. 2000. "Distance Matters." *Human Computer Interaction* 15(2/3): 139–79.

Orlikowski, Wanda. 2000. "Using Technology and Constituting Structures: A Practice Lens for Studying Technology in Organizations." *Organization Science* 11(4): 404–28.

Ring, Peter S., and Andrew H. van de Ven. 1994. "Development Process of Cooperative Interorganizational Relationships." *Academy of Management Review* 19(1): 90–118.

Rousseau, Denise M., Sim B. Sitkin, Ronald S. Burt, and Colin Camerer. 1998. "Not So Different After All: A Cross-Discipline View of Trust." *Academy of Management Review* 23(3): 393–404.

Shapiro, Susan P. 1987. "The Social Control of Impersonal Trust." *American Journal of Sociology* 93(3): 623–58.

Sheppard, Blair H., and Dana M. Sherman. 1998. "The Grammars of Trust: A Model and General Implications." *Academy of Management Review* 23(3): 422–37.

Sproull, Lee, and Sara Kiesler. 1991. *Connections: New Ways of Working in the Networked Organization.* Cambridge, Mass.: MIT Press.

Strickland, Lloyd H. 1958. "Surveillance and Trust." *Journal of Personality* 26: 200–15.

Walther, Joseph B. 1997. "Group and Interpersonal Effects in International Computer-Mediated Collaboration." *Human Communication Research* 23(3): 342–68.

Weisband, Suzanne. 2002. "Maintaining Awareness in Distributed Team Collaboration: Implications for Leadership and Performance." In *Distributed Work,* edited by Pamela J. Hinds and Sara Kiesler. Cambridge, Mass.: MIT Press.

Wilson, Jeanne M. 2001. "The Development of Trust in Distributed Groups." Ph.D. diss., Carnegie Mellon University.

Zack, Michael H., and James L. McKenney. 1995. "Social Context and Interaction in Ongoing Computer-Supported Management Groups." *Organization Science* 6(4): 394–422.

Zaheer, Akbar, Bill McEvily, and Vicenzo Perrone. 1998. "Does Trust Matter? Exploring the Effects of Interorganizational and Interpersonal Trust on Performance." *Organization Science* 9(2): 141–59.

Zajonc, Robert B. 1968. "Attitudinal Effects of Mere Exposure." *Journal of Personality and Social Psychology* 9: 1–27.

Zolin, Roxanne, Pamela J. Hinds, Renate Fruchter, and Raymond E. Levitt. 2004. "Interpersonal Trust in Cross-Functional, Geographically Distributed Work: A Longitudinal Study." *Information and Organization* 14(1): 1–26.

Chapter 10

Psychological Safety, Trust, and Learning in Organizations: A Group-Level Lens

AMY C. EDMONDSON

There's much greater openness on this team—it's intangible.
—Marketing member, new-product development team,
manufacturing company

[In this team] people are put down for being different.
—Accountant, publications team, manufacturing company

Mistakes [in this unit] are serious, because of the toxicity of the drugs—
so you're never afraid to tell the nurse manager.
—Nurse, team A, "Memorial Hospital"

[The team leader] treats you as guilty if you make a mistake. . . . I was
called into her office and made to feel like a two-year old. . . . You get
put on trial.
—Nurse, team B, "Memorial Hospital"

MUCH WORK in today's organizations is accomplished collabora-
tively and involves sharing information and ideas, integrating
perspectives, and coordinating tasks. Teams provide a structural mechanism through which this collaboration often occurs. A defining characteristic of teams is the need for different individuals to work

together to achieve a shared outcome (Hackman 1987). Both the research literature and anecdotal experiences of people who have worked on teams suggest that working interdependently with others is not always easy. Put simply, some teams work—members collaborate well—and others don't (Hackman 1990). What allows people to openly share ideas and contribute a part of themselves to a collaborative undertaking? This paper argues that understanding how people perceive the interpersonal climate in the teams in which they work is an important part of the larger question of understanding both teamwork and learning in organizations. Trust, the unifying theme of this volume, is a critical input to this interpersonal climate, as is mutual respect. In this chapter I show that such a climate, which I refer to as one of psychological safety, enables the willing contribution of oneself—of one's ideas and actions—to collective work.

A recent increase in research on trust in organizations suggests a growing interest in intrapsychic states that affect performance and other organizational outcomes (Kramer 1999). Most research on trust has focused on either the experiences of individuals or on organizations as entities and on the ways trust can facilitate interorganizational relationships, such as with suppliers or customers. This paper examines *psychological safety,* an intrapsychic state that is especially salient at the group level of analysis. Later I suggest that psychological safety has particular salience for small groups, in the same way that trust is particularly relevant for the dyadic relationship.

The presence and absence of psychological safety can be inferred from the statements of people working in team situations. The four quotations presented here are selected from hundreds of similar statements in which team members almost immediately volunteer descriptions that reveal the presence or absence of psychological safety in their teams in response to an open-ended question such as "What is it like to work in this team?" Despite the important relationship of psychological safety to trust, trust does not accurately capture a particular dimension of interpersonal experience conveyed in these descriptions: a sense of how valued and comfortable an employee feels in that work setting. This paper presents evidence from recent studies of operating-room (OR), nursing, new-product development, management, service, and production teams to illustrate how the construct of psychological safety differs from the related construct of trust and to propose antecedents and consequences of psychological safety in work teams. I also examine implications of team psychological safety for organizational learning, limitations of the construct, and areas for future research.

Psychological Safety and Trust

Psychological safety and trust both describe intrapsychic states related to interpersonal experience, and so it is important to clarify conceptual differences between these related constructs, as well as to establish empirical evidence of the existence and value of psychological safety—the less familiar concept. I highlight psychological safety as a distinct, complementary phenomenon that, like trust, can affect various behavioral and organizational outcomes. This section thus distinguishes psychological safety from trust and illustrates this difference by drawing on my own and others' research.

Psychological Safety Defined

Psychological safety describes individuals' perceptions about the consequences of interpersonal risks in their work environment. It consists of taken-for-granted beliefs about how others will respond when one puts oneself on the line, such as by asking a question, seeking feedback, reporting a mistake, or proposing a new idea. I argue that individuals engage in a tacit calculus at behavioral micro-decision points, whereby they assess the interpersonal risk associated with a given behavior against the particular interpersonal climate: "If I do X here, will I be hurt, embarrassed, or criticized?" A negative answer indicates psychological safety, so that the actor can proceed. Thus, an action that might be unthinkable in one work group can be readily taken in another, owing to different beliefs about probable interpersonal consequences.

Others have defined psychological safety similarly. William A. Kahn (1990, 708) described it as "feeling able to show and employ one's self without fear of negative consequences to self-image, status, or career." In a qualitative field study, Kahn found that psychological safety was one of three psychological conditions that "shaped how people inhabited their roles" (703) in an organization. Recent empirical research shows that psychological safety promotes work engagement (May, Gilson, and Harter, forthcoming). Similarly, in classic research on organizational change, Edgar Schein and Warren Bennis (1965) proposed that a work environment characterized by psychological safety is necessary for individuals to feel secure and thus capable of changing their behavior.

More recently, Schein (1985, 298–99) argued that psychological safety helps people overcome the defensiveness, or "learning anxiety," that occurs when they are presented with data that disconfirm their expectations or hopes, which can thwart productive learning behavior. Psychological safety does not imply a cozy environment in which people are necessarily close friends, nor does it suggest an absence of pressure or problems. Rather, it describes a climate in which the focus can be on productive discussion that enables early prevention of problems and accomplishment of shared goals, because people are less likely to focus on self-protection. For this reason, particular attention has been paid to psychological safety in the clinical psychology literature, as an important element of the therapeutic context (Rappoport 1997; Swift and Copeland 1996; Waks 1988).

Unlike most research on psychological safety, my work has focused specifically on the experience of people in organizational work teams. Work teams are groups within the context of a larger organization, with clearly defined membership and shared responsibility for a team product or service (Alderfer 1987; Hackman 1987); such teams may contain five to twenty people. I focus on the team rather than the individual as the locus of psychological safety. I posit *team psychological safety* as a group-level construct, meaning that the construct characterizes the team as a unit rather than individual team members. Consistent with this, I argue that perceptions of psychological safety tend to be highly similar among people who work closely together, such as members of an intact team, both because team members are subject to the same set of contextual influences and because these perceptions develop out of salient shared experiences (Edmondson 1999a). For example, most members of a team will conclude that making a mistake does not lead to rejection when they have had team experiences in which appreciation and interest are expressed in response to discussion of their own and others' mistakes. The similarity of beliefs in social systems such as organizations or work groups is the subject of much inquiry (see reviews by Klimoski and Mohammed 1994; Walsh 1995).

Definitions of Trust

Although a concise and universally accepted definition of trust has remained elusive (Creed and Miles 1995; Kramer 1999), most definitions include an aspect of perceived risk of vulnerability—also an element of psychological safety as noted above. As discussed below, however, the nature of this vulnerability is more narrowly defined for psychological safety than for trust. Roger C. Mayer, James H. Davis, and F. David Schoorman (1995, 712) conceptualize trust as "the willingness of a party to be vulnerable to the actions of another party, based on the expectation that the other will perform a particular action important to the truster, irrespective of the ability to monitor or control the other party." Similarly, Gareth R. Jones and Jennifer M. George (1998, 531–32) maintain that trust is "an expression of confidence between the parties in an exchange of some kind—confidence that they will not be harmed or put at risk by the actions of the other party or confidence that no party to the exchange will exploit the other's vulnerability." These authors argue that "trust leads to a set of behavioral expectations among people, allowing them to manage the uncertainty or risk associated with their interactions so that they can jointly optimize the gains that will result from cooperative behavior" (532).

Trust is often conceptualized in terms of choice—that is, in terms of the truster's decision-making process. Roderick Kramer (1999) identifies two approaches in the trust literature, rational and relational models of choice. Although psychological safety also involves an element of choice—generally a tacit choice—its definition is easily distinguished from definitions of trust within the rational model, in which individuals are presumed to make efficient choices on the basis of risk evaluation by maximizing expected gains or minimizing expected losses. In this model, people choose to trust when it is rational to do so. Such rational choices are made through "conscious calculation of advantages, a calculation that in turn is based on an explicit and internally consistent value system" (Schelling 1960, 4; cited in Kramer 1999). This includes evaluating the incentives of the other person to honor that trust (see discussion in Kramer 1999). The relational model, in contrast, takes into consideration social aspects, conceptualizing trust "not only as a calculative orientation toward risk, but also a social orientation toward other people and towards society as a whole" (Kramer 1999, 573). In this model, choices are more affective and intuitive than calculative.

Psychological Safety Versus Trust

As noted above, the concepts of psychological safety and trust have much in common: they both describe psychological states involving perceptions of risk or vulnerability and making choices to minimize negative consequences, and both have potential positive consequences for work groups and organizations. However, they are also distinct interpersonal beliefs. Three elements of psychological safety are described to distinguish it from trust: the object of focus, time-frame, and level of analysis.

Focus on "Self" Versus "Other"   People often equate trust with giving others the benefit of the doubt—indicating a focus on *others'* potential actions or trustworthiness. In discussing psychological safety, the question is instead whether others will give *you* the benefit of the doubt, when, for instance, you have made a mistake. When two nurses in different teams at Memorial Hospital described the interpersonal context in which they worked, one reported that she was "never afraid" to tell her team's manager about mistakes, while the other reported being "made to feel like a two-year-old" by the manager in her team.[1] Although it might be the case that the first nurse trusted her manager and the second did not, the meaning of these descriptions is not captured by the construct of trust. Instead, they depict an interpersonal belief that pertains to feelings of safety in interpersonal interactions. A nurse who reports being made to feel like a two-year-old is likely to monitor her *own* actions to protect herself, rather than trying to protect herself by monitoring *others'* actions.

Narrow Temporal Bounds   The tacit calculus inherent in psychological safety considers the very short-term interpersonal consequences one expects from engaging in a specific action. For example, a nurse facing the decision of whether to ask a physician in the unit about a questionable medication dosage may be so focused on the potential immediate consequences of this question, such as being scolded or humiliated for being uninformed, that she temporarily discounts the longer-term consequence of *not* speaking up—the harm that may be caused to a patient. Although the differential weighting of consequences in this example is clearly irrational, I have heard countless similar stories across markedly different organizational settings. The experience of the nurse in team B highlights this point. After embarrassing past encounters with her manager, she was inclined to avoid speaking up about errors for fear of getting "put on trial," thereby unwittingly discounting the longer-term consequences for patients and for the team of her silence. In contrast to these short-term calculations, the construct of trust pertains to anticipated consequences across a wide temporal range, including the relatively distant future.

Group-Level Analysis   As noted earlier, team psychological safety is proposed to characterize groups, rather than describing individual or temperamental differences. It is conceptualized as an emergent property of the collective that describes the level of interpersonal safety experienced by people in a particular group. Members of work teams tend to hold similar perceptions about this, about "the way things are around here," because they are subject to the same influences (for example, by having a common manager) and because many of their beliefs develop out of shared experiences. Thus, team members of the team B nurse who reported being "made to feel like a two-year-old" independently reported similar feelings of discomfort about speaking up, commenting, for example, that "nurses are blamed for mistakes" and if you make a mistake, "doctors bite your head off." These nurses, either from personal or vicarious experience, came to the conclusion that, on this team, reporting mistakes was interpersonally penalized. In summary, the presence or absence of psychological safety tends to be experienced at the group level of analysis (Edmondson 1999a), unlike trust, which pertains primarily to a dyadic relationship, whether between individuals or collectives such as firms (as in supplier relationships).

Studying and Measuring Psychological Safety

I start by reviewing methods I have used in studies of work groups in health care and business organizations. I then review other research on groups in settings ranging from a summer camp to a social science organization.

Recent Research on Psychological Safety in Work Groups

Field research in four distinct organizational settings has explored the nature and role of psychological safety in work groups. Each has taken a slightly different approach to measuring psychological safety, in part driven by ongoing refinement of the construct and in part driven by constraints inherent in a given research site or situation. To clarify how psychological safety can be measured these projects are summarized below.

Medication Error Study   In a study designed to investigate the effects of team structure on the rate of medication errors, an unexpected result suggested the possibility of differences in psychological safety across eight nursing teams in two hospitals. The highest-performing of these teams, with the most skilled nurse managers, had higher detected error rates than teams lower on these dimensions. Using interviews, observation, and archival data, I found significant differences in members' beliefs about the social consequences of reporting medication errors (Edmondson 1996). These beliefs could be characterized as tacit; they were automatic, taken-for-granted assessments of the "way things are around here," like those of the nurses. These beliefs varied markedly across the teams: in some teams, members saw it as self-evident that speaking up is natural and necessary, and in others speaking up was viewed as a last resort. The level of psychological safety thus could be inferred from members' spontaneous reports about what it was like to work in their team and how they viewed the reporting of errors. These inferences, made by a research assistant unaware of my hypotheses, were highly correlated with detected error rates. Finally, the study included a single survey question, "If you make a mistake in this team, is it held against you?" This also provided a rough index of team psychological safety.

Change Program Study   Amy Edmondson and Anita Woolley (2003) used interviews and a survey to study an organization-wide change program in a large manufacturing company, and found that psychological safety was associated with the acceptance and perceived usefulness of the program. First, in interviews we noticed that people who supported the new program were more likely to report a sense of psychological safety; for example, one subordinate successfully using the program's guidelines with his manager explained, "I could be myself, I don't have to put on an act of anything, worry about saying the wrong thing because something [bad] may happen if I do." In contrast, a manager in a dyad in which the program was regarded cynically reported, "I've been stepped on a few times for being too straightforward. . . . I'm not real comfortable that there wouldn't be repercussions" for speaking up about problems. From the interview data we developed a six-item survey variable (see table 10.1) to assess psychological safety. This measure had adequate psychometric properties and was a significant predictor of program acceptance and success, also measured by the survey. The focus in this study was on dyadic relationships, and psychological safety was measured at the individual level of analysis, with several items focusing specifically on the manager relationship.

Manufacturing Company Study   In a study of fifty-one teams of different types (including management, new-product development, sales and production teams), I developed and tested a new seven-item survey measure of team psychological safety, shown in table 10.1 (Edmondson 1999a). This measure displayed internal consistency reliability and discriminant validity, and predicted team learning behavior and team performance as rated by independent observers. Other survey variables (from Hackman 1990) assessing team characteristics were included in the study, allowing me to examine the relationship between psychological safety and well-designed teams. The study included extensive observation of and interviews with subsets of the teams to establish the correspondence between qualitative and quantitative data assessing psychological safety and other variables. Analysis of the individual-level survey data (n = 427) demonstrated the convergence of team members' perceptions of psychological safety, using the intraclass correlation coefficient. These results supported aggregation to a group-level data set (n = 51), with which substantive relationships were tested.

Cardiac Surgery Team Study   Amy Edmondson, Richard M. Bohmer, and Gary P. Pisano (2001) studied cardiac surgery operating-room teams in sixteen hospitals to explore the role of psychological safety in interdisciplinary teams learning to use a radical new technology for minimally invasive cardiac surgery.[2] We used a structured interview protocol and a few open-ended questions to interview 165 informants, including all members of each operating-room team as well as others in each hospital who might provide additional information or perspective about the implementation of the new technology. Both because of the

Table 10.1   Survey Scales Used to Measure Psychological Safety

Edmondson (1996)
  If you make a mistake in this team, it is held against you.

Edmondson and Woolley (2003)
  If I make a mistake in this job, it is often held against me. (Reverse scored)
  It is difficult to ask others in this department for help. (Reverse scored)
  My manager often encourages me to take on new tasks or to learn how to do
    things I have never done before.
  If I was thinking about leaving this company to pursue a better job elsewhere, I
    would talk to my manager about it.
  If I had a problem in this company, I could depend on my manager to be my
    advocate.
  Often when I raise a problem with my manager, she or he does not seem
    very interested in helping me find a solution. (Reverse scored)

Edmondson (1999a)
  If you make a mistake on this team, it is often held against you.
  Members of this team are able to bring up problems and tough issues.
  People on this team sometimes reject others for being different.
  It is safe to take a risk on this team.
  It is difficult to ask other members of this team for help.
  No one on this team would deliberately act in a way that undermines my
    efforts.
  Working with members of this team, my unique skills and talents are valued
    and utilized.

Anderson and West (1994b; as used by Kivimaki et al. 1997)
  We share information generally in the team rather than keeping it to
    ourselves.
  We have a "we are together" attitude.
  We all influence each other.
  People keep each other informed about work-related issues in the team.
  People feel understood and accepted by each other.
  Everyone's view is listened to, even if it is in a minority.
  There are real attempts to share information throughout the team.
  There is a lot of give and take.

Source: Author's compilation.

small number of teams and because of the busy schedule of surgeons
and other operating-room team members, it was impractical to use a
team survey in this setting.

Instead, we developed two measures of psychological safety by coding qualitative data as follows: First, notes from informants' responses to
several questions about the team, including what they would do if faced
with a specific potential complication, were rated by the interviewers
using a three-point scale: "The atmosphere and interaction in this team

is characterized by (3) open reciprocal communication (very free and effortless), (2) respectful but guarded communication (picking the right moment to speak, pronounced awareness of status differences), and (1) communication that is quite limited, with some members extremely hesitant to speak up (low-status members walk on eggshells)." Second, we asked two research assistants to rate 168 quotes previously coded as relevant to psychological safety on a three-point scale from high (easy to speak up about anything on one's mind) to low (people appear to be very uncomfortable speaking up and only do with extreme difficulty), using anchors we developed together in a preparatory training session. One-way ANOVA (Analyses of Variance) showed highly significant differences in ratings across teams, and these data were aggregated to produce a group-level measure that was significantly correlated with the interviewers' ratings (Edmondson 2003).

These four studies have investigated and measured psychological safety using both quantitative and qualitative data, and the resulting data have consistently supported aggregation to the group level of analysis. Findings and examples from these studies are used throughout this paper to illustrate several new theoretical propositions.

Other Measures of Psychological Safety

In a qualitative field study in an architecture firm and a summer camp, Kahn (1990) used a series of open-ended questions to measure the constructs of psychological safety, meaningfulness and availability. The study examined the effect of psychological safety on team members' willingness to *engage*, that is, "employ or express themselves physically, cognitively, and emotionally during role performances," versus *disengage*, that is, "withdraw and defend their personal selves" (694).

Michael A. West (1990, 311) investigated a related construct, "participative safety," in work teams, defining it as "a construct in which the contingencies are such that involvement in decision-making is motivated and reinforced while occurring in an environment which is perceived as interpersonally non-threatening." Neil Anderson and West (1994b) developed a survey instrument, the Team Climate Inventory (TCI), to measure participative safety and three other "team climate" factors.[3] "Team climate" refers to "the norms, atmosphere, practices, interpersonal relationships, enacted rituals and ways of working developed by a team" (Anderson and West 1994a, 81). The TCI's participative-safety scale includes such issues as level of influence over decision making, information sharing, interaction frequency, and safety (Anderson and West 1994a; see table 10.1.) Versions of the instrument have been used by several researchers in health-care, community psychiatric care, social service, and industrial management settings (Kivimaki et al. 1997; Schippers 2003).

Antecedents of Psychological Safety

Understanding how to create these positive states is a central challenge in organizational research on both trust and psychological safety.[4] This section proposes antecedent conditions likely to give rise to psychological safety in work teams. Some of these propositions are supported by past research; others will require future work to support arguments presented here. Five factors that may increase the chances of intact work groups' having psychological safety are presented below. Although I draw upon others' research on individuals' experiences, these propositions focus on the work group or team context.

Leader Behavior

There can be little doubt that formal power relations affect perceptions of interpersonal risk in the workplace. The research literature has demonstrated this in numerous ways, showing for example that bad news is rarely transmitted up the hierarchy (Lee 1993) and that subordinates are less likely to ask for help from bosses than from peers or others (Lee 1997). In a related vein, supportive managerial behavior has been shown to have a positive effect on creativity (see, for example, Amabile, Conti, and Herron 1996 and Deci, Connell, and Ryan 1989). Creativity, a form of free self-expression, is likely to require some degree of psychological safety in an organizational setting.

Research has also shown that team members are particularly aware of the behavior of the leader (Tyler and Lind 1992), such that his or her responses to events and behaviors are likely to influence other members' perceptions of appropriate and safe behavior. One implication of the finding that leader behavior is especially influential is that leaders of work groups may have to go out of their way to be open and coaching-oriented to create an atmosphere of psychological safety. A benefit of this effort for the leaders is that they are more likely to learn what people are really thinking and feeling if psychological safety is present (see discussion of consequences in the next section). In short, leader behavior sets a salient example for how to behave, and beliefs about how leaders will use their power are likely to affect psychological safety. At the group level of analysis, the behaviors that directly influence members' perceptions are generally not those of the organization's chief executive or senior managers but are instead those of team leaders, middle managers, and front-line supervisors, who interact face-to-face with team members. I speculate that three aspects of leader behavior in particular will promote psychological safety: being available and approachable, explicitly inviting input and feedback, and modeling openness and fallibility.

Accessibility   By making themselves available and approachable, leaders may reduce perceived barriers that prohibit discussion. In contrast, if leaders assume authoritative stances or act in punitive ways, team members are likely to feel that their opinions are not welcomed or valued (Edmondson 1996). In our study of operating-room (OR) teams, we found that surgeon accessibility varied significantly and that this was associated with differences in team members' perceptions of psychological safety. An OR nurse at Suburban Hospital implicitly makes this association, describing the surgeon leading her team as "very accessible. He's in his office, always just two seconds away. He can always take five minutes to explain something, and he never makes you feel stupid." In striking contrast, the surgeon in another team requested that nonphysician team members go through his residents rather than speak to him directly. These two surgeons' behavior conveyed vastly different messages to their respective teams. The first surgeon increased the likelihood that people would come to him with questions or problems, whereas the second surgeon closed off potential discussion by making it difficult to reach him. Overall, our measures of psychological safety showed that teams with accessible, coaching-oriented surgeons were more likely to perceive the team environment as safe.

Inviting Input   Similarly, leaders who explicitly ask for team members' input are likely to encourage team psychological safety. Soliciting feedback suggests to others that their opinion is respected; it may also contribute to a norm of active participation. At the other end of the spectrum, when leaders, verbally or otherwise, discourage input or discussion, team members are less likely to express their opinions, fearing potential negative consequences. The extent to which surgeons encouraged input and feedback from OR team members varied greatly across the sixteen hospitals we studied. To illustrate, the OR technician, called a perfusionist, who runs the heart-lung bypass machine at Suburban Hospital, recalled that the surgeon "gave us a talk about what minimally invasive surgery is about—the kind of communication he wanted in the OR, what results he expected, and told us to immediately let him know—let us know if anything is out of place."

In contrast, the surgeon at Decorum Hospital, described by several team members as "the commander of the ship," did not actively encourage discussion from his team. This team's perfusionist commented, "He's a tough man. He doesn't openly invite input from my point of view. He may get it elsewhere, but there is no open forum. For example, sitting in a room and talking about [the device] and what we can do to make it better and keep it going; no, there is none of that communication at all."

Modeling Openness and Fallibility   How team leaders behave is likely to create an implicit model of acceptable behavior in the team, because of the implications of power in organizations. Team members are likely to mimic the behavior of leaders, so that if leaders are taciturn and their behavior indicates that certain matters are best not discussed, others will follow their example. Explicitly demonstrating fallibility or vulnerability can help reduce counterproductive barriers created by status differences. Team members who hear their leader admit to the group that he or she made a mistake are likely to remember this the next time they make mistakes and feel more comfortable bringing this up. One perfusionist in the OR team at Eastern Medical Center reported that the surgeon had "created an atmosphere where that happens. He models the behavior. He'll say 'I screwed up. My judgment was bad in this case.' " By admitting mistakes himself, this surgeon signaled to the team that errors and concerns could be discussed without fear of punishment (Edmondson, Bohmer, and Pisano 2001). In sum, team members are likely to conclude that their team environment is safe if the leader is coaching-oriented, invites questions and feedback, and responds nondefensively to questions and challenges.

> *Proposition 1:* The coaching behavior of team leaders—such as being accessible, inviting input, and modeling openness—promotes team psychological safety.

Trusting and Respectful Interpersonal Relationships

Much research examines the cognitive and affective bases for interpersonal trust (for example, McAllister 1995; Zucker 1986). Others have studied the role of interpersonal trust with respect to psychological safety; for example, a recent study (May, Gilson and Harter, forthcoming) showed that coworker trust had a significant positive effect on psychological safety. Kahn (1990) concluded that in the architecture firm he studied, "interpersonal relationships promoted psychological safety when they were supportive and trusting." Informants in his study felt free to share ideas and concepts about designs when they believed that any criticism would be viewed as constructive rather than destructive (Kahn 1990). The belief that others see one as competent (an aspect of respect) is particularly salient in this context; those who feel that their capability is in question are more likely to feel judged or monitored and thus may keep their opinions to themselves for fear of harming their reputation (Moingeon and Edmondson 1998). In sum, if relationships within a group are characterized by trust and respect, individuals are likely to believe they will be given the benefit of the doubt—a defining characteristic of psychological safety.

Proposition 2: Trust and respect in horizontal group relationships promote team psychological safety.

"Practice Fields"

"Practice fields," a term introduced by Peter M. Senge (1990), describes forums deliberately set up to practice important skills rather than take action and to reflect upon the results. Senge points out that it is difficult for managers to learn because they lack the practice or rehearsal settings used by other kinds of teams, such as professional sport teams, orchestras, or cockpit crews; instead, management teams typically must learn in the real playing field, where the stakes are high. As a former hospital chief commented about airplane pilots, "Nobody says, 'Well, you read the book on the 727, now take it up' " (Ellen Goodman, "Getting It Right in the O.R.," *Boston Globe*, January 13, 2000, p. A19). Cockpit crews in training use simulations to help them learn in a safe environment—to see which strategies work, what they will require of each member, and where the weak links are, and to practice responding to unexpected events—prior to their first flight.

In contrast, managers and most physicians must make decisions on the real-life playing field, without the benefit of a practice field in which to try out different strategies and learn from failure. To correct this situation, managers can set up a kind of off-line, practice-field environment where they can deliberately try to cultivate an environment of psychological safety by removing or suspending the harmful consequences of mistakes and failures. These practice fields can take the form of trial ("dry") runs, off-site or off-line meetings, and multiple kinds of simulations. (See Isaacs and Senge 1992 and Sterman 1989 for descriptions of the use of management simulation exercises to promote learning.)

Practice fields are likely to contribute to psychological safety not only because real financial or medical consequences are removed but also because they convey to the members of the team that learning is important and that getting it right the first time is not always possible. Discussing and experiencing aspects of the team task off-line highlights potential problems, and because there are no material consequences of errors individuals are likely to speak up about them. This use of practice fields is related to leader behavior in that leaders are most often in a position to suggest and implement them.

Across the cardiac surgery teams, we found striking differences in the use of "dry-run" sessions, in which the team ran through the operation without a patient present, following formal training and in advance of the first real case. Some teams conducted thorough dry runs with all team members present, running through all of the steps of the procedure as if it were happening, and even discussing how they wished to communicate with each other as a team in the real operation. Other teams conducted practice sessions without the potentially intimidating high-status surgeons present; some reviewed only technical aspects of the equipment, rather than including communication, and some teams reported only reading the manual to prepare. A particularly thorough dry run was carried out by an OR team at Suburban Hospital, which also had a high level of psychological safety. This team went through the entire procedure step-by-step while talking about how they would communicate with each other differently than in conventional cases. The perfusionist reported the rehearsal they had the night before their first case:

> We had a couple of talks in advance, and the night before we walked through the process step by step. Took two and half or three hours to do it. We communicated with each other as if it were happening, i.e., the balloon is going in, and so on. The surgeon gave us a talk about what [the new technology] is about. The kind of communication he wanted in the OR, what results he expected, and told us to immediately let him know—let us know if anything is out of place.

In striking contrast, at another hospital the team that conducted the first operation included none of the members who had attended training, other than the surgeon; in fact, the operation was the first time many of them had seen any of the equipment. The extent to which a team engaged in a thorough dry run was significantly correlated with team psychological safety across all sixteen teams.[5] Surgeons who conducted such practice fields signaled to other team members that mistakes were inevitable and that input and communication were required for success. This allowed other team members to perceive their environment as safe to discuss mistakes and offer observations.

Proposition 3: The use of "practice fields" promotes team psychological safety.

Organizational Context Support

Past research has shown that structural features of team design, including organizational context that provides timely information and resources, increase team effectiveness (Hackman 1987; Wageman 1998). The extent of such context support experienced by a team is proposed to foster team psychological safety as well, because access to resources and information is likely to reduce insecurity and defensiveness in a team that could be caused by concerns about unequal distribution of resources within or between an organization's teams.

Survey measures of team psychological safety and organizational context supportiveness were highly correlated in the manufacturing company study; however, this association was a rule with some striking exceptions.[6] Some teams with notably high psychological safety in this sample faced substantial organizational barriers, such as having members frequently pulled away to work on other tasks, yet continued to have a sense of openness and cohesion that may have been strengthened by the shared experience of surmounting hurdles (Edmondson 1999a). In sum, this study suggested that context support may be helpful but not essential in promoting psychological safety.

Proposition 4: A supportive organizational context promotes team psychological safety.

Emergent Group Dynamics

Not only formal power and leadership behavior but also informal, emergent dynamics in a team are likely to affect psychological safety. The notion of emergent group dynamics describes the interplay of roles and "characters" that people assume or are assigned in typical work relationships (Kahn 1990; Bales and Strodtbeck 1951). Kahn proposes that team members assume roles and unacknowledged characters in the unconscious plays that develop in organizations, such as those dealing with authority, competition, and sexuality. These roles are often formed independent of formal assignments. He further proposes that the psychological safety experienced by a group member will depend on where their "character" stands in the informal group play.

In Kahn's (1990) study of an architecture firm, the firm's president was viewed as the "father figure," with other members taking supporting roles such as "mother" or "son." Each of these "family members" experienced different degrees of safety to express themselves according to their relationship to the "father." The "mother" felt that her role "lets me interact with him and with others pretty much as I want to, within limits" (710). Similarly, a "favored son" claimed, "I tend to be seen as the next generation of designers that he lays out. My designs aren't questioned as much as those of others, and I think it's because I'm seen as following his tradition, but in my own way" (710). In contrast, the team member who took on the persona of the "bad son" wore earrings, cracked jokes, dyed his hair red, and was "frustrated" because he felt that he was seldom able to engage. This study showed that differences in psychological safety can emerge as a consequence of group interactions.

Proposition 5: Team psychological safety is influenced by informal dynamics in the team.

Consequences of Psychological Safety

As noted earlier, the level of psychological safety in a team is likely to affect the way members interact with each other. In particular, psychological safety is likely to affect behaviors related to learning and improvement (Edmondson 1999a). Five specific learning-oriented behaviors may be enabled by team psychological safety.

Help Seeking

Each member of a team can look to other members to provide information or perspective to help them solve a challenging problem. Help seeking can increase others' awareness of opportunities for cooperative behavior (Anderson and Williams 1996). Yet power dynamics often cause people in organizations to avoid seeking the help they need. Using an experimental paradigm, Fiona Lee (1997) showed that coworker power (whether confederates were labeled bosses or subordinates) affected participants' help-seeking behavior. In the presence of a high-power colleague, participants confronted with a difficult problem-solving task were significantly less likely to ask for help than if the colleague had low power—despite the fact that help was essential for task completion. As this result suggests, seeking help from those in a position to judge your performance or ability involves interpersonal risk. Asking for help brings a potential risk of appearing incompetent, and—as psychological safety alleviates excessive concern about others' reactions—it is likely to promote help seeking in teams.

To illustrate this association, I found substantial differences in self-reported help-seeking behavior across teams in the manufacturing company. Members of a factory production team volunteered reports of seeking help to assess their product, for example, "If we have a quality issue—we're not sure about something we've just done—we'll bring others in without telling them what the issue is to ask them if they see a problem with this part." This team stood in striking contrast to another production team in the same company, whose members, according to an internal consultant, didn't ask for help because they "don't want to look like brown-nosers." And a local supervisor noted, "If there's a technical problem, they don't ask the engineers for help," and similarly "They were having problems with the glue, but they didn't get help; they just sit and don't work, then they get overtime on Saturday." The survey measure of team psychological safety was significantly correlated with responses to a single survey item measuring help-seeking behavior filled out by two or three independent observers of each team ($r = .37$, $p < .01$), supporting the following proposition.[7]

Proposition 6: Psychological safety promotes help-seeking behavior in work teams.

Feedback Seeking

Attention to feedback has been shown to promote learning (Schön 1983) and enhance performance of individual managers (Ashford and Tsui 1991) and teams (Ancona and Caldwell 1992). Like help seeking, feedback-seeking is often essential to successful task completion, and carries similar interpersonal risk. Requests for feedback from other team members or other groups place the seekers in a vulnerable situation, where they are poised to hear negative criticism. This may cause them "learning anxiety," driven by the fear of losing "effectiveness and self-esteem" (Schein 1995). Team psychological safety, which diminishes the concern that others will respond in a way that is cruel or humiliating, is likely to encourage feedback seeking.

Two new product development teams in the manufacturing company represented extremes of feedback-seeking behavior. The "Sidekick" team actively sought feedback from more experienced people in the company. A senior manager noted that Sidekick's leader "asks me to come [to some meetings]; she wants my view, my industry experience and how Sidekick fits with [the company's] systems strategy." In contrast, a team working on a similar project, the "Radar" team, remained strikingly insular. Members reported spending considerable time developing details of a new product design before soliciting customer input, only to discover that customers were not interested in the product idea in the first place. Members of this team also did not feel comfortable offering ideas or bringing up problems in the team, and one explained that the team leader "doesn't want to hear it." Another member noted that the leader of the team "would be afraid to tell [the senior manager] when things weren't going well—so we didn't always get his feedback."

A team's ability to seek feedback can have a significant effect on its performance. Because Radar received little external input, the team was less able to notice and fix what they were doing wrong. One team member noted, "We did make changes, but too slowly. . . . We found ourselves going in circles a lot. Sometimes this took a lot of time." Another member explained that there were a lot of "blind alleys. . . . We had a preconceived notion of what was important that prevented us from seeing" the solution. Sidekick had greater team psychological safety than Radar, and overall, team psychological safety was correlated with observers' ratings of team feedback-seeking behavior, a three-item scale $(r = .51, p < .001)$.[8]

Proposition 7: Psychological safety facilitates feedback-seeking behavior in and by a team.

Speaking Up About Errors and Concerns

In both the management and medical literatures, noted scholars have advocated discussion of concerns and failures in organizations (Kohn, Corrigan, and Donaldson 2000; Leonard-Barton 1995; Michael 1976; Schein 1993; Sitkin 1992), but less attention has been paid to the social psychological factors enabling people to do this. It is proposed that psychological safety allows team members to speak up about concerns and problems directly by alleviating fears about repercussions or embarrassment. Psychological safety makes it possible for people to believe that the benefits of speaking up outweigh the costs.

The role of psychological safety was particularly salient in the cardiac surgery and nursing team studies. Health care provides a good context in which to draw examples of speaking up—especially given recent public attention to the widespread problem of error in hospitals (Robert Pear, "Report Outlines Medical Errors in V.A. Hospitals," *New York Times*, December 19, 1999, p. A1; Abigail Zuger, "The Healing Arts, Cast in Shades of Gray," *New York Times*, December 14, 1999, p. F7). Remaining silent about a questionable medication order in a nursing team could lead to serious patient injury. Similarly, in an OR team, not speaking up about a potential problem can critically affect clinical outcomes. Yet in some of the OR teams we studied, speaking up about potentially life-threatening problems was often seen as difficult or impossible to do, with the result that team members would wait to see if someone else noticed the same problem and spoke up first.

In the cardiac surgery study, psychological safety was assessed in part on the basis of team members' reports of how easy or difficult it was to speak up, confounding our measures of psychological safety and speaking up. However, these data shed light on *how* perceptions related to the interpersonal context affect people's willingness to speak up and also show that the willingness to speak up can vary across otherwise highly similar teams. The homogeneity of OR teams in cardiac surgery in terms of structural features such as the team's composition, its tasks, and its goals highlights the role of interpersonal and intrapsychic factors in explaining observed behavioral differences across teams. For example, members of the OR team at Decorum reported being uncomfortable mentioning potential problems they observed during the minimally invasive operation. One nurse explained that if she noticed that the balloon pressure was a little low, she'd

> tell the adjunct. Or I might whisper to the anesthesiologist, "Does it look like it migrated?" In fact I've seen that happen. It drives me crazy. They are talking about it, the adjunct is whispering to the anesthesiologist, it looks like it moved or there is a leak in the ASD or something and I'm

saying you've got to tell him. Why don't you tell him? But they are not used to saying anything. They are afraid to speak out. But for this procedure you have to say stuff.

Similarly, the perfusionist at Decorum described an interaction with the surgeon after he had noticed and mentioned having some trouble with the venous return. "The surgeon said, 'Jack, is that you?' I said yes. He said, 'Are you 'doing' this case?' I said, 'No, I'm assisting.' 'Well in the future, if you are not doing this case I don't want to hear from you.' It is a very structured communication."

Other members of this team reported that they would only speak up if they had caused the problem, not if it was someone else's mistake. This was not the case with other teams in the sample. For example, an anesthesiologist at Saints Hospital noted that everyone in the OR team was very comfortable speaking up: "We speak up easily. At the beginning, we spoke up about everything; after a while, we realized what was really important. No one is intimidated by the surgeons or the situation. I think the surgeons make it so. They make it easy to speak up. . . . It is not a problem even for an RN to speak up."

A perfusionist in a Memorial Hospital team explained, "You have to level with these guys. I feel comfortable when admitting a mistake." At Urban Hospital, a senior OR nurse reported an incident in which a junior nurse pointed out the senior's mistake: "In the last case, we needed to reinsert a guide wire and I grabbed the wrong wire and I didn't recognize it at first. My circulating nurse said, 'Sue, you've grabbed the wrong wire.' This shows how much the different roles don't matter. We all have to know about everything. You have to work as a team." Her ease in sharing this story about an error being pointed out by a subordinate itself suggests a high level of comfort admitting mistakes in her team.

These examples show how a sense of psychological safety can make it easier to speak up across status and role boundaries. Like many work settings, the hospital environment is highly structured, including having well defined status differences within the OR team. Some surgeons recognized a need to work to reduce these kinds of barriers to be able to learn to carry out minimally invasive surgery. An anesthesiologist at Eastern Medical Center highlighted this point:

> The perception that the surgeon has to know everything has to change. . . . Each person has an important job. For minimally invasive surgery you can't ever stop talking. . . . I have to be able to tell the surgeon to stop. This is very new. I would never have dared to say anything like that before, nothing was that important. So you have to develop a way to deal with communication in advance, such as "anesthesia can be telling the surgeon what to do." It has got to be legitimate. This is really important.

Speaking up, especially in ways that can reflect on others' performance, means crossing the lines that delineate roles. In particularly stratified work environments, this can require courage on the part of the speaker; however, psychological safety can reduce concerns about sanctions from crossing status lines.

Finally, evidence of this relationship is provided by the nursing team study in which the reverse-scored survey item—"If you make a mistake in this team, it is held against you"—was correlated with errors made that were actually intercepted by other team members before reaching patients (Edmondson 1996). Some teams thus reported being comfortable speaking up about errors. A member of team C at Memorial Hospital said, "People feel more willing to admit errors here because [the nurse manager] goes to bat for you." This is in sharp contrast with statements from team D such as "People are nervous about being called into the principal's office" and "People don't advertise errors here. If there's no adverse event, then don't report it."

> *Proposition 8:* Team psychological safety promotes speaking up about errors and concerns.

Innovative Behavior and Innovation

Innovative behavior can be defined as doing novel or different things intelligently, to produce useful outcomes. West (1990) argued that "participative safety" in teams encourages the freedom to offer new ideas and experiment with different behaviors without fear of looking stupid or being embarrassed. Innovative behavior has much in common with "voice," defined by Linn Van Dyne and Jeffery A. LePine (1998, 109) as being comfortable "making innovative suggestions for change and recommending modifications to standard procedures even when others disagree."

West (1990, 320) theorizes that "participative safety is a necessary but not sufficient condition for high levels of innovation." He draws on developmental and clinical psychology to show a basis for this relationship, noting that research on child development shows that children with secure bonds with their parents are more likely to explore new situations sooner than children whose bonds are less secure (Ainsworth and Bell 1974; West 1990). Similarly, research indicates that patients whose therapeutic alliances are characterized by interpersonal safety, lack of judgment, and consistency of support are more likely to explore the most threatening aspects of their experiences (West 1990; Rogers 1961). West argues similarly that innovation will occur more frequently if people feel safe. Psychological safety, by enabling risk taking and the willingness to suggest new ideas without fear of embarrassment, may support innovative behavior and innovation in teams.

Other research has shown that participation leads to less resistance to change (Wall and Lischeron 1977; West 1990), and that the more frequently people participate in decision making, the more likely they are to offer ideas for new and improved ways of working (West and Wallace 1991). This increased interaction leads to cross-fertilization of ideas (Mumford and Gustafson 1988; West 1990), which is important to creativity and innovation. Similarly, to the extent that psychological safety promotes information sharing, it gives individuals more knowledge with which to develop new ideas.

West argues that participative safety influences quality of innovation as well as quantity. For example, cross-fertilization of ideas can increase an innovation's significance or novelty. Moreover, innovations developed in this way are likely be implemented because high levels of participation lead to less resistance to change (Wall and Lischeron 1977) and because thorough discussion may surface potential weaknesses or errors in the early stages in the process of producing an innovation, thus preventing future problems.

I found substantial differences in innovation across cardiac surgery teams learning to use a new technology. As an administrator at University Hospital reported, "Our surgeons are very creative. They see something that works well here and they see it will apply elsewhere." In contrast, an anesthesiologist at State University Hospital commented, "It is best not to stick your neck out. Innovation is tolerated, at best." Consistent with this argument, a quantitative measure of innovation from the structured interview protocol (Edmondson 2003) was correlated with measures of psychological safety ($r = .51$, $p < .05$).[9]

> *Proposition 9:* Team psychological safety promotes innovative behavior and innovation.

Boundary Spanning

Boundary-spanning behavior is external communication with other groups, such as that needed to coordinate objectives, schedules, or resources. Boundary spanning can also involve interpersonal risk, including asking for help or resources, seeking feedback, and delivering bad news such as that there are delays or design problems. It is through such activities that teams can clarify performance requirements, obtain information and resources, and coordinate their tasks with other groups. Past research has shown that boundary spanning promotes effective team performance (Ancona 1990; Ancona and Caldwell 1992). However, these benefits will be unrealized if team members are unwilling to incur the risks involved because they wish to avoid appearing to have problems. It is argued here that team psychological safety is likely to foster boundary-spanning behavior because team members who are accustomed to taking interpersonal risks within the team may be able to transfer that behavior to other, external interactions (Edmondson 1999b).

The operating-room teams I studied varied considerably in boundary-spanning activities. Some surgeons spoke informally on a daily basis with or attended frequent meetings with other groups. Other members of the same OR teams also tended to have a high level of boundary spanning. One OR team members said, "It is informal at my level; there are no formal meetings, just informal networking with the catheter lab and the SICU. . . . I try to put my face out there and let them know we're available." In contrast, a perfusionist in another team reported, "In this hospital everyone acts independently and assumes everyone is doing their job. There are not meetings to see how stuff is going. It just doesn't happen. It has the feel of a factory sometimes. The key players talk team, but it is not practice." Quantitative measures of team boundary spanning as measured with a structured interview protocol were highly correlated with team psychological safety (Edmondson 2003).[10] Similarly, in the manufacturing study team, psychological safety and boundary spanning, measured in two surveys, were significantly correlated both for self-reported[11] and observer-rated[12] boundary spanning behavior (Edmondson 1999b).

Proposition 10: Psychological safety enables team members to engage in boundary spanning.

Implications and Issues

This section reviews implications and limitations of past work on psychological safety. In particular, I discuss the role of psychological safety in organizational learning, the risks of creating psychological safety in organizations, and the opportunities for future research.

Psychological Safety and Organizational Learning

The behavioral consequences of psychological safety (see figure 10.1) fall under the broad rubric of activities through which learning occurs in organizations. Research on trust has identified numerous benefits of trusting attitudes and behaviors in organizations: trusting environments reduce transaction costs within an organization (Kramer 1999; Uzzi 1997; Williamson and Craswell 1993); increase spontaneous sociability among organization members (Fukuyama 1995; Messick et al. 1983); and facilitate appropriate forms of deference to organizational authorities (Arrow 1974; Gabarro 1978; Miller 1992; Tyler 1994; Tyler and Lind 1992). A unifying theme in trust research is the view of trust as a substitute for

**Figure 10.1   Model of Antecedents and Consequences of Team
Psychological Safety**

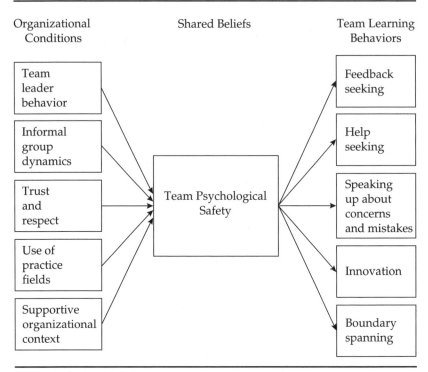

Organizational   Shared Beliefs   Team Learning
Conditions   Behaviors

Team leader behavior		Feedback seeking
Informal group dynamics	Team Psychological Safety	Help seeking
Trust and respect		Speaking up about concerns and mistakes
Use of practice fields		Innovation
Supportive organizational context		Boundary spanning

Source: Author's compilation.

control (Handy 1995); unlike the case in research on psychological safety, the theme of learning has not played a central role in this work.

An extensive literature on organizational learning has paid little attention to the behaviors at the level of work teams that allow organizations to learn, with notable exceptions (for example, Edmondson 2002; Kasl, Marsick, and Dechant 1993; Senge 1990). Much essential learning in organizations takes place in the interpersonal interactions between members of work groups (Edmondson 2002), yet learning behaviors are limited when individuals have concerns about interpersonal consequences. Chris Argyris (1990) suggested that when people experience interpersonal threat, they utilize "defensive routines" that thwart their own and their organization's learning. Similarly, Schein (1995) proposes that the "learning anxiety" created by the fear of confronting disconfirming data increases "in direct proportion to the amount of disconfirmation, leading to the maintenance of the equilibrium by defensive avoidance of the disconfirming information." The anxiety associated with not learning must be greater than the anxiety associated with the risk of looking or feeling incompetent for individuals to engage in learning behavior.

One implication of research on psychological safety is that interpersonal threat in an organization is subjective and inconsistent. The studies discussed in this paper indicate that interpersonal beliefs vary from team to team, even within strong organizational cultures and contexts. Thus, the interpersonal risk inherent in learning in organizational settings can be mitigated by a climate of psychological safety among colleagues or coworkers. A face-to-face work team can provide a safety net for learning, or, in contrast, it may be a place where the risk of learning behavior is magnified. Some teams are therefore likely to learn faster than others. The phenomenon of organizational learning may be better described as a patchwork quilt than as a uniform fabric, so that an organization does not learn (or fail to learn) as an entity but rather encompasses varying pockets of learning (Edmondson 2002). One implication of this for practice is that managers must focus on creating psychological safety in face-to-face work units throughout the organization. Attempts to enhance organizational learning through top-down, uniform approaches are likely to have limited effectiveness without attention to the way interpersonal climate can vary across groups (Edmondson and Woolley 2003).

Limits of Psychological Safety

If psychological safety promotes learning behavior in work groups, does this suggest that more psychological safety is always good? First, the size of the teams examined in the studies reviewed here presents a potential boundary condition for this proposition. The surgery, nursing, new-product development, production, and management teams studied were all relatively small, ranging from five to twenty or, infrequently, thirty members. Yet in some organizational environments, such as the automotive or semiconductor industries, groups of two hundred or more people often share responsibility for designing or developing a new product or bringing it to market. Given the reduced salience of face-to-face interaction in planning and executing work in a team of two hundred than in a team of five, psychological safety may not play a critical a role in the learning of such a team, and further research is needed to investigate this. Moreover, the increased number of relationships and complex interdependencies in a very large group may diminish the amount of repeated interaction between any subset of members and thereby reduce the degree to which consistent perceptions of psychological safety take shape. Finally, the role of psychological safety in dispersed, or "virtual," teams (Leonard et al. 1998; Sole and Edmondson 2002) may be very different from that in the teams discussed in this paper.

Second, psychological safety is not sufficient to ensure learning behavior. Without a clear and compelling shared goal, members of a team may lack motivation to engage in learning-oriented actions, which require both effort and thought. People are more likely to offer ideas, ask for help, and seek or provide feedback if they believe that their effort makes a difference in achieving an outcome that they care about. Similarly, effective learning behavior involves effort and thought, for example, to identify gaps that could be filled through help seeking. This suggests that a sense of safety from harmful personal consequences must be combined with a need and capacity for thoughtful, intelligent action if effective learning behavior is to occur. The advice to create an environment of psychological safety could be counterproductive if managers believe that this is all that is needed to promote learning. Furthermore, managers should not equate structural supports, such as standard operating procedures, with barriers to psychological safety.

The results of the research discussed in this paper suggest certain consistent positive effects of team psychological safety and negative effects of an interpersonal climate that lacked safety. In these examples, the question of whether a team can have too much psychological safety has not been addressed. Excessive psychological safety could be detrimental if people are so comfortable with each other that they spend an inappropriate amount of time in casual conversation at the expense of their work. A complete lack of censorship could create such a low barrier to seeking feedback and help or speaking up with concerns that valuable time could be wasted on unimportant things.

On the other hand, an argument can be made that no amount of *interpersonal* fear is helpful in promoting performance. Although fear of not achieving goals, or anxiety about survival in an ever more competitive environment may motivate productive work, anxiety triggered by interpersonal fear may not be helpful. Schein (1995) noted that learning occurs in organizations when survival anxiety exceeds anxiety about learning—and certainly fails to occur when the opposite is the case. In practice, such theoretical distinctions are likely to blur; distinguishing interpersonal and other sources of fear may be unrealistic. Envisioning the possibility of a team with excessive safety, somehow lacking an edge to drive them forward, is not difficult. Managers thus may face a tension in trying to draw a line somewhere to set high standards and prevent sloppy work—such as by discouraging questions or comments unrelated to the task at hand—without closing down communication about important issues. If they inadvertently communicate that suppression of questions and concerns is wise, they are likely to suppress learning.

A third potential limitation is that excessive team psychological safety may promote intergroup tensions in organizations. Teams that are actively engaged in exciting projects and enjoying the intense sense of camaraderie that such collaboration often implies may inadvertently communicate an impression of self-satisfaction and arrogance that other organizational groups interpret as denigrating of them. Many effective new-product development teams assigned to a strategically important project have fallen into this trap (see Wheelwright and Verlinden 1999). Although these teams often have psychological safety and open, direct confrontation inside the team, they often have done less to encourage others in the organization to speak openly to them.

Finally, there may be situations in which the lack of an interpersonal barrier to speaking up may actually exacerbate problems rather than help them. Randall S. Peterson (1999) hypothesized that group member "voice" may be more useful in groups characterized by common understanding than in those where such understanding is absent. An implication of this for teams in which people fundamentally disagree about task-related issues is that psychological safety may open the door for getting stuck in counterproductive discussions, which they lack the interpersonal skill to resolve. This suggests the need for psychological safety to be accompanied by interpersonal competence (Argyris 1993) for maximum learning to take place.

Future Research

The propositions presented in this paper suggest several directions for future research. First, further work is needed to develop and operationalize the construct of team psychological safety with additional kinds of teams. To develop a consistently reliable and valid measure of psychological safety, future research must continue to collect data from a variety of team and organizational settings. For example, the effect of psychological safety in culturally diverse teams warrants further research, since foreign-born workers may be hesitant to ask questions, admit a lack of understanding, or make negative statements (Thiederman 1988). The use of multiple methods to triangulate across assessments would serve to further solidify the survey measure of team psychological safety used in the studies discussed here and shown in table 10.1.

Second, further research is needed to test many of the propositions in this paper. Preliminary data from many teams were offered to illustrate the viability of these arguments; however, more systematic research is clearly required. Similarly, conceptual and empirical work is warranted to explore the relationships *among* the proposed antecedents and consequences of psychological safety. For instance, the decisions and actions of the team leader are likely to have a significant effect on each of the other antecedent variables. Leaders can pay attention to informal group dynamics that arise, elicit trust and respect, implement practice fields, and make sure the team has sufficient access to resources (see, for example, Hackman and Walton 1986). Similarly, the relationship between practice fields and other antecedent factors can be explored. Do off-line practice sessions increase the likelihood of trusting interpersonal relationships or alter informal group dynamics? Relationships among the proposed consequences of psychological safety thus may also prove to be fruitful avenues for further exploration.

Conclusion

At this stage of research on team psychological safety, a few preliminary conclusions can be articulated. First, the existence of psychological safety as a distinct concept with implications for organizational behavior is supported by data from a variety of organizational settings. The notion that psychological safety tends to be shared by members of face-to-face work teams has strong empirical support from several studies. Moreover, despite a lack of extensive systematic empirical research thus far, the proposition that psychological safety exists and may influence certain kinds of behaviors in organizations has considerable face validity.

Second, evidence from several types of work groups in very different organizational contexts suggests an important role for psychological safety in facilitating collaborative work, particularly when work groups face uncertainty and change and need to learn together. Thus, psychological safety may have important consequences for understanding organizational learning. The studies reviewed above point to specific actions that team leaders can take to promote psychological safety and to thereby catalyze a process of encouraging learning in an organization, work group by work group.

Neither scholarly nor lay notions of trust precisely capture the concept of psychological safety. Although interpersonal trust is likely to be an essential prerequisite for team psychological safety, this paper argues and illustrates that it is not the same construct. This work thus contributes to the literature by expanding the range of salient intrapsychic experiences likely to influence organizational behavior.

Notes

1. All hospital names have been changed.
2. Minimally invasive cardiac surgery differed from traditional cardiac surgery in two ways. It promised shorter and less painful recovery for patients (rather than cutting open the patient's chest and splitting the breastbone the surgeon accessed the heart through a tiny incision between the ribs). In addition, the

small incision transformed a routine procedure with well-established roles and tasks into one that required communication and coordination among members of the operating-room team. Direct tactile and visual data previously available to surgeons was replaced by information displayed on monitors that had to be communicated to the surgeon by others. The OR team thus had to learn a new work routine that altered the surgeon's role as sole authority with privileged access to data.

3. The others are vision, task orientation, and support for innovation. TCI can be obtained from the Institute of Work Psychology at Sheffield University, Sheffield, England.

4. Kramer (1999, 575–81) identified individual and organizational factors that affect trust: (1) the truster's disposition—his or her generalized attitude toward people, developed as a result of past experiences with trust in general; (2) the past history or cumulative interaction between the truster and the trustee, or a combination of the truster's expectations and the extent to which they are validated over time; (3) the input of third parties; (4) the category or role of the trustee (for example, successful role occupation signals trust in competence); and (5) explicit and tacit organizational rules and norms that filter down to the micro-level, such as "open-door" policies.

5. Both variables were measured by structured interview scales; the correlation was $r = .50$, $p < .05$.

6. Context support items include "This team gets all the information it needs to do our work and plan our schedule," and "Good work is rewarded in this organization." The correlation was $r = .70$, $p < .01$, for $n = 51$ teams.

7. The item was "This team asks for help from others in the company when something comes up that team members don't know how to handle." The response alternatives were "Never," "Infrequently," "Sometimes," "Often," or "Always," and "observer" means responses provided a group-level measure.

8. A representative item is "This team asks its internal customers [those who receive or use its work] for feedback on its performance." Cronbach's alpha for this scale, created for this paper, is .79.

9. Team innovation was measured as the sum of three correlated variables: innovative modification of surgical procedures; novel application of the procedure (used to something previously considered impossible); and expansion of patient eligibility criteria as a result of reflection on accumulated experiences.

10. $r = .70$, $p < .01$, $N = 16$.

11. $r = .78$, $p < .01$, $N = 51$.

12. $r = .48$, $p < .01$, $N = 51$.

References

Ainsworth, Mary D. S., and Silvia M. Bell. 1974. "Mother-Infant Interaction and the Development of Competence." In *The Growth of Competence*, edited by Kevin J. Connolly and Jerome S. Bruner. New York: Academic Press.

Alderfer, Clayton P. 1987. "An Intergroup Perspective on Organizational Behavior." In *Handbook of Organizational Behavior*, edited by Jay W. Lorsch. Englewood Cliffs, N.J.: Prentice-Hall.

Amabile, Teresa M., Regina Conti, and Michael Herron. 1996. "Assessing the Work Environment for Creativity." *Academy of Management Journal* 39(5): 1154–83.

Ancona, Deborah G. 1990. "Outward Bound: Strategies for Team Survival in the Organization." *Academy of Management Journal* 33(3): 334–65.

Ancona, Deborah G., and David F. Caldwell. 1992. "Bridging the Boundary: External Activity and Performance in Organizational Teams." *Administrative Science Quarterly* 37(4): 634–55.

Anderson, Neil, and Michael West. 1994a. "The Personality of Teamworking." *Personnel Management* 26(11): 81.

———. 1994b. *The Team Climate Inventory*. Windsor, U.K.: Berks ASE.

Anderson, Stella E., and Larry J. Williams. 1996. "Interpersonal, Job, and Individual Factors Related to Helping Processes at Work." *Journal of Applied Psychology* 81(3): 282–96.

Argyris, Chris. 1990. *Overcoming Organizational Defenses: Facilitating Organizational Learning*. Boston: Allyn & Bacon.

———. 1993. *Knowledge for Action: A Guide to Overcoming Barriers to Organizational Change*. San Francisco: Jossey-Bass.

Arrow, Kenneth. 1974. *The Limits of Organization*. New York: Norton.

Ashford, Susan J., and Anne S. Tsui. 1991. "Self-Regulation for Managerial Effectiveness: The Role of Active Feedback Seeking." *Academy of Management Journal* 34(2): 251–80.

Bales, Robert F., and Fred L. Strodtbeck. 1951. "Phases in Group Problem Solving." *Journal of Abnormal and Social Psychology* 46: 485–95.

Creed, Doug W. E., and Robert E. Miles. 1995. "Trust in Organizations: A Conceptual Framework Linking Organizational Forms, Managerial Philosophies, and the Opportunity Cost of Controls." In *Trust in Organizations: Frontiers in Theory and Research*, edited by Roderick M. Kramer and Tom R. Tyler. Thousand Oaks, Calif.: Sage.

Deci, Edward L., James P. Connell,, and Richard M. Ryan. 1989. "Self-Determination in a Work Organization." *Journal of Applied Psychology* 74(4): 580–91.

Edmondson, Amy C. 1996. "Learning from Mistakes Is Easier Said Than Done: Group and Organizational Influences on the Detection and Correction of Human Error." *Journal of Applied Behavioral Science* 32(1): 5–28.

———. 1999a. "Psychological Safety and Learning Behavior in Work Teams." *Administrative Science Quarterly* 44(2): 350–83.

———. 1999b. "A Safe Harbor: Social Psychological Conditions Enabling Boundary Spanning in Work Teams." *Research on Managing Groups and Teams* 2: 179–99.

———. 2002. "The Local and Variegated Nature of Learning in Organizations: A Group-Level Perspective." *Organization Science* 13(2): 128–46.

———. 2003. "Speaking Up in the Operating Room: How Team Leaders Promote Learning in Interdisciplinary Action Teams." *Journal of Management Studies* 40(6): 1419–52.

Edmondson, Amy C., Richard M. Bohmer, and Gary P. Pisano. 2001. "Team Learning and New Technology Adaptation." *Administrative Science Quarterly* 46(December): 685–716.

Edmondson, Amy C., and Anita W. Woolley. 2003. "Understanding Outcomes of Organizational Learning Interventions." In *International Handbook on Organizational Learning and Knowledge Management*, edited by Mark Easterby-Smith and Marjorie Lyles. London: Blackwell.

Fukuyama, Francis. 1995. *Trust: The Social Virtues and the Creation of Prosperity.* New York: Free Press.

Gabarro, John. 1978. "The Development of Trust and Expectations." In *Interpersonal Behavior: Communication and Understanding in Relationships*, edited by Anthony Athos and John Gabarro. Cambridge: Blackwell.

Hackman, J. Richard. 1987. "The Design of Work Teams." In *Handbook of Organizational Behavior*, edited by Jay W. Lorsch. Englewood Cliffs, N.J.: Prentice-Hall.

———, ed. 1990. *Groups that Work and Those that Don't.* San Francisco: Jossey-Bass.

Hackman, J. Richard, and Richard E. Walton. 1986. "Leading Groups in Organizations." In *Designing Effective Work Groups*, edited by Paul S. Goodman. San Francisco: Jossey-Bass.

Handy, Charles. 1995. "Trust and the Virtual Organization." *Harvard Business Review* 73(May–June): 40–50.

Isaacs, William, and Peter Senge. 1992. "Overcoming Limits to Learning in Computer-Based Learning Environments." *European Journal of Operations Research* 59(1): 183–96.

Jones, Gareth R., and Jennifer M. George. 1998. "The Experience and Evolution of Trust: Implications for Cooperation and Teamwork." *Academy of Management Review* 23(3): 531–46.

Kahn, William A. 1990. "Psychological Conditions of Personal Engagement and Disengagement at Work." *Academy of Management Journal* 33(4): 692–724.

Kasl, Elizabeth, Victoria J. Marsick, and Kathleen Dechant. 1993. "Teams as Learners: A Research Based Model of Team Learning." *Journal of Applied Behavioral Science* 33(2): 227–46.

Kivimaki, Mika, George Kuk, Marko Elovainio, Louise Thomson, Tiina Kalliomäki-Levanto, and Armo Heikkilä. 1997. "The Team Climate Inventory TCI—Four or Five Factors? Testing the Structure of TCI in Samples of Low and High Complexity Jobs." *Journal of Occupational and Organizational Psychology* 70(4): 375–89.

Klimoski, Richard, and Susan Mohammed. 1994. "Team Mental Model: Construct or Metaphor?" *Journal of Management* 20(2): 403–37.

Kohn, Linda T., Janet M. Corrigan, and Molla Donaldson. 2000. *To Err Is Human: Building a Safer Health System.* Washington, D.C.: National Academy Press.

Kramer, Roderick M. 1999. "Trust and Distrust in Organizations: Emerging Perspectives, Enduring Questions." *Annual Review of Psychology* 50: 569–98.

Lee, Fiona. 1993. "Being Polite and Keeping MUM: How Bad News Is Communicated in Organizational Hierarchies." *Journal of Applied Social Psychology* 23(14): 1124–49.

———. 1997. "When the Going Gets Tough, Do the Tough Ask for Help? Help Seeking and Power Motivation in Organizations." *Organizational Behavior and Human Decision Processes* 72(3): 336–63.

Leonard, Dorothy A., Paul A. Brands, Amy Edmondson, and Justine Fenwick. 1998. "Virtual Teams: Using Communications Technology to Manage Geographically Dispersed Development Groups." In *Sense and Respond: Capturing Value in the Network Era,* edited by Stephen P. Bradley and Richard L. Nolan. Boston: Harvard Business School Press.

Leonard-Barton, Dorothy. 1995. *Wellsprings of Knowledge: Building and Sustaining the Sources of Innovation.* Boston: Harvard Business School Press.

May, Douglas R., Richard L. Gilson, and L. Harter. Forthcoming. "The Psychological Conditions of Meaningfulness, Safety, and Availability and the Engagement of the Human Spirit at Work." *Journal of Occupational and Organizational Psychology.*

Mayer, Roger C., James H. Davis, and F. David Schoorman. 1995. "An Integrative Model of Organizational Trust." *Academy of Management Review* 20(3): 709–34.

McAllister, Daniel J. 1995. "Affect- and Cognition-Based Trust as Foundations for Interpersonal Cooperation in Organizations." *Academy of Management Journal* 38(1): 24–59.

Messick, David M., Henk A. M. Wilke, Marilyn Brewer, Roderick M. Kramer, Patricia E. Zemke, and Layton Lui. 1983. "Individual Adaptations and Structural Change as Solutions to Social Dilemmas." *Journal of Personality and Social Psychology* 44(2): 294–309.

Michael, Donald N. 1976. *On Learning to Plan and Planning to Learn.* San Francisco: Jossey-Bass.

Miller, Gary. 1992. *Managerial Dilemmas: The Political Economy of Hierarchy.* New York: Cambridge University Press.

Moingeon, Bertrand, and Amy C. Edmondson. 1998. "Trust and Organisational Learning." In *Trust, Learning and Economic Expectations,* edited by Nathalie Lazaric and Edward Lorenz. London: Edward Elgar.

Mumford, Michael S., and Sigrid B. Gustafson. 1988. "Creativity Syndrome: Integration, Application and Innovation." *Psychological Bulletin* 103(1): 27–43.

Peterson, Randall S. 1999. "Can You Have Too Much of a Good Thing? The Limits of Voice for Improving Satisfaction with Leaders." *Personality and Social Psychology Bulletin* 25(3): 313–24.

Rappoport, Alan. 1997. "The Patient's Search for Safety: The Organizing Principle in Psychotherapy." *Psychotherapy* 34(3): 250–61.

Rogers, Carl. 1961. *On Becoming a Person.* Boston: Houghton Mifflin.

Schein, Edgar. 1985. *Organizational Culture and Leadership.* San Francisco: Jossey-Bass.

———. 1993. "How Can Organizations Learn Faster? The Challenge of Entering the Green Room." *Sloan Management Review* 34(2): 85–92.

———. 1995. "Kurt Lewin's Change Theory in the Field and in the Classroom: Notes Toward a Model of Managed Learning." Working paper. Available at: www.a2zpsychology.com/articles/kurt_lewin's_change_theory.htm.

Schein, Edgar, and Warren Bennis. 1965. *Personal and Organizational Change Through Group Methods*. New York: Wiley.

Schelling, Thomas. 1960. *The Strategy of Conflict*. New Haven, Conn.: Yale University Press.

Schippers, Michaela. 2003. "Reflexivity in Teams." Ph.D. diss., Free University, Amsterdam.

Schön, Donald. 1983. *The Reflective Practitioner*. New York: Basic Books.

Senge, Peter M. 1990. *The Fifth Discipline: The Art and Practice of the Learning Organization*. New York: Doubleday.

Sitkin, Sim B. 1992. "Learning Through Failure: The Strategy of Small Losses." In *Research in Organizational Behavior*, edited by Larry L. Cummings and Barry Staw. Volume 14. Greenwich, Conn.: JAI Press.

Sole, Deborah, and Amy Edmondson. 2002. "Situated Knowledge and Learning in Dispersed Teams." *British Journal of Management* 13(special issue, September): S17–S34.

Sterman, John. 1989. "Modeling Managerial Behavior: Misperceptions of Feedback in Dynamic Decision-Making." *Management Science* 35(3): 321–39.

Swift, Wendy, and Jan Copeland. 1996. "Treatment Needs and Experiences of Australian Women with Alcohol and Drug Problems." *Drug and Alcohol Dependence* 40(3): 211–19.

Thiederman, Sondra. 1988. "Managing the Foreign-Born Work Force: Keys to Effective Cross-Cultural Motivation." *Manage* 40(3): 26–29.

Tyler, Tom R. 1994. "Psychological Models of the Justice Motive: Antecedents of Procedural and Distributive Justice." *Journal of Personality and Social Psychology* 67(5): 850–63.

Tyler, Tom R., and E. Allen Lind. 1992. "A Relational Model of Authority in Groups," In *Advances in Experimental Psychology*. Volume 25. New York: Academy Press.

Uzzi, Brian. 1997. "Social Structure and Competition in Interfirm Networks: The Paradox of Embeddedness." *Administrative Science Quarterly* 42(1): 35–67.

Van Dyne, Linn, and Jeffery A. LePine. 1998. "Helping and Voice Extra-Role Behaviors: Evidence of Construct and Predictive Validity." *Academy of Management Journal* 41(1): 108–19.

Wageman, Ruth. 1998. "The Effects of Team Design and Leader Behavior on Self-Managing Teams: A Field Study." Working paper. New York: Columbia University.

Waks, Leonard J. 1988. "Design Principles for Laboratory Education in the Creative Process." *Person-Centered Review* 3(4): 463–78.

Wall, Toby D., and Joseph A. Lischeron. 1977. *Worker Participation: A Critique of the Literature and Some Fresh Evidence*. Maidenhead, U.K.: McGraw-Hill.

Walsh, James. 1995. "Managerial and Organizational Cognition: Notes from a Trip Down Memory Lane." *Organization Science* 6(3): 280–321.

West, Michael A. 1990. "The Social Psychology of Innovation in Groups." In *Innovation and Creativity at Work: Psychological and Organizational Strategies*, edited by Michael A. West and James L. Farr. Chichester, U.K.: Wiley.

West, Michael, and Michaela Wallace. 1991. "Innovation in Health Care Teams." *European Journal of Social Psychology* 21(4): 303–15.

Wheelwright, Steve C., and Matthew C. Verlinden. 1999. "Eli Lilly: The Evista Project." HBS case #699-016. Boston: Harvard Business School Publishing.

Williamson, Oliver E., and Richard Craswell. 1993. "Calculativeness, Trust, and Economic Organization." *Journal of Law and Economics* 36(1, part 2): 453–502.

Zucker, Lynne G. 1986. "Production of Trust: Institutional Sources of Economic Structure, 1840–1920." *Research in Organizational Behavior* 8: 53–111.

PART III

CHALLENGES TO SECURING AND SUSTAINING TRUST

Chapter 11

Managing Images of Trustworthiness in Organizations

KIMBERLY D. ELSBACH

To POSSESS an image of interpersonal trustworthiness is to be perceived by others as displaying (now and in the future) competence, benevolence, and integrity in one's behaviors and beliefs (Mayer, Davis, and Schoorman 1995; Mayer and Davis 1999). In this definition, interpersonal trustworthiness is defined as a perception of trustworthiness from and about social interactions. In a corporate context, competence refers to the abilities and skills that allow a manager to have power and influence in the organization, benevolence refers to a manager's desire to do good on behalf of organizational members, and integrity refers to a manager's adherence to principles or ideals that an organization's members find acceptable. This definition is based on recent frameworks which define trust as "a willingness to be vulnerable to the actions of another party." (Mayer and Davis 1999, 124). That is, where trust is defined as a willingness or intent to submit to the actions of another, trustworthiness is defined as a perception that a trusted person, a trustee, will exhibit specific behaviors that commonly engender a willingness to submit to that person's actions. These definitions of trust and trustworthiness are supported by recent research that identifies both motivation and ability as bases of trust in organizations (Mishra 1996; Brockner and Siegel 1996), and uses the components of intention and belief to define trust (McKnight, Cummings, and Chervany 1998).[1]

Such definitions seem particularly appropriate in managerial settings, where trust often means submitting to the direction of leaders with little knowledge about the consequences of those directions. In such risky or ambiguous situations, perceived trustworthiness has been shown to be an important factor in engendering people's willingness to subject themselves to the actions of others (Kramer and Tyler 1996). For example, F. David Schoorman, Roger C. Mayer, and James H. Davis (1996) found that perceived trustworthiness in a staff member contributed significantly to a veterinarian's willingness to delegate to that staff member risky tasks such as administering anesthesia. Similarly, in a fourteen-month field study of management performance appraisal systems, Mayer and Davis (1999) found that enhancing perceived benevolence, integrity, and competence by means of implementing a new performance appraisal system increased employees "willingness to let top management have control over" employee and organizational well-being.

Effects of Trustworthiness Perceptions

In general, research on the effects of trustworthiness perceptions provides evidence that such impressions can lead individuals to cooperate and support the trustworthy person by, for example, voting for a trustworthy politician (Sigal et al. 1988) or cooperating with a trustworthy negotiator (Schurr and Ozanne 1985). Further, such impressions can lead individuals to view the trustworthy person as more positive on a number of other traits such as effectiveness as a teacher (Freeman 1988) and believability as a communicator (Lui and Standing 1989). In a similar vein, when organization members perceive managers to be trustworthy, they have been shown to exhibit a number of positive attitudes and behaviors, including citizenship behavior and attentiveness to the needs of others (McAllister 1995), willingness to express opinions in decision-making processes (Dooley and Fryxell 1999), and willingness to obtain help for substance-abuse problems (Harris and Fennell 1988). These behaviors result in positive outcomes for the organization, such as enhanced decision quality (Dooley and Fryxell 1999) and enhanced managerial performance (McAllister 1995).

Antecedents of Trustworthiness Perceptions

Given the important effects of perceptions of interpersonal trustworthiness, organizational researchers have recently begun to explore their antecedents. This research has focused on two factors that have the greatest potential to be changed: behaviors and cognitions.[2]

Behavioral factors. Organizational researchers have examined the behavioral factors that contribute to perceived trustworthiness. A recent review of this work (Whitener et al. 1998) suggests five primary behaviors that managers can exhibit to increase their perceptions of trustworthiness among employees: behavioral consistency; behavioral integrity; sharing control; accurate, open, and thorough communication; and demonstrating concern.

Behavioral consistency—reliability or predictability—on the part of managers increases employees' confidence in managers' competence and increases employees' willingness to take risks on managers' behalf (Butler 1991; Robinson and Rousseau 1994). Behavioral integrity— telling the truth and keeping promises—reduces employees' perceived risk in working with a manager (Mayer, Davis, and Schoorman 1995). Sharing control by managers enhances employees' abilities to protect their own interests and affirms their self-worth as valued parts of the organization, which increases their perception of managers' benevolence (Tyler and Lind 1992). Accurate, open, and thorough communication about decisions and organizational issues helps employees to feel that there is a sharing and exchanging of ideas, and increases perceptions of managers' integrity (Butler 1991; Hart et al. 1986). Finally, demonstrating concern for employees' well-being—for example, by showing consideration and sensitivity for employees' needs and interests, acting in a way that protects their interests, and refraining from exploiting employees—leads employees to perceive managers as loyal and benevolent.

While this research confirms the notion that, behaviors that exhibit the dimensions of competence, ability, and benevolence will enhance perceptions of trustworthiness, it does not go very far in explicating *how* people interpret such behaviors as evidence of trustworthiness. As Ellen M. Whitener and colleagues (1998, 526) note, "boundary conditions" such as cognitions of perceived similarity and competence may "limit the extent to which managerial trustworthy behavior affects employees' perceptions of trust." Whitener et al. (1998) go on to suggest that understanding how such processes affect perceptions of trustworthiness is an important component to evolving frameworks of managerial trust.

Cognitive factors. In response to the work on behavioral factors, another group of organizational theorists have begun to explore the cognitive factors that might lead to perceptions of trustworthiness. Recent reviews of organizational research suggest that the cognitive processes of social categorization and comparison might explain how perceptions of trustworthiness are established in the minds of organization members. For example, in their framework describing initial trust formation among organization members, D. Harrison McKnight, Larry L. Cummings, and Norman L. Chervany (1998) suggest that social categorization processes influence perceptions of managerial trustworthiness by defining managers in terms of group membership, viz.: (1) in-groups (vs. out-groups); (2) groups that have an organizational reputation for competence, benevolence, or integrity; and (3) stereotypically trustworthy groups, such as certain religious groups. In the same vein, Michelle Williams (2001) suggests that in most situations, individuals will be more likely to trust in-group members over out-group members because there is less known about out-group members and stereotypes of out-group members are likely to exist (Cox 1993; Donnellon 1996)—but that in certain situations individuals may openly trust out-group members, for example, in situations where there is a professional norm of "goodwill" between groups (Meyerson, Weick, and Kramer 1996). Williams (2001) also suggests that categorizations that highlight professional legitimacy and professional norms of trustworthy behavior are likely to enhance perceptions of trustworthiness.

Taken together, the organizational research on behavioral and cognitive antecedents to perceptions of trustworthiness suggest that, in order to improve their image of trustworthiness, managers might exhibit behaviors that elicit in observers social categorizations and comparisons highlighting their similarity to observers, their institutional certification as competent, and their reputation for benevolence, competence, and integrity. Thus, the reviewed research provides the theoretical grounding needed to design effective tactics for managing images of interpersonal trustworthiness. Yet few organizational researchers have taken this step (Elsbach and Elofson 2000). Moreover, there appears to be no general framework that discusses how to use displayed behaviors and social cognitions to maintain or manage interpersonal trustworthiness.

In the remainder of this chapter, I develop a framework that defines some of the image management tactics managers and other organizational members might use to enhance their image of trustworthiness. This framework is grounded in the research on the antecedents of trustworthiness perceptions and in empirical findings from practitioner studies of perceptions of trustworthiness in, for example, counselors, educators, and politicians. The latter research provides a useful empirical lens for examining the relationship between behaviors and cognitions in managing impressions of trustworthiness because of its setting in practical, real-life contexts.

Tactics for Managing Images of Trustworthiness

Over the last two decades, a number of education and counseling researchers have examined the predictors of positive perceptions of trustworthiness between practitioners and their clients (Carter and Motta 1988; Arokiasamy et al. 1994). In addition, a number of social-psychological studies have examined the predictors of trustworthiness perceptions in contexts involving politicians or other leaders and their followers (Bless et al. 2000). This research focuses on visible behaviors and displays that enhance perceptions of trustworthiness.

A review of this research (summarized in table 11.1) indicates three types of tactics available to individuals attempting to manage their trustworthiness images in interpersonal relationships:

1. Self-presentation behaviors—verbal accounts, references to titles, self-disclosures

2. Choice of language—formal or informal, specific, technical, easy or hard to understand

3. Physical appearance—dress, posture, facial expression, maturity

Further examination of this research reveals that these tactics may affect images of trustworthiness by suggesting one or more of the specific characteristics associated with trustworthiness: similarity to observers, belonging to a group that is stereotypically trustworthy, and having a reputation for competence, benevolence, or integrity.

In the following sections I discuss these three tactics, as well as some specific examples of each. I also discuss how each tactic might lead to specific trustworthiness categorizations. (See figure 11.1 for a summary of these tactics and their predicted effects on perceptions of trustworthiness.)

Self-Presentation Behaviors and Trustworthiness Images

Research in the area of impression management provides substantial evidence that interpersonal images may be enhanced through self-presentation behaviors (Giacalone and Rosenfeld 1989, 1991). Findings from several studies of practitioner-client interaction, such as counselors and patients or educators and students, suggest that trustworthiness may be one such image. One common self-presentation tactic that has been shown to enhance trustworthiness perceptions in these contexts is the revelation that one is similarly "human" to one's audience, that is, that one possesses the same human emotions, limits, or failings as one's audience. Such revelations may improve perceptions of trustworthiness by prompting clients to categorize practitioners as "in-group" members. For example, Edward J. Lundeen and W. John Schuldt (1989) showed a videotaped session between a counselor and a client to undergraduate students, and asked those students to empathize with the client. Their study found that the counselor was rated as more trustworthy if he disclosed information about himself that was similar to the difficult issues discussed by the client. In a similar study design with retired persons as raters of counselors, Bert Hayslip, Lawrence J. Schneider, and Kay Bryant (1989) found that a

Table 11.1   Research on Perceptions of Interpersonal Trustworthiness

Citation	Factors Enhancing Trustworthiness Images	Factors Reducing Trustworthiness Images	Categorizations Suggested[a]
Self-presentation behaviors			
Bless et al. (2000)	Reference to one untrustworthy exemplar in category (such as politicians) increases trustworthiness of other contrasting category members.	Reference to one untrustworthy exemplar in category (such as politicians) reduces trustworthiness of general category.	Members of stereotypically untrustworthy group (politicians). Members of group dissimilar to out-group.
Newcomb et al. (2000)	Rock stars' testimonials in antidrug-use commercials.		Members of in-group. Members of group with competent reputation.
Lundeen and Schuldt (1989)	Therapist's self-disclosure about similar problems in video-taped mock-therapy session.		Members of in-group.
Arokiasamy et al. (1994)	Good attending skills by counselor in videotaped therapy session: attended to client's feelings, asked pertinent questions, made responses reflective of client's feeling statements.		Members of stereotypically legitimate group. Members of in-group.
Hayslip, Schneider, and Bryant (1989)	Client's ability to identify with individual counselor.		Members of in-group.
Myers and Dugan (1996)		Sexist behavior by professors in real-life classroom experiences (use of stereotypical examples of male and female roles, sexist language, calling only on males).	Members of stereotypically untrustworthy group (for example, bigots, sexists). Members of out-group.
Redfern, Dancey, and Dryden (1993)	Empathetic treatment of client by counselor.		Members of in-group.

Language			
Hurwitz, Miron, and Johnson (1992)	Words that connote power, status.	Passive voice.	Members of competent group.
Elsbach and Elofson (2000)	Easy-to-understand, colloquial language used by an expert communicating a decision explanation.	Hard-to-understand, technical language used by an expert communicating a decision explanation.	Members of in-group or out-group. Members of stereotypically untrustworthy group.
Physical appearance			
Roll and Roll (1984)	Informal dress.	Formal dress.	Members of in-group or stereotypically competent group. Members of out-group or stereotypically incompetent group.
Carter and Motta (1988)	Informal dress, counselors address others by first name.	Formal dress, counselors address others by surname.	Members of in-group or stereotypically competent group. Members of out-group or stereotypically incompetent group.
Heitmeyer and Goldsmith (1990)	Moderately formal dress.	Overly formal or informal dress.	Members of out-group or stereotypically incompetent group.
Brownlow (1992)	"Baby-faced" speaker.	"Mature-faced" speaker.	Members of stereotypically trustworthy or untrustworthy groups.
Lee, Uhlemann, and Haase (1985)	Perceptions by client: warm, concerned facial expression; spontaneous head nod; soft, pleasing voice; expressive gesture; timely smile; slow fluent speech; relaxed, approaching posture; steady eye contact for beginning counselors.		Members of stereotypically competent group.

Source: Author's compilation.
[a]Suggested by research, but not explicitly tested.

Figure 11.1   Tactics for Enhancing Interpersonal Perceptions of Trustworthiness

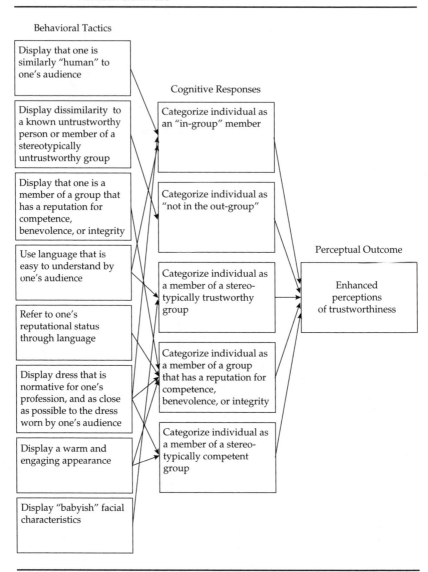

Behavioral Tactics

Display that one is similarly "human" to one's audience

Cognitive Responses

Display dissimilarity to a known untrustworthy person or member of a stereotypically untrustworthy group

Categorize individual as an "in-group" member

Display that one is a member of a group that has a reputation for competence, benevolence, or integrity

Categorize individual as "not in the out-group"

Use language that is easy to understand by one's audience

Categorize individual as a member of a stereotypically trustworthy group

Perceptual Outcome

Refer to one's reputational status through language

Enhanced perceptions of trustworthiness

Display dress that is normative for one's profession, and as close as possible to the dress worn by one's audience

Categorize individual as a member of a group that has a reputation for competence, benevolence, or integrity

Display a warm and engaging appearance

Categorize individual as a member of a stereotypically competent group

Display "babyish" facial characteristics

Source: Author's compilation.

client's ability to identify with a particular counselor (perceive a "one-ness" with the counselor [Ashforth and Mael 1989]) increased ratings of the counselor's trustworthiness.

By contrast, other studies of client and practitioner interactions have shown that revealing or displaying how one *differs* from a known *untrust-*

worthy person or member of a stereotypically untrustworthy group can also enhance perceptions of that practitioner's trustworthiness. These revelations may improve trustworthiness perceptions by prompting clients to categorize practitioners as "not in the out-group." Although not mentioned by organizational frameworks describing the categorizations required for perceptions of trustworthiness (Whitener et al. 1998), such categorizations have been shown to be important in defining social identities because they connote "disidentifications" with an undesirable group (Elsbach and Bhattacharya 2001). An illustration of this process comes from a study by Daniel J. Myers and Kimberly B. Dugan (1996). They found that graduate students' perceptions of their professors' trustworthiness was negatively associated with reports of sexist behavior in the classroom by those professors, as evidenced by use of only masculine pronouns, calling on men more than women, and using course materials that don't include women and are not written by women. Their findings suggest that sexist behaviors may have prompted students to categorize the offending professor as a member of an out-group, that is, "sexists," as a well as a stereotypically untrustworthy group, that is, "bigots."

By contrast, a few studies by social psychologists have shown that presenting oneself as dissimilar to an untrustworthy other may improve one's image of trustworthiness. For example, Herbert Bless et al. (2000) studied German students' perceptions of real-life politicians after a short exercise that brought specific politicians to mind: they were required to identify the German state headed by four specific politicians. Results showed that including, as one of the four, a politician who was associated with a recent, widely known scandal decreased students' perceptions of the trustworthiness of politicians in general, but increased perceptions of the other three politicians' trustworthiness. The authors suggest that the judgment of German politicians in general was negative because the scandalous politician elicited the stereotypically untrustworthy category "politicians." Yet the other politicians, because of the contrast between them and the scandalous politician, were judged more positively; the students viewed these other politicians as different from the scandalous politician. Bless et al. (2000, 1042) describe these results as evidence of an inclusion-exclusion model of social judgment (see also Schwarz and Bless 1992). They note:

> Superordinate categories (such as German politicians) allow for the inclusion of subordinate context information (in this case, exemplars of the category "German politicians"). This results in assimilation effects [such as stereotyping] on judgments of superordinate targets. Lateral categories, however, such as different exemplars, are mutually exclusive. Hence the accessible context information is used in constructing a standard of comparison, resulting in contrast effects [in-groups vs. out-groups] on judgments of other lateral targets.

Finally, a few studies by social psychologists and counseling and education theorists have shown that revealing or displaying evidence that one is a member of a group that has a reputation for competence, benevolence, or integrity may enhance perceptions that one is trustworthy. For example, Michael D. Newcomb, Claire St. Antoine Mercurio, and Candace A. Wollard (2000) examined the effects of using unknown actors or widely known rock stars (Gene Simmons, Jon Bon Jovi, Belinda Carlysle, and Aimee Mann) in antidrug-use commercials aimed at high school students in Los Angeles. In a pre-test, Newcomb et al. found that 67 percent of a sample of these high school students expected heavy-metal rock stars to use "a lot of drugs." Further, recent studies suggested that a majority of these students would identify with rock stars (Arnett 1995). These findings suggest that high school students might categorize rock stars as members of a group that is "competent" to talk about the negative effects of drug use and also that is "similar" with respect to students' beliefs and attitudes. Both of these categorization processes would enhance students' perceptions of rock stars' trustworthiness as spokespersons in antidrug-use campaigns. Consistent with this prediction, Newcomb et al. (2000) found that the high school students perceived the rock stars, especially those admitting to personal drug use, as significantly more trustworthy than unknown actors.

In sum, the use of self-presentational behaviors—self-revelations, stereotypical behavior, labeling—may be used by organizational members to signal that they are similar to observers because they are either members of an in-group or not members of an out-group, and that they possess benevolence, competence, and integrity because they are members of groups with reputations for such traits. These relationships between self-presentation tactics and trustworthiness categorizations are depicted in figure 10.1.

Language and Trustworthiness Images

Research in the area of communication and language (Scherer and Giles 1979) as well as social influence and social judgment (Fiske and Taylor 1991) suggests that the language one uses to communicate with others, regardless of the content of one's message, affects perceptions of one's trustworthiness. Findings from a small set of studies of trustworthiness and language suggest this effect may be due, at least in part, to the social categorizations that language elicits.

First, using language that is easy to understand by one's audience may improve images of a speaker's trustworthiness by prompting observers to categorize the speaker as similar to themselves and as members of an in-group. By contrast, the use of difficult-to-understand language containing technical jargon not familiar to the audience may reduce images of trustworthiness by leading observers to categorize the speaker as a member of an out-group. Further, using technical jargon and difficult-to-understand explanations may also lead observers to categorize the speaker as a member of a "stereotypically untrustworthy" group, for example, experts who hide behind jargon because they do not really understand the issue. Kimberly Elsbach and Greg Elofson (2000) found that the use of common or colloquial language and avoiding technical jargon improved managers' perceptions of a hypothetical consultant's trustworthiness in an exercise where students received advice about a foreign investment. The consultant who explained the logic of his investment decision in clear, simple terms understandable to a layperson was viewed as significantly more trustworthy than the one who used difficult-to-understand language.

Second, it appears that referring to one's status by means of titles and identifiers that connote status such as "head of organization," "New York State Police," or "Marshall fellow" or using language that indicates power (demanding and commanding as opposed to requesting) may enhance a person's image of trustworthiness. Such language may lead observers to categorize the speaker as "institutionally certified as competent." For example, Steven D. Hurwitz, Murray S. Miron, and Blair T. Johnson (1992) showed that "words that connote power" increased students' perceptions of the trustworthiness of videotaped expert witnesses, who had testified in actual medical malpractice trials. In their study, "power" words included remarks about the experts' official status, degree of prominence, and recognition in the field.

In sum, members of an organization may use specific types of language (technical jargon, common language, power words) (1) to signal that they are similar to observers because they are either members of an in-group or not members of an out-group, and (2) to signal that they are institutionally certified as competent. These relationships between language tactics and trustworthiness categorizations are depicted in figure 11.1.

Appearance and Trustworthiness Images

Finally, a number of studies of counselor-client interactions suggest that physical appearance can play an important role in the construction and maintenance of images of trustworthiness. Specifically, the dress, interpersonal demeanor, and facial characteristics of a counselor appear to affect perceptions of trustworthiness by clients.

First, a number of studies have shown that moderately informal dress—not too informal and not overly formal—enhances clients' perceptions of counselors' trustworthiness (Heitmeyer and Goldsmith 1990). For example, Randi I. Carter and Robert W. Motta (1988) had undergraduates view videotapes of simulated therapy sessions between a male therapist and a patient. In cases where the therapist was dressed informally, wearing an open-collar sports shirt, students perceived him as significantly more trustworthy than when he wore a tie and jacket. In a similar study, Stephen A. Roll and Bonnie M. Roll (1984) engaged undergraduates in an actual fifty-minute counseling session with a female therapist in which they talked about stressors of college life. In sessions in which the counselor was informally dressed, wearing clean blue jeans and a sweater, students rated her as being significantly more trustworthy than in sessions in which she was formally dressed, in a tailored suit and dress shoes. Here, the authors suggest that moderately informal dress may signal that the counselor is similar to the client, a member of the in-group, because most clients dress informally. Further, it seems plausible that informal dress may signal that the counselor is a member of a stereotypically competent group—the stereotypical perception of competent counselors and therapists, supported by television and movie depictions, is that they wear sweaters and comfortable shoes and not suits and ties. Although not mentioned by organizational frameworks describing the categorizations required for perceptions of trustworthiness (Whitener et al. 1998), *stereotypical competence* seems like a relevant antecedent categorization of trustworthiness, similar to the more general categorization of stereotypical trustworthiness. Thus, while moderately informal dress may be important for eliciting trustworthy categorizations for counselors, the more general lesson to be learned from these studies is that individuals should display dress that is normative for their profession, and as close as possible to the dress worn by their audiences, those to whom they wish to project an image of trustworthiness.

Second, several studies suggest that a warm and engaging appearance may improve counselors' images of trustworthiness among clients. In one particularly thorough study, Dong Yul Lee, Max R. Uhlemann, and Richard F. Haase (1985) found that during a twenty-minute therapy session, clients perceived beginning counselors as more trustworthy the more they displayed a warm and engaging appearance, a warm and concerned facial expression, spontaneous head nod at appropriate times during the session, used expressive gestures, a timely smile, a relaxed, approachable posture, and steady eye-contact. They were perceived as less trustworthy the more they displayed a more distanced, formal appearance. In the former cases, clients may have perceived the beginning counselors as displaying appearances that they expected a seasoned counselor to display. That is, these beginning counselors were categorized as stereotypically competent. It should be noted, however, that Lee et al. (1985) also found that clients and counselors differed in their interpretation of the same appearances, so that appearances that clients interpreted as engaging were not necessarily the same as the appearances counselors interpreted as engaging. So it is important, when you employ this tactic, to obtain reliable information about one's audience's preferences and perceptions of what constitutes an engaging appearance.

Finally, a few studies have shown that "babyish" facial characteristics may improve perceptions of trustworthiness by eliciting stereotypes about the physical appearance of honest and trustworthy people. Facial characteristics that are considered "babyish" include large heads and eyes and a youthful appearance. In one study examining perceived trustworthiness of a female student campaigning for an elected office on campus, Sheila Brownlow (1992) found that potential voters found a "baby-faced" candidate more trustworthy than a "mature-faced" candidate. In this case, the authors suggest that the baby-faced candidates were perceived as stereotypically honest and trustworthy, since we think of babies as innocent and free of guile.

In sum, appearance tactics (dress, engaging appearance, babyish facial characteristics) may be used by organizational members to signal that they are (1) similar to observers, (2) members of groups that are stereotypically thought to be competent, or (3) members of groups that are stereotypically thought to be honest and to possess integrity (see figure 11.1).

Conclusion

In this chapter, I have reviewed research that describes how cognitive and behavioral factors contribute to our perceptions of interpersonal trustworthiness. On the basis of this research I have proposed a set of linkages between specific cognitions—social categorizations—and enhanced perceptions of trustworthiness. On the basis of empirical research on practitioner-client relationships, I have in turn proposed a set of linkages between these specific social categorizations that enhance trustworthiness perceptions and a number of specific image management tactics. In this manner I have explicitly identified a framework of tactics that members of organizations might use to construct and maintain images of trustworthiness.

The implications of this framework are both theoretical and practical. First, this framework synthesizes theory about behavioral and cognitive antecedents of trustworthiness by indicating how specific behaviors might elicit specific cognitions relevant to trustworthiness perceptions. In doing so, it begins to fill some of the gaps in understanding of trustworthiness perceptions outlined by Whitener et al. (1998). It identifies some of the boundary conditions—the types of social categorizations most easily prompted by image management behaviors—that may limit the effectiveness of managers' attempts to improve trustworthiness perceptions among their employees. Further, it identifies at least two new categorizations that might lead to perceptions of trustworthiness: that one is not in the out-group and thus is dissimilar from untrustworthy group members and that one is a member of a stereotypically competent group. These two categorizations are suggested by empirical findings from client-practitioner research and provide enhancements to existing frameworks describing the cognitive antecedents of trustworthiness.

Second, this framework provides some practical guidance about the kinds of image management tactics that specific organizational members may effectively use. For example, it may be relatively easy for many organizational members to alter their dress to improve perceptions of trustworthiness, but relatively difficult for most to alter their physical characteristics—their facial appearance, posture, or smile. In cases where written communication is used as a means of improving trustworthiness perceptions, easy-to-understand language should be used in communications in general, but references to technical titles and degrees etc. might be used when it is important to gain trust by appearing "institutionally legitimate." It is also important to note that the findings upon which this framework is based show that it the audience's perceptions of the behavior, not the image maker's, determine the management tactic's effectiveness in eliciting desired social categorizations. Thus, before choosing any tactic, an impression manager must understand how his or her audience defines "in-groupness," legitimacy, competence, integrity, and benevolence.

These contributions notwithstanding, the ideas presented in the current framework may present an ethical dilemma for managers who do not wish to "cultivate a belief that managers merely need to display the appearance of trustworthiness (Greenberg 1990) to create trusting relationships" (Whitener et al. 1998, 525). Yet, as Whitener et al. (525) go on to note: "[I]mpression management attempts need not be manipulative or insincere (Goffman 1959; Liden and Mitchell 1988). Indeed, a focus on behavior calls attention to what organizations can do to initiate and manage trustworthy behavior and to engender and support trusting relationships that are self-perpetuating and sustainable."

In the end, then, the present framework may best serve organizations as a means to identify the types of behavior they wish to naturally elicit from their members.

Notes

1. It is significant that Roger C. Mayer, James H. Davis, and F. David Schoorman (1995) define the components of trustworthiness in purely cognitive terms (perceptions of others), and differentiate their framework from those that

include affective components of trustworthiness such as feelings of shared values (McAllister 1995). My focus on image management in this chapter leads me to rely on the cognitive framework.

2. I omit stable personality traits as an antecedent factor to images of trustworthiness because of the difficulty in influencing such traits, meaning that they are not good targets for image management tactics.

References

Arnett, Jeffrey Jensen. 1995. "Adolescents' Uses of the Media for Self-Socialization." *Journal of Youth and Adolescence* 24(5): 519–33.

Arokiasamy, Charles V., Douglas C. Strohmer, Sherri Guice, Rose Angelocci, and Michelle Hoppe. 1994. "Effects of Politically Correct Language and Counselor Skill Level on Perceptions of Counselor Credibility." *Rehabilitation Counseling Bulletin* 37(4): 304–14.

Ashforth, Blake E., and Fred Mael. 1989. "Social Identity Theory and the Organization." *Academy of Management Review* 14(1): 20–39.

Bless, Herbert, Eric R. Igou, Norbert Schwarz, and Michaela Wanke. 2000. "Reducing Context Effects by Adding Context Information: The Direction and Size of Context Effects in Political Judgment." *Personality and Social Psychology Bulletin* 26(9): 1036–45.

Brockner, Joel, and Phyllis Siegel. 1996. "Understanding the Interaction Between Procedural and Distributive Justice: The Role of Trust." In *Trust in Organizations: Frontiers of Theory and Research,* edited by Roderick M. Kramer, and Tom R. Tyler. Thousand Oaks, Calif.: Sage.

Brownlow, Sheila. 1992. "Seeing Is Believing: Facial Appearance, Credibility, and Attitude Change." *Journal of Nonverbal Behavior* 16(2): 101–15.

Butler, John K. 1991. "Towards Understanding and Measuring Conditions of Trust: Evolution of Conditions of Trust Inventory." *Journal of Management* 17(3): 643–63.

Carter, Randi I., and Robert W. Motta. 1988. "Effects of Intimacy of Therapist's Self Disclosure and Formality on Perceptions of Credibility in an Initial Interview." *Perceptual and Motor Skills* 66(2): 167–73.

Cox, Taylor H. 1993. *Cultural Diversity in Organizations.* San Francisco: Berrett-Koehler.

Donnellon, Anne. 1996. *Team Talk: The Power of Language in Team Dynamics.* Boston: Harvard Business School Press.

Dooley, Robert S., and Gerald E. Fryxell. 1999. "Attaining Decision Quality and Commitment from Dissent: The Moderating Effects of Loyalty and Competence in Strategic Decision Making Teams." *Academy of Management Journal* 42(4): 389–402.

Elsbach, Kimberly D., and C. B. Bhattacharya. 2001. "Defining Who You Are by What You're Not: A Study of Social Identity and the National Rifle Association." *Organization Science* 12(4): 393–413.

Elsbach, Kimberly D., and Greg Elofson. 2000. "How the Packaging of Decision Explanations Affects Perceptions of Trustworthiness." *Academy of Management Journal* 43(1): 80–89.

Fiske, Susan, and Shelley Taylor. 1991. *Social Cognition*. New York: McGraw-Hill.

Giacalone, Robert A., and Paul Rosenfeld. 1989. *Impression Management in the Organization*. Hillsdale, N.J.: Erlbaum.

————. 1991 *Applied Impression Management: How Image Making Affects Managerial Decisions*. Newbury Park, Calif.: Sage.

Goffman, Erving. 1959. *The Presentation of Self in Everyday Life*. Garden City, N.Y.: Doubleday.

Greenberg, Jerald. 1990. "Looking Fair vs. Being Fair: Managing Impressions of Organizational Justice." In *Research in Organizational Behavior*, edited by Barry M. Staw and Larry L. Cummings. Volume 12. Greenwich, Conn.: JAI Press.

Freeman, Harvey R. 1988. "Perceptions of Teacher Characteristics and Student Judgments of Teacher Effectiveness." *Teaching of Psychology* 15(3): 158–60.

Harris, Michael M., and Mary L. Fennell. 1988. "Perceptions of an Employee Assistance Program and Employees' Willingness to Participate." *Journal of Applied Behavioral Science* 24(4): 423–38.

Hart, Kerry M., H. Randall Capps, Joseph P. Cangemi, and Larry M. Caillouet. 1986. "Exploring Organizational Trust and Its Multiple Dimensions: A Case Study of General Motors." *Organizational Development Journal* 4(1): 31–39.

Hayslip, Bert, Lawrence J. Schneider, and Kay Bryant. 1989. "Older Women's Perceptions of Female Counselors: The Influence of Therapist Age and Problem Intimacy." *Gerontologist* 29(2): 239–44.

Heitmeyer, Jeanne R., and Elizabeth B. Goldsmith. 1990. "Attire, an Influence on Perceptions of Counselors' Characteristics." *Perceptual and Motor Skills* 70(3): 923–29.

Hurwitz, Steven D., Murray S. Miron, and Blair T. Johnson. 1992. "Source Credibility and the Language of Expert Testimony." *Journal of Applied Social Psychology* 22(24): 1909–39.

Kramer, Roderick M., and Tom R. Tyler. 1996. *Trust in Organizations. Frontiers of Theory and Research*. Thousand Oaks, Calif.: Sage.

Lee, Dong Yul, Max R. Uhlemann, and Richard F. Haase. 1985. "Counselor Verbal and Nonverbal Responses and Perceived Expertness, Trustworthiness, and Attractiveness." *Journal of Counseling Psychology* 32(2): 181–87.

Liden, Robert C., and Terence R. Mitchell. 1988. "Ingratiatory Behavior in Organizational Settings." *Academy of Management Review* 13(4): 572–87.

Lui, Louisa, and Lionel Standing. 1989. "Communicator Credibility: Trustworthiness Defeats Expertness." *Social Behavior and Personality* 17(2): 219–21.

Lundeen, Edward J., and W. John Schuldt. 1989. "Effects of Therapist's Self Disclosure and a Physical Barrier on Subjects' Perceptions of the Therapist: An Analogue Study." *Psychological Reports* 64(3): 715–20.

Mayer, Roger C., and James H. Davis. 1999. "The Effect of the Performance Appraisal System on Trust for Management: A Field Quasi Experiment." *Journal of Applied Psychology* 84(1): 123–36.

Mayer, Roger C., James H. Davis, and F. David Schoorman. 1995. "An Integrative Model of Organizational Trust." *Academy of Management Review* 20(3): 709–34.

McAllister, Daniel J. 1995. "Affect- and Cognition-Based Trust as Foundations for Interpersonal Cooperation in Organizations." *Academy of Management Journal* 38(1): 24–59.

McKnight, D. Harrison, Larry L. Cummings, and Norman L. Chervany. 1998. "Initial Trust Formation in New Organizational Relationships." *Academy of Management Review* 23(3): 473–90.

Meyerson, Debra, Karl E. Weick, and Roderick M. Kramer. 1996. "Swift Trust and Temporary Groups." In *Trust in Organizations: Frontiers of Theory and Research,* edited by Roderick M. Kramer and Tom R. Tyler. Thousand Oaks, Calif.: Sage.

Mishra, Aneil K. 1996. "Organizational Responses to Crisis: The Centrality of Trust." In *Trust in Organizations: Frontiers of Theory and Research,* edited by Roderick M. Kramer and Tom R. Tyler. Thousand Oaks, Calif.: Sage.

Myers, Daniel J., and Kimberly B. Dugan. 1996. "Sexism in Graduate School Classrooms: Consequences for Students and Faculty." *Gender and Society* 10(3): 330–50.

Newcomb, Michael D., Claire St. Antoine Mercurio, and Candace A. Wollard. 2000. "Rock Stars in Anti–Drug Abuse Commercials: An Experimental Study of Adolescents' Reactions." *Journal of Applied Social Psychology* 30(6): 1160–85.

Redfern, Sheila, Christine P. Dancey, and Windy Dryden. 1993. "Empathy: Its Effect on How Counselors Are Perceived." *British Journal of Guidance and Counseling* 21: 300–9.

Robinson, Sandra L., and Denise M. Rousseau. 1994. "Violating the Psychological Contract: Not the Exception but the Norm." *Journal of Organizational Behavior* 15(3): 245–59.

Roll, Stephen A., and Bonnie M. Roll. 1984. "Neophyte Counselor Attire and College Student Perceptions of Expertness, Trustworthiness, and Attractiveness." *Counselor Education and Supervision* 4(4): 321–27.

Scherer, Klaus Ranier, and Howard Giles, eds. 1979. *Social Markers in Speech.* Cambridge: Cambridge University Press.

Schoorman, F. David, Roger C. Mayer, and James H. Davis. 1996. "Empowerment in Veterinary Clinics: The Role of Trust in Delegation." Paper presented at the eleventh annual meeting of the Society for Industrial and Organizational Psychology. San Diego, Calif. (April 1996).

Schurr, Paul H., and Julie L. Ozanne. 1985. "Influences on Exchange Processes: Buyers' Preconceptions of a Seller's Trustworthiness and Bargaining Toughness." *Journal of Consumer Research* 11(4): 939–53.

Schwarz, Norbert, and Herbert Bless. 1992. "Scandals and the Public's Trust in Politicians: Assimilation and Contrast Effects." *Personality and Social Psychology Bulletin* 18(5): 574–79.

Sigal, Janet, Louis Hsu, Stacey Foodim, and Jeffrey Betman. 1988. "Factors Affecting Perceptions of Political Candidates Accused of Sexual and Financial Misconduct." *Political Psychology* 9(2): 273–80.

Tyler, Tom R., and E. Allan Lind. 1992. "A Relational Model of Authority in Groups." In *Advances in Experimental Social Psychology,* edited by Mark Zanna. Volume 25. San Francisco: Jossey-Bass.

Whitener, Ellen M., Susan E. Brodt, M. Audrey Korsgaard, and Jon M. Werner. 1998. "Managers as Initiators of Trust: An Exchange Relationship Framework for Understanding Managerial Trustworthy Behavior." *Academy of Management Review* 23(3): 513–30.

Williams, Michelle. 2001. "In Whom We Trust: Group Membership as an Affective Context for Trust Development." *Academy of Management Review* 26(3): 377–96.

Chapter 12

Paradoxes of Trust: Empirical and Theoretical Departures from a Traditional Model

J. Keith Murnighan, Deepak Malhotra, and J. Mark Weber

T HE CONCEPT of exchange is central to social action (Homans 1961). In essence, anything that we might label as "social" depends on the give-and-take of more than a single individual. Many of these exchanges are informal or implicit, like the reciprocation of a smile upon meeting or the fulfillment of expectations that other drivers will conform to the driving norms of a particular locale. When exchanges become more formal or explicit, the parties typically reach agreements that regulate the transfer of objects or ideas between them, like the sale and delivery of goods in a market or the exchange of marriage vows. These kinds of exchanges are often accompanied by written documents, contracts, which stipulate many of the parameters of the exchange. However, what are often implicit in these contracts are the fundamental, sometimes value-laden expectations of the parties. In addition, in formal contracts it is literally impossible to cover all of the past, present, and future issues and concerns of the parties. Thus, every chemical and physical detail of the goods being exchanged is not stipulated in buyer-seller contracts, nor are all of the commitments that marriage partners expect of each other stated in their wedding vows.

Most people understand, at least implicitly, that contracts are limited and cannot be all-encompassing. As a result, formal exchanges often rely on a more generalized trust that extends beyond contractual obligations. This chapter begins by describing common conceptions of trust, based on early literature and everyday notions of the concept. We then discuss various definitions of trust, choosing a recent definition as the basis for our subsequent discussion. In the remainder of the chapter, we address some converse, counterintuitive findings with regard to trust and trusting acts, some of which constitute paradoxes, in other words, sets of statements that are self-referential and contradictory, establishing a vicious cycle (Hughes and Brecht 1975). We focus most of our review on our own recent research: it shows that a rational-choice approach to trusting behavior does not provide a clear basis for behavioral predictions. We then present a preliminary model that expands current conceptualizations of trust and the processes that help establish it. We conclude by discussing a variety of theoretical and practical implications.

Common Conceptions of Trust

Most treatments of trust suggest that it builds slowly (see Kelley 1979; Rempel, Holmes, and Zanna 1985).[1] Repeated positive interactions between two (or more) parties contribute to attributions of benevolence that in turn engender trust (Mayer, Davis, and Schoorman 1995). The development of trust tends to be initially gradual but increasingly rapid, as each additional positive interaction becomes more valuable in establishing mutual trust (see figure 12.1). In essence, positive interactions form an accumulating foundation that allows both parties to have increasing confidence in each other's actions. After rising markedly, the impact of additional positive interactions becomes less important—only because trust may not be able to continue to increase exponentially. Even so, trust is likely to continue increasing, however marginally, as additional positive interactions accumulate.[2]

Common conceptions of trust suggest that the occurrence of a negative interaction where trust and positive outcomes were expected can be devastating. Once trust is broken, it may be lost completely and forever. According to John K. Rempel, John G. Holmes, and Mark P. Zanna (1985), not only is trust difficult to establish, it also "is doubly difficult to reestablish" (111). Figure 12.2 shows what happens when trust that has been built on long, repeated positive interactions has been violated. (There is an implicit assumption that some of these interactions entailed vulnerability and resulted from voluntary action by one party or the other.) The immediate result is the dramatic reduction or disappearance of trust, entering the realm of distrust. Now, the reestablishment of trust between the same parties becomes particularly problematic. The negative event must be cognitively resolved before trust can be reestablished, but because negative events carry considerably more weight than positive events, the task of trust reestablishment is considerably more difficult than the task of initial trust establishment.

Figure 12.1   Traditional Model of Trust Development

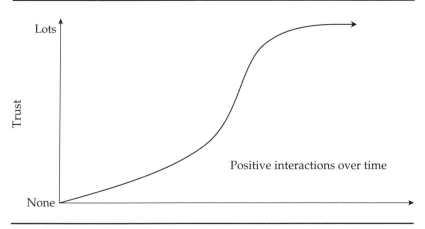

Source: Authors' compilation.

This depiction of the trust formation process might be called "a rational-choice approach" (see Kramer 1999). In essence, it suggests that people do not take big risks in new relationships. Instead, trust builds slowly. It is almost as if people implicitly calculate the probabilities that their trust will be honored; if they have had repeated positive experi-

Figure 12.2   The Impact of a Breach of Trust

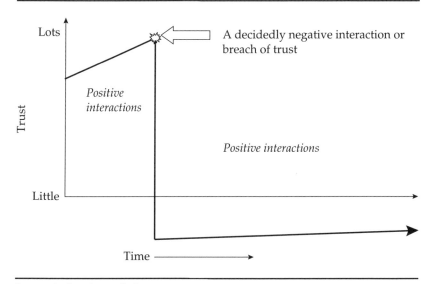

Source: Authors' compilation.

ences, they are willing to increase the stakes with greater confidence. This process matches rational models of decision making, and considerable data support this approach (Howard 1966; Rapoport and Mowshowitz 1966; Boyle and Bonacich 1970).

Although trust is obviously a critical issue in all sorts of exchanges, the literature seems to have paid only moderate attention to it until recently (see Kramer 1999). Recent progress on its definition and conceptualization has stimulated considerable research interest. Prior to turning to some of that research, we briefly summarize some of the recent conceptual discussions and present a definition of trust that helps guide our subsequent analyses.

Defining Trust

The psychological and organizational literatures have historically been populated by many different definitions of trust, and competing conceptualizations have at times been problematic. For instance, Roger C. Mayer, James H. Davis, and F. David Schoorman (1995) suggested that advances have been hindered by "a lack of clear differentiation among factors that contribute to trust, trust itself, and outcomes of trust" (711).

One of Mayer, Davis, and Schoorman's (1995) most important contributions was to focus on vulnerability as an essential element in trust. This theoretical emphasis built on Diego Gambetta's (1988) classic definition as well as earlier observations that the "willingness to take risks may be one of the few characteristics common to all trust situations" (Johnson-George and Swap 1982, 1306). More recently, in a special issue of *The Academy of Management Review* on trust (Rousseau et al. 1998), the "willingness to be vulnerable" was the most frequently cited definition of trust.

Mayer, Davis, and Schoorman (1995) were careful to point out that "trust is not taking risk per se, but rather it is a willingness to take risk" (712). They further distinguished trust from the related constructs of cooperation, confidence, and predictability. All three have a history of being confounded with trust, yet all three can quite clearly be distinguished from trust. For example, although cooperation sometimes involves risk, as in many social dilemmas, "trust is not a necessary condition for cooperation to occur, because cooperation does not necessarily put a party at risk" (713). Niklas Luhmann (1988) differentiates between confidence and trust by noting that trust requires the recognition and acceptance of risk. "If you do not consider alternatives (every morning you leave the house without a weapon!), you are in a situation of confidence. If you choose one action in preference to others in spite of the possibility of being disappointed by the action of others, you define the situation as one of trust" (102). Following Morton Deutsch (1958), Mayer, Davis, and Schoorman (1995) also note that trust is not predictability: "To equate the two is to suggest that a party who can be expected to consistently ignore the needs of others and act in a self-interested fashion is therefore trusted, because the party is predictable" (714). All three of these sometimes-associated constructs fail tests of necessity, sufficiency, or both.

After reviewing current research on trust in several disciplines, Rousseau et al. (1998) presented this definition: "Trust is a psychological state comprising the intention to accept vulnerability based upon positive expectations of the intentions or behavior of another" (395). We use this definition as a foundation for our conceptual analysis of the dynamics of trust. At the same time, like other scholars we differentiate between trust and trusting actions. Whereas trust is a psychological construct that represents a willingness to risk, those who take trusting actions actually take those risks. Thus, trusting actions must necessarily include a potential for additional gain as well as the potential for loss. Reciprocity following a trusting action typically generates gain for the initial trustor; exploitation or even a simple nonresponse may cause a loss for the initial trustor.

As an empirical foundation for our analyses, we focus on a series of five recent research papers. Four represent our own work; the fifth comes from a decidedly different literature, and employs both different methods and a different general theoretical approach. All five, however, reach the same underlying conclusion: that observable instances of trust do not *necessarily* play out in a slowly increasing, rational fashion. Thus, these data provide the basis for a new conceptualization of the dynamics that can lead to and motivate trust.

We begin by summarizing a project on contracts and how they interact with the establishment of trust. We follow this with a summary of an ongoing project on the strategic interplay of executives and MBA students who might trust each other but often do not, to their mutual detriment. Then we turn to the discussion and description of a study that directly investigates the dissolution and potential rebuilding of trust. We follow with an investigation of the concept of reciprocity, one of the backbones of a rational-choice approach to trust. The final research project, which differs considerably from the rest, investigates the sexual choices of the members of committed gay couples in light of the threat of AIDS. Although this study offers results that are more socially jarring than the others, as part of this set of research endeavors it helps to provide the backdrop for some new theoretical ideas about the dynamics of trust.

Contracts and Trust

To varying degrees, all organizations face problems of agency, control, and uncertainty. Many of these problems stem from the simple fact that the relationships between individuals and organizations largely represent mixed-motive interactions. On the one hand, many individuals feel a sense of organizational loyalty and identify with their organization and its goals. On the other, their own individual needs may be at odds with their organization's needs. Many organizations address these self-interest concerns by investing in costly technology to monitor employee behavior (Enzle and Anderson 1993). Companies also structure rules and incentive contracts to minimize the possibility of behavior that might conflict with organizational goals (Jensen and Meckling 1976). Employees also seek the security of employment contracts that specify their rights and responsibilities (Nye 1988). To this end, formal, binding contracts have become favored, routinized solutions to the problems of agency, control, and uncertainty in organizations and in many interpersonal domains as well. These formal agreements help reduce uncertainty (Williamson 1979), eliminate (certain kinds of) risk (Williamson 1996), enhance control (Klein 1993), and mitigate agency problems (Jensen and Meckling 1976).

Cooperation between individuals or between individuals and organizations can, however, develop without the use of contracts. When individuals trust each other, they are more likely to cooperate in strategic interactions (Mayer, Davis, and Schoorman 1995), share information in negotiations (Thompson 1991), and engage in mutually beneficial relationships (Siamwalla 1978). Trust helps to reduce uncertainty (Kollock 1994) and can lead to an increase in joint gains (Carnevale and Isen 1986). Trust can help solve agency problems (Das and Teng 1998), facilitate market processes (Arrow 1974), and lead to greater cooperation within and between organizations (Smith, Carroll, and Ashford 1995).

Contracts and trust can and do substitute for one another. Thus, a lack of trust suggests that the parties might want to create a contract to specify their rights and responsibilities (Coffrin and Cochran 1982; Sitkin and Roth 1993). Alternatively, when trust is strong, the parties may feel no need for the specifics or constraints of a contract. Instead, they may be able to fulfill a mutually beneficial agreement without having to resort to a contract's restrictions (Uzzi 1997).

Most approaches, whether slanted toward formal contracts or toward trust, acknowledge the value of both, even for the same agreement. Thus, even though contracts are important, they cannot possibly address all of the contingencies that might develop in a relationship (Parkhe 1998). This makes it necessary to cultivate trust. At the same time, it may be crucial for the parties not to underestimate the need to "get it in writing" (Nye 1988). Their task then becomes one of creating contracts while simultaneously cultivating trust. Our recent research investigates the dynamics and consequences of this process (Malhotra and Murnighan 2002).

Attributions of Trust

As we have noted, trust often depends in large part on the interaction history of the engaging parties (Boon and Holmes 1991; Lindskold 1978; Swinth 1967; Solomon 1960). A cooperative, mutually beneficial relationship gives both parties confidence that they can trust each other.

A potential difficulty with contracts is that the parties may attribute their resulting mutual cooperation to the contract, a situational attribution, rather than to each other. Contracts are likely to prompt situational attributions for two reasons. First, the situational constraint, the contract, is likely to be particularly salient. Shelley E. Taylor and Susan T. Fiske (1975, 1978) suggest that perceptually salient stimuli are more likely to be perceived as causal. Second, when there is high "consensus" (if it is thought that most people act this way), situational attributions become more likely (Kelley 1967). Contracts (and their threat of enforcement) typically generate compliance, that is, high consensus. Thus, cooperative behavior that is contractually mandated may not be seen as particularly indicative of an individual's dispositions. Also, even with a cooperative history, it is necessary that each party interpret the other's cooperation as being the result of their dispositions or motives rather than the result of other, situational factors. For instance, someone who has been obviously coerced to cooperate would not necessarily be perceived as trustworthy.

Contracts, then, may act as double-edged swords. On the one hand, they foster cooperation and help bring people together by reducing or eliminating the risk of exploitation. This is particularly true when the stakes are high and the risks of loss increase. In such interactions, contracts may be a necessary prerequisite for cooperation. On the other hand, they may make it difficult for trust to develop (Shapiro, Sheppard, and Cheraskin 1992; Sitkin and Roth 1993; Lewicki, McAllister, and Bies 1998).

Empirical Research on Contracts and Trust

Our research operationalized trust in the context of the Trust Game (Snijders 1996; Dasgupta 1988; Kreps 1990), an interaction between two people who each have two choices, made sequentially. Player 1s choose to "trust" or "not trust" player 2s. If player 1s choose not to trust, the game ends, and player 1s receive a moderate outcome and player 2s receive a small outcome (often nothing). If player 1s choose to trust, player 2s have the option of rewarding ("honoring the trust") or exploiting player 1s ("abusing the trust"). When trust is honored, both players receive a moderately high outcome. When trust is abused, player 2s maximize their personal gain to the detriment of player 1s, who receive

Figure 12.3   Structure of the Game

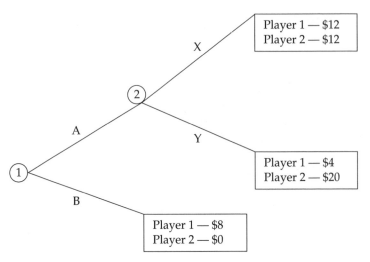

The figure is interpreted by reading it from left to right. Each node in the figure is a decision made by one of the players (identified by a circled number). Player 1 makes the first choice by choosing A or B. If player 1 chooses B, the game ends, since there are no more nodes after we follow the B path. The payoffs are in the boxes at the end nodes. If player 2 chooses A, then player 2 makes a choice of X or Y. The payoffs for each player are listed in the end nodes following each path.

Source: Authors' compilation.

less than if they had chosen not to trust. Figure 12.3 displays an extended form of the Trust Game.

In a first study (Malhotra and Murnighan 2002), we observed people playing the Trust Game repeatedly (three or four times) with the same partners. Cooperation between some dyads was facilitated in early rounds by allowing them to use contracts. A contract proposed by player 2s and accepted by player 1s meant that player 1s would necessarily choose to trust and player 2s would necessarily honor their trust. In their third and fourth interactions, contracts were no longer possible or no longer chosen. This provided a basis for comparing the trusting behaviors of player 1s with and without contracts. We predicted that the use of contracts would rob the parties of the opportunity to make trustworthy attributions regarding their counterparts and that the subsequent removal of contracts would have a damaging effect on trust. In other words, when player 2s could not or did not offer a contract after having done so in previous rounds, we predicted that player 1s would be less trusting than if they had not experienced contracts at all.

In this study, the removal of contracts was sometimes due to a choice by player 2s; other times contracts were removed exogenously. We predicted that player 2s' active choices would have a detrimental effect on trust. That is, trust would be least when player 2s rather than an outside force made the decision not to use a contract. Previous research indicates that people can accept a poor outcome more when they can attribute it to chance rather than to another person's choices (for example, Blount, Thomas-Hunt, and Neale 1996). Because player 1s are always better off with a contract, they may be less willing to accept the risk (to trust) when their counterpart no longer proposes one. Further, if player 2s have not proposed a contract when contracts are possible, player 1s might suspect that player 2s might exploit them.

The Experiment

All of the participants played the role of player 1 and made their choices via computer. Unknown to participants, there were no player 2s. Instead, player 2s' responses were programmed. Participants knew that one of their interactions would be randomly chosen to determine their monetary payoffs.

In a baseline condition, the "no-contracts" condition, participants interacted for four rounds with no mention of contracts. Player 1s simply made either "A" or "B" decisions, that is, to trust or not. Player 2s were programmed always to choose X, which was to honor trust. At the end of each round, the payoffs were announced. When the fourth round began, a message on the screen informed participants that this would be the last round. They were told that their counterpart also received this announcement.

In the other conditions, participants were told that player 2s could propose a contract. Player 2s' purported cost for proposing the contract was two dollars. Player 1s could accept or reject proposed contracts. It was in their best interest to accept. When they did, the computer automatically enforced the contract, ending the interaction and displaying a message that both players would receive twelve dollars for that interaction.

Player 2s proposed contracts in the first two rounds, but not in rounds 3 or 4. Player 1s were told that player 2s were either "not allowed" or had "chosen not" to propose a contract after the second round.

Results and Implications

In figure 12.4, player 1s chose to trust a great majority of the time (86.4 percent, or nineteen of twenty-two players) in their first three interactions, even with no mention of contracts. On the fourth and last round in the no-contracts condition, significantly fewer player 1s trusted (59.1 percent, or thirteen of twenty-two).

Figure 12.4   Data from Key Conditions in Malhotra and Murnighan (2002)

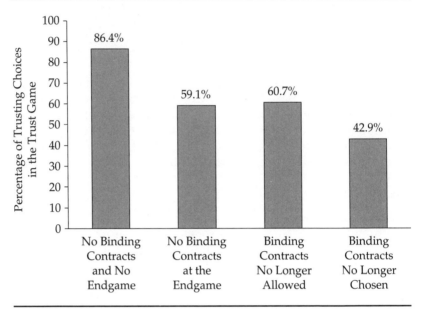

Source: Malhotra and Murnighan (2002).

Player 2s' active choices were powerful: when they chose not to propose contracts (in round 3) after having proposed contracts in the first two rounds, only 42.9 percent of the player 1s were willing to trust, significantly less than in round 3 of the no-contracts condition. In addition, there was significantly less trust after player 2s had offered contracts on rounds 1 and 2 and then chose not to (round 3) than in the first round of the no-contracts conditions. This suggests that, in this situation, a cooperative history under contracts results in less trust than no history at all.

When contracts were allowed and chosen (in the first two rounds) but then not allowed (in round 3), trust also dropped, to 60.7 percent. This was significantly less than the level of trust in the third round of the no-contracts condition (86.4 percent), suggesting that the removal of contracts, even when the decision is not in the hands of the other person, results in a drop in trust. In addition, as in the active-choice condition, there was significantly less trust after player 2s had offered contracts and then were not allowed to than in the first round of the no-contracts condition. Even without active choice, then, the use of contracts interfered with the development of trust.

These results suggest that binding contracts generate situational attributions for cooperation and can keep trust from developing. In addition, not only does trust have less chance to develop in a contractual interaction, but also any existing (presumptive) trust appears to diminish when contracts are employed.

Prevailing wisdom often encourages people to "get it in writing" and to "read the fine print" (see, for example, Nye 1988). This may be why the use of contracts in employment relationships is increasing (Morishima 1996). At the same time, recent research on trust consistently highlights the benefits of, and need for, cultivating trust (Coleman 1990; Fukuyama 1995; Kramer and Tyler 1996; Mayer, Davis, and Schoorman 1995; McAllister 1995; Putnam 1993; Misztal 1996; Seligman 1997; Sitkin and Roth 1993). Some authors have suggested that contracts might set the foundation for mutual trust (Coffrin and Cochran 1982; Lorenz 1999). The current findings provide a stark contrast, suggesting that one common prescription (contracts are helpful) might undermine the other (trust is essential). In essence, the use of binding contracts may make it difficult to cultivate trust. In addition, trust was less likely with a cooperative interaction history that was mandated by the presence of binding contracts than in cases with no interaction history at all. This suggests that contracts kept the interacting parties from seeing each other's cooperative behaviors as indicative of trustworthiness. As Gambetta (1988, 219) notes, "[I]f other people's actions were heavily constrained, the role of trust in governing our decisions would be proportionately smaller, for the more limited people's freedom, the more restricted the field of actions in which we are required to guess ex ante the probability of their performing them."

This study explored the relationship between explicit, formal arrangements and implicit, informal understandings. These two forms of agreement characterize many human relationships, particularly within organizations. The irony is that the relationship between the two is far from clean or simple. Whereas formal agreements such as contracts help to reduce risk and enhance the likelihood of cooperative interaction, they can work against the development of informal understanding and mutual trust. The converse may also be true: people with strong trust bonds may shy away from contracts, even though these may reduce their risks.

This is our first paradox: *Long-term cooperation may require the simultaneous use of contracts and trust, but the use of one can undermine the other.*

Trust Development in Strategic Interactions

In the contracts project just described, we focused on how binding contracts affected the trustors' perceptions of their counterparts. We now consider how a trusted party's own actions might affect their perceptions of the trustors. We investigated this issue in a recent study (Malhotra and Murnighan 2003) involving an iterated prisoner's dilemma framed as the gas station game (Murnighan 1991).

Table 12.1   The Profit Table in the Gas Station Game

		Team 2	
		Maintain Price (Cooperate)	Cut Price (Compete)
Team 1	Maintain price (cooperate)	Team 1: $1,200 Team 2: $1,200	Team 1: $400 Team 2: $1,600
	Cut price (compete)	Team 1: $1,600 Team 2: $400	Team 1: $800 Team 2: $800

Source: Authors' compilation.

In this exercise, two groups represent owners of competing gas stations. The goal of each group is to maximize profits for their station. In each round ("each week") participants make a simple, strategic choice: they cut their price or keep it the same. The groups make their decisions simultaneously, and the other's choice is not known before one's own decision is made. The payoff for each round is determined by the two groups' choices (depicted in table 12.1). The payoffs fit the definition of a prisoner's dilemma (Rapoport and Chammah 1965): if both groups keep their prices unchanged, both make a moderately high profit (fictitious amounts of $1,200 each); if one cuts and the other doesn't, the station with the lower price receives the maximum payoff ($1,600) and the status quo station receives the minimum payoff ($400); and if both groups cut their prices, they both make a moderately low profit ($800 each). In a one-shot interaction, the strictly dominant strategy is to cut: regardless of the other group's choice, cutters get $400 more than they would have received from remaining constant. Since both groups are in the same position, the unique Nash Equilibrium prediction (where neither party has any motivation to change their behavior) is that they will both cut and each will receive $800 each round. Cutting prices may be individually rational (in the short term), but it is collectively suboptimal: both groups can do better by leaving their prices alone. This choice, however, entails obvious risks. Without communication, trust, or the prospects of future interaction, both groups may find it difficult to avoid cutting.

Our research investigated the effects of these three factors—communication, trust, and expectations of future interaction—in multiple rounds (seven) of gas station games with the opportunity to communicate starting with the third round. This context gave the parties an opportunity to develop trust. The fact that the first two rounds of their interaction did not allow them to communicate meant that we could also evaluate the dynamics of trust development when some of the parties had initially cooperated and others had not. Thus, we investigated the development of trust in dyads that had begun their interactions cooperatively, competitively, or with a combination of cooperation and competition. Because of the repeated nature of the interactions, we were also able to track the effectiveness of cooperative and competitive strategies.

The Interactions

The participants in this study were two hundred groups of three, four, or five executives, M.B.A. students, or executive M.B.A.s. Each session included from six to twelve groups, yielding three to six interacting pairs, all in the same room. Participants did not know how long their interaction would last. At the beginning of each round, groups privately made their decision to cut or maintain prices. Once all groups had made their choices, each group's profits were displayed on the board for all to see. These payoffs were visible throughout the seven rounds of their interactions. During rounds 1 and 2 the groups were not allowed to communicate with each other. After round 2, the experimenter announced that the groups could send representative(s) to the other group; they could say anything they wished. In addition, the gas stations were "not in the United States and informal conversations between competitors were neither illegal nor unethical." Groups were still required to make their decisions privately.

After round 4, the experimenter announced that the interaction would end after three more rounds. Communication continued to be possible on each of the last five rounds. The participants were reminded of the approaching endpoint prior to rounds 5, 6, and 7.

Results and Discussion

Of the two hundred groups in this study, exactly half chose to cut their prices on the first round and half chose to maintain the same price. This suggests that the initial choice was not easily made. In fact, strong strategic arguments can be made for either choice (Murnighan 1991).

Thirty pairs (sixty groups) mutually cooperated (both groups maintained prices) on round 1. Not surprisingly, they tended to continue cooperating at a relatively high rate (twenty-eight pairs mutually cooperated on round 2; sixteen mutually cooperated on the last round) and accumulated the greatest total profits. They also tended to enjoy the interaction more than other groups did.

We were interested in finding out which combination of first-round choices would lead to the greatest difficulty in fostering trust and longer-term cooperation: pairs in which one party initially competed and the other cooperated, or those in which both parties initially competed? Forty pairs included one group cooperating (maintaining prices) and one group competing (cutting prices) on round 1; thirty pairs included both groups cutting. Competitive choices are signals that a group either expects the other to act competitively or hopes to take advantage of the other's possible cooperation, or both. If initial competition predicts future trust (or lack of it), then pairs of mutual competitors should develop the worst relationship and perform poorest. In other words, pairs in which both groups are initially distrustful (and perhaps untrustworthy) are likely to have the greatest difficulty in building trust. Alternatively, because pairs in which one group cooperates and the other competes immediately post different profits ($1,600 for one and $400 for the other), asymmetric choices may instigate feelings and perceptions of inequity, especially for the initial cooperators. Moreover, because initial competitors are unlikely to share perspectives, asymmetric first-round choices may also generate communication and coordination difficulties after round 2.

The results showed that groups that made different initial choices had more trouble building a positive relationship over the next six rounds than mutually competitive groups. Their overall joint gains (across seven rounds), however, did not differ. The reason for this is that dyads in which groups made different initial choices had lower joint gains than mutual competitors when communication first became available (rounds 3 and 4), but higher joint gains as the endgame approached (rounds 6 and 7). Asymmetric outcomes in round 1 made trusting each other difficult, even when communication was possible; mutual competition made subsequent cooperation easier. This pattern reversed, however, when the endgame was announced, as more initial mutual competitors reverted to the competitive Nash Equilibrium prediction. Thus, the "absolute" level of initial distrust seemed to do more to reduce uncertainty than it did to create bad feelings.

In the few cases (n = 7; 17.5 percent) when initial competitors and their cooperative counterparts both changed their choices (to cooperative and competitive, respectively) on round 2, profitability increased markedly. This development was particularly rare, however, because most initial competitors thought of themselves as winners: they had just received the maximum payoff of $1,600 and were unwilling to either apologize for their actions or provide payback. Instead, they often thought of their first-round choice as smart. Thus, when the groups could communicate with each other, they were on decidedly different wavelengths: initial cooperators claimed that they had been cheated and demanded reparations; initial competitors suggested that past outcomes were history and were no longer relevant. Round 1 competitors often indicated that, since no promises were ever made (because there was no communication in rounds 1 or 2), no one could have been cheated. Their cooperative counterparts, however, felt that their trust had already been violated. Communication, rather than being an opportunity to move toward joint gain, then, often contributed to mutual distrust that became increasingly difficult to overcome.

The data indicate that in these dyads, the first-round competitors would actually have profited more over the seven rounds if they had provided immediate payback to their cooperative counterparts. The data show that "substantive penance" could have had positive effects in either round 2 or round 3. After round 3, however, payback was both less likely and less effective (taking a "hit" now cost more than the subsequent gains from mutual cooperation). Had the interaction lasted longer than seven rounds, this kind of penance would likely have been even more effective for initial competitors. In general, the longer the shadow of the future, the more important it becomes to repair a relationship, even if it is costly in the short run.

Interestingly, the worst mistake, in terms of profits, for an initial cooperator who was paired with an initial competitor was to cooperate again on round 2. Instead, a tough stance (after having been the "sucker" in round 1) was associated with higher subsequent profits. This suggests that, in the current context, tit-for-tat (starting cooperatively and then choosing your counterpart's previous choice) was an excellent strategy after the initial round had been lost. In general, however, over all of the groups, cooperating in round 1 was no more effective than competing (average outcomes of $7,285 and $7,230). For interactions that are longer than seven rounds, however, cooperating in round 1 will likely provide greater payoffs than competing in round 1, making tit-for-tat, which prescribes a cooperative first move, even more effective.

The results of this study suggest a number of implications for contexts in which early decisions are made with imperfect information and later decisions depend in part on the results of prior decisions. First, a party's own choices are likely to influence their attributions about the trustworthiness and morality of others. Even when we choose noncooperatively, we are likely to see ourselves as more trusting (and trustworthy) than others see us (for example, Tenbrunsel 1998). When we choose cooperatively, we are likely to consider the choice situation as a trustworthiness test that we have passed and that our counterparts might not. Just as pointedly, our perceptions of ourselves and of others are not likely to match the perceptions of those who do not choose as we have chosen. Second, mutual distrust may be a source of useful certainty that allows for relatively accurate attributions of each other's behaviors. These attributions seem to reflect convergent expectations that stem from symmetric initial strategies. Finally, it is beneficial for initial losers to take a strong stand in round 2; it is similarly beneficial, and more difficult, for initial winners to cooperate in round 2.

Thus, this study generated our second and third paradoxical results. First: *Noncooperative behavior is damaging to joint outcomes, and it is more damaging to joint outcomes if one party is cooperative when the other party is non-cooperative.* Second: *To repair a damaged relationship, it may be impor-*

tant for those who were initially trustworthy and those who were initially untrustworthy to switch roles.

The next section builds on issues of substantive penance, which we have touched on only briefly, by investigating the process of the breakdown and potential reestablishment of trust.

The Power of Penance

Organizations are dense with interdependencies and exposures to risk. Because trust provides a basis for cooperative action in organizations (Kahn et al. 1964) maintaining trust in relationships is crucial. The empirical literature, however, provides little in the way of systematic evidence on the dynamics of reestablishing trust once it has been violated (a recent paper by Kim et al. [forthcoming] is a notable exception). Some of our own recent research (Bottom et al. 2002) also began to address this issue. This research examined the dynamics and effectiveness of different kinds of penance on the restoration of cooperation in a repeated prisoner's dilemma.

Once a string of cooperative actions has occurred, expectations of continued cooperation increase for both parties. When one party changes course and chooses noncooperatively, the conditions surrounding that choice (expressed and perceived intentions), the benefits from reverting to cooperation, and the length of their prior cooperative interaction can all contribute to the potential for the relationship to be resurrected—or not. The philosophical literature on forgiveness (for example, North 1987) suggests that an apology, substantive amends, and forgiveness may all be required to return a relationship to a trusting, cooperative state. This experiment investigated all of these issues.

The experiment's procedures paired individuals with a programmed counterpart. Participants did not know their counterparts were programmed, but reported believing that they were interacting with another person. The program reinforced (and successfully stimulated) early, cooperative action. Later, the programmed counterpart breached the participant's trust by choosing competitively after sending messages promoting cooperation. The breach was followed by a sequence of mutual competition and then by initiatives (by the program) to reestablish cooperation.

The study manipulated three variables: intent, penance, and the duration of the parties' interaction prior to the breach of trust. The manipulation of intent occurred immediately after the breach. The programmed participant either denied intent ("I didn't mean to do that; the experimenter took the wrong card"), or acknowledged it ("I must admit that I meant to do that; I was just trying to do a little better for myself"). The duration of their interaction was manipulated by providing participants with a series of five or fifteen choices (almost always mutually cooperative) prior to the breach. After the breach, four rounds of non-cooperative play ensued to extinguish any residual cooperation. Then, the programmed counterpart began a sequence of actions that included the penance manipulation, first sending all participants an apology and a request for a return to the original cooperative behavioral norm. The apology was "I am sorry for doing this. I think we should go back to cooperation." Offers of penance were added to this message. The different versions were (1) mere talk: "I would be willing to do this if you are"; (2) small penance: "I would be willing to lose on the next round and let you win"; (3) large penance: "I would be willing to lose on the next two rounds and let you win"; or (4) an open-ended offer of penance: "What will it take for you to cooperate again?", which solicited penance requests. A follow-up condition was also run that presented the open-ended penance offer more personally: "What can I do to get you to cooperate again?"

After all of the acts of penance had occurred, participants were notified that the end of the interaction would come in five more rounds of choices. Game theory predicts that once a definite endpoint is known, a purely rational participant will choose strictly competitively (Luce and Raiffa 1957). Consequently, the last five rounds gave the participants an opportunity to choose cooperatively in conditions that entailed risk, in other words, they needed to trust their counterparts to choose cooperatively, especially in the last round. Participants' choices in the last five rounds determined the effectiveness of the different forms of penance, along with the dynamics of intent and the duration of the interaction on subsequent trusting choices.

The results showed that substantive offers of penance both large and small led to more cooperative choices in the final rounds of play than did mere talk. However, mere talk—sometimes called "cheap talk" (Farrell and Gibbons 1989)—led to many cooperative choices in the last five rounds, which runs counter to game theory's predictions. An apology alone was not as effective as an apology plus substantive penance, but it was considerably better than nothing.

Early breaches (after five rounds) typically led to cognitive rather than emotional reactions. Later breaches (after fifteen rounds) prompted many more questions about the counterpart's actions, prompting both cognitive and emotional reactions, for example, "What the hell!?"

The duration of the interactions prior to the breach and the acknowledgment or denial of intent also interacted to influence later cooperative choices in the open-ended penance conditions. Acknowledging rather than denying noncooperative intent was more effective at generating future cooperation in short interactions but the reverse was true for long interactions. It seems that a longer period of trustworthy behavior on another's part may incline people to be more open to denials of intent, as much as to say, "We knew they couldn't have meant to do that." Perhaps it is easier to believe that you have not misjudged a person than to assume you have been wrong about them for a long time. An examination of the penance requests in the open-ended penance conditions also revealed that when faced with denials, people in shorter interactions made larger penance requests than people in longer interactions. In contrast, an admission of intent from a long-time trustworthy partner could be experienced as a particularly profound violation, and might therefore be better to deny. Conversely, during the early, uncertain period in which people feel particularly vulnerable to new partners, denials of intent apparently seemed implausible. These results suggest a fourth paradox: *As trust in a relationship increases, it is simultaneously less likely that the parties will exploit each other and more likely that they will get away with exploiting each other.*

Open-ended offers of penance that acknowledged the wrongdoer's responsibility for harm were most effective. Yet requests for penance were similar in size to the offers of small (fixed) penance, which could not fully compensate the participants for the economic opportunities that they lost due to the breach of trust. This suggests that it was not the size of penance that mattered as much as its voluntary nature. In some sense, the ultimate value of penance may have been symbolic rather than economic.

Several pictures emerge from this study. The most effective explanations for a breach of trust in reestablishing cooperation depended in part on the duration of the relationship prior to the breach. Breakdowns in longer relationships had more emotional implications, while those in shorter relationships led to a more calculated, economic approach to penance by the wronged party. Sincerity in offers of penance was critical, but the size of a penitent's offer was less significant in reestablishing trust than its voluntary nature. In addition, these data suggest that, unlike the expectations of a rational-choice approach, the reestablishment of some level of trust was possible with an apology and no substantive penance (even though substantive penance was more effective).

Reciprocity and the Perception of Trust

The rational choice approach suggests that trust development is an iteratively reciprocating process. Thus, consideration of the trusted parties' perceptions is necessary to understand and predict how trust development will evolve in a given relationship. Reciprocity models (Cialdini 1993; Gouldner 1960) suggest that trusted parties who interpret trustors' choices to accept vulnerability as completely voluntary may respond by being trustworthy. Further, higher levels of perceived trust are likely to trigger even greater trustworthiness. Thus, as individuals choose to become more and more vulnerable, the target of their trust may feel more and more obligated to reciprocate and honor their trust—if, that is, trusted parties perceive the trustor's actions as trustors do, that is, as risky or potentially costly.

Trusting interactions can be conceptualized as non-zero-sum games, in other words, mutual trust can increase both parties' payoffs, often in both economic and in social terms. When someone trusts, the trusted parties' benefits typically increase, and if a trusted party reciprocates by being trustworthy, the trustor's benefits also increase. Thus, if we lend people money when they are in need, we make them better off. When they return what they owe, we gain, possibly monetarily but certainly socially, making the prospects for future "win-win" interactions more likely. The continued exchange of positive interpersonal acts can build trust and expand the possibilities for both parties to obtain individual and joint benefits. All this fits the rational-choice approach to trust.

An essential component of reciprocity is the perception of being trusted. If the parties who received our loan do not perceive our actions as acts of trust, they may be less likely to reciprocate. In many situations, people make positive attributions of their own actions (Taylor and Brown 1988) and devalue the contributions or concessions of others (Stillinger et al. 1990). Problems surface when the parties' perceptions of their interaction are incompatible (Bettenhausen and Murnighan 1985). Because shared understandings are necessary for effective cooperation and trust development, the variation in the perceptions of the trusting and trusted party can be critical.

We investigated these kinds of processes in two experiments (Pillutla, Malhotra, and Murnighan 2003). In particular, we manipulated the amount of trust that trustors exhibited and measured how much the trusted parties reciprocated. This allowed us to map the pattern of trust and reciprocity in a situation that involved an easily measured economic outcome (money).

Trust and Reciprocity

Joyce Berg, John Dickhaut, and Kevin McCabe (1995) developed a version of the Trust Game that differs from the version developed by Chris Snijders (1996), Partha Dasgupta (1988), and David M. Kreps (1990), described earlier. This version is particularly appropriate for investigating reciprocity. In Berg, Dickhaut, and McCabe's (1995) initial experiment, participants received ten dollars for participating. They were then directed to one of two rooms. Participants in room A (player 1s) were told that they could offer as much of their ten dollars as they wished to one of the people in room B (where the player 2s waited). They knew that the recipients would receive three times the amount that they sent. Thus, if a player 1 sent five dollars, the player 2 would received fifteen dollars (in addition to the ten dollars he or she would receive at the outset). Player 2s would then freely decide how much to return to player 1s. Everyone acted anonymously.

Since this one-shot situation provided no opportunity for reputation building, player 2s had no incentive to return any money. Game theoretic analysis, then, suggests that player 1s should send no money. The unique Nash Equilibrium prediction for this game is that player 1s will not send any money and, if player 2s receive any money, they will return none of it to player 1s. This outcome is far from collectively efficient, since player 1s who send their entire ten dollars can create an additional twenty dollars of joint value.

By sending money to player 2s, player 1s signal that they trust player 2s to return enough to make their trusting action individually as well as jointly profitable. This choice, however, is a unilateral gamble: player 1s cannot ensure that player 2s will act benevolently. Thus, the structure of this game perfectly fits, in a simple, easily observable way, our working definition of trusting action.

Berg, Dickhaut, and McCabe's (1995) results suggest that player 1s often trusted and player 2s often reciprocated player 1s' trust, but reciprocity was not universal, either in frequency or size. In particular, player 2s rarely returned enough to make the two parties' outcomes equal. Berg, Dickhaut, and McCabe (1995, 137) concluded that "some of the subjects who did not reciprocate may not have interpreted room A behavior as initiating a trust." This suggests that trusting actions may only be reciprocated if player 2s view them as trusting.

An important strategic question for player 1s is how much they should send for their act to be seen as trusting. Berg, Dickhaut, and McCabe (1995) provide only a partial answer to this question because their data are restricted to the actual amounts that player 1s sent. We explored this issue further by explicitly manipulating the amounts that player 1s sent. Thus, we presented player 2s with a variety of different amounts. We also varied player 1s' initial endowments. Manipulating these factors allowed us to provide a clear picture of a broad range of the consequences of different degrees of trusting acts.

A simple reciprocity model suggests that the higher the amount sent, the higher the return should be (Cialdini 1993; Gouldner 1960). That is, as trust increases, so should reciprocity. From player 2's perspective, however, player 1s have many choices. For instance, sending small amounts may prompt player 2s to ask, "Why didn't they send more?" Player 2s might answer this question by deciding that player 1s are not particularly trusting. Small offers might also be viewed as insulting, leading to negative attributions and consequently little reciprocation (compare Pillutla and Murnighan 1996).

In contrast, player 2s might view large amounts as favors that create an obligation. Receiving a large amount from player 1 may make it difficult to justify keeping the lion's share of the gains. When more has been received, it becomes more difficult for player 2 to deny that player 1's act is an act of trust. Many self-serving and other interpolations are possible following the transferral of small amounts. Few are possible for very large amounts. Not reciprocating would indicate that they themselves are not fair, an identity attribution that people generally seek to avoid (Greenberg 1990; Murnighan, Oesch, and Pillutla 2001). The desire to think of themselves as fair, or trustworthy, then, might compel player 2s to reciprocate sizable offers more than they reciprocate less than sizable offers.

The Experiments

Participants were all player 2s; we experimentally manipulated player 1s' endowments and offers. Player 2s each received offers from one player 1 (experiment 2) or from 16 different player 1s (experiment 1). Player 2s knew that player 1s started with either ten or twenty dollars; their offers were two, three, four, five, six, nine, ten, twelve, eighteen, or twenty. Player 2s were given no initial endowment. As in Berg et al. (1995), player 2s received three times the amount that player 1s sent. Participants in experiment 1 knew that one of their decisions would be randomly chosen to determine their actual monetary payoff. After being informed of the amount that a player 1 had sent, player 2s indicated how much they would return. All decisions were anonymous.

The data across the two experiments were consistent and reliable. The more player 2s received, the more they returned. Also, except for one condition, player 2s returned less for comparable offers (for the same amount of money offered) when player 1s had a twenty- rather than a ten-dollar endowment. Thus, the proportion that player 1s sent was clearly important. In almost all of the conditions, if it was possible, player 2s' modal returns equalized their outcomes and player 1s' outcomes. For instance, when player 1s sent nine of ten dollars, the most frequent player 2 response was a return of thirteen dollars, leaving both players with fourteen. This equalizing pattern held even for the most lucrative condition: when player 1s sent twenty, more player 2s returned thirty than any other response.

These data suggest that reciprocity increases as trust increases. On average, however, player 1s were better off only when they had sent all of their ten-dollar endowment or almost all, eighteen or twenty dollars, of their twenty-dollar endowment. In trust terms, player 1s only benefited from trusting player 2s when they fully (or almost fully, in the twenty-dollar case) trusted. In contrast, partial trusting acts led, on average, to small monetary losses for player 1s.

This result may be explained, at least partially, by player 2s' equality motives (see Messick 1993). For example, when player 1s send five dollars of a twenty-dollar endowment and player 2s desire equality, they should return nothing. This means that they neither return as much as was sent nor do they reward player 1s for freely sending them money. However, even when player 2s received enough to allow them to equalize their outcomes and reward player 1s—say, when player 1s sent twelve dollars of twenty, player 2s could return fourteen to give each of them twenty-two dollars—their average returns gave player 1s final outcomes that were less than their initial endowment. In this case, player 2s' average return was ten dollars and forty-five cents, leaving player 1s with eighteen dollars and forty-five cents and player 2s with twenty-five dollars and fifty-five cents.

The data clearly indicate that player 1s do better by not engaging in trusting acts rather than by trusting partially. However, when they maximize their trusting acts, the data suggest that, on average, they come out slightly ahead (by forty-eight cents when they send their ten-dollar endowment and by thirty-three cents when they send their twenty-dollar endowment). At the same time, by offering the entire amount they risk receiving nothing: in both endowment conditions, sending everything led to over 20 percent of player 2s keeping the entire amount, leaving full trustors with nothing.

Postexperiment questionnaires indicated that player 2s felt obligated by receiving money; they also perceived, in general, that sending money was a smart, trusting act. Both sets of feelings—of obligation and the combination of perceptions of intelligence and a trusting act—mediated the amount sent–amount returned relationship. Thus, player 2s' attributions may have been as important as player 1s' acts in determining player 1s' ultimate monetary outcomes.

This study suggests that many player 2s constructed negative attributions of partial trustors and that, unlike sending nothing, which entails no risk, sending everything may be jointly profitable but was tremendously risky for trustors. Trusting fully is effective, on average, because it seems to compel most trusted parties to feel obligated and reciprocate. The fifth paradox, then, is clear: *Trust, by definition, entails risk and vulnerability, which is important to manage, but trustors are punished for hedging, and may need to choose between large acts of trust, or none at all.*

Risking as Part of Loving

At the beginning of this paper, we described common conceptions of trust as fitting many of the parameters of a rational-choice approach. We also presented an S-curve to depict the normal trust development process (figure 12.1). As our research has shown, in several contexts, the trust development process is neither neat nor strictly rational. Instead, degrees of risk and perceptions of interdependence can lead to a variety of trust development patterns. These patterns also appear in a recent field study that presents a striking perspective on the paradoxes of trust.

Paul R. Appleby, Lynn C. Miller, and Sadina Rothspan (1999) surveyed forty-six long-term homosexual male couples on their reasons for engaging in safe or unsafe sexual behavior. They note that stable relationships do not, at least in the context studied, make unprotected sex safe among gay men. For example, 73 percent of gay men in stable relationships reported having sex with someone besides their partner at least once during their relationship (Peplau and Cochran 1988). With estimates that HIV infection among gay men in urban populations range anywhere from 21 percent to 51 percent (Valdiserri et al. 1988), promiscuity becomes a serious source of concern.

In Appleby, Miller, and Rothspan (1999), 21 percent of the couples had been completely monogamous. Thus, a majority of the survey respondents admitted to having sex outside of their committed relationship. Only 30 percent of those who reported having sex outside the relationship, however, claimed to have consistently used condoms. The risks that unprotected sex had for their committed relationships may also have been apparent to their partners, as 84 percent reported knowing about their partners' outside sexual activities.[3] Surprisingly, and tragically, those couples in which one or both partners engaged in extra-relationship sexual contact were no more safe in their sexual behavior within their primary relationships (by using condoms) than were couples who did not engage in any extra-relationship sexual contact.

Clearly, many of the men in this study chose to be vulnerable to a potentially life-threatening degree. Appleby, Miller, and Rothspan's survey probed the rationales for the choices they made in their primary relationships. Individuals who engaged in risky (unprotected) sex were more likely to use love, trust, and commitment as explanations for their behavior than those who engaged in safer sex. In addition, individuals who were "more dependent upon their relationships and who desired a stable and lasting relationship practiced riskier sex" (1999, 81). This is consistent with an earlier finding that people who feel that their partner is someone "special" engage in more risky sexual behavior (Kelly et al. 1991). Respondents consistently indicated that making requests for safer sex conveyed a negative message to their partners.

Beyond being profoundly troubling, these data suggest that people often take risks to build trust in relationships rather than building trust so that they can take risks. Our definition of trusting incorporates a willingness to assume risk as an essential element, and the rational-choice approach to trust suggests that trust will grow gradually, will become established after many positive interactions, and that greater risk taking will follow. The Appleby, Miller, and Rothspan (1999) data suggest the exact converse, that people take (large) risks as a way to build or maintain trust. In other words, to establish mutual trust, individuals must act as if they are trusting. If they do not, then trust may not develop at all. The sixth paradox that this suggests cuts to the heart of traditional conceptions of trust development: *While building trust is necessary to accommodate large risk taking, large risk taking may be necessary to build trust.*

This conclusion strengthens the conclusion drawn from our reciprocity study (Pillutla, Malhotra, and Murnighan 2003): to build trust, individuals may have to take more risks than are actually warranted, at least in terms of rational choice. The Appleby, Miller, and Rothspan (1999) findings point out that, for relationships that are highly valued or are perceived as being of great future importance, the risks that are necessary to establish a person as both trusting and trustworthy may be significant. There is another related, and striking, similarity between the Appleby, Miller, and Rothspan data and our reciprocity study. In the reciprocity study we found that the greatest returns accrued to those who demonstrated absolute trust in their counterparts; partial trusting actually had negative effects. There are not many more powerful examples of absolute trusting acts than sexually active men in a contemporary urban gay community choosing to practice unsafe sex. Furthermore, the participants in the Appleby, Miller, and Rothspan (1999) study seem to intuit what our data demonstrated: acts that might be viewed as "partial" trust (for example, sex with a condom) can actually undermine trust.

Whether these results apply to other kinds of relationships, for example, between two organizations, becomes an intriguing research question. Small, dependent firms that envision considerable long-term profitability, for instance, may be willing to engage in considerable risk taking (for example, operating without a contract) to establish themselves with new partners. Further, a suggestion that would reduce the "trust-related" risk, say through the formalization of informal agreements in contractual form, may be experienced as negative or suspicious. This may be particularly true when one of the two parties values a developing relationship more than the other. In such situations, we might expect to see the pattern we frequently observed in our prisoner's dilemma research (Malhotra and Murnighan 2003): the more dependent party choosing cooperatively and the less dependent party choosing competitively. Whether the inequities that follow lead to the same difficulties that we observed in our research is yet another intriguing empirical question.

Discussion and Conclusions

This chapter began with the notion that common conceptions of the trust development process might not be so simple or so rational as traditional rational-choice theories might lead us to expect. After defining trust and trusting actions and considering these common conceptions, we reviewed a series of research projects that clearly call into question the assumptions underlying what we, and others, have called a rational-choice approach to trust.

The first project, on the impact of contracts, concentrated on the actions and thoughts of trustors. It showed that contractually mandated interactions interfered with the trust establishment process. Providing an opportunity to use binding contracts reduced the likelihood that two parties would be able to easily develop trust. Attribution theory suggests that the parties gave credit to the contracts rather than to their counterparts for their early cooperation and these attributions made it more difficult for them to cooperate with and trust each other later.

The second project focused on the strategic interplay of pairs of parties who could create mutual benefits for each other if they interacted effectively. Communication opportunities and repeated interactions allowed them to develop trust and a mutually beneficial cooperative relationship. Pairs of groups that were lucky enough to experience mutually cooperative choices initially were particularly effective over the course of their interactions. Pairs of groups that experienced mutually competitive choices initially were less effective but were able to work from a common basis of understanding. Their communications were less troubled and they were often able to build a cooperative relationship, if only for a short time. As the end of their interaction approached, their ability to cooperate diminished markedly. Thus, their early competitive choices were harbingers of their later choices, and both parties seemed to expect this. When one of two groups cooperated initially and its counterpart competed, they had a difficult time establishing trust. Only in the rare instances when both groups reversed their initial choices early in their interaction, thereby cleaning the slate and reestablishing equivalent outcomes, were they able to reap the benefits of cooperation. In essence, the strategic interplay of the parties in this potentially competitive context made the establishment of trust a difficult task and one that often required counterintuitive strategies by those involved.

The third project pursued the topic of strategic interactions and trust even further by investigating the potential antecedents of trust reestablishment following a breach. Unlike many conceptions of the breakdown of trust, this experiment showed that some level of trust could be reestablished without the exchange of anything more than a sincere apology. In addition, offers of substantive penance were more effective than apologies alone, but the size of these offers was not particularly important. Thus, penance appeared to be more important symbolically than substantively. Reestablishing trust, however, does appear to require active intervention and is far from automatic.

Project number four shifted the focus from the trustor and the two parties' strategies and interactions to the perceptions of the trusted party. It investigated the likelihood of reciprocity when an initial trustor made trusting choices that varied widely in degree. The results suggest that actions that communicate partial rather than complete trust lead to negative attributions and less reciprocity by the trusted parties. Many trusted parties acted to equalize their financial outcomes and those of their trustors but on average, trustors lost resources if they did anything other than trust completely or not at all. Linear models of reciprocity do not fit these data. Instead, attributional processes appear to be causal forces in the choice to potentially reciprocate trusting actions.

The final project reviewed here concerned the sexual choices of gay men in committed homosexual relationships. Most of the respondents in the Appleby, Miller, and Rothspan (1999) survey reported engaging in sexual encounters outside their primary relationship, and many of those were unsafe. Yet they also reported engaging in unsafe sex within their relationships, even though most were aware of their own or their partners' past extrarelationship activities. Response patterns suggested that participants may have been motivated to put themselves at risk to signal love, trust (or trustworthiness), and commitment, and to avoid signaling distrust (or a lack of trustworthiness). These data also do not fit the rational-choice approach to trust.

Reconsidering Definitions

Early in this paper we adopted Rousseau et al.'s (1998) definition of trust: "a psychological state comprising the intention to accept vulnerability based upon positive expectations of the intentions or behavior of another." A rational approach to the establishment of positive expectations would require small, positive exchanges first and larger exchanges later, rather than the reverse. In many ways, this matches Charles E. Osgood's (1962) GRIT approach, which he proposed as a means for establishing peaceful relations in competitive contexts. GRIT—graduated reciprocation in tension reduction—is a process that begins with a unilateral, cooperative act that entails minimal risk (much like the first cooperative choice in tit-for-tat). When the other party reciprocates, larger, riskier cooperative acts follow until both sides trust each other enough to make serious concessions.

Needless to say, the risks of unsafe sex in the gay community, or anywhere else for that matter, are not minimal. One event can ultimately mean an individual's untimely death. Similarly, participants in the reciprocity study demonstrated the inefficacy of small and moderate acts of trust. Moreover, all five studies demonstrate the need to better understand the attributional processes that underlie trust (and reciprocity) decisions, the effects of perceived dependence on trust, and the differing perspectives of trustors and trusted parties. These issues suggest that the rational-choice approach to trust is not universally applicable. Instead, the data we have summarized here suggest the need for an alternative model. In the next section, we outline the beginnings of such a model. We elaborate on it more completely in another paper (Weber, Malhotra, and Murnighan, under review).

The Attributional Basis of Trust

The data that we have summarized in this paper consistently and repeatedly focus our attention on the attributional analyses of interacting parties who must decide whether they can trust each other. All of their analyses, in turn, are intimately connected to considerations of their counterparts' intentions—their trustworthiness. We think that an attributional model is needed to complement the rational-choice approach to trust. In essence, it would suggest that, to develop trust, individuals attempt to (and feel that they need to) influence others' attributions of their actions. Not only do initial trustors want their trust honored, but they also want to become the recipients of trust—they want to be trusted. To do so, they must not only judge their counterparts to be trustworthy, but they must also influence them to think that they themselves are trustworthy. To create such attributions, they implicitly invoke reciprocity and act (much sooner than the rational model would predict) as if they truly trust these relevant others. Thus, if Sandy wants to build trust with Chris, Sandy may act as if she has considerable trust in Chris. Sandy's hope is that Chris will think that Sandy is very trusting, as Sandy has obviously taken an action that is particularly risky. Sandy hopes that this risky act will communicate to Chris that Sandy can be trusted and that Chris will then take a similar (or greater) risk. In the process, Sandy may overestimate Chris's desire to augment their relationship and build trust. Thus, Sandy may expect that Chris will look at Sandy's action as a golden opportunity to create a stronger bond between them and will reciprocate in kind. But if Chris has more modest intentions, the reciprocation that Sandy hopes for may not be forthcoming.

This process differs from the rational-choice approach in many ways. First, it explicitly differentiates the perceptions of the two parties, with greater risks being taken by trustors earlier in their interaction. In addition, the trusted party's responses can vary widely. In Pillutla, Malhotra, and Murnighan (2003), for instance, the modal response was to equalize outcomes. This strategy honored and rewarded trust. But many recipients of the other party's trust did not honor it at all and kept all of the money (this was the second most frequent response). Others simply returned an amount that was equal to the initial trustors' offer (providing them with no benefit) and some reacted in ways that seemed to mix these three responses. A motivated attributions model of trust would suggest that initial trustors who take considerable risks may suffer considerably from their choices, sometimes very quickly. The paradox here is that because partial trustors are judged harshly, greater risks are necessary to increase the chance that the trusted party will reciprocate and that trust will develop. But the greater risks are serious gambles that can result in considerable net losses for trusting initiators.

The rational-choice approach to trust suggests that the parties should only risk more when they have a foundation of previous, positive experiences. Risky choices should only increase in magnitude following sufficient reciprocity. The rational choice approach also implies, however, that trustors will consciously evaluate their risks before they take them. Even after repeated positive interactions, then, rational choice suggests that the parties will suspect counterparts who could be less than honorable and will therefore temper their risk taking.

An attributional model would suggest that dependent actors who see considerable benefit from a stronger relationship may take these kinds of disproportionate risks, even without an elaborated, positive history. Their vision of the future may dominate, interfere with, and overcome any of their rational calculations. And if their initial trusting act is honored, attributional euphoria may make subsequent rational analysis even less likely. The paradox here is that trust may be based more on the expectations of one's own benefits than on rational calculations or clear consideration of the other party's needs and likely responses. Historical evidence and its potential predictability can be overwhelmed by expectations of potential benefits.

It is interesting to note that if dependent initial trustors do not take a big risk and the other party realizes that they have held back, significant reciprocity is not likely, and a weak foundation of moderately positive acts may limit the likelihood of encouraging cooperative actions by either party. One contributor to these kinds of relationship problems is that each party is likely to overestimate its own contribution and underestimate the other's contribution to the trust development process (Taylor and Brown 1988). In the extreme, this will result in mutually perverse attributions regarding the other's trustworthiness (Kramer 1998). Then neither party is likely to step in and make the contributions that are necessary to create the basis for a positive, cooperative spiral. Instead, if both parties are likely to feel that they are already giving more to the relationship (by being more trusting, accepting more risks, and so forth) and the inequity that they perceive is likely to increase, positive attributions of the other party become increasingly less likely.

A further complicating factor is that an individual's own actions can influence his or her conclusions about another's intentions. This was certainly the case among the participants in the gas station game (Malhotra and Murnighan 2003), where groups that made an initially competitive choice often expressed an unwillingness to trust their initially cooperative counterparts. Similarly, Ann Tenbrunsel (1998) found that when stakes are high, misrepresentation became more likely in negotiations and the misrepresenters often assumed that their counterparts had been less than truthful as well, even when they had no real evidence for drawing this conclusion.

An attributional model of trust would build on the foundation of paradoxes and counterintuitive empirical results identified here. At its core, it would suggest that people often take large risks to develop trust and may not have the option of developing trust gradually because recipients of trusting acts judge partial trustors harshly. This makes it difficult for interacting parties to use (or suggest) contracts or to accept small doses of initial vulnerability. While this may not dissuade particularly dependent parties from engaging in (risky) collaborations, other partnerships may be less likely. The ultimate paradox here is that the very thing that trust is supposed to facilitate, namely, cooperation, may be threatened by the processes that underlie trust development. With that said, a silver lining in this review is that the reestablishment of trust, while by no means easy, might not be as improbable as originally suspected. More research on rebuilding trust and on the effects of communication and expectations of future interaction is clearly necessary, and perhaps critical, with regard to this issue. In particular, this kind of research holds the promise of discovering encouraging news about the initial trust-building process. Our final observation is that our attributional conceptualization of the trust development process suggests that people can, at times, effect more rapid development of trust by straying from the risk-averse behavioral prescriptions of a rational incremental model. Given people's apparent propensity for acting "irrationally" in the social domain, this is good news, indeed.

This project benefited from the assistance and support of several organizations and many people. First, we gratefully acknowledge the financial assistance of the Russell Sage Foundation and the Dispute Resolution Research Center at the Kellogg Graduate School of Management at Northwestern University. We also thank Rod Kramer, Karen Cook, and all of the participants in the conference at Stanford for their constructive comments on earlier versions of this manuscript.

Notes

1. Debra Meyerson, Karl E. Weick, and Roderick M. Kramer's (1996) article on swift trust may be an exception that proves the rule.
2. This discussion is admittedly general and does not address the possibility that people might trust each other in one domain but not in another. Expanding our discussion to deal with these conceptual issues goes far beyond the scope of this paper. We can visualize a model that is domain-specific and can accommodate a variety of different domains that, in the most trusting of interactions, might expand the "total" trust to phenomenal amounts. (With appropriate scaling, these conceptualizations can be kept to a manageable size.)
3. However, it is not clear from the data when partners became aware of the extrarelationship sexual contacts.

References

Appleby, Paul R., Lynn C. Miller, and Sadina Rothspan. 1999. "The Paradox of Trust for Male Couples: When Risking Is a Part of Loving." *Personal Relationships* 6(1): 81–93.

Arrow, Kenneth. 1974. *The Limits of Organizations*. New York: Norton.

Berg, Joyce, John Dickhaut, and Kevin McCabe. 1995. "Trust, Reciprocity, and Social History." *Games and Economic Behavior* 10(1): 122–42.

Bettenhausen, Kenneth, and J. Keith Murnighan. 1985. "The Emergence of Norms in Competitive Decision-Making Groups." *Administrative Science Quarterly* 30(3): 350–72.

Blount, Sally, Melissa C. Thomas-Hunt, and Margaret A. Neale. 1996. "The Price Is Right—Or Is It? A Reference Point Model of Two-Party Price Negotiations." *Organizational Behavior and Human Decision Processes* 68(1): 1–12.

Boon, Susan D., and John G. Holmes. 1991. "The Dynamics of Interpersonal Trust: Resolving Uncertainty in the Face of Risk." In *Cooperation and Prosocial Behavior*, edited by Robert A. Hinde, and Jo Groebel. New York: Cambridge University Press.

Bottom, William, Steven Daniels, Kevin S. Gibson, and J. Keith Murnighan. 2002. "When Talk Is Not Cheap: Substantive Penance and Expressions of Intent in Rebuilding Cooperation." *Organization Science* 13(5): 497–513.

Boyle, Richard, and Phillip Bonacich. 1970. "The Development of Trust and Mistrust in Mixed-Motive Games." *Sociometry* 33(2): 123–39.

Carnevale, Peter J., and Alice Isen. 1986. "The Influence of Positive Affect and Visual Access on the Discovery of Integrative Solutions in Bilateral Negotiations." *Organizational Behavior and Human Decision Processes* 37(1): 1–13.

Cialdini, Robert B. 1993. *Influence: Science and Practice*. New York: HarperCollins.

Coffrin, Clyde, and Gavin Cochran. 1982. "Management Contracts: Against/For." *Credit Union Magazine* 48(5): 52–54.

Coleman, James. 1990. *Foundations of Social Theory*. Cambridge, Mass.: Harvard University Press.

Das, T. K., and Bing-Sheng Teng. 1998. "Between Trust and Control: Developing Confidence in Partner Cooperation in Alliances." *Academy of Management Review* 23(3): 491–512.

Dasgupta, Partha. 1988. "Trust as Commodity." In *Trust: Making and Breaking Cooperative Relations*, edited by Diego Gambetta. Oxford: Blackwell.

Deutsch, Morton. 1958. "Trust and Suspicion." *Journal of Conflict Resolution* 4(2): 265–79.

Enzle, Michael E., and Sharon C. Anderson. 1993. "Surveillant Intentions and Intrinsic Motivation." *Journal of Personality and Social Psychology* 64(2): 257–66.

Farrell, Joseph, and Robert Gibbons. 1989. "Cheap Talk Can Matter in Bargaining." *Journal of Economic Theory* 48(1): 221–37.

Fukuyama, Francis. 1995. *Trust: The Social Virtues and the Creation of Prosperity.* New York: Free Press.

Gambetta, Diego. 1988. "Can We Trust Trust?" In *Trust: Making and Breaking Cooperative Relationships,* edited by Diego Gambetta. Cambridge, Mass.: Blackwell.

Gouldner, Alvin W. 1960. "The Norm of Reciprocity: A Preliminary Statement." *American Sociological Review* 25(1): 161–78.

Greenberg, Jerald. 1990. "Looking Fair Versus Being Fair: Managing Impressions of Organizational Justice." In *Research in Organizational Behavior,* edited by L. L. Cummings and B. Staw. Volume 12. Greenwich, Conn.: JAI Press.

Homans, George C. 1961. *Social Behavior: Its Elementary Forms.* New York: Harcourt Brace and World.

Howard, Neil. 1966. "The Theory of Meta-Games." *General Systems* 11(1): 167–86.

Hughes, Patrick, and George Brecht. 1975. *Vicious Circles and Infinity: A Panoply of Paradoxes.* New York: Penguin.

Jensen, Michael C., and William H. Meckling. 1976. "Theory of the Firm: Managerial Behavior, Agency Costs, and Ownership Structure." *Journal of Financial Economics* 3(2): 305–60.

Johnson-George, Cynthia, and Walter Swap. 1982. "Measurement of Specific Interpersonal Trust: Construction and Validation of a Scale to Assess Trust in a Specific Other." *Journal of Personality and Social Psychology* 43(6): 1306–17.

Kahn, Robert L., Donald M. Wolfe, Robert P. Quinn, J. D. Snoek, and Robert A. Rosenthal. 1964. *Organizational Stress: Studies in Role Conflict and Ambiguity.* New York: McGraw-Hill.

Kelley, Harold H. 1967. "Attribution Theory in Social Psychology." In *Nebraska Symposium on Motivation,* edited by David Levine. Volume 15. Lincoln: University of Nebraska Press.

———. 1979. *Personal Relationships: Their Structures and Process.* Hillsdale, N.J.: Erlbaum.

Kelly, Jeffrey A., Seth C. Kalichman, M. R. Kauth, H. G. Kilgore, H. V. Hood, P. E. Compos, S. M. Rao, T. L. Brasfield, and J. S. St. Laurence. 1991. "Situational Factors Associated with AIDS Risk Behavior Lapses and Coping Strategies Used by Gay Men Who Successfully Avoid Lapses." *American Journal of Public Health* 81(10): 1335–38.

Kim, Peter H., Donald L. Ferrin, Cary C. Cooper, and Kurt T. Dirks. Forthcoming. "Removing the Shadow of Suspicion: The Effects of Apology Versus Denial for Repairing Competency-Based Versus Integrity-Based Trust Violations." *Journal of Applied Psychology.*

Klein, Benjamin. 1993. "Contracts and Incentives: The Role of Contract Terms in Assuring Performance." In *Contract Economics*, edited by Lars Werin, and Hans Wijkander. Cambridge, Mass.: Blackwell.

Kollock, Peter. 1994. "The Emergence of Exchange Structures: An Experimental Study of Uncertainty, Commitment and Trust." *American Journal of Sociology* 100(2): 313–45.

Kramer, Roderick M. 1998. "Paranoid Cognition in Social Systems: Thinking and Acting in the Shadow of Doubt." *Personality and Social Psychology Review* 2(2): 251–75.

———. 1999. "Trust and Distrust in Organizations: Emerging Perspectives, Enduring Questions." *Annual Review of Psychology* 50(1): 569–98.

Kramer, Roderick M., and Tom R. Tyler, eds. 1996. *Trust in Organizations.* Thousand Oaks, Calif.: Sage.

Kreps, David M. 1990. "Corporate Culture and Economic Theory." In *Perspectives on Positive Political Economy*, edited by James E. Alt and Kenneth A. Shepsle. Cambridge: Cambridge University Press.

Lewicki, Roy J., Daniel J. McAllister, and Robert J. Bies. 1998. "Trust and Distrust: New Relationships and Realities." *Academy of Management Review* 23(3): 438–512.

Lindskold, Sven. 1978. "Trust Development, the GRIT Proposal, and the Effects of Conciliatory Acts on Conflict and Cooperation." *Psychological Bulletin* 85(4): 772–93.

Lorenz, Edward. 1999. Trust, Contract and Economic Cooperation. *Cambridge Journal of Economics* 23(3): 301–15.

Luce, R. Duncan, and Howard Raiffa. 1957. *Games and Decisions: Introduction and Critical Survey.* New York: Wiley.

Luhmann, Niklas. 1988. "Familiarity, Confidence, Trust: Problems and Alternatives." In *Trust: Making and Breaking Cooperative Relations*, edited by Diego Gambetta. Oxford: Blackwell.

Malhotra, Deepak, and J. Keith Murnighan. 2002. "The Effects of Formal and Informal Contracts on Interpersonal Trust." *Administrative Science Quarterly* 47(3): 534–59.

———. 2003. "Strategies, Trust, and Consequences in Repeated, Finite Prisoner's Dilemma Games." Unpublished paper. Draft under revision, Kellogg School of Management, Northwestern University.

Mayer, Roger C., James H. Davis, and F. David Schoorman. 1995. "An Integrative Model of Organizational Trust." *Academy of Management Review* 20(3): 709–34.

McAllister, Daniel. J. 1995. "Affect- and Cognition-Based Trust as Foundations for Interpersonal Cooperation in Organizations." *Academy of Management Journal* 38(1): 24–59.

Messick, David M. 1993. "Equality as a Decision Heuristic." In *Psychological Perspectives on Justice: Theory and Applications*, edited by Barbara A. Mellers and Jonathan Baron. Cambridge: Cambridge University Press.

Meyerson, Debra, Karl E. Weick, and Roderick M. Kramer. 1996. "Swift Trust in Temporary Groups." In *Trust in Organizations*, edited by Roderick M. Kramer and Tom R. Tyler. Thousand Oaks, Calif.: Sage.

Misztal, Barbara A. 1996. *Trust in Modern Societies.* Cambridge, Mass.: Blackwell.

Morishima, M. 1996. "Renegotiating Psychological Contracts: Japanese Style." *Journal of Organization Behavior* 3(1): 139–58.

Murnighan, J. Keith. 1991. *The Dynamics of Bargaining Games.* Englewood Cliffs, N.J.: Prentice Hall.

Murnighan, J. Keith, John Oesch, and Madan M. Pillutla. 2001. "Player Types and Self-Impression Management in Dictatorship Games: Two Experiments." *Games and Economic Behavior* 37(3): 388–414.

North, Joanna. 1987. "Wrongdoing and Forgiveness." *Philosophy* 62(3): 449–508.

Nye, David. 1988. "Trust Is a Well-Drawn Employment Contract." *Across the Board* 25(10): 32–41.

Osgood, Charles E. 1962. *An Alternative to War or Surrender.* Urbana: University of Illinois Press.

Parkhe, Arvind. 1998. "Understanding Trust in International Alliances." *Journal of World Business* 33(3): 219–40.

Peplau, Letitia A., and Susan D. Cochran. 1988. "Value Orientations in the Intimate Relationships of Gay Men." In *Gay Relationships,* edited by John De Cecco. New York: Harrington Park Press.

Pillutla, Madan M., Deepak Malhotra, and J. Keith Murnighan. 2003. "Attributions of Trust and the Calculus of Reciprocity." *Journal of Experimental Social Psychology* 39(3): 448–55.

Pillutla, Madan M., and J. Keith Murnighan. 1996. "Unfairness, Anger, and Spite: Emotional Rejections of Ultimatum Offers." *Organizational Behavior and Human Decision Processes* 68(2): 208–24.

Putnam, Robert D. 1993. *Making Democracy Work: Civic Traditions in Modern Italy.* Princeton, N.J.: Princeton University Press.

Rapoport, Anatol, and Albert N. Chammah. 1965. *Prisoner's Dilemma: A Study in Conflict and Cooperation.* Ann Arbor: University of Michigan Press.

Rapoport, Amnon, and Abbe Mowshowitz. 1966. "Experimental Studies of Stochastic Models for the Prisoner's Dilemma." *Behavioral Science* 6: 444–58.

Rempel, John K., John G. Holmes, and Mark P. Zanna. 1985. "Trust in Close Relationships." *Journal of Personality and Social Psychology* 49(1): 95–112.

Rousseau, Denise M., Sim B. Sitkin, Ronald S. Burt, and Colin Camerer. 1998. "Not So Different After All: A Cross-Discipline View of Trust." *Academy of Management Review* 23(3): 393–404.

Seligman, Adam B. 1997. *The Problem of Trust.* Princeton, N.J.: Princeton University Press.

Shapiro, Debra, Blair H. Sheppard, and Lisa Cheraskin. 1992. "Business on a Handshake." *Negotiation Journal* 8(4): 365–77.

Siamwalla, Ammar. 1978. "Farmers and Middlemen: Aspects of Agricultural Marketing in Thailand." *Economic Bulletin for Asia and the Pacific* (June): 38–50.

Sitkin, Sim B. 1995. "On the Positive Effect of Legalization on Trust." In *Research on Negotiation in Organizations,* edited by Robert J. Bies, Roy J. Lewicki, and Blair H. Sheppard. Volume 5. Greenwich, Conn.: JAI Publishing.

Sitkin, Sim B., and Nancy L. Roth. 1993. "Explaining the Limited Effectiveness of Legalistic 'Remedies' for Trust/Distrust." *Organization Science* 4(3): 367–92.

Smith, Ken, Stephen Carroll, and Susan Ashford. 1995. "Intra- and Inter-organizational Cooperation: Toward a Research Agenda." *Academy of Management Journal* 38(1): 7–23.

Snijders, Chris. 1996. *Trust and Commitments*. Groningen: Interuniversity Center for Social Science Theory and Methodology.

Solomon, Leonard. 1960. "The Influence of Some Types of Power Relationships and Game Strategies Upon the Development of Interpersonal Trust." *Journal of Abnormal Social Psychology* 61(2): 23–30.

Stillinger, Constance A., Michael Epelbaum, Dacher Keltner, and Lee Ross. 1990. "The 'Reactive Devaluation' Barrier to Conflict Resolution." Unpublished paper (mimeographed). Palo Alto, Calif.: Stanford University.

Swinth, Robert L. 1967. "The Establishment of the Trust Relationship." *Journal of Conflict Resolution* 11(3): 335–44.

Taylor, Shelley E., and Jonathan D. Brown. 1988. "Illusion and Well-Being: A Social-Psychological Perspective on Mental Health." *Psychological Bulletin* 103(2): 193–210.

Taylor, Shelley E., and Susan T. Fiske. 1975. "Point-of-View and Perceptions of Causality." *Journal of Personality and Social Psychology* 32(3): 439–45.

———. 1978. "Salience, Attention, and Attribution: Top of the Head Phenomena." In *Advances in Experimental Social Psychology*, edited by Leonard Berkowitz. Volume 11. New York: Academic Press.

Tenbrunsel, Ann E. 1998. "Misrepresentation and Expectations of Misrepresentation in an Ethical Dilemma: The Role of Incentives and Temptation." *Academy of Management Journal* 41(3): 330–39.

Thompson, Leigh. 1991. "Information Exchange in Negotiation." *Journal of Experimental Social Psychology* 27(2): 161–79.

Uzzi, Brian. 1997. "Social Structure and Competition in Interfirm Networks: The Paradox of Embeddedness." *Administrative Science Quarterly* 42(1): 35–67.

Valdiserri, Ronald O., David W. Lyder, Laura C. Leviton, Catherine M. Callahan, Lawrence A. Kingsley, and Charles R. Rinaldo. 1988. "Variables Influencing Condom Use in a Cohort of Gay and Bisexual Men." *American Journal of Public Health* 78(7): 801–5.

Weber, J. Mark, Deepak Malhotra, and J. Keith Murnighan. Under review. "Normal Acts of Irrational Trust and the Attributional Process of Trust Development."

Williamson, Oliver E. 1979. "Transaction Cost Economics: The Governance of Contractual Relations." *Journal of Law and Economics* 22(0): 3–61.

———. 1996. *The Mechanisms of Governance*. New York: Oxford University Press.

Chapter 13

Untangling the Knot of
Trust and Betrayal

Sandra L. Robinson, Kurt T. Dirks, and Hakan Ozcelik

Trust is critical to organizational effectiveness. Trust enhances cooperation, improves communication, facilitates citizenship behaviors, in addition to improving group and organizational performance (Davis et al. 2000; Dirks 1999; O'Reilly and Roberts 1976; Podsakoff et al. 1990). Despite the importance of trust, however, current organizational environments often challenge the trust that employees bestow on organizations. Indeed, as trends toward downsizing, restructuring, and temporary employment continue, perceptions of unfair treatment (Brockner, Tyler, and Cooper-Schneider 1992), broken contracts (Robinson 1996), and experiences of betrayal will remain a part of the organizational landscape. And although it is an accepted assumption that these organizational changes and actions increase the frequency of breach and betrayal, we know very little about how existing trust in the employment relationship may impact those experiences of betrayal when they do occur.

The purpose of this chapter is to explore the potential relationship between trust and betrayal, with a special focus on how prior trust influences one's experience of breach and betrayal. In doing so, we put forth a theory suggesting that prior trust may either mitigate or enhance the negative effects of betrayal, but that this relationship is dependent upon other conditions in the betrayal context.

Exploration of this question is important for a number of reasons. First, the current literature is unclear about the role of trust in the betrayal experience. As we will explicate, employees' prior trust in management may either intensify the experience of betrayal or inoculate against it. To date we have yet to either fully articulate these differing perspectives or to reconcile the paradox they present. To do so will not only benefit future theoretical and empirical research on trust, but may also help to inform related literatures, such as the research on psychological contracts and justice in the workplace.

From a practical perspective, this is a valuable question to address because organizations not only need to understand how their actions affect employees' reactions but also need information on what they can do to positively influence those reactions. Will organizations' attempts to increase and maintain employees' trust create a greater risk of reaction to subsequent challenges to that trust? Or will increased trust offset the potential negative reactions of employees?

The Experience of Breach and Betrayal

Research suggests that employees' experiences of breach and betrayal are common. Sandra L. Robinson, Matthew Kraatz, and Denise Rousseau (1994) found that 55 percent of their sample of managers perceived that their organizations had failed to fulfill one or more promised obligations in the first two years of the employment relationship. Moreover, the negative repercussions of these experiences of breach and betrayal have been well documented; they result in reductions in employees' trust, job satisfaction, intentions to remain with the organization, sense of obligation, and in-role and extra-role performance (Robinson 1996; Robinson, Kraatz, and Rousseau 1994; Robinson and Morrison 2000; Robinson and Rousseau 1994).

The emotional impact of breach and betrayal alone can be significant and traumatic (Morrison and Robinson 1997). Such emotions emanate not only from the disappointment of having not gotten something expected, but, more important, from a sense of injustice and mistreatment by someone with whom one shared a trusting relationship. As Denise M. Rousseau (1989) states, "[T]he intensity of the reaction [to violation] is directly attributable not only to unmet expectations of specific rewards or benefits, but also to more general beliefs about respect of persons, codes of conduct and other patterns of behavior associated with relationships involving trust."

Although the experience of breach and betrayal may lead to intense and negative behavioral and emotional reactions, one must recognize that the individuals may have different reactions to similar or identical events: a betrayal to one may go unnoticed by another; a breach may evoke intense rage in one individual and forgiveness in another. Robert J. Bies and Thomas M. Tripp (1996) found that responses to betrayals ranged from violence to forgiveness. Although the universality of breach and betrayal in organizations is well known, we have yet to address the variance in experiences and why individuals have different reactions to potential and actual betrayals.

The Role of Trust

One particularly promising explanation for why individuals may have different reactions to potential betrayal experiences lies in the domain of trust. Research on interpersonal relationships suggests that trust is a central component of relationship schemas (Berscheid 1994). Likewise, within the context of employment relationships, one may consider trust to be a critical and fundamental attitude (Robinson 1996). Indeed, some would argue that an exchange relationship cannot exist without the basic glue of trust (Blau 1964; Deutsch 1958; Zand 1972).

A primary function of attitudes, such as trust, is to serve as an appraisal heuristic, enabling individuals to efficiently assess objects and events and people in their environment and to make sense of their world (Pratkanis 1989; Pratkanis and Greenwald 1989; Smith, Bruner, and White 1957). An attitudinal heuristic uses a stored evaluation of an object as a guide for understanding the actions of that object (Pratkanis and Greenwald 1989). If trust is one of the fundamental and influential attitudes within an employment relationship, then one can assume that trust will play a pivotal role in influencing how one perceives, interprets, and reacts to a breach or betrayal within one's work relationships.

But what role might trust play? Prior research and theory suggest two very different, potentially paradoxical, arguments for how trust may influence betrayal experiences. Using a romantic relationship metaphor, when a lover is betrayed, one may ask "Is it true that love is blind?" Or is the saying "Hell hath no fury like that of a woman scorned" more apt? Each of these perspectives is addressed in depth below.

The Love-Is-Blind Perspective

One possible way in which prior trust may affect the experience of betrayal is by mitigating the negative effects of broken promises. Robinson (1996) found that employees with high prior trust were less affected by their employers' contract breaches than were those with low prior trust. A similar finding comes from the literature on interpersonal relationships. John G. Holmes and John K. Rempel (1989) found that marital partners with high trust tend toward a more charitable orientation, making attributes about behavioral transgressions that do not affect their beliefs about their partner's central motives. Thus, behavioral transgressions can be more easily endured because they have been largely discounted in advance of their occurrence.

Alan Benton and colleagues (1969) found evidence that trust influenced the relationship between deceit by a marital or romantic partner and doubting the partner's word. Specifically, after being deceived by a partner to a limited extent, individuals with high levels of trust in their partner tended to hold little doubt about the partner's truthfulness. Individuals with low levels of trust in their partner, however, with the same level of deceit, tended to have significant doubt about their partner's truthfulness. Prior trust seemed to impact the extent to which individuals actually detected the occurrence of a transgression by their partner. Thus, high prior trust offsets, or mitigates, the impact of breach or betrayal.

This effect of prior trust can be explained in different ways. First, it may emanate from tendencies toward cognitive consistency. A long history of research has found that individuals act in ways that preserve their established knowledge structures, perceptions, schemata, and memories (Greenwald 1980). Cognitive consistency is maintained through selective perception: by one's seeking out, attending to, and interpreting one's environment in ways that reinforce one's prior knowledge, beliefs, and attitudes (Fiske and Taylor 1991). A rich body of empirical evidence has identified a variety of encoding and decoding biases that tend toward confirming, rather than disconfirming, prior beliefs (Lord, Ross, and Lepper 1979; Snyder and Swann 1976). Anthony G. Greenwald (1980) reviews much of this literature, citing evidence of confirmation bias in numerous contexts: responding to persuasion (for example, Anderson and Hubert 1963; Greenwald 1968; Hovland, Janis, and Kelley 1953; Petty, Ostrom, and Brock 1981), information search (Mischel, Ebbesen, and Zeiss 1973; Snyder and Swann 1976), memory and recall (Mischel, Ebbesen, and Zeiss 1973; Snyder and Uranowitz 1978), and primacy in person impression formation (review by Schneider, Hastorf, and Ellsworth 1979).

This cognitive consistency bias suggests that when an individual perceives evidence of a betrayal, that individual's prior trust in the reneging party will influence his or her recognition of, and interpretation or understanding of, that transgression. Thus, an individual with high prior trust will be more inclined to perceive the breach in ways that are consistent with that high prior trust, interpreting it in relatively neutral or positive terms. Thus, in a high-trust relationship, the transgression may be viewed as an unintentional event, a misunderstanding, a temporary lapse, or outside the responsibility or control of the reneging party. In contrast, in a low-trust relationship the transgression is likely to be viewed as being within the control of the other party—of being an intentional, perhaps even malevolent act—because this fits existing perceptions of the other party. For instance, research on suspicion suggests that suspicious individuals are more likely to view another individual's behavior and motives negatively, despite strong evidence to the contrary (Fein and Hilton 1994).

Another way to understand this effect of prior trust is in terms of emotional costs. In high-trust relationships, the psychological or emotional costs of discovering a breach extend far beyond the need for cognitive consistency. Indeed, to recognize that one has been betrayed by close, trusted others may be a particularly offensive blow to one's self-esteem (Morrison and Robinson 1997). Moreover, evidence suggesting that one was duped or fooled, or naïve enough to trust someone who was actually untrustworthy, may also be emotionally painful. Our sense of esteem and identity is influenced by how we are treated in our important relationships by trusted others (Lind and Tyler 1988). The stronger one's trust, and the closer the relationship, the greater that blow.

Although one might assume that a victim of psychological contract transgression would prefer the truth, this may not be the case. Research has shown that although we have motivations to seek accurate information and feedback, we also have a strong need to protect our sense of self and self-esteem (Janis and Mann 1977). Indeed, research suggests people tend to avoid information that may be ego threatening (Swann and Read 1981).

The mitigating effects of prior trust on experiences of betrayal may also occur because of individual and relationship differences in how partners evaluate each other's behavior. Trust not only influences individuals' reactions to specific incidents but also shapes the psychological perspective they adopt in the overall evaluation process of a partner (Holmes 1981). Trusting individuals tend to assess the flow of events in their relationships over a more extended period of time. This broader time perspective, involving a larger sample of behaviors, helps to hold perceptions constant because attributions of another's behavior are moderated by the aggregation of evidence over a longer period. Thus, those in high-trust relationships are likely to use a longer-term metric and thus discount one incident of breach or betrayal more readily than those with low trust, who will tend to focus on the more immediate evidence of one betrayal.

In summary, one can argue that prior trust will mitigate the experience of betrayal. This mitigating effect comes as a result of the need for cognitive consistency, the need to reduce the emotional and psychological costs of recognizing a betrayal, and the unique attribution process engaged in by partners within a close relationship.

The Hell-Hath-No-Fury Perspective

A contrasting perspective on the role of prior trust in the experience of betrayal is that those with high prior trust will actually feel *more* betrayed than those with low prior trust when a promise is broken; thus, high prior trust does not mitigate but rather exacerbates the negative effects of betrayal. This is consistent with a study by Joel Brockner, Tom Tyler, and Rochelle Cooper-Schneider (1992), in which they found that to the extent that subjects had high prior commitment to an authority, commitment dropped after they discovered that the authority was unfair in their layoff policies. In other words, the stronger the relationship with the organization, the greater the decline in the relationship following a perceived mistreatment by the organization.

This phenomenon might be termed a contrast effect. To the extent that the betrayed party had high trust, there was a greater contrast or discrepancy between the prior trusting expectations and the evidence of a betrayal. This great contrast leads to the strongest emotional reaction. The notion of contrast creating strong emotions underlies a number of areas of study, such as the research on unmet expectations and realistic job previews (Wanous et al. 1992). Negative emotions, such as disappointment, dissatisfaction, or anger will match the extent to which actual experiences are found to be in contrast with prior beliefs.

In accordance with the saying "Hell hath no fury . . . ," the strongest feelings of anger, betrayal, and hurt may come from the recognition that one gave to, committed to, and trusted another and that trusted other then took advantage of that trust. When individuals trust, they purposefully make themselves vulnerable (Mayer, Davis, and Schoorman 1995) and thus the experience of breach or betrayal may be perceived as exploitation—of one's vulnerability, of one's trusting attitude.

Prior trust may also lead to a greater sense of betrayal because of the factor of unpredictability. In high-trust relationships, the occurrence of betrayal will be much less predictable than in low-trust relationships, where one may actually anticipate such an event. Research on stress demonstrates that stress emanating from an event is greater to the extent that the event was not anticipated (Finkelman and Glass 1970).

The greater sense of betrayal in a high-prior-trust situation may also emanate from a reality shock or a perceived discrepancy between one's prior expectations and the betraying incident itself. Stronger affect is generated to the extent that stimuli are discrepant with prior expectations (McClelland et al. 1953). In fact, some scholars analyze emotion as the result of interruptions in expectations (for a summary of this research see Fiske and Taylor 1991). Disruptions in plans or discrepant expectations create arousal and cognitive appraisals. The extent of the interruption and the subsequent arousal are proposed to determine the intensity of the emotional reaction. Research suggests that not only the size of the discrepancy per se matters but also the direction of the discrepancy (Verinis, Brandsma, and Cofer 1968). As Elliot Aronson and J. Merrill Carlsmith (1962) showed, when an expectation of an event is disconfirmed, dissonance is experienced, which may lead the individual to dislike the event even more than if no initial expectation had existed. Research on realist job previews has long demonstrated that dissatisfaction can be decreased by lowering employees' expectations about a new job to align them with what they will actually experience on the job (Wanous et al. 1992). In a low-trust relationship, the impact of a violation would be expected to be less severe. Although the outcome (for example, broken promise) is disappointing, the transgression itself would not be unexpected or surprising—hence, the shock or interruption that would evoke strong emotion is lacking.

The emotional costs associated with an injured sense of self-esteem could also create the strong negative reaction of betrayal in a trusting relationship. As noted in the previous section, our sense of well-being and self-identity come from knowing we are treated well by others with whom we have a relationship (Lind and Tyler 1988). The betrayal is likely to signal an apparent disregard for the valued relationship by the other party, as evidenced by the actions of the trusted other. Consequently, the individual is likely to feel a loss of self-worth. The emotional costs may also be compounded by a feeling that one was a "fool" or a "sucker" to trust the other party.

In summary, prior trust may not mitigate, but actually make worse the negative repercussions of betrayal. This relationship may exist because of the victims' sense that their trust and vulnerability were taken advantage of or exploited, the unpredictability of the betraying event, and the huge discrepancy between the prior trusting expectations and the betraying event.

Reconciliation

So where does this leave us? It appears that prior trust can either exacerbate or mitigate the negative emotional trauma of betrayal that follows when a trusted other breaks a promise. Are these perspectives in conflict, or is there some way to reconcile this apparent paradox, making both of these conclusions true? We reconcile these competing perspectives on the role of trust by examining how the impact of trust may differ at different points in the cognitive process of the betrayal experience. Let us explain.

First, we propose that prior trust will moderate the relationship between the breach experience and the *appraisal* or *interpretation* of breach evidence. Individuals work very hard to maintain cognitive consistency and protect against the emotional costs of betrayal in a trusted relationship. Thus, in the interpretation of the betrayal, prior trust really does mitigate the experience of the event. The stronger the trust, the greater the motivation to interpret the betrayal in a positive light.

Under some conditions, this tendency to interpret the potential betrayal as a nontransgression will be much more likely to occur. These conditions, in a sense, serve as a pushing force, maintaining the high prior trust. First, it is more likely that one will maintain one's high level of trust and discount evidence of a betrayal when the information regarding the event is ambiguous, conflicting, or incomplete. Such conditions provide more leeway for the positive interpretation that the high-trusting individual prefers.

This positive tendency is also more likely when the perpetrator conspires to help the victim interpret the evidence in a positive light. For example, the use of social accounts and justifications may aid in a positive interpretation, influencing the victim's perception of the intentionality or foreseeability of the event (Bies 1987). Again, because of the need for consistency and the need to protect oneself from emotional costs, the desire is strong to discount the evidence. Thus, both parties may actually engage in a sense-making process whereby excuses, justifications, and explanations are used to hold the sense of betrayal at bay.

When the individual holds strong emotional ties to the perpetrator, one would also expect a stronger resistance to recognizing a breach. Such would be the case when the relationship is of a long duration or the emotional investments in the relationship are high. In addition, the emotional costs of betrayal, and hence the tendency to positively interpret such an event, will be greater when the victim is unable to leave the relationship or few alternatives exist. For example, in cultures or industries where it is difficult to move from one organization or another, one would expect the emotional costs of a betrayal to be very high since the victims may feel they must live the rest of their life with the betrayer. Similarly, if one has few skills, is nearing retirement, or the unemployment rate is high, the costs of recognizing a betrayal by one's current organization will be large.

Despite this tendency toward preservation of initial trust levels, especially when the need for consistency and protection from emotional costs is high, eventually "reality" will compete with pressures toward a positive interpretation. That is, the tendency and pressures toward maintaining consistency can only work *up to a degree*. Under some conditions, the "reality" of the actual betrayal will win out and the victim will have no choice but to interpret the evidence as a betrayal.

Certainly, when the prior trust is not particularly high, or the cognitive belief is not particularly solid, the "threshold for persuasion" will not be very high. In such cases, one will readily interpret evidence as a betrayal. Similarly, if the relationship and the context are such that the emotional costs were not particularly strong, the pressures toward cognitive consistency will be less and reality may easily dominate. When the evidence of betrayal is unambiguous, clear, and strong, it may be difficult or impossible to maintain one's prior trust no matter what the emotional or cognitive costs. Thus, while there is a tendency toward maintenance of high prior trust, there are *many* situations in which a victim cannot help but recognize a painful betrayal for what it is: a painful betrayal.

Once that threshold is reached, and despite one's prior trust, the evidence wins out and the party is perceived as having reneged, then the impact of prior trust works in the opposite direction. At this point, prior trust will moderate the relationship between the *appraisal* or *interpretation* of breach evidence and one's *reaction*. The individual with the higher prior trust feels *most betrayed* and reacts with the strongest of negative emotions. The sense of betrayal will be extremely acute, and those with high trust will be much more hurt, angry, and upset than those who had low initial trust.

For those with high trust, not only will the magnitude of the betrayal be greater than for those with low trust but the type of outcomes may also differ. For instance, high-trust individuals who are betrayed by a trusted other may experience self-doubt or feelings of diminished self-worth ("I must have done something to deserve this") in their attempt to make sense of the unexpected and painful act. Also, the lasting effects of a betrayal may be significantly greater when it occurs in a high-trust relationship. For example, a study of betrayal by Robert Hansson, Warren Jones, and Wesla Fletcher (1990) indicated that 50 percent of subjects reported incidents that had occurred more than twenty years earlier. Our own experience of interviewing betrayed individuals suggest that individuals who experienced betrayals by a trusted employer occurring up to three decades ago can still describe the incidents in vivid emotional detail.

In sum, we propose that trust will moderate the relationship between the appraisal of the breach and emotional and behavioral reactions. Other factors being equal, the more the victim attributes the act to the transgressor, the more negative the reaction, so that a transgression interpreted as being intentional or malevolent in nature would be more likely to result in a negative reaction. This effect, is however, moderated by the level of trust. A transgression interpreted as being intentional would elicit a much more severe, and potentially different, effect in a high-trust relationship because the shock of being intentionally taken advantage of would be large, and such an action may also injure the victim's self-esteem.

The contrast effect may be amplified under some conditions or for some types of individuals. Individuals with high levels of self-esteem may, for instance, react to a breach by a trusted partner in a particularly severe manner. Research by Roy F. Baumeister, Laura Smart, and Joseph M. Boden (1996) suggests that individuals with high self-esteem tend to react with aggression, perhaps even with physical violence, when their ego is affronted. As discussed above, a betrayal by a trusted partner can be considered an affront to an individual's ego as it makes the person feel as if he has been "played the sucker" or that the act of betrayal destroys an important part of himself. Therefore, when an individual with high-self esteem experiences betrayal by a trusted partner, intense reactions punctuated by emotional distress, aggression, and perhaps even violence may occur.

In summary, high prior trust can be said to mitigate the negative repercussions of betrayal by increasing the likelihood that the victim will interpret the breach in a positive light. If, however, the breach is ultimately interpreted in a negative light, then high prior trust can be said to accentuate the negative repercussions of betrayal. To further illustrate, we argue that prior trust will impact two segments of the cognitive processes in a betrayal experience. First, the level of prior trust will impact the relationship between a breach per se and an individual's cognitive appraisal of the breach. Under high trust, a breach is most likely to result in no recognition or acknowledgment that a breach has taken place or, if a breach is acknowledged, a benign appraisal of the party's role in causing the breach. In contrast, under low trust, a breach is most likely to result in a recognition that an obligation was unfulfilled and a negative appraisal of the other party's role in causing the breach.

Second, the level of prior trust will impact the relationship between the cognitive appraisal of the breach and the individual's emotional, attitudinal, and behavioral response. When the individual perceives that a breach has occurred, the effect will be substantially greater under high trust than under low trust.

Implications

This proposed theory has a number of implications for both the study of organizational behavior and the practice of management. First, it suggests that we cannot be overly simplistic in our claims regarding the building of trust and its importance. Most organizational scholars and consultants would direct organizations and managers to increasing employee trust—touting it as the panacea of many organizational problems. Indeed, trust has been seen as critical to organizational effectiveness in numerous ways (Davis et al. 2000; Dirks 1999). This theory, however, suggests a potential but important downside to trust, namely, that trust is positive only so long as it is maintained. Although there is a tendency toward maintaining prior high levels of trust, if the evidence is too strong, high trust can produce very strong feelings of betrayal, which is potentially damaging to the parties and the organization involved. Furthermore, the theory suggests that trust may not always be as easy to break as conventional wisdom suggests. In fact, the ideas articulated above suggest that in high-trust relationships, trust may be relatively resilient to transgressions. This idea is consistent with evidence from Robinson (1996). The analysis above also implies, however, that once the resilient shell provided by high trust is breached, the effects of betrayal may be more appropriately called "shattering" than merely a breaking of trust.

From a practical perspective, organizations should perhaps accept the advice to build employee trust, but do so with informed caution. On the one hand, established trust may help organizations and their employees to weather the storms of change and the minor bumps of injustice or breach of trust that comes with organizational change. Organizations cannot entirely avoid breaching the contracts of their employees or breaking promises from time to time. Firms that have inoculated employees with a degree of trust are likely to find that their employees take the minor bumps and potential breaches more softly than if their prior trust level was initially low. On the other hand, our theory suggests that high trust does carry with it a certain degree of risk and obligation. Although it may inoculate employees from the effects of more minor betrayals, it may actually make the betrayal experience much worse in some situations. Organizations that follow a trust-building strategy must also take on the responsibility to live up to that trust—there is little room for serious violation. Once destroyed by betrayal, trust of that prior high level may be very difficult, if not impossible, to repair.

Our model suggests that an employee's interpretation of the breach plays a pivotal mediating role in determining whether prior high trust will result in a strong negative reaction. Clearly, the interpretation may be impacted by a number of factors other than those specified in our model. In attempting to prevent employees from experiencing the strong negative reaction, organizations may try to manage or influence this interpretation, for example, by focusing attention on factors outside of transgressor's control that caused breach. Future research might help determine which factors may be most effective at influencing interpretations when a breach has occurred.

Future Research Directions

Where does this leave us? Although we believe our theory reconciling these differing perspectives on the role of trust in the breach experience is valid, there are a number of challenges to obtaining empirical proof of this theory. First, the phenomenon that we seek to understand is truly intrapsychic, and getting "inside heads" remains difficult. Our more common methodological approaches, such as field surveys and laboratory experiments, may be insufficient to capture the depth of what we seek to understand; hence, researching this topic relies on skilled interviewing techniques and other qualitative approaches that can garner better insights into individuals' thought processes. That said, individuals may themselves not be capable of sharing the inner workings of their cognitions, motivations, and emotions, so even interviews and other qualitative approaches may fail to capture what we need to support our theory.

Second, this phenomenon that we seek to understand changes over time. Seeking to gain insights from interviews based on past experiences may result in only biased, fragmented, after-the-fact perspectives from those who have experienced betrayal. Future research must attempt to explore this cognitive and emotional process over time, *as it occurs*.

A final challenge to empirically examining the proposed theory is that although it is easy to capture the salient betrayal experience, it is very difficult to capture the "nonevent"—when evidence of a betrayal is interpreted positively and then forgotten—which is more common. Thus, researchers of this topic may find that they can get one side of the experience, when a betrayal is felt, but miss the equally important side of the experience when the evidence of betrayal is not interpreted as a betrayal. Thus, we must be careful not to err by "sampling on the dependent variable," or only looking where the light shines, lest we miss the complete picture.

Conclusion

In our discussion of our theory regarding the effect of trust on the experience of betrayal, the integration of various literatures suggests that prior trust can either mitigate or exacerbate the experience of betrayal. It may mitigate the experience of betrayal by leading the trustor to create positive interpretations of evidence of a breach of trust, but it may also exacerbate the negative reaction when evidence is finally perceived as a betrayal. Although this theory has yet to be tested, we believe it has value to both our study of trust and betrayal and the management of such experiences.

References

Anderson, Norman H., and Stephen Hubert. 1963. "Effects of Concomitant Verbal Recall on Order Effects in Personality Impression Formation." *Journal of Verbal Learning and Verbal Behavior* 2(4): 379–91.

Aronson, Elliot, and J. Merrill Carlsmith. 1962. "Performance Expectancy as a Determinant of Actual Performance." *Journal of Abnormal and Social Psychology* 65(3): 178–82.

Baumeister, Roy F., Laura Smart, and Joseph M. Boden. 1996. "Relation of Threatened Egotism to Violence and Aggression: The Dark Side of High Self-Esteem." *Psychological Bulletin* 103(1): 5–33.

Benton, Alan, Eric Gelber, Harold Kelly, and Barry Liebling. 1969. "Reactions to Various Degrees of Deceit in a Mixed-Motive Relationship." *Journal of Personality and Social Psychology* 12(2): 170–80.

Berscheid, Ellen. 1994. "Interpersonal Relationships." *Annual Review of Psychology* 45: 79–129.

Bies, Robert J. 1987. "The Predicament of Injustice: The Management of Moral Outrage." In *Research in Organizational Behavior,* edited by Larry L. Cummings and Barry M. Staw. Volume 9. Greenwich, Conn.: JAI Press.

Bies, Robert J., and Thomas M. Tripp. 1996. "Beyond Distrust: Getting Even and the Need for Revenge." In *Trust in Organizations,* edited by Roderick M. Kramer and Tom R. Tyler. Thousand Oaks, Calif.: Sage.

Blau, Peter M. 1964. *Exchange and Power in Social Life.* New York: Wiley.

Brockner, Joel, Tom R. Tyler, and Rochelle Cooper-Schneider. 1992. "The Influence of Prior Commitment on Reactions to Perceived Unfairness: The Higher They Are, the Harder They Fall." *Administrative Science Quarterly* 37(2): 241–61.

Davis, James H., F. David Schoorman, Roger C. Mayer, and Hwee Hoon Tan. 2000. "The Trusted General Manager and Business Unit Performance: Empirical Evidence of a Competitive Advantage." *Strategic Management Journal* 21(5): 563–76.

Deutsch, Morton. 1958. "Trust and Suspicion." *Journal of Conflict Resolution* 2(4): 265–79.

Dirks, Kurt T. 1999. "The Effects of Interpersonal Trust on Work Group Performance." *Journal of Applied Psychology* 84(3): 445–55.

Fein, Steven, and James L. Hilton. 1994. "Judging Others in the Shadow of Suspicion." *Motivation and Emotion* 18(2): 167–98.

Finkelman, Jay M., and David C. Glass. 1970. "Reappraisal of the Relationship Between Noise and Human Performance by Means of a Subsidiary Task Measure." *Journal of Applied Psychology* 54(3): 211–13.

Fiske, Susan T., and Shelley E. Taylor. 1991. *Social Cognition.* New York: Random House.

Greenwald, Anthony G. 1968. "Cognitive Learning, Cognitive Response to Persuasion and Attitude Change." In *Psychological Foundations of Attitudes,* edited by Anthony G. Greenwald, Timothy C. Brock, and Thomas M. Ostrom. New York: Academic Press.

———. 1980. "The Totalitarian Ego: Fabrication and Revision of Personal History." *American Psychologist* 35(7): 603–18.

Hansson, Robert O., Warren H. Jones, and Wesla L. Fletcher. 1990. "Troubled Relationships in Later Life: Implications for Support." *Journal of Social and Personal Relationships* 7(3): 451–63.

Holmes, John G. 1981. "The Exchange Process in Close Relationships: Microbehavior and Macromotives." In *The Justice Motive in Social Behavior,* edited by Melvin J. Lerner and S. C. Lerner. New York: Plenum.

Holmes John G., and John K. Rempel. 1989. "Trust in Close Relationships." In *Close Relationships,* edited by Clyde Hendrick. Newbury Park, Calif.: Sage.

Hovland, Carl Iver, Irving L. Janis, and Harold H. Kelley. 1953. *Communication and Persuasion.* New Haven, Conn.: Yale University Press.

Janis, Irving L., and Leon Mann. 1977. *Decision Making: A Psychological Analysis of Conflict, Choice, and Commitment*. New York: Free Press.

Lind, E. Allan, and Tom R. Tyler. 1988. *The Social Psychology of Procedural Justice*. New York: Plenum.

Lord, Charles G., Lee Ross, and Mark R. Lepper. 1979. "Biased Assimilation and Attitude Polarization: The Effects of Prior Theories on Subsequently Considered Evidence." *Journal of Personality and Social Psychology* 37(11): 2098–2109.

Mayer, Roger C., James H. Davis, and F. David Schoorman. 1995. "An Integrative Model of Organizational Trust." *Academy of Management Review* 20(3): 709–34.

McClelland, David C., John William Atkinson, Russell A. Clark, and Edgar L. Lowell. 1953. *The Achievement of Motive*. New York: Appleton-Century-Crofts.

Mischel, Walter, Ebbe B. Ebbesen, and Antonette Raskoff Zeiss. 1973. "Selective Attention to the Self: Situational and Dispositional Determinants." *Journal of Personality and Social Psychology* 27(2): 213–25.

Morrison, Elizabeth W., and Sandra L. Robinson. 1997. "When Employees Feel Betrayed: A Model of How Psychological Contract Violation Develops." *Academy of Management Review* 22(1): 226–56.

O'Reilly, Charles, and Karlene Roberts. 1976. "Relationships Among Components of Credibility and Communication Behaviors in Work Units." *Journal of Applied Psychology* 61(1): 99–102.

Petty, Richard E., Thomas M. Ostrom, and Timothy C. Brock. 1981. *Cognitive Responses in Persuasion*. Hillsdale, N.J.: Erlbaum.

Podsakoff, Philip M., Scott MacKenzie, Robert H. Moorman, and Richard Fetter. 1990. "Transformational Leader Behaviors and Their Effects on Followers' Trust in Leader, Satisfaction, and Organizational Citizenship Behaviors." *Leadership Quarterly* 1(2): 107–42.

Pratkanis, Anthony R. 1989. "The Cognitive Representation of Attitudes." In *Attitude Structure and Function*, edited by Anthony R. Pratkanis, Steven J. Breckler, and Anthony G. Greenwald. Hillsdale, N.J.: Erlbaum.

Pratkanis, Anthony R., and Anthony G. Greenwald. 1989. "A Sociocognitive Model of Attitude Structure and Function." *Advances in Experimental Social Psychology* 22: 245–85.

Robinson, Sandra L. 1996. "Trust and Breach of the Psychological Contract." *Administrative Science Quarterly* 41(4): 574–99.

Robinson, Sandra L., Matthew Kraatz, and Denise M. Rousseau. 1994. "Changing Obligations and the Psychological Contract: A Longitudinal Study." *Academy of Management Journal* 37(1): 137–52.

Robinson, Sandra L., and Elizabeth W. Morrison. 2000. "The Development of Psychological Contract Breach: A Longitudinal Study." *Journal of Organizational Behavior* 21(5): 525–46.

Robinson, Sandra L., and Denise M. Rousseau. 1994. "Violating the Psychological Contract: Not the Exception but the Norm." *Journal of Organizational Behavior* 15(3): 245–59.

Rousseau, Denise M. 1989. "Psychological and Implied Contracts in Organizations." *Employee Responsibilities and Rights Journal* 2(2): 121–39.

Schneider, David J., Albert H. Hastorf, and Phoebe C. Ellsworth. 1979. *Person Perception*. Reading, Mass.: Addison-Wesley.

Smith, Mahlon Brewster, Jerome S. Bruner, and Robert W. White. 1957. *Opinions and Personality*. New York: Wiley.

Snyder, Mark, and William B. Swann. 1976. "When Actions Reflect Attitudes: The Politics of Impression Management." *Journal of Personality and Social Psychology* 34(5): 1034–42.

Snyder, Mark, and Seymour Uranowitz. 1978. "Reconstructing the Past: Some Cognitive Consequences of Person Perception." *Journal of Personality and Social Psychology* 36(9): 941–50.

Swann, William B., and Stephen J. Read. 1981. "Acquiring Self-Knowledge: The Search for Feedback That Fits." *Journal of Personality and Social Psychology* 41(6): 1119–28.

Verinis, J. Scott, Jeffrey M. Brandsma, and Charles N. Cofer. 1968. "Discrepancies from Expectation in Relation to Affect and Motivation: Tests of McClelland's Hypothesis." *Journal of Personality and Social Psychology* 9(1): 47–58.

Wanous, John P., Timothy D. Poland, Stephen L. Premack, and K. Shannon Davis. 1992. "The Effects of Met Expectations on Newcomer Attitudes and Behaviors: A Review and Meta-Analysis." *Journal of Applied Psychology* 77(3): 288–97.

Zand, Dale E. 1972. "Trust and Managerial Problem Solving." *Administrative Science Quarterly* 17(2): 229–39.

Chapter 14

Power, Uncertainty, and the Amplification of Doubt: An Archival Study of Suspicion Inside the Oval Office

RODERICK M. KRAMER AND DANA A. GAVRIELI

I N HIS thoughtful meditation on the relationship between power and presidential performance, Garry Wills (1994) provocatively observed, "There is something twistable in the hand about power—something tricky and unpredictable—*amphisbaenic* or backward-striking" (297). Wills's observation brings to mind the familiar caveat that "power corrupts." But does power corrupt trust? Is there something "twistable in the hand" about the relationship between power and the capacity to trust?

Broadly construed, this question directs our attention to the seeming fragility of trust in many organizational settings: Trust is hard-won, yet easily lost—or so, at least, it seems (see Janoff-Bulman 1992). Is it even harder won and more easily lost for those in power? It is sometimes asserted that it is lonely at the top. Is it lonely in part because those in power cannot know so easily who among them is trustworthy and can be counted on for their advice and loyalty?

At first glance, it might seem as if power buffers us somewhat from many of the problems associated with the development and maintenance of trust. When we are in a position of power we may seem less dependent on others and able to summon the resources needed to verify others' reliability and loyalty. Thus, problems of assessing others' trustworthiness might seem lessened. Yet, rather than insulating us from the problems of trust, power might instead compound them. In highly competitive or political environments, the cost of misjudgment when it comes to trusting others can be steep—especially for those on the top who have much to lose. Consequently, concerns about trustworthiness are likely to loom very large for the leader in power. As the historian Doris Kearns-Goodwin (1976) once aptly noted, "When every relationship is translated into one of power lost or gained, all relationships, including friendships, are reduced to a series of shifting and undependable alliances. In such a world it is easy to succumb to the belief that even one's closest friends must be watched for signs of treason" (388). When even a single misstep with respect to trust can prove fatal, the shadow of suspicion is likely to be broadly cast over the political landscape.

In this chapter we examine this provocative but largely unexplored relationship between power and the potential fragility of trust from a rather unique vantage point: one that takes us, quite literally, inside the Oval Office. Drawing on a large body of recently available archival data, we explore some of the antecedents and consequences of presidential suspicions regarding others' trustworthiness. On the basis of these data, we inductively develop a conceptual framework that explicates some of the cognitive components of leader suspicion.

To better set the stage for this inductive inquiry, we offer first a few remarks regarding the relationship between power and doubt.

Power, Uncertainty, and Doubt in Organizations

The relationship between power and trust is obviously a complex one. Those who achieve positions of power in organizations typically confront a variety of vexing dilemmas surrounding the issue of trust. Because of the demands of high office, individuals in positions of power obviously cannot know every nuance of every decision. They cannot possess the expertise required for every decision task. As a consequence, they must rely on others around them for their judgment and counsel. Similarly, they cannot monitor every transaction and must depend on others to faithfully implement their initiatives.

The vulnerabilities leaders labor under were made all too clear to the newly elected President Kennedy in the early days of his administration. Kennedy had decided to rely on the expert advice provided by the CIA and the Joint Chiefs of Staff regarding the wisdom of the proposed Bay of Pigs operation—an operation initially formulated by the Eisenhower administration. He also relied on those in control of this covert operation to fully implement his directives to scale it down and minimize the risk of political damage. In both instances, Kennedy came to believe his trust had been seriously misplaced. Of the members of the Joint Chiefs of Staff, Kennedy bitterly complained, "Those sons-of-bitches with all the fruit salad just sat there nodding, saying it would work" (Reeves 1993, 103). As Kennedy learned too late, when a leader's attention is increasingly taken up by the rush and press of multiple concerns and competing claims, scant time is available for assessing others' trustworthiness, loyalty, or competence.

Because power alters the relationship between power holders and those who serve them, there are additional reasons why trust—or, more precisely, the problem of assessing others' trustworthiness—may be fraught with difficulty. It may be more difficult for leaders to discern others' true feelings, thoughts, and loyalties. Advisers around the leader are likely to shade their true views in order to curry favor and, equally important, avoid disfavor. If they harbor ambitions of their own, they are likely to keep those ambitions hidden. As a consequence, those in power confront a potentially daunting task when trying to take the measure of others' trustworthiness and loyalty. Just as the extraordinarily wealthy or exceptionally attractive individual must wonder about the true depth of others' affections, so must the truly powerful leader wonder whether others' seeming trustworthiness and loyalty are as transparent and profound as they seem. Power almost necessarily enshrouds such judgments in a fog of ambiguity.

At a psychological level, this ambiguity is animated by uncertainty or doubt regarding one's attribution of motives and intentions to other actors on whom the leader depends. It is our inherent inability to fully discern or truly know others' real character that renders trust at the top tricky, however essential or desirable it may be. As Diego Gambetta (1988) aptly observed, "The condition of ignorance or uncertainty about other people's behavior is central to the notion of trust. It is related to the limits of our capacity ever to achieve a full knowledge of others, their motives . . ." (218). For those in power, the dilemma of trust created by such uncertainty is amplified.

Despite the importance of the topic of leader's distrust, there has been surprisingly little systematic theory or research on how individuals in positions of power cope with such trust dilemmas. Instead—and for understandable reasons—much of the extant trust literature has examined how the relatively powerless cope with dependence and vulnerability (see, for example, Kramer 1996). Accordingly, in attempting to better understand how those in positions of power respond to doubt regarding others' trustworthiness, we adopted a qualitative theory-building approach, exploiting an unusually rich and in many respects rather remarkable archival data set. For a variety of reasons, President Lyndon Baines Johnson decided early in his presidency to install listening devices in several locations in the White House, including the Oval Office.[1] This system enabled the President secretly to tape-record many

of his Oval Office conversations and telephone calls, providing an intimate record of the deliberations of a powerful leader as he struggled
with the deepening quagmire of Vietnam and the related floundering of
his Great Society initiatives. Johnson was, it should be noted, neither the
first nor last President to create a secret record of his presidential decisions (see Doyle 1999 for a history of presidential taping systems). His
use of such a system, however, was considerably more extensive than
most others': to date over four thousand hours of recorded conversations have come to light.

Although Johnson expressed his desire that these covertly recorded
calls be destroyed upon his death, the tapes were preserved by his secretary. As a result, scholars today possess an extraordinary chronicle of
the decision making processes of a president as he went about his day-
to-day deliberations in the Oval Office (Beschloss 1997 and 2001 provides
commentary on verbatim transcripts of these tapes).

To develop a better understanding of Johnson's deliberations regarding whom he could trust and whom he could not, we examined the currently declassified taped and transcribed conversations. Each tape was
searched for statements bearing on Johnson's trust or distrust of his
advisers, other members of his administration, and his political allies
and adversaries. To supplement the evidence from these tapes, we also
searched available oral histories on the Johnson administration, most
notably Merle Miller's extensive 1980 compilation. We also examined
recently declassified files and records of meetings involving Lyndon
Johnson and his advisers (Barrett 1993; Berman 1982, 1988; Burke and
Greenstein 1989), as well as memoirs by key participants in the decision-
making process scrutinized (Califano 1991; Clifford 1991; Goodwin
1988; Kearns-Goodwin 1976; Valenti 1977). These accounts were supple-
mented by the president's own detailed personal account (Johnson 1971)
and Doris Kearns-Goodwin's (1976) insider perspective on Johnson
and his administration. Finally, interviews were conducted with a
number of surviving members of Johnson's administration, including
McGeorge Bundy, Alain Entoven, John Gardner, Carl Kaysen, and Robert
McNamara. When viewed in concert, these data provide an unusually
broad window through which to peer into the mind of a President of
the United States as he wrestled with profound and troubling questions
regarding the trustworthiness and loyalty of those around him.

Conceptualizing Leader Doubt: Insights from Social-Psychological Theory and Research on Suspicion

In setting the stage for this inductive inquiry into the origins and
dynamics of Lyndon Johnson's suspicions, it may be helpful first to

undertake a brief tour of some of the relevant theory and research on suspicion from the social sciences. Over the past forty years, a small but informative scholarly literature on suspicion has accumulated (see Kramer 1998 and 2002 for more complete literature reviews). Although trust theorists have differed considerably with respect to how they conceptualize suspicion, several points of convergence are discernible within this literature. First, suspicion has generally been construed as an active psychological state that is closely linked to individuals' attitudes, beliefs, and expectancies about other people. Stephen Fein and James Hilton (1994) have defined suspicion as a "psychological state in which perceivers actively entertain multiple, possibly rival, hypotheses about the motives or genuineness of a person's behavior. Moreover, suspicion involves the belief that the actor's behavior may reflect a motive that the actor wants hidden from the target of his or her behavior" (168–69).

Thus, suspicion arises when individuals worry about such things as others' potential lack of credibility or attribute deceptive intentions to their actions, especially in situations where uncertainty or ambiguity is present regarding the true causes of their behavior.

In much of the social psychological literature, the social inference processes associated with resolving suspicion have been construed as reasonably orderly forms of induction, consistent with the idea that social perceivers often resemble "intuitive scientists" as they try to make sense of the social worlds they inhabit. While recognizing the importance of prior history and experience in the development of suspicion, a number of researchers have noted that some forms of suspicion appear to be far less rational in origin (Barber 1983; Deutsch, 1973) than those based on experience and prior history. For example, Morton Deutsch (1973) proposed an irrational form of suspicion that he characterized in terms of an "inflexible, rigid, unaltering tendency to act in a suspicious manner, irrespective of the situation or the consequences of so acting" (171). The pathology of such suspicion, he noted, is reflected in "the indiscriminateness and incorrigibility of the behavioral tendency" (171). Irrational suspicion reflects an exaggerated propensity to doubt, which can arise even in the absence of specific experiences that justify it.

Paranoid cognitions constitute one form of such irrational suspicion. Paranoid cognitions have been defined by Kenneth Colby (1981, 518) as "persecutory delusions and false beliefs whose propositional content clusters around ideas of being harassed, threatened, harmed, subjugated, persecuted, accused, mistreated, wronged, tormented, disparaged, vilified, and so on, by malevolent others, either specific individuals or groups." One of the most conspicuous symptoms of this disorder is the paranoid person's profound suspicion that he or she is the focus of others' thoughts or the target of their actions (Cameron 1943). As Colby (1981) noted, "Around the central core of persecutory delusions [that preoccupy the paranoid person] there exists a number of attendant properties such as suspiciousness, hypersensitivity, hostility, fearfulness, and self-reference that lead the paranoid individual to interpret events that have nothing to do with him as bearing on him personally" (518). For example, Norman Cameron (1943) recounts the case of a woman who was so preoccupied with her looks that she became convinced other people were constantly noticing her looks as well and were making disparaging remarks about her appearance behind her back.

Within clinical psychology, paranoid cognitions have usually been regarded as symptomatic of a psychiatric disorder (American Psychological Association 1987; Cameron 1943). In particular, it has been assumed that such cognitions are caused by abnormal personality factors, which reflect unresolved psychodynamic conflicts (Siegel 1994). In sharp contrast to these psychiatric conceptions, recent social cognitive research suggests a very different perspective on paranoid cognitions, one that affords considerably more attention to their social and situational determinants (see in particular Fenigstein and Vanable 1992; Kramer 1994; Zimbardo, Andersen, and Kabat 1981). This latter conception is predicated on the informal observation that, in milder form, paranoid cognitions appear to be rather prevalent and can be observed even among "normal" individuals, especially when they find themselves in certain social situations. As Allen Fenigstein and Paul Vanable (1992, 130–32) have cogently observed in this regard, ordinary people

> in their everyday behavior often manifest characteristics—such as self-centered thought, suspiciousness, assumptions of ill will or hostility, and even notions of conspiratorial intent—that are reminiscent of paranoia. . . . On various occasions, one may think one is being talked about or feel as if everything is going against one, resulting in suspicion and mistrust of others, as though they were taking advantage of one or were to blame for one's difficulties.

Recent research suggests that a variety of situational forces can contribute to the development of these extreme and seemingly irrational forms of paranoid suspicion. Of particular relevance to the present chapter is evidence that threats to decision makers' autonomy, power, and security can foster a debilitating form of such paranoid cognition (see Kramer 2002 for a recent literature review). As we argue in the next section, many of these conditions came together for Lyndon Johnson in the late 1960s, as he confronted the most serious political crisis in his long and extraordinary career.

An Inductive Analysis of the Origins and Dynamics of Presidential Doubt

To explore the cognitive structure of leader doubt, we take as a point of departure recent evidence that late in his presidency, Lyndon Johnson began to display patterns of perception and behavior that bear striking similarities to clinical accounts of paranoia. According to a number of accounts by aides within the Oval Office, Johnson became deeply suspicious of those around him. At first this circle of suspicion encompassed primarily his political foes, including members of Congress and the press who opposed his Vietnam policies or distrusted Johnson in general. As opposition to his Vietnam policy spread and his plans for a Great Society floundered, his circle of suspicion enlarged to embrace even his closest advisers and long-trusted friends. These growing paranoid suspicions led Johnson to isolate himself from others and to engage in a variety of uncharacteristically ineffective political behaviors.

Evolution of Johnson's Paranoia

In tracing the evolution of his suspicions, it is important to note that Lyndon Johnson unexpectedly inherited the office of the presidency on a moment's notice on November 22, 1963, after the assassination of President John Kennedy. Although he found himself holding the reins of power unexpectedly, he was already fully prepared to exercise it. Throughout much of his political life, Lyndon Johnson had harbored dreams of one day occupying the Oval Office and had labored long and hard to make these dreams comes true (Dallek 1991). He knew, moreover, just what he wanted to do should the opportunity present itself. Foremost in his mind was fulfilling his ambition of becoming one of the greatest presidents in American history. His aide Jack Valenti said of him, "He had one goal really: to be the greatest president doing the greatest good in the history of the nation" (Valenti 1977, 24). He himself said that he wanted to be "the greatest father the country had ever had" (quoted in Gruber 1991).

In Johnson's eyes, presidential greatness had two cornerstones. The first was a record of dramatic domestic achievement. Here Johnson sought, as the journalist Nicholas Lemann once commented, to "set world records in politics the way a star athlete would in sports" (quoted in Dallek 1991, 109). In pursuit of this goal Johnson unleashed a whirlwind of legislative activity, passing more sweeping domestic legislation than any other president in history. He was determined to eclipse the record of Franklin Roosevelt as a president who knew how to throw the enormous machinery of government into high gear in pursuit of great if difficult aims. In this spirit he embarked on a broad set of initiatives that he brought together under the umbrella of what he called the Great Society program. In large measure he felt that this program would be the crowning achievement of his presidency—the banner proclaiming his presidential legacy.

The second cornerstone to presidential greatness in Johnson's eyes was the ability of a president to keep his country out of harm's way. Every U.S. president who had achieved greatness, Johnson knew, had prevailed in wartime, even on the battlefield itself. Here the images of Lincoln and Roosevelt loomed large as comparisons in Johnson's mind. Consequently, he believed that however much he achieved, presidential greatness would elude him should he fail to resolve favorably the conflict raging in Vietnam.

If Johnson was clear about the ends to which he would apply his power in his quest for presidential greatness, he was equally sure of the means he would use in pursuit of those ends. He would do whatever it took and use whomever he needed to achieve his goals. Throughout his political life, Lyndon Johnson had displayed a remarkable degree of perceptiveness when it came to assessing the reliability and loyalty of those around him. He could readily discern whom he could trust and whom he should distrust. "If Lyndon Johnson was not a reader of books," Robert Caro (1982) once observed, "he was a reader of men's minds" (103).

What seemed to some observers to be an almost intuitive or instinctive ability to size up others, however, was the result of disciplined and determined vigilance and study of human nature. Jim Heath (1975, 179) has noted that Johnson "studied, analyzed, catalogued, and remembered the strengths and weaknesses, the likes and the dislikes, of fellow politicians as some men do stock prices, batting averages, and musical compositions. He knew who drank Scotch and who bourbon, whose wife was sick, who needed new post offices . . . who was in trouble with organized labor . . . and who owed him for a past favor."

Such vigilance helped Johnson recognize subtle opportunities and threats strewn across the political terrain—and helped him steer clear of the untrustworthy (Caro 1982; Dallek 1991). Chris Matthews (1988, 27) remarked on the utility of Johnson's intense vigilance and scrutiny of others' needs and vulnerabilities:

> It may seem all the more surprising that a man with [Johnson's] towering ego should have climbed to such heights by studying the inner as well as the outer needs of others. Yet it was his willingness to focus on other people and their concerns, no matter how small, that contributed to the near-total communication or at least access that Johnson achieved with those he sought to influence.

Johnson's vigilance also helped him figure out how best to tailor his approach to the specific person he was trying to influence. "To gain a senator's vote on a bill, Johnson would spend hours studying every conceivable motivation. . . . The fellow never knew what hit him" (Matthews 1988, 30). Johnson himself noted that in order to successfully influence someone and to gain their trust, "You've got to understand the beliefs and values common to them all as politicians, the desire for fame and the thirst for honor, [but] then you've got to understand the emotion most controlling that particular senator when he thinks about this particular issue" (Goodwin 1988, 261).

Jeffrey Pfeffer (1992) has argued that the ability to take the perspective of the other party is crucial to success in acquiring and maintaining power and cultivating trust: "One has to be able, at least for the moment, to stop thinking about oneself and one's own needs and beliefs" (173).

To push his domestic agenda ahead and make sense of Vietnam, Johnson brought all of his powers of perception and persuasion to bear. George Herring (1993) noted that Johnson "brought to [his contemplation of] the war this same enormous energy and compulsive attention to detail that characterized his approach to politics, the presidency, and life in general" (89). He admonished the Joint Chiefs of Staff during an early briefing on Vietnam in April 1964, "Remember, they are going to write stories about this like they did in the Bay of Pigs. Stories about me and my advisers. That is why I want you to think carefully, very, very carefully about alternatives and plans" (Califano 1991, 37).

Initially, Johnson was confident that all of his tried-and-true methods would work their usual magic and that he would be able to enact his domestic agenda while at least maintaining U.S. commitments in Vietnam. But as victory eluded him and as his Great Society plans began to collapse under the weight of the Vietnam War, his Vietnam-related decisions put enormous psychological pressure on him (Berman 1989; Janis 1983).

As Johnson's attempts to win the war in Vietnam floundered, he began to believe that his perceived political adversaries and critics were lining up against him. As the pressures continued unabated, a number of individuals who enjoyed intimate access to Johnson's personal views and were close observers of his presidential actions all commented in strikingly similar fashion that his behavior was starting to bear striking similarities to clinical accounts of paranoia (see Califano 1991; Dallek 1991; Goodwin 1988; Kearns-Goodwin, 1976; although see Rusk et al., *New York Times*, August 24, 1988, for a dissenting view). So alarming were their observations that at least two presidential aides, Bill Moyers and Richard Goodwin, actually went to the library and looked up the clinical symptoms of paranoia in a medical book.

The most detailed and compelling of these descriptions are provided by Johnson's aide, confidante, and eventual biographer, Doris Kearns-Goodwin (1976, 316), who wrote:

Members of the White House staff who had listened to the President's violent name-calling were frightened by what seemed to them signs of paranoia. Suddenly, in the middle of a conversation, his voice would become intense and low-keyed. He would laugh inappropriately and his thoughts would assume a random, almost incoherent quality, as he began to spin a vast web of accusations.

No less dramatic incidents are recounted by Johnson's former speechwriter and adviser Richard Goodwin. Goodwin (1988, 401–2) noted that it was not so much what he said or did that sounded paranoid, but rather the

> disjointed, erratic flow of thought, unrelated events strung together, yet seemingly linked by some incomprehensible web of connections within Johnson's mind. . . . It was a giant, if always partial, leap into unreason, an outward sign that the barriers separating rational thought and knowledge from delusive belief were becoming weaker, and more easily crossed.

At first, Johnson's doubts and suspicions were leveled primarily at his political adversaries and critics and were explained by him primarily in terms of what he regarded as individual failures of vision or resolve. He thus characterized them as "nervous nellies" and "half-brights" (a derogatory reference to William Fulbright, one of his most vocal critics) who, he felt, had neither the stomach or will to persevere on the difficult but necessary course of action. Over time, the scope of the conspiracy he imagined to be marshaled against him grew, seemingly in perverse proportion to the extent to which he felt besieged. It was almost as if he explained to himself why his enormous personal skills and institutional advantages as President weren't enough by conjuring up opponents with comparable power and cunning comparable to his own.

Commenting on the evolution and amplification of Johnson's doubts about others, Kearns-Goodwin (1976) noted further that although "sometimes it seemed as if Johnson himself did not believe what he was saying . . . at other times [his] voice carried so much conviction that his words produced an almost hypnotic effect. . . . The worse the situation in Vietnam became, the more Johnson intruded his suspicions and his fears into every aspect of his daily work" (317). He began to withdraw socially, drawing the political wagons in an ever tighter circle around the White House.

As the attacks on his policy and character continued, Johnson became suspicious even of his closest aides and advisers, including individuals like Robert McNamara, whom he had once affectionately called his "lard-hair man" and characterized as the "the most competent man . . . the most objective man I've ever met" (quoted in Gruber 1991).

Whereas before Johnson had drawn a sharp line between his loyal aides and those outside his administration, the boundary between friend and foe began to shift more and more toward the center of his inner circle—at first almost imperceptibly and then, as his frustrations mounted, with increasing momentum. "I can't trust anybody anymore," he finally complained bitterly to Goodwin (Goodwin 1988, 392).

These accounts provide a number of clues to the origins and dynamics of Lyndon Johnson's growing suspicions regarding others' trustworthiness and loyalty. More generally, they suggest some of the psychological forces that contribute to leader suspicion within organizational settings.

The data suggest first that beginning in 1964 Johnson began to manifest a style of hypervigilant social information processing. In particular, he began to scrutinize every interaction for evidence of defection or disloyalty—not only those involving his obvious enemies, but even those of his once-trusted aides and advisers.

In sharp contrast with the sort of adaptive vigilance that Johnson had displayed throughout his rise to power, this hypervigilance exerted a debilitating effect on his thinking about whom he could trust. For instance, Johnson felt that he was being assaulted from all directions: "I feel like a hound bitch in heat in the country," he complained. "If you run, they chew your tail off. If you stand still, they slip it to you" (Berman 1989, 183). Thus, any attempt at persuasion or reconciliation that Johnson made to satisfy or appease one constituency seemed to alienate others. Each new attempt to cope with the threats he confronted seemed to entrap him further in a painful avoidance-avoidance conflict, with no attractive alternatives. He felt that any course of action he proposed was sabotaged by critics who simply did not understand the special difficulties Vietnam posed.

Construing the threat in such personal terms seemed to bring to the surface with renewed intensity Johnson's longstanding doubts and insecurities about his ability to lead and to be admired and liked. As Berman (1989) noted, "As his political maneuverings failed to achieve their anticipated goals, Johnson's great personal insecurities manifested themselves. All presidents feel ill-treated by the press, but with Johnson [this feeling] became an obsession" (183).

Those in power live under the continual scrutiny of multiple audiences and constituencies to whom they feel accountable and on whom their power depends (see Tetlock, Skitka, and Boettger 1989). Pfeffer (1992) observed, "To be in power is to be watched more closely, and this surveillance affords one the luxury of few mistakes" (302). Being in the limelight in this way was hardly a new or unique experience for Johnson. In fact, Johnson had always displayed a keen appreciation of the expectations and interests of the various groups who influenced his power, and had responded with a deft and often devious touch. What was different in his musings about Vietnam was the extent to which Johnson *personalized* this scrutiny. Every expression of doubt and criticism, even from close friends and even when intended as constructive, was transformed by Johnson into a personal assault on his character or the legitimacy of his claim on the nation's leadership. And when these comments concerned Vietnam, he felt as if every presidential gesture and deed were being severely and unfairly condemned. As Herring (1993, 95) commented, "If Ronald Reagan was the Teflon president, to whom nothing stuck, Johnson was the flypaper president, to whom everything clung. A compulsive reader, viewer, and listener who took every criticism personally and to heart, he was at first intent on, and then obsessed with, answering every accusation, responding to every charge."

Johnson began to view himself as being betrayed by an unruly mob of hostile critics, including many of those he had helped the most with his Great Society programs. The circle of critics was vast and included not only his all-too-familiar political enemies in Washington but also the national press, whose approval he had assiduously courted, and a vast citizenry whose love and affection he had long sought. Johnson himself said (Kearns-Goodwin 1976, 329),

> I felt that I was being chased on all sides by a giant stampede coming at me from all directions. . . . I was forced over the edge by rioting blacks, demonstrating students, marching welfare mothers, squawking professors, and hysterical reporters. And then the final straw. The thing I feared from the first day of my Presidency was actually coming true. Robert Kennedy had openly announced his decision to reclaim the throne in the memory of his brother. And the American people, swayed by the magic of the name, were dancing in the streets. The whole situation was unbearable.

Johnson's perception that he was under hostile scrutiny was no doubt fueled by the way in which he had acquired his presidency. With the death of President Kennedy, Johnson had at long last achieved his ultimate political goal (indeed, when asked by a colleague in 1960 why he had accepted Kennedy's offer of the vice presidency, against the advice of so many close aides, Johnson confided, "I'll be a heartbeat away from the Presidency"). However, the dubious circumstances surrounding his inheritance made the victory hollow: Johnson regarded himself as an accidental president, especially during his first term. Even in his own eyes he was the undeserving beneficiary of a tragic turn of fate rather than the recipient of a legitimate mandate. More important, he feared that others regarded him as a mere pretender to the throne, an illegitimate heir to Camelot (Gruber 1991).

There is a revealing irony here. On the one hand, Johnson felt as if he were under relentless scrutiny—trapped in the harsh and lugubrious limelight of public attention. At the same time he was consumed by doubts as to whether or not he would even be remembered after his presidency had expired. The psychiatrist R. D. Laing (1961, 136–37) has provided a perceptive observation about the complex and somewhat paradoxical phenomenology of paranoid cognitions:

> In typical paranoid ideas of reference, the [paranoid] person feels that the murmurings and mutterings he hears as he walks past a crowd are all about him. . . . When one gets to know such a person more than superficially, however, one often discovers that what tortures him is not so much his delusions of reference, but his harrowing suspicion that he is of no importance to anyone, that no one is referring to him at all. . . . He is persecuted by being the center of everyone else's world, yet he is preoccupied with the thought that he never occupies first place in anyone's affection.

Johnson's hypervigilance fed this sense of being under intense scrutiny, so much so that he became increasingly self-conscious, not only about his role in the war's escalation but also about his responsibility for the economic and social costs it was inflicting on the country.

Even within the cloistered recesses of the White House Johnson found little respite from these painful feelings of self-consciousness. "Johnson felt a stranger among his inherited advisers," noted Barber (1972, 79), "extraordinarily sensitive to the slurs by all the 'overbred smart alecks who live in Georgetown and think in Harvard.' And he wondered continually about his adequacy to be what he so desperately wanted to be, a Great President." He imagined that those around him, especially the carryovers from the Kennedy administration, were continually making invidious comparisons between him and his predecessor (Henggeler 1991). As a result he felt trapped: unable to relax with them, yet reluctant to remove them, fearing the public would view any change in his cabinet as an act of disrespect towards the recently slain leader (Gruber 1991).

Johnson's painful self-consciousness also reflected his fear that the unfulfilled promise of the Kennedy administration would continue to cast a pall over his own efforts to sculpt the Great Society. As Goodwin (1988, 396) commented, "The enduring shadow of Camelot—glamorous, popular, intellectual, enshrined in steadily growing myth—seemed to him to obscure the achievements of his own presidency, preventing others from seeing how much more he was accomplishing than had his predecessor."

Not only did his aspirations for the Great Society seem endangered, but his concrete accomplishments in bringing it to life seemed to be eclipsed. This Great Society that he had once graphically described as like a beautiful and desirable lady now seemed to him like a withered old woman: "She's getting thinner and thinner and uglier and uglier all the time. . . . Soon she'll be so ugly the American people will refuse to look at her; they'll stick her in a closet to hide her away and there she'll die. And when she dies, I, too, will die" (Kearns-Goodwin 1976, 286–87).

Another factor that contributed to Johnson's hypervigilance was the way he construed his loss of control over the management of political opposition to the war. Throughout his career Johnson labored to control every facet of his political climb and tried to leave as little as possible to chance. In his rise to power he had demonstrated a remarkable ability to orchestrate myriad social and political forces around him as he saw fit to achieve his ends (Caro 1982; Dallek 1991; Gruber 1991). With Vietnam, however, Johnson found himself "for almost the first time, encompassed by men and events that he could not control: Vietnam and the Kennedys, and, later, the press, Congress, and even the public whose approval was essential to his own esteem" (Goodwin, 1988, 399).

Johnson also found himself increasingly isolated and removed from critical sources of social support and political solace. In the past, he had often relied on the counsel and reassurance of a number of close colleagues and advisers when working his way through a political crisis. Now, Johnson perceived many of these same people as no longer entirely trustworthy. He felt they were pulling back, either to cover their own political backs or because they were simply lacked the resolve needed to stay a difficult course. Rather than the unconditional support he now sought and felt he deserved, Johnson saw those around him as jumping ship.

What Johnson seemed to fail to appreciate during this period is the role his own rigid behavior and irrational persistence were playing in driving away some of the best, brightest, and most loyal of his advisers, including Robert McNamara, Clark Clifford, and Hubert Humphrey. Although he felt they had deserted him, he had in fact driven them away.

In what he perceived as an egregious assault on not only his presidency but also his legacy in the history books, Johnson may have experienced what Karl Weick (1993b) has characterized as "cosmology episodes" in organizations. A cosmology episode occurs when people "suddenly and deeply feel that the universe they inhabit is no longer a rational, orderly, system. . . . A cosmology episode feels like *vu jade*—the opposite of *déjà vu:* I've never been here before, I have no idea where I am, and I have no idea who can help me" (633–34).

Also evident from the data is that as the escalation of his conflict with his political adversaries and critics continued, Lyndon Johnson began to engage in a pattern of intense, *dysphoric rumination* about his inability to extricate America from the conflict in Vietnam. Dysphoric rumination is a psychological process characterized by the intense, intrusive reexperiencing and rehashing of past events. As Kearns-Goodwin (1976, 299) observed, Johnson often

> consciously and deliberately decided not to think another thought about Vietnam. Nonetheless, discussions that started on poverty or education invariably ended up on Vietnam. If Johnson was unhappy thinking about Vietnam, he was even less happy not thinking about it. . . . He found himself unwilling, and soon unable, to break loose from what had become an obsession.

Other accounts describe how Johnson often woke in the middle of the night to prowl the corridors of the White House and ponder the next day's bombing targets and to check casualty figures as they arrived. Secretary of State Dean Rusk recalled, "We could never break him of the habit, even for health reasons, of getting up at 4:30 or 5:00 every morning to go down to the operations room and check on the casualties from Vietnam, each one of which took a little piece out of him" (Berman 1988, 144).

Nor he could not understand the seemingly sudden erosion of trust and loss of affection of the public, who only months before had sent an enormously strong mandate in the 1964 election. "Why don't people like me?" he once asked Dean Acheson. To which Acheson reportedly replied, "Because, Mr. President, you are not a very likable man" (Barber 1972, 77).

Rumination in political contexts is a complex cognitive process. In the context of highly competitive or political environments—where even a single misstep with respect to trust can be enormously costly—leaders' willingness to devote scarce attentional resources to ruminating about events around them may greatly enhance the likelihood they will avoid mistakes. Thus, constructive rumination can contribute potentially to the development of more cognitively complex views of trust-related situations. This type of rumination can be contrasted with more superficial, heuristic modes of information processing that are designed to limit the demands on decision makers' limited attentional resources and expedite sense making. Thus, precisely *because* those in power are so willing to allocate cognitive resources to sense-making tasks, they might be more likely to detect opportunities and threats that others underestimate or overlook.

What is striking about Johnson's rumination during this period, however, is its clearly destructive impact on his judgments regarding whom he could or should trust for advice. In searching for answers to his difficulties, Johnson directed his attention not inward, toward his own failings and faults, but outward, toward others, scrutinizing his relationships for signs of other people's doubt, disloyalty, or betrayal, and always pondering their presumably concealed motives and intentions. "Discussions on legislation would be interrupted by diatribes against the 'critics,' " writes Kearns-Goodwin (1976). "Private luncheons and dinners would be dominated by complaints about 'the traitors' " (317).

The data suggest three distinct and rather interesting patterns of misperception, which we characterize as (1) the sinister attribution error, (2) the overly personalistic construal of events, and (3) the exaggerated perception of conspiracy.

The term *sinister attribution error* reflects a tendency for individuals to overattribute hostile intentions and malevolent motives to others' actions (Kramer 1994). Several writers have noted that throughout his career, Johnson frequently expressed suspicions regarding others' motives and intentions, convinced that he was detecting slights and snubs that less discerning observers simply failed to see. For example, Clark Clifford (1991) commented that Johnson "saw real or imagined slights everywhere" (390). Even the seemingly most benign events could take on sinister import in Johnson's mind. For example, when relatives of the Kennedy family accompanied him on a world tour, he became convinced they were acting as spies for Robert Kennedy (Henggeler, 1991, 62).

These suspicions intensified dramatically as the Vietnam situation unfolded. Johnson believed that many of the actions of his political enemies, especially those of Robert F. Kennedy, were intended not only to challenge his foreign policy but also to mock and humiliate him personally. Later, a bemused Bobby Kennedy, perhaps underestimating the threat he posed to Johnson, asked Goodwin, "Why does he keep worrying about me? I don't like him, but there's nothing I can do to him. Hell, he's the President and I'm only a junior senator" (cited in Goodwin 1988, 396).

Overly personalistic construal refers to a tendency for individuals involved in a conflict or crisis to construe their adversaries' actions in purely personal—and often self-serving—terms (Kahn and Kramer 1990). "Self-serving" in this context may mean "punctuating," or interpreting, social interactions and events in a way that reinforces or confirms their suspicions. For example, Johnson once observed,

> Look what happened whenever I went to make a speech about the war. The week before my speech, the St. Louis Post–Dispatch or the Boston Globe or CBS News would get on me over and over, talking about what a terrible speaker I was . . . pretty soon the people began to wonder, they began to think that I really must be uninspiring if the papers and the TV said so. (Kearns-Goodwin 1976, 315–17)

On another occasion he suggested,

> "Isn't it funny that I *always* received a piece of advice from my top advisers *right after* each of them had been in contact with someone in the communist world? And isn't it funny that you could *always* find [the Soviet

foreign minister Anatoly] Dobrynin's car in front of [the American journalist James] Reston's house the *night before* Reston delivered a blast on
Vietnam?" (Kearns-Goodwin 1976, 315–17, emphasis added)

Exaggerated perceptions of conspiracy reflect a tendency for individuals to overestimate the extent to which their perceived enemies are
engaged in concerted or coordinated actions against them (see Pruitt
1987; Stein 1988; Kramer 1994). Just as overly personalistic construal and
biased punctuation of interactions entail the overperception of causal
linkages among events, the exaggerated perception of conspiracy entails
an overperception of social linkages among actors. Johnson believed
that a conspiracy of enormous proportions existed to undermine U.S.
efforts in Vietnam. He once confided to Kearns-Goodwin (1976, 316):

> Two or three intellectuals started it all, you know. They produced all the
> doubt, they and the columnists in the *Washington Post*, the *New York
> Times*, *Newsweek*, and *Life*. And it spread and spread. . . . Bobby began
> taking it up as his cause and, with Martin Luther King on his payroll, he
> went around stirring up the Negroes. . . . Then the communists stepped
> in. They control the three networks, you know, and the forty major out-
> lets of communication. It's all in the FBI reports. They prove everything.
> Not just about the reporters, but about the professors too.

Gradually the scale and scope of the conspiracy broadened:

> No longer satisfied with impugning the motives of his critics . . . or
> attributing his difficulties to "those Kennedys" or "those Harvards" or
> to the traitorous citizens who lived in seeming innocence along the
> banks of Boston's Charles River, Johnson began to hint privately . . . that
> he was the target of a gigantic communist conspiracy in which his
> domestic adversaries were only players—not conscious participants per-
> haps, but unwitting dupes. (Goodwin 1988, 402)

Johnson was so convinced his perceptions regarding this international conspiracy were correct that he berated CIA Director Richard
Helms for his inability to find evidence of the "money trail" linking
American opposition to the war to its Communist origins. "I simply
don't understand why it is that you can't find out about that foreign
money," he complained bitterly (Miller 1980, 626).

Ironically, the more Johnson ruminated about such linkages and patterns, the more convinced he became of the veracity of his suspicions. It
might seem surprising that rumination would have increased Johnson's
confidence in his misperceptions. One might argue just the opposite:
that the more people ruminate about the causes of their difficulties, the
more likely they should be to generate alternative—and perhaps more
realistic—interpretations of their causes. However, research suggests

that rumination often works in exactly the opposite direction, fostering an unrealistic confidence in a person's construals of events as they find more "evidence" to support their suspicions. As Timothy Wilson and Dolores Kraft (1993) have noted, "Because it is often difficult to get at the exact roots of feelings, repeated introspections may not result in better access to the actual causes. Instead, people may repeatedly focus on reasons that are plausible and easy to verbalize" (410).

Once in Doubt, Always in Doubt: The Self-Entrapping Nature of Suspicion at the Top

All else being equal, it might seem as if these types of judgmental distortions would be difficult to sustain. As noted earlier, there is a considerable body of theory and research which suggests that when making judgments about others' trustworthiness, people act much like Bayesian statisticians, recalibrating or updating their judgments on the basis of their experiences (see Kramer 1999, for a recent review). Thus, even if one can understand the initial circumstances that give rise to suspicion, one might expect that such misperceptions and errors should over time be self-correcting. If evidence that one's fears and suspicions about others turn out to be exaggerated or groundless, they should weaken and eventually disappear. In fact, however, a number of dynamics may contribute to the resilience of paranoid cognitions. These autistic or self-sustaining characteristics of paranoid perceptual systems arise, arguably, from both the paranoid perceivers' difficulty in learning from their trust-related experiences and also their difficulty in generating useful trust-building (diagnostic) experiences. In other words, the systematic and adaptive auditing processes described earlier are easily short-circuited or corrupted.

Difficulty Learning from Experience

One problem that the highly suspicious perceiver confronts is that because of the presumption that others are untrustworthy and that things may not be what they seem, the perceived diagnostic value of any particular cue or piece is evidence is tainted from the outset. As Weick (1979) noted, all cues are corruptible and may in fact be corrupted. He cites an interesting historical example that illustrates this inherent corruptibility of cues. The day before the Japanese attack on Pearl Harbor, an American naval attaché had informed Washington that he did not believe a surprise attack by the Japanese was imminent because the fleet was still stationed at its home base. As evidence for this conclusion, he noted that large crowds of sailors could be observed casually strolling the streets of Tokyo. What the attaché did not know was that these "sailors" were in actuality Japanese soldiers disguised as sailors to conceal the fact that the Japanese fleet had already sailed. From the perspective of the Japanese, this was a brilliant example of what intelligence experts call strategic disinformation, which is intended to mislead an adversary about one's capabilities or intentions.

In elaborating on the implications of this incident, Weick noted that the very fact that the attaché had searched for a foolproof cue made him, ironically, more vulnerable to being fooled. Weick underscored his point by quoting a passage from the social psychologist Erving Goffman:

> The very fact that the observer finds himself looking to a particular bit of evidence as an incorruptible check on what is or might be corruptible, is the very reason he should be suspicious of this evidence; for the best evidence for him is also the best evidence for the subject to tamper with. . . . When the situation seems to be exactly what it appears to be, the closest likely alternative is that the situation has been completely faked. (Goffman 1969, 172–73)

For the already suspicious perceiver, of course, the attaché's experience dramatically illustrates what happens when one's social vigilance is too lax and innocence regarding others' motives and actions is too readily or naïvely assumed. In a world presumed to be sinister, such cues are always corrupted and always in a predictably dangerous direction. Figuratively speaking, sailors are never just sailors, and the fleet must always be presumed to have stealthily sailed.

Ironically, even the *nonexistence* of evidence can become a powerful form of confirmatory evidence for the actively suspicious social perceiver. Robyn Dawes (1988) provides a nice illustration of this possibility in his discussion of the debate over internment of Japanese Americans at the beginning of the Second World War. When Earl Warren, then the governor of California, testified before a congressional hearing regarding this policy, one of his interrogators noted that absolutely no evidence of espionage or sabotage on the part of any Japanese Americans had been presented or was available to the committee. Warren's response about how to construe this fact was revealing: "I take the view that this lack [of evidence] is the *most ominous sign* in our whole situation. It convinces me more than perhaps any other factor that the sabotage we are to get, the Fifth Column activities we are to get, are timed just like Pearl Harbor was timed. . . . I believe we are just being lulled into *a false sense of security*" (Dawes 1988, 251; emphasis added).

Research on trust suggests other cognitive "toeholds" for paranoid cognition. Numerous scholars have noted that trust is easier to destroy than to create or sustain (Barber 1983; Janoff-Bulman 1992; Slovic 1993). Paul Slovic (1993) noted in trying to explain this fact that a variety of cognitive factors contribute to asymmetries in the trust-building versus trust-destroying process. First, negative (trust-destroying) events are more visible and noticeable than positive (trust-building) events. Second, trust-destroying events carry more weight in judgment than trust-building events of comparable magnitude. As evidence for this *asymmetry principle,* Slovic evaluated the impact of hypothetical news events on people's trust judgments and found that negative events had more impact on trust judgments than positive events. Slovic noted further that asymmetries between trust and distrust may be reinforced by the fact that sources of bad (trust-destroying) news tend to be perceived as more credible than sources of good news.

Other evidence suggests that violations of trust tend to loom larger in people's minds than confirmations of trust. Studies of individuals' reactions to trust betrayals suggest that violations of trust are highly salient to victims, prompting intense ruminative activity and a persistent search for the causes of the violation (Janoff-Bulman 1992). Furthermore, to the extent that violations of trust are coded as interpersonal losses, they should loom larger than "mere" confirmations of trust of comparable magnitude. For instance, failure to keep a promise should have more impact on judgments about trustworthiness than "merely" keeping it.

Difficulties in Generating Disconfirming Experience

In addition to impairing perceivers' ability to learn from experience, situations that induce suspicion may also impede their ability to generate the kind of diagnostic information needed to accurately calibrate others' trustworthiness. Learning about the distribution of trustworthiness in a population entails risk taking. People must engage in trust-taking experiments if they are to generate the diagnostic data necessary to learn who among them can be trusted, and how much. Such experiments require that individuals expose themselves to the prospect of misplaced trust and misplaced distrust. Any systematic bias in the generation of data samples can of course influence the inferences that result from these experiments. Trust theorists such as Gambetta (1988) have argued that asymmetries in the presumptive trust benchmark of low and high trusters may differentially impact both the frequency with which they generate useful learning opportunities and their ability to extract reliable cues from the opportunities they do generate. Gambetta noted that distrust is very difficult to invalidate through experience, because it either "prevents people from engaging in the appropriate kind of social experiment, or, worse, it leads to behavior which bolsters the validity of distrust itself" (234). Consequently, presumptive distrust tends to become perpetual distrust.

Because of their heightened suspicion of others' motives and intentions, paranoid perceivers approach social interactions with an orientation of presumptive distrust. An instructive parallel can be drawn from research on the dynamics of hostile attribution—attribution of hostile intent to others—among aggressive boys. Such boys approach social interactions almost "pre-offended" and prepared for the worst. They thus elicit through their own behaviors the very outcomes they most dread. Much like these overly aggressive boys, who are perceptually vigilant when it comes to detecting hostility, so the paranoid perceiver is prepared to distrust and to be confirmed in this stance. Not surprisingly, the paranoid perceiver's behavior also ends up eliciting the sort of uncomfortable, distant interactions that reinforce mutual wariness and suspicion and discomfort.

Contributions and Implications of the Present Study

The primary aim of the present study was to explore some facets of the relationship between power and trust. The chapter took the tack of backing into this problem by examining some of the ways in which trust becomes more problematic for those in positions of power. We suggest that examining some of the factors that contribute to the development and amplification of leader suspicions enables us to better understand some of the necessary and sufficient conditions for more resilient trust.

The present study makes a number of specific contributions to our understanding of the cognitive structure of leader doubts about others' trustworthiness and the dynamics underlying the amplification of that doubt. A distinctive feature of the framework presented here is that it avoids construing leader suspicion merely in terms of aberrant personality dynamics, as have more traditional psycho-historical or psycho-biographical approaches to such material (such as Greenstein 1975). Instead, this paper has suggested how various "normal" cognitive heuristics and social information processing strategies that leaders use can, under certain circumstances, go awry. For example, it is clear that vigilance and rumination are often useful cognitive processes from the standpoint of helping leaders make sense of the crises and predicaments they face. Such processes can contribute to effective appraisal and decision making (see Janis 1989). The cognitive drift into the dysfunctional range of hypervigilance and destructive rumination occurs only when the right confluence of dispositional and situational forces obtains.

In concluding, it may be worth elaborating on a few caveats regarding the internal and external validity of the inductively driven analysis presented here. In building our case we have relied primarily on historical data regarding Lyndon Johnson's paranoid perceptions and behaviors.

Much of this qualitative data, to be sure, is based on direct observation and recording of Johnson's expressed thoughts and his behavior. Moreover, there is considerable convergence in these observations. Nonetheless, in focusing so heavily on one decision maker's apparent display of paranoia during the height of an unusually protracted and intense organizational crisis, questions inevitably arise as to the external validity of the theoretical arguments. To what extent are these general processes?

In attempting to address such concerns, it is worth considering some other contemporary examples of irrational and emergent leader suspicion. Perhaps the most obvious and compelling case that springs to mind pertains to President Richard Nixon's behavior during the Watergate crisis (see, among others, Ambrose 1991). A number of writers have commented on Nixon's deep paranoia about the motives and machinations of his political adversaries as his presidency unraveled. Admiral Elmo Zumwalt, who was Richard Nixon's chief of naval operations, described a meeting with Nixon in terms that echo many of the themes discussed with respect to Johnson. He noted that

> the President . . . saw the various attacks on [him] as part of a vast plot by intellectual snobs to destroy a president who was representative of the man in the street. . . . It was clear he perceived himself as a fighter who was . . . involved in mortal battle with the forces of evil. . . . [Nixon] repeatedly expressed the thought that the eastern liberal establishment was out to do us all in and that we should beware. (quoted in Ambrose 1991, 285)

In addition, and as noted earlier, there is considerable qualitative evidence of a tendency for certain organizational leaders and power brokers to display signs of paranoia. Reeves's (1993) more recent and amply documented investigation corroborates and elaborates on this picture.

Although the conceptual framework presented in this chapter provides a reasonably parsimonious account of the historical data pertaining to Johnson's political paranoia, it is not intended as a complete or comprehensive account. The data suggest several obvious areas that merit fuller elaboration and differentiation. For example, a more systematic development of the links between suspicion and other forms of misperception and judgmental biases would be useful. It would also be helpful to articulate more carefully the role group and institutional dynamics might play in the development of "collective" forms of paranoia among policy makers. Clearly, these unanswered questions and lacunae in the present formulation should be construed as opportunities for future research, rather than intrinsic shortcomings of the model itself.

Toward a Functionalist Account of Leader Suspicion: The Virtues of Doubt in an Uncertain and Dangerous World

In concluding, we would like to offer a final caveat regarding the way the function of leader suspicion might be construed. To the extent that heightened suspicions contribute to misperceptions and self-defeating behaviors, they obviously represent maladaptive forms of leader cognition. The analysis up to this point has emphasized primarily these dysfunctional consequences. However, it is important to consider as well the possibility that such cognitions might play an adaptive role.

There are several reasons for thinking paranoid cognitions may not be entirely dysfunctional or maladaptive in certain political contexts. Distrust and suspicion are not always irrational. In highly political environments there may be legitimate cause for profound suspicion and concern about one's well-being. Jerome Frank (1987) noted that the fears and suspicions of organizational leaders are not always in error: "In their rise to power, leaders are almost certain to encounter superiors who wish to hold them back, rivals who seek to displace them, and subordinates seeking to curry favor" (339). In such environments, the cost of misplaced trust may be substantial. Thus, even though the fears and suspicions of paranoid leaders may seem exaggerated or inappropriate to others, this does not mean that their suspicions are entirely misplaced or that their seeming preternatural wariness is unwarranted.

Under such circumstances, prudence and caution may be far preferable to regret, and increased vigilance of others' behavior and a propensity to ruminate about their motives may be quite functional. In discussing Lyndon Johnson's paranoia, Goodwin (1988) noted that because presidents do have real adversaries and genuine reasons for suspicion, the tendency to perceive others "as a potential source of opposition or even danger" can help them remain "on the alert—observing and listening—to discern the hidden intentions of others, thus sharpening skills that can give them a remarkable intuitive understanding of others—their concealed ambitions, weaknesses, greeds, and lusts" (398). As Henry Kissinger once quipped in defense of Richard Nixon, "Even paranoids can have real enemies."

There also may be some self-presentational advantages associated with leaders' strategic displays of suspicious behavior. First, when viewed as an influence strategy, the *reputation* for being a bit paranoid may confer considerable bargaining leverage, especially against individuals whose taste for confrontation or willingness to bear the risks and costs of an escalating conflict are low. At the margin, such individuals may decide someone else can carry the conflict, while they will simply ride it out. For example, Seymour Hersh (1983) provides an account of those who were reluctant to take Kissinger on in the early days of the Nixon presidency. Thus, a carefully nurtured reputation for being irrational, unpredictable, and explosive may be a useful deterrent to challenges to one's power. In this sense, strategic displays of paranoia may function much like strategic displays of anger and other forms of negative affect to keep others in line (compare Hedrick Smith's 1988 discussion of "porcupine power").

A related point is that by strategically framing their problems and conflicts in terms of powerful, united enemies, leaders may be able to recruit and mobilize other individuals to come to their assistance. Thus, to the extent it can be "collectively" instilled, a leader's paranoia can be used to build cohesiveness by suggesting the existence of a common enemy against which a group can unite.

A little paranoia may also serve a self-protective role by helping sustain a leader's motivation and persistence, especially during periods when that leadership is being questioned or threatened. In much the same way that defensive pessimism has been shown to enhance individuals' motivation to engage in efficacious preemptive behavior to fend off failure (Norem and Cantor 1986), paranoid cognitions might help individuals detect emerging threats and help them maintain their motivation to overcome perceived dangers and obstacles, even in situations where those dangers and obstacles, from the perspective of a more neutral observer, seem grossly exaggerated. In fact, we would argue that precisely *because* they are so willing to expend considerable cognitive resources, including a willingness to ruminate at length about others' intentions, motives, and plans, such individuals might actually be more likely to detect patterns of threat that others fail to see.

In this regard, the seemingly exaggerated and extreme forms of suspicion of the leader may in fact reflect a heightened (even if exaggerated) sensitivity to the interpersonal dangers that surround him or her. This raises the tantalizing possibility that—at least in highly competitive and political organizational environments—paranoid cognition may contribute to an expedient and sensible kind of organizational sense making (Weick 1993a). As J. David Lewis and Andrew Weigert (1985) have cogently noted in this regard, distrust and suspicion help reduce complexity and uncertainty in organizational life by "dictating a course of action based on suspicion, monitoring, and activation of institutional safeguards" (969). In an world of "zero-sum" thinkers, having a positive-sum mentality can be fatal.

The present analysis acknowledges those potential advantages of paranoid cognitions but also raises the prospect of their leading to ironic and potentially tragic errors in political sense making. In this regard it is interesting to consider the final months of Ernest Hemingway's life. Much to the dismay of his wife and friends, Hemingway began to display signs of apparent clinical paranoia late in his life. For example, when drinking with his friends in local bars he would often point out to his startled drinking companions various men in dark suits who, he asserted, were FBI agents sent by J. Edgar Hoover to follow his movements and harass him. Moreover, he claimed, his mail was being intercepted and his telephone lines were regularly being tapped by the FBI. At the time, these claims—and the certitude and vehemence with which they were asserted—were viewed as evidence of Hemingway's clinical paranoia. To be sure, Hemingway was suffering from a variety of mental difficulties linked to chronic alcohol abuse and depression over his writing. Nevertheless, several decades later we now know that at least some of Hemingway's perceptions were in fact veridical: documents released under the Freedom of Information Act have revealed that, in fact, he *was* under FBI surveillance and that the FBI *was* engaged in an intense program of harassment, apparently stimulated by Hoover's dislike of Hemingway and suspicions about his association with leftist political causes (Federal Bureau of Investigation 2001).

Even Lyndon Johnson's suspicions that some conspiracy had taken place that resulted in all his advisers turning against him were not entirely misplaced. When Clark Clifford became Johnson's secretary of defense following Robert McNamara's exit in 1968, Clifford quickly became convinced that there was no way the war could be won in the current circumstances. When he asked the generals what the strategy for winning the war was, they told him there was none. Thus, Clifford set about bringing a halt to the madness—but he recognized that a lone voice of doubt and dissent would be ineffective. It would lead at best to Johnson's dismissing what he said and even removing him from his post. Accordingly, Clifford decided to turn to Johnson's advisers as a group—the very counselors who had unanimously given their approval to Johnson's policy only months before. Clifford (Gruber 1991) recounted,

> Although it might sound somewhat conspiratorial, I thought it wise to contact a good many of them first. So I did. I knew them all. . . . They all came back, went through the same process (reading cables, getting briefed). . . . I got a feeling from them. I made 4,5, or 6 contacts. And found that in each instance, Tet [the March 1968 Tet Offensive] had changed their mind—so profoundly that [Johnson] thought something had gone wrong and he used the expression, "I think someone has poisoned the well."

In a very real sense someone had poisoned the well, and Lyndon Johnson—the ever-vigilant sense maker—had accurately discerned the hidden hand of a betrayer, even if a benignly motivated one, working behind the scenes. This possibility is the other edge of the sword of suspicion. As David Shapiro (1962) aptly observed, "Suspicious thinking is unrealistic only in some ways, while, in others, it may be sharply perceptive. . . . Suspicious people are not simply people who are apprehensive and 'imagine things.' They are, in fact, extremely keen and often penetrating observers" (55–56).

As the old and familiar adage reminds us—or alerts us, "Just because you are paranoid doesn't mean they aren't out to get you."

This research was supported by funds provided by the John F. Kennedy School of Government at Harvard University and the Stanford Graduate School of Business. We also acknowledge the generous assistance of the librarians and archivists at the John F. Kennedy and Lyndon Baines Johnson Presidential Libraries. We wish to thank a number of individuals, including Max Bazerman, Irving Janis, Carl Kaysen, David Gergen, Dutch Leonard, David Messick, Richard Hackman, Robert McNamara, McGeorge Bundy, and Jack Valenti for their comments related to preparation of this chapter. We are also extremely grateful for the insightful comments provided by the anonymous Russell Sage reviewers.

Notes

1. To be sure, Lyndon Johnson had displayed a propensity toward paranoid-like suspicion throughout his political life (Caro, 1982; Dallek, 1991). Moreover, he had a well-developed penchant for secrecy and covert maneuvering which may have heightened his sensitivity to others' use of these same approaches. Arguably, much of this early paranoia was even prudent, as we argue in our functional analysis subsequently in this chapter. However, what is striking is the extent to which his paranoia escalated once he was in the White House.

References

Ambrose, Stephen. 1991. *Nixon: Ruin and Recovery, 1973–1990*. New York: Simon & Schuster.
American Psychological Association. 1987. *Diagnostic and Statistical Manual of Mental Disorders*. Washington, D.C.: APA.
Barber, Bernard. 1983. *The Logic and Limits of Trust*. New Brunswick, N.J.: Rutgers University Press.
Barber, James David. 1972. *The Presidential Character: Predicting Performance in the White House*. Englewood Cliffs, N.J.: Prentice-Hall.
Barrett, David M. 1993. *Uncertain Warriors: Lyndon Johnson and His Vietnam Advisors*. Lawrence: University Press of Kansas.
Berman, Larry. 1982. *Planning a Tragedy: The Americanization of the War in Vietnam*. New York: Norton.

———. 1988. Lyndon B. Johnson: Paths Chosen and Opportunities Lost. In *Leadership in the Modern Presidency*, edited by Fred I. Greenstein. Cambridge, Mass.: Harvard University Press.

———. 1989. *Lyndon Johnson's War*. New York: Norton.

Beschloss, Michael R. 1997. *Taking Charge: The Johnson White House Tapes, 1963–1964*. New York: Simon & Schuster.

———. 2001. *Reaching for Glory: Lyndon Johnson's Secret White House Tapes, 1964–1965*. New York: Simon & Schuster.

Burke, John P., and Fred I. Greenstein. 1989. *How Presidents Test Reality: Decisions on Vietnam, 1954 and 1965*. New York: Russell Sage Foundation.

Califano, Joseph A. 1991. *The Triumph and Tragedy of Lyndon Johnson*. New York: Simon & Schuster.

Cameron, Norman. 1943. "The Development of Paranoic Thinking." *Psychological Review* 50: 219–33.

Caro, Robert A. 1982. *The Path to Power: The Years of Lyndon Johnson*. New York: Vintage Books.

Clifford, Clark. 1991. *Counsel to the President*. New York: Random House.

Colby, Kenneth M. 1981. "Modeling a Paranoid Mind." *The Behavioral and Brain Sciences* 4: 515–60.

Dallek, Robert. 1991. *Lone Star Rising: Lyndon Baines Johnson*. New York: Oxford University Press.

Dawes, Robyn. 1988. *Rational Choice in an Uncertain World*. New York: Harcourt Brace.

Deutsch, Morton. 1973. *The Resolution of Conflict*. New Haven, Conn.: Yale University Press.

Doyle, William. 1999. *Inside the Oval Office: The White House Tapes from FDR to Clinton*. New York: Kodansha.

Federal Bureau of Investigation. 2001. *20th-Century FBI Files: Declassified from the Federal Bureau of Investigation. Volume 3: Celebrities and Public Figures*. Washington: U.S. Government Printing Office.

Fein, Stephen, and James L. Hilton. 1994. "Judging Others in the Shadow of Suspicion." *Motivation and Emotion* 18(2): 167–98.

Fenigstein, Allan, and Peter A. Vanable. 1992. "Paranoia and Self-Consciousness." *Journal of Personality and Social Psychology* 62: 129–38.

Frank, Jerome D. 1987. "The Drive for Power and the Nuclear Arms Race." *American Psychologist* 42(4, April): 337–44.

Gambetta, Diego. 1988. "Can We Trust Trust?" In *Trust*, edited by Diego Gambetta. Cambridge: Blackwell.

Goffman, Erving. 1969. *Strategic Interaction*. Philadelphia: University of Pennsylvania Press.

Goodwin, Richard N. 1988. *Remembering America: A Voice from the Sixties*. New York: Harper & Row.

Greenstein, Fred I. 1975. *Personality and Politics*. In *Handbook of Political Science*, edited by Fred I. Greenstein and Nelson W. Polsby. Volume 2, *Micropolitical Theory*. Reading, Mass.: Addison-Wesley.

Gruber, David. 1991. *LBJ: A Biography*. Video. Dallas: North Texas Public Broadcasting.

Heath, Jim F. 1975. *Decade of Disillusionment: The Kennedy-Johnson Years.* Bloomington: Indiana University Press.

Henggeler, Paul R. 1991. *In His Steps: Lyndon Johnson and the Kennedy Mystique.* Chicago: Dee.

Herring, George C. 1993. "The Reluctant Warrior: Lyndon Johnson as Commander in Chief." In *Shadow on the White House: Presidents and the Vietnam War, 1945–1975,* edited by David L. Anderson. Lawrence: University of Kansas Press.

Hersh, Seymour M. 1983. *The Price of Power: Kissinger in the Nixon White House.* New York: Summit Books.

Janis, Irving L. 1983. *Groupthink.* 2nd ed. Boston: Houghton Mifflin.

———. 1989. *Crucial Decisions.* New York: Free Press.

Janoff-Bulman, Ronnie. 1992. *Shattered Assumptions: Towards a New Psychology of Trauma.* New York: Free Press.

Johnson, Lyndon Baines. 1971. *The Vantage Point: Perspectives on the Presidency, 1963–1969.* New York: Holt, Rinehart, and Winston.

Kahn, Robert L., and Roderick M. Kramer. 1990. "Untying the Knot: De-Escalatory Processes in International Conflict." In *Organizations and Nation-States: New Perspectives on Conflict and Cooperation,* edited by Robert L. Kahn and Mayer N. Zald. San Francisco: Jossey-Bass.

Kearns-Goodwin, Doris. 1976. *Lyndon Johnson and the American Dream.* New York: New American Library.

Kramer, Roderick M. 1994. "The Sinister Attribution Error: Antecedents and Consequences of Collective Paranoia." *Motivation and Emotion* 18(2): 199–231.

———. 1996. "Divergent Realities and Convergent Disappointments in the Hierarchic Relation: Trust and the Intuitive Auditor at Work." In *Trust in Organizations,* edited by Roderick M. Kramer and Tom R. Tyler. Thousand Oaks, Calif.: Sage.

———. 1998. "Revisiting the Bay of Pigs and Vietnam Decisions 25 Years Later: How Well Has the Groupthink Hypothesis Stood the Test of Time?" *Organizational Behavior and Human Decision Processes* 73(2 and 3): 236–71.

———. 1999. "Trust in Organizations: Emerging Perspectives, Enduring Questions." *Annual Review of Psychology* 50: 569–98.

———. 2002. "Organizational Paranoia: Origins and Dynamics." In *Research in Organizational Behavior,* edited by Robert I. Sutton and Barry M. Staw. Volume 23. New York: Elsevier.

Laing, Ronald David. 1961. *Self and Others.* New York: Penguin Books.

Lewis, J. David, and Andrew Weigert. 1985. "Trust as a Social Reality." *Social Forces* 63(4): 967–85.

Matthews, Chris. 1988. *Hardball.* New York: Summit Books.

Miller, Merle. 1980. *Lyndon: An Oral Biography.* New York: Ballantine.

Norem, Julie K., and Nancy Cantor. 1986. "Defensive Pessimism: Harnessing Anxiety as Motivation." *Journal of Personality and Social Psychology* 51: 1208–17.

Pfeffer, Jeffrey. 1992. *Managing with Power.* Cambridge, Mass.: Harvard Business School Press.

Pruitt, Dean G. 1987. "Conspiracy Theory in Conflict Escalation." In *Changing Conceptions of Conspiracy,* edited by Carl F. Graumann and Serge Moscovici. New York: Springer-Verlag.

Reeves, Richard. 1993. *President Kennedy: Profile of Power.* New York: Simon & Schuster.

Shapiro, David. 1962. *Neurotic Styles.* New York: Basic Books.

Siegel, Ronald K. 1994. *Whispers: The Voices of Paranoia.* New York: Crown.

Slovic, Paul. 1993. "Perceived Risk, Trust, and Democracy." *Risk Analysis* 13(6): 675–82.

Smith, Hedrick. 1988. *The Power Game.* New York: Random House.

Stein, Janice G. 1988. "Building Politics into Psychology: The Misperception of Threat." *Political Psychology* 9: 245–71.

Tetlock, Phillip E., Linda Skitka, and Richard Boettger. 1989. "Social and Cognitive Strategies for Coping with Accountability: Conformity, Complexity, and Bolstering." *Journal of Personality and Social Psychology* 57(4): 632–40.

Valenti, Jack. 1977. *A Very Human President.* New York: W. W. Norton.

Weick, Karl E. 1979. *The Social Psychology of Organizing.* Reading, Mass.: Addison-Wesley.

———. 1993a. "Sensemaking in Organizations." In *Social Psychology in Organizations: Advances in Theory and Practice,* edited by J. Keith Murnighan. Englewood Cliffs, N.J.: Prentice-Hall.

———. 1993b. "The Collapse of Sensemaking in Organizations: The Mann Gulch Disaster." *Administrative Science Quarterly* 38(4): 628–52.

Wills, Garry. 1994. *The Kennedy Imprisonment: A Meditation on Power.* Boston: Little, Brown.

Wilson, Timothy D., and Dolores Kraft. 1993. "Why Do I Love Thee? Effects of Repeated Introspection About a Dating Relationship on Attitudes Towards the Relationship." *Personality and Social Psychology Bulletin* 19(4): 409–18.

Zimbardo, Philip G., Susan M. Andersen, and Loren G. Kabat. 1981. "Induced Hearing Deficit Generates Experimental Paranoia." *Science* 212: 1529–31.

Index

Boldface numbers refer to figures and tables.

371

372   Index